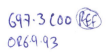

Warm Air Heating
for Climate Control

Warm Air Heating
for Climate Control

SECOND EDITION

William B. Cooper and Raymond E. Lee
Professors, Mechanical Technology
Macomb County Community College

Raymond A. Quinlan
Mechanical Contractor, State of Michigan
Air Conditioning, Heating, Refrigeration

LINCOLN TECHNICAL INSTITUTE

PRENTICE HALL, Englewood Cliffs, New Jersey 07632

ISBN 0-13-952789-3

Editorial/production supervision and interior design: Tom Aloisi
Manufacturing buyer: Bob Anderson

This 1991 Edition is a Special Edition
for the Lincoln Technical Institute.

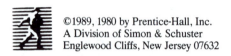 ©1989, 1980 by Prentice-Hall, Inc.
A Division of Simon & Schuster
Englewood Cliffs, New Jersey 07632

Printed in the United States of America

10 9 8 7 6 5 4 3 2 1

ISBN 0-13-952789-3

Prentice-Hall International (UK) Limited, *London*
Prentice-Hall of Australia Pty. Limited, *Sydney*
Prentice-Hall Canada Inc., *Toronto*
Prentice-Hall Hispanoamericana, S.A., *Mexico*
Prentice-Hall of India Private Limited, *New Delhi*
Prentice-Hall of Japan, Inc., *Tokyo*
Prentice-Hall of Southeast Asia Pte. Ltd., *Singapore*
Editora Prentice-Hall do Brasil, Ltda., *Rio de Janeiro*

X43201

Contents

2 COMFORT 12

3 ESTIMATING THE HEATING LOAD 23

4 EVALUATING A HEATING SYSTEM 32

5   INSTALLATION PRACTICE   57

Contents

6 COMBUSTION AND FUELS 84

Contents

7 PARTS COMMON TO ALL FURNACES 107

8 COMPONENTS OF GAS-BURNING FURNACES 132

9   COMPONENTS OF OIL-BURNING FURNACES   149

10   HIGH-EFFICIENCY FURNACES   171

11   HEAT PUMPS   194

12 BASIC ELECTRICITY AND ELECTRICAL SYMBOLS 231

13 SCHEMATIC WIRING DIAGRAMS 255

14 USING ELECTRICAL TEST INSTRUMENTS 266

15   EXTERNAL FURNACE WIRING   295

Contents

18   OIL FURNACE CONTROLS   358

19 ELECTRICAL HEATING 379

20 HEATING SYSTEM MAINTENANCE AND CUSTOMER RELATIONS 394

21   ENERGY CONSERVATION 418

Preface

This text is designed to provide the necessary facets of theory and practice for anyone interested in the subject of comfort heating with gas, oil, electricity, coal, or solar energy.

The performance-based objectives provided at the beginning of each chapter give the student an indication of what minimum knowledge he can expect to receive from that portion of the text.

Warm Air Heating for Climate Control, Second Edition provides not only the necessary theory for the student and service technician alike, but also gives examples to help reinforce that theory. Many actual manufacturers' service and/or maintenance and operating instructions are incorporated as well.

Upon completion of this study, the student will have the knowledge and confidence necessary for the proper servicing and installation of heating equipment.

Warm Air Heating
for Climate Control

1 Climate

OBJECTIVES

After studying this chapter, the student will be able to:

- Define the common terms used in the text pertaining to warm air heating for climate control
- Determine the Btu added to a substance by the application of heat
- Convert Fahrenheit temperatures to Celsius temperatures

INDOOR CLIMATE

Climate is the condition of the weather. Weather refers to the character of the atmosphere. It may be hot or cold, wet or dry, calm or windy. This text is concerned with indoor climate. Broadly speaking, indoor climate includes conditions of temperature, humidity, air motion, air cleanliness, noise or sound levels, odors, even conditions of some materials that occupy or surround the space.

The fundamental concepts that will be discussed in this unit are:

- Temperature
- Heat
- Humidity

- Air motion

- Laws of thermodynamics

Since people engaged in the heating business are responsible for controlling indoor climate conditions, this text discusses the means that are available to produce changes in the indoor climate. One of these is the addition or removal of heat to produce a temperature change.

TEMPERATURE

Temperature is a relative term that can be defined as something that is responsible for the sensations of hot and cold. Temperature can be accurately measured using a thermometer.

Thermometers

A *thermometer* is a device for measuring temperature. There are many shapes and sizes of thermometers available using a variety of scales. However, in general, two types of thermometers are most frequently used. One type is used in the British or English system and is known as the Fahrenheit thermometer. The other type is used in the metric system and is called the Celsius thermometer. Both of these thermometers measure temperature, but the scales are different. A comparison of the two thermometer scales is shown in Figure 1-1.

The scale selected for the Celsius thermometer is the easier of the two to understand. Zero degrees (0°) on the Celsius scale refers to the freezing point of water and 100° refers to the boiling point of water. There are 100 equal divisions between the zero point and the 100° mark on the scale. On the Fahrenheit scale, the freezing point of water is 32° and the boiling point of water is 212°. The Fahrenheit thermometer has 180 equal divisions between the freezing point of water and its boiling point.

It is important to understand both of these thermometer scales. Some temperature information is given in Fahrenheit degrees and some in Celsius degrees. To prevent confusion about which scale is involved, a capital C is placed after the number of Celsius degrees and a capital F is placed after the number of Fahrenheit degrees. For example, 40°C means 40 degrees Celsius; 40°F means 40 degrees Fahrenheit.

When working continuously with one scale or the other, there is no problem in recording and using the information. However, there are times when it is necessary to change from one scale to the other. Such *conversions* can be done by using the following formulas:

$$\text{Degrees Fahrenheit} = (\tfrac{9}{5} \times \text{degrees Celsius}) + 32°$$
$$\text{Degrees Celsius} = \tfrac{5}{9} \times (\text{degrees Fahrenheit} - 32°)$$

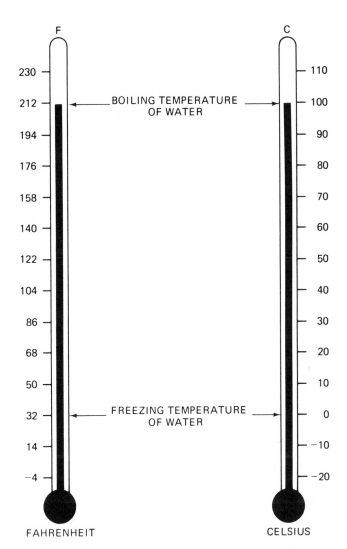

Figure 1-1 A comparison of Fahrenheit and Celsius thermometer scales.

EXAMPLE: 70°F is converted to Celsius degrees as follows:

$$°C = \tfrac{5}{9} \times (°F - 32°)$$
$$= \tfrac{5}{9} \times (70° - 32°)$$
$$= \tfrac{5}{9} \times (38)$$
$$= \frac{190}{9}$$
$$= 21°C$$

EXAMPLE: 27°C is converted to Fahrenheit degrees as follows:

$$°F = (\tfrac{9}{5} \times °C) + 32°$$
$$= (\tfrac{9}{5} \times 27°) + 32°$$
$$= \left(\frac{243}{5}\right) + 32°$$
$$= 49 + 32$$
$$= 81°F$$

HEAT

Heat is the quality that causes an increase in the temperature of a body when it is added or a decrease in the temperature of a body when it is removed, provided that there is no change in state in the process.

The stipulation "no change in state" requires some explanation. A substance changes its state when it changes its physical form. For example, when a solid changes to a liquid, that is a change in state. When a liquid changes to a vapor, that is also a change in state. *Sublimation* is the change in state from a solid to a vapor without passing through the liquid state. A good example of this is the evaporation of mothballs or the evaporation of dry ice (solid carbon dioxide).

The unit of measurement of heat in the British system is the *British thermal unit (Btu)*. One Btu is the amount of heat required to raise 1 pound (lb) of water 1°F, as shown in Figure 1-2.

In the original metric system the unit of heat was the *kilocalorie (kcal)*. This is the amount of heat required to raise the temperature of 1 *kilogram (kg)*, or 1000 *grams (g)*, of water 1°C. This unit of heat is still in use. However, the present metric unit or

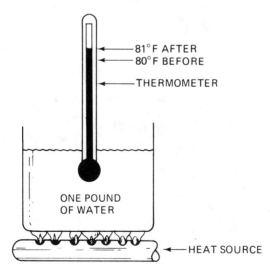

81°F AFTER
80°F BEFORE
THERMOMETER
ONE POUND OF WATER
HEAT SOURCE

Figure 1-2 One Btu is the amount of heat required to raise 1 lb of water 1°F.

Climate   Chap. 1

International System (SI) unit for heat, comparable to a Btu, is the joule (J). The joule is defined in terms of work, being equivalent to the movement of a force of one neuton for a distance of 1 meter (m). When the unit of heat includes a time element comparable to Btu per hours, the metric unit is watts (W), which is equivalent to joules per second.

It is important in most cases to note the rate of heat change. How fast or how slow does a piece of heating equipment produce heat? Therefore, a more precise term is *Btu per hour (Btuh)*. Sometimes figures get quite large, so, using *M* to represent 1000, the abbreviation *MBh* is used to represent *thousands of Btu per hour*. For example, a furnace may have an output of 100,000 Btu per hour, or 100 MBh.

Types of Heat

There are two types of heat: one type changes the temperature of a substance and the other changes its state. The type that changes the temperature is called *sensible heat*. The type that changes the state is called *latent heat*.

The formula used to determine the sensible heat added or removed from a substance is

$$Q = W \times \text{SH} \times \text{TD}$$

where: Q = quantity of heat, Btu

  W = weight, lb

  SH = specific heat, Btu/lb/°F

  TD = temperature difference or change, °F

The formula used to determine the change in latent heat is:

$$Q = W \times L$$

where: L = change in latent heat per pound

When heat is added to a solid to change it to a liquid, the latent heat is called *heat of melting*. When a liquid is changed to a solid, the latent heat is called *heat of fusion*.

When a liquid is changed to a vapor, the latent heat is called *heat of vaporization*. When a vapor is changed to a liquid, the latent heat is called *heat of condensation*. Latent heat is always related to a change in state.

A good example to indicate the effects of heat is its reaction on water, as shown in Figure 1-3. In this figure, ice is taken at 0°F and heated to steam. Note that there are five parts to the diagram, and the following is a description of what takes place.

PART 1:

Ice at 0°F is heated to 32°F; 16 Btu is added. The amount of heat required is found by substituting values in the sensible heat formula.

Heat   **5**

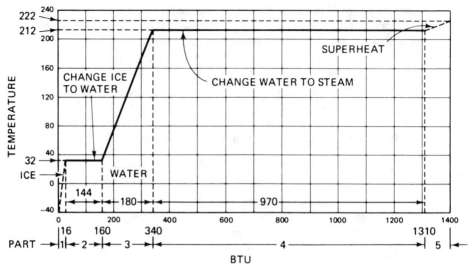

Figure 1-3 A temperature heat diagram, showing the effects of heat on water.

$$Q = 1 \text{ lb} \times 0.5 \text{ Btu/lb/}°F \times (32°F - 0°F)$$

$$= 1 \times 0.5 \times 32$$

$$= 16 \text{ Btu}$$

PART 2:

Ice at 32°F is changed to water at 32°F. Since the heat of melting of water is 144 Btu/lb and, using the latent heat formula, 144 Btu is added:

$$Q = 1 \text{ lb} \times 144 \text{ Btu}$$

$$= 144 \text{ Btu}$$

PART 3:

Water at 32°F is heated to 212°F, by adding 180 Btu. Using the formula and substituting in the values yields

$$Q = 1 \text{ lb} \times 1.0 \text{ Btu/lb/}°F \times (212°F - 32°F)$$

$$= 1 \times 1 \times 180$$

$$= 180 \text{ Btu}$$

PART 4:

Water at 212°F is changed to steam by adding 970 Btu. Since the heat of vaporization of water is 970 Btu/lb, using this formula we obtain

$$Q = 1 \text{ lb} \times 970 \text{ Btu (latent heat)}$$

$$= 970 \text{ Btu}$$

PART 5:

The steam is superheated. Superheating means heating steam (vapor) above the boiling point. If the steam is superheated 10°F, the amount of heat added is 5 Btu. Since the specific heat of steam is 0.48 Btu/lb/°F, the amount of heat added is determined by the formula

$$Q = 1 \text{ lb} \times 0.48 \text{ Btu/lb/°F} \times (222°\text{F} - 212°\text{F})$$

$$= 1 \times 0.48 \times 10$$

$$= 5 \text{ Btu (rounded to the nearest whole number)}$$

Both heat of fusion and heat of vaporization are reversible processes. The change in state can occur in either direction. Water can be changed to ice or ice to water. The amount of heat added or subtracted is the same in either case. Tables are available giving the heat of fusion and the heat of vaporization for various substances.

Specific heat. When most substances are heated, they absorb heat, thereby raising their temperatures, except where a change in state occurs. The temperature of the substance increases rapidly or slowly, depending on the nature of the material. Since the standard heating unit is defined in terms of the temperature rise of water, it is fitting to use water as a basis for comparison for the heat-absorbing quality of other substances.

The definition of specific heat is much like the definition of Btu. The specific heat of a substance is the amount of heat required to raise 1 lb of a substance 1°F. Figure 1-4 lists specific heat values for various substances.

These specific heat values make it easy to calculate the amount of heat added to or removed from a substance when the temperature rise or drop is known. The amount of heat required is equal to the weight of the substance, times the specific heat, times the rise in temperature in degrees Fahrenheit.

EXAMPLE: How much heat is required to heat 10 lb of aluminum from 50°F to 60°F?

SOLUTION: Btu = pounds of aluminum × specific heat × °F temperature rise

$$= 10 \text{ lb} \times 0.22 \text{ Btu/lb/°F} \times (60°\text{F} - 50°\text{F})$$

$$\text{Btu} = 10 \times 0.22 \times 10$$

$$= 22$$

Transfer of Heat

Three different ways to transfer heat are by convection, conduction, and radiation, as shown in Figure 1-5. Modern heating plants make use of all three ways to transfer heat.

SPECIFIC HEAT VALUES

MATERIAL	SPECIFIC HEAT BTU/LB./DEG F
WATER	1.00
ICE	0.50
AIR (DRY)	0.24
STEAM	0.48
ALUMINUM	0.21
BRICK	0.20
CONCRETE	0.16
COPPER	0.09
GLASS (PYREX)	0.20
IRON	0.10
PAPER	0.32
STEEL (MILD)	0.12
WOOD (HARD)	0.45
WOOD (PINE)	0.67

THESE VALUES MAY BE USED FOR COMPUTATIONS
WHICH INVOLVE NO CHANGE OF STATE.

Figure 1-4 A table of the specific heat values for some common substances.

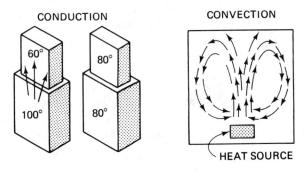

CONDUCTION

CONVECTION

HEAT SOURCE

RADIATION

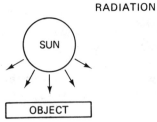

SUN

OBJECT

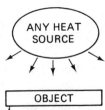

ANY HEAT SOURCE

OBJECT

AT TEMPERATURE
LOWER THAN SOURCE

Figure 1-5 Three ways to transfer heat: conduction, convection, and radiation.

Convection is the circulatory motion in air due to the warmer portions rising, the denser cooler portions sinking. For convection to take place, there must be a difference in temperature between the source of heat and the surrounding air. The greater the difference in temperature, the greater the movement of air by convection. The greater the movement of air, the greater the transfer of heat.

Conduction is the flow of heat from one part of a material to another part in direct contact with it. The rate at which a material transmits heat is known as its conductivity. The amount of heat transmitted by conduction through a material is determined by the surface area of the material, the thickness, the temperature difference between two surfaces, and the conductivity.

Radiation is the transfer of heat through space by wave motion. Heat passes from one object to another without warming the space in between. The amount of heat transferred by radiation depends upon the area of the radiating body, the temperature difference, and the distance between the source of heat and the object being heated.

HUMIDITY

Humidity is the amount of water vapor within a given space. There are two types of humidity: absolute and relative.

Absolute humidity is the weight of water vapor per unit of volume. *Relative humidity* is the ratio of the weight of water vapor in 1 lb (or in 1 kg) of dry air compared to the maximum amount of water vapor 1 lb (or 1 kg) of air will hold at a given temperature, expressed in percent.

In a heating system, during the winter months it is usually desirable to increase the percentage of humidity within the space being conditioned. For every pound of water that is evaporated, approximately 970 Btu is required.

Humidity is measured using a *sling psychrometer*, an instrument for determining the moisture content of air. The use of a sling psychrometer is discussed in Chapter 2.

AIR MOTION AND ITS MEASUREMENT

Air motion means changing the position of air. Most heating systems transfer warm air to cold areas by the movement of air. As in other aspects of indoor climate, the control of air movement is a necessary factor in a satisfactory heating system.

The velocity (speed) of air can be measured by instruments such as an *anemometer*. The unit of measurement of indoor velocities is usually feet per minute (ft/min) in the English system and meters per second (m/s) in the metric system.

LAWS OF THERMODYNAMICS

Thermodynamics is the science that deals with the relationship between heat and mechanical energy. Energy is the ability to do work. If a force is applied to an object moving it a given distance, work has been performed. Heat is a form of energy. Other forms of energy include light, chemical, mechanical, and electrical.

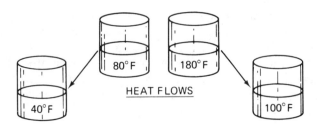

Figure 1-6 Heat flows from hot to cold.

Since heat is a form of energy, it follows the natural laws that relate to energy. These laws are useful in the study of heating. From the laws of thermodynamics, two helpful facts are derived:

1. Energy can be neither created nor destroyed, but it can be converted from one form of energy to another

2. Heat flows from hot to cold

An example of the conversion of energy is the changing of electrical energy to heat in an electric heating unit. An example of heat flowing from hot to cold is illustrated in Figure 1-6.

CHAPTER 1 STUDY QUESTIONS

Answers to the study questions are found in sections of this chapter under the chapter topic indicated.

STUDY QUESTIONS	CHAPTER TOPIC
1. What factors are included in indoor climate?	*Indoor climate*
2. Define temperature.	*Temperature*
3. Describe the two types of scales for measuring temperature.	*Thermometers*
4. Give the formula for converting degrees Fahrenheit to degrees Celsius and degrees Celsius to degrees Fahrenheit.	*Thermometers*
5. Give two definitions of a British thermal unit (Btu), one for Fahrenheit temperatures and one for Celsius temperatures.	*Heat*

6. What are the formulas for calculating sensible and latent heat? — *Types of heat*

7. Define specific heat in terms of British units. — *Specific heat*

8. Name the three ways to transfer heat. — *Transfer of heat*

9. What is the difference between absolute and relative humidity? — *Humidity*

10. Define energy. — *Laws of thermodynamics*

11. What is meant by change of state? — *Types of heat*

12. Give the specific heats of ice, water, and steam. — *Specific heat*

2 Comfort

OBJECTIVES

After studying this chapter, the student will be able to:

- Describe the conditions produced by the warm air heating system that are necessary for human comfort

CONDITIONS THAT AFFECT COMFORT

Comfort is the absence of disturbing or distressing conditions—it is a feeling of contentment with the environment.

The study of human comfort concerns itself with two aspects:

1. How the body functions in respect to heat
2. How the area around a person affects the feeling of comfort

HUMAN REQUIREMENTS

The body can be compared to a heat engine. A heat engine has three characteristics:

1. It consumes fuel.

2. It performs work.

3. It dissipates heat.

The body consumes fuel, in the form of food, which produces energy to perform work. The body also dissipates heat to the surrounding atmosphere.

The body has a unique characteristic in that it maintains a closely regulated internal body temperature, 97 to 100°F (36 to 38°C). Any excess energy that is not used to produce work or to perform essential body functions is expelled to the atmosphere. It is, therefore, important that any loss of body heat be at the proper rate to maintain body temperature. If the body loses heat too fast, a person has the sensation of being cold. If the body loses heat too slowly, a person has the sensation of being too warm.

There are two additional factors that must be taken into consideration:

1. The amount of activity of a person. The greater the activity, the more heat produced by the body that must be dissipated to the atmosphere (Figure 2-1).

2. The amount of clothing worn by a person. Clothing is a form of insulation and insulation slows down the transfer of heat. Therefore, the warmer the clothing, the greater the insulation value and the less the amount of heat dissipated. Thus, heat that would normally be lost to the atmosphere is used to warm the surface of the body.

Excess heat must be transferred from the body to the area around it. This is accomplished in three ways (Figure 2-2):

1. Convection

2. Radiation

3. Evaporation

ACTIVITY	TOTAL HEAT ADJUSTED* BTUH	SENSIBLE HEAT BTUH	LATENT HEAT BTUH
SCHOOL	420	230	190
OFFICE	510	255	255
LIGHT WORK	640	315	325
DANCING	1280	405	875
HEAVY WORK	1600	565	1035

*ADJUSTED TOTAL GAIN IS BASED ON NORMAL PERCENTAGE OF MEN, WOMEN AND CHILDREN FOR THE APPLICATION LISTED.

Figure 2-1 Heat from people.

Human Requirements

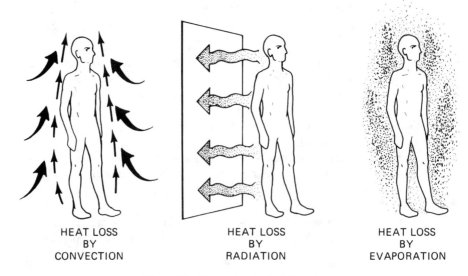

HEAT LOSS
BY
CONVECTION

HEAT LOSS
BY
RADIATION

HEAT LOSS
BY
EVAPORATION

Figure 2-2 Three ways the body loses heat.

Convection

For convection to take place, the area around the body must be at a lower temperature. The greater the difference in temperature, the greater the movement of convection currents around the body and the greater the heat transfer.

If the temperature difference is too great, a person will feel the sensation of being cold. If the temperature difference is too small, a person will feel the sensation of being hot.

Radiation

The body radiates heat to cooler surfaces just as the sun radiates heat to the earth. The greater the temperature difference between the body and the exposed surfaces, the greater the rate of heat transfer.

It has been found that the most comfortable conditions are maintained if the inside surface of the outside walls and windows are heated to the room temperature. If these surface temperatures are too low, the body radiates heat to them too fast and this produces a feeling of discomfort.

Evaporation

Water (or moisture) on the surface of the skin enters the surrounding air by means of evaporation. Evaporation is the process of changing water to vapor by the addition of heat. As the water absorbs heat from the body, it evaporates, thus transferring heat to the air.

If the rate of evaporation is too great, the skin has a dry, uncomfortable feeling.

The membranes of the nose and throat require adequate humidity to maintain their flexible condition. If the rate of evaporation is too slow, the skin has a clammy, sticky feeling.

Evaporation of moisture requires approximately 970 Btu of heat per pound of water evaporated. Heat required for evaporation is lost from the body, cooling it.

Space

Space is defined as the enclosed area in which one lives or works. Conditions for comfort are maintained within the space by mechanical heating. The requirement for comfort is that the space supply a means for dissipating the heat from the body at the proper rate to maintain proper body temperature.

The conditions for comfort in the space may be divided into two groups: thermal and environmental. The thermal conditions include temperature, relative humidity, and air motion. The environmental conditions include clean air, freedom from disturbing noise, and freedom from disagreeable odors. Because of the importance of the thermal factors, these will be discussed first.

Temperature

The ability to produce the correct space temperature is probably the most important single factor in providing comfortable conditions. Two types of temperature are considered:

1. The temperature of the air that surrounds the body

2. The temperature of exposed surface enclosing the room

For the maximum degree of comfort, both the air temperature and the surface temperature should be the same.

Air temperature is measured with an ordinary thermometer. Surface temperature is more difficult to measure, and is usually read by using either an electronic thermometer or a special surface temperature thermometer. The best comfort temperature level for both air and surface within the space is 76°F (24.5°C), according to the American Society of Heating, Refrigerating and Air Conditioning Engineers (ASHRAE) Comfort Standard 55-80.

However, in view of the need for conserving energy, interior temperature levels for heating have been lowered. This text uses 70°F (21.1°C) as a design inside temperature. In some cases lower temperatures are recommended when energy must be conserved. It is acknowledged that some individuals will have to put on additional clothing to remain comfortable at this temperature.

Relative Humidity

For our purposes, relative humidity indicates the percent of water vapor actually in the air compared to the maximum amount that the air could hold at the same temperature.

There are two types of psychrometers used to determine the relative humidity. The sling psychrometer and the power psychrometer are shown in Figure 2-3. The difference

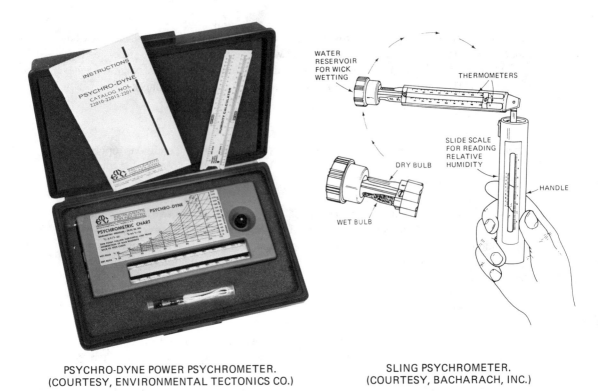

PSYCHRO-DYNE POWER PSYCHROMETER.
(COURTESY, ENVIRONMENTAL TECTONICS CO.)

SLING PSYCHROMETER.
(COURTESY, BACHARACH, INC.)

Figure 2-3 Two types of psychrometers.

between the instruments is that the sling psychrometer is manual and the power psychrometer utilizes a fan powered by a battery.

To take readings using a sling psychrometer, dip the wick on the wet bulb thermometer in water (distilled, if possible). (Use only one dipping per determination of relative humidity, but never dip between readings.) The evaporation of the moisture on the wick is the determining factor of the wet bulb reading.

Whirl the sling psychrometer for 30 s. Quickly take the reading on the wet bulb thermometer first; then read the dry bulb and record the readings. Continue to whirl the psychrometer, taking readings at 30 s intervals for five successive readings, recording the temperatures each time until the lowest readings for wet bulb and dry bulb have been obtained.

The power psychrometer is designed to provide a 15-ft/s air flow over the thermometers. When the fan operates, the wet bulb temperature will be rapidly lowered. A reading should *not* be taken until the temperature drops to its lowest point. This may take from 1 min to 2 min, depending on the dryness of the air. Take two readings; use a psychrometric chart or table to obtain the relative humidity (rh).

Figure 2-4 is a simplified psychrometric chart that can be used to determine the relative humidity of a sample of air. Note that the wet-bulb lines slope downward to the right, the dry bulb lines are vertical, and the relative humidity lines curve upward to the right. Any point on the chart, therefore, represents some wet bulb, dry bulb, and relative humidity condition.

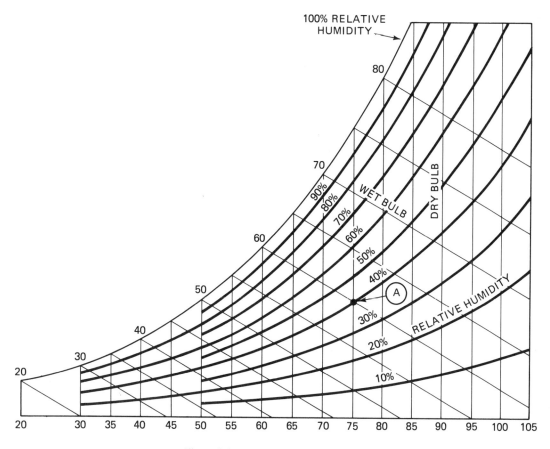

Figure 2-4 Simplified psychometric chart

EXAMPLE: What is the relative humidity for the condition of 75°F db (dry bulb) and 60°F wb (wet bulb)?

SOLUTION: Locate 75° db on the base line and trace vertically upward until it meets the 60° wb line. The relative humidity at this point is 40%.

A high relative humidity may become objectionable if moisture begins to condense on the inside of the windows. Figure 2-5 can be used to determine the maximum rh under varying sets of conditions.

EXAMPLE: If the outside temperature is 20°F db, and the window is single glass; what is the maximum relative humidity that can be maintained inside a 70°F db room?

SOLUTION: Locate 20 db on the base line and trace vertically upward to the single glass line; then go across to the rh scale. The maximum relative humidity is 25%.

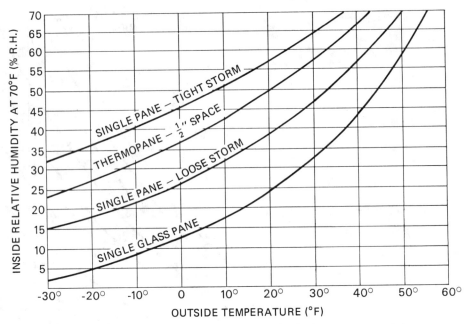

Figure 2-5 Outside temperatures at which condensation begins to appear on windows with an inside temperature of 70°F (courtesy, Research Products Corporation).

Air Motion

Most heating systems require some air movement to distribute heat within the space. In a forced-air heating system, air is supplied through registers and returned to the heating unit through grilles. High-velocity air, measured in feet per minute (ft/min), enters the room through the supply registers. Air at these velocities may be required to properly heat cold exterior walls. The velocity is greatly reduced by natural means before the air reaches the occupants of the room.

According to the ASHRAE Comfort Standard, provided that other recommended conditions are maintained (76°F db, 40% rh), the air that comes in contact with people should not exceed a velocity of 45 ft/min or 0.23 m/s.

Air Quality

One of the desirable qualities of a forced warm air heating system is its ability, through air filters, to remove certain portions of the dust and dirt that are carried by the air. There are three types of residential air filters: disposable (throwaway), permanent (cleanable), and electronic, as shown in Figure 2-6.

Disposable filters are made of oil-impregnated fibers. When dirty, they are noncleanable and are replaced with new ones.

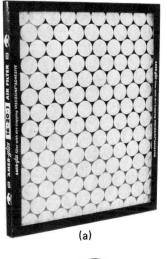

(a)

(b)

(c)

Figure 2-6 Three types of air filters: (a) disposable-type air filter; (b) permanent type air filter; (c) electronic air filter.

Permanent filters are made of metal or specially constructed fibrous material. The dirt is collected on the surface of the filtering material as the air passes through. When properly cleaned, these filters can be reused.

Electronic filters remove dust particles by first placing an electrical charge on the dust particle and then attracting the dust to collector plates having the opposite electrical charge. They are usually used with cleanable-type prefilters because the electronic filter removes only extremely small particles.

Figure 2-7 shows the size of various dust particles. The size is indicated in *microns* (μm). A micron is 1/25,4000 inch (in.) [0.001 millimeter (mm)]. The ordinary throwaway or cleanable-type home air filter will remove particles down to 10 μm. The electronic air filter will remove particles from 0.1 to 10 μm.

Human Requirements

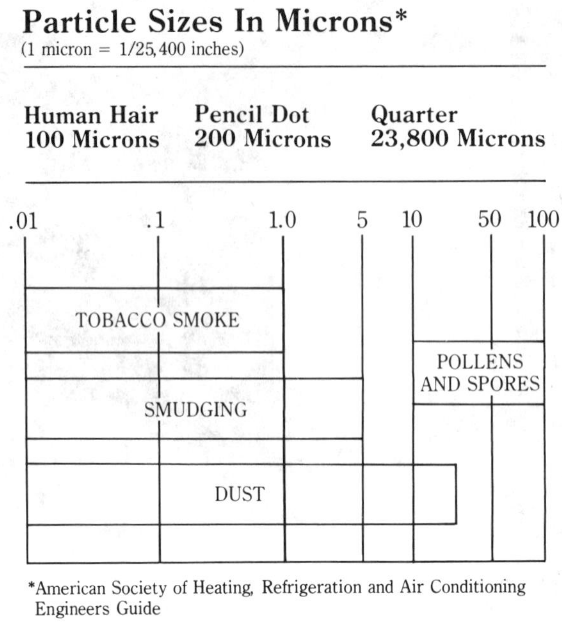

Particle Sizes In Microns*

(1 micron = 1/25,400 inches)

Human Hair	Pencil Dot	Quarter
100 Microns	200 Microns	23,800 Microns

```
 .01        .1         1.0      5   10      50  100
  |          |          |       |   |       |   |
  |          |          |                       |
  |     TOBACCO SMOKE    |                       |
  |          |          |                       |
  |          |          |            POLLENS    |
  |          |          |          AND SPORES    |
  |       SMUDGING       |                       |
  |          |          |                       |
  |          |          |                       |
  |        DUST          |        |              |
  |          |          |        |
  |          |          |
```

*American Society of Heating, Refrigeration and Air Conditioning
Engineers Guide

Figure 2-7 Particle size in microns. (courtesy, Research Products Corporation).

Freedom From Disturbing Noise

Noise or objectionable sound can be airborne or travel through the structure of a building.

Airborne noise can be caused by mechanical equipment being located too near a building's occupants or by the mechanical noise being transmitted through connecting air ducts.

Noise that travels through the structure of a building is caused by the vibration of equipment mounted in direct contact with the building.

To remove noise problems, equipment should be properly selected from a noise-level standpoint. Where noise or vibration does exist, equipment should be properly isolated (separated from sound-transmitting materials) (Figure 2-8).

Sound can be measured by acoustical instruments. The unit of sound-level measurement is the decibel (dB).

Freedom from Disagreeable Odors

Any closed space occupied by people will develop odors. Ventilation is the most effective means of reducing odors.

Some outside air leaks into a building through the cracks around windows and through the building construction. In modern construction this is occasionally not enough to provide adequate ventilation.

A provision can be made in the air supply to the heating unit to provide an additional quantity of outside air. Some designers use 10 cubic feet per minute (ft^3/min) per occupant of the house as a reasonable amount of ventilation air. A damper arrangement can be used to regulate or close off the outside air if desired.

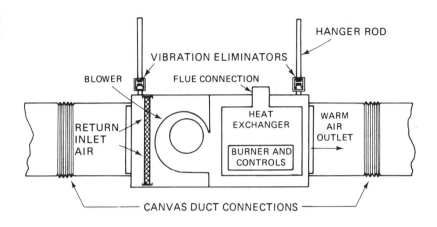

HORIZONTAL FORCED WARM AIR FURNACE

Figure 2-8   Noise and vibration eliminators. (By permission of ASHRAE Handbook).

Ventilation air should not be confused with combustion air, since combustion air must be provided to properly burn the furnace fuel. This must not in any way subtract from the air (oxygen) available for the occupants of the house.

CHAPTER 2 STUDY QUESTIONS

Answers to the study questions are found in the sections of this chapter under the chapter topic indicated.

STUDY QUESTIONS	CHAPTER TOPIC
1. Define comfort.	*Conditions that effect comfort*
2. How can the body be compared to a heat engine?	*Human requirements*
3. What is the normal body temperature?	*Human requirements*
4. What are the conditions for body comfort from the standpoint of heat loss?	*Human requirements*
5. How does the body transfer heat?	*Human requirements*
6. How does the temperature of exposed room surfaces affect comfort?	*Temperature*
7. How much heat is required to evaporate 1 lb of water?	*Evaporation*
8. How does the activity of a person affect the amount of heat dissipated?	*Human requirements*
9. What is a sling psychrometer? How do you use it in measuring relative humidity?	*Relative humidity*

10. Referring to the psychrometric chart, what is the relative humidity for 75°F db and 60°F wb?

Relative humidity

11. Name and describe the three types of air filters.

Air quality

12. What is the size range of particles removed by the electronic air filter?

Air quality

3 Estimating the Heating Load

After studying this chapter, the student will be able to:

- Utilize heating load calculation procedures described in the Air Conditioning Contractors of America's *Manual J*

OVERVIEW OF HEATING LOADS

The primary purpose of a heating system is to provide comfort conditions with the expenditure of a minimum amount of energy. This process requires that the heating system be properly sized to fit the building requirements.

Although most heat load calculations are derived from ASHRAE information, *Manual J*, published by the Air Conditioning Contractors of America (ACCA), has become the standard of the residential heating industry.

Manual J provides an orderly procedure for calculating the total load of a structure, which is then used as the basis for selecting furnace size. The J calculation also provides the loads of the individual rooms, which can be used to design the duct system using ACCA's *Manual D*. This chapter deals only with the use of *Manual J*. Selecting the correct furnace size is very important, since an undersized unit will not handle the load, whereas an oversized unit with excess capacity can result in poor control, inefficiency, excessive operating costs, and so on.

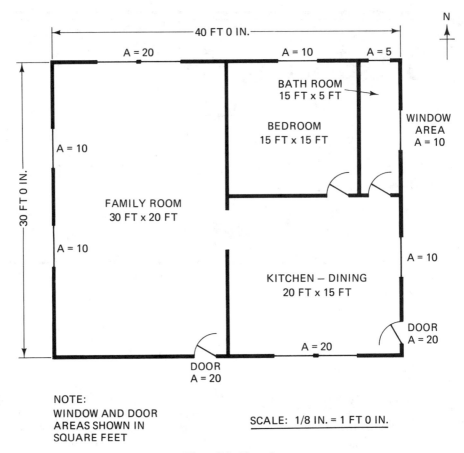

Figure 3-1 Floor plan.

A TYPICAL CALCULATION

In order to illustrate the method of using *Manual J*, a typical calculation is shown. An abbreviated floor plan is given in Figure 3-1. For simplicity, the outside walls and partitions are shown as single lines. In actual practice the outside dimensions of the house would be used for the "entire house" calculation. The inside dimensions of the outside walls would be used in calculating the individual room loads.

Determining Outside Design Temperature

In the example shown, the city selected from Table 1* is Detroit, Michigan, which has a winter design temperature of +6°F. This is not the lowest temperature reached in the area, but 97½% of the time the temperature will be above the +6°F outdoor design temperature.

---

* All tables used in this chapter are from ACCA's *Manual J*. Therefore, the ACCA table numbers are used.

TABLE 1

Outdoor Design Conditions for Representative Cities in the States of Georgia and Michigan.

Location	Latitude (degrees)	Winter	
		97½% design (db)	Heating D.D. below 65°F
Georgia			
Atlanta	33	+22	2990
Augusta	33	+23	2410
Savannah	32	+27	1850
Michigan			
Detroit	42	(+6)	6290
Grand Rapids	42	+5	6890
Lansing	42	+1	6940

Selecting Inside Design Temperature

The recommended selection is 70°F.

Determining Design Temperature Difference

Design temperature difference is the difference between the inside design temperature of 70°F and the outside design temperature of 6°F:

$$70°F - 6°F = 64°F$$

Rounding this figure to the nearest 5°F interval, the value used is 65°F. (This is done to comply with the 5°F temperature increments shown in the tables.)

Determining Construction Numbers

The construction numbers for windows, doors, walls, ceilings, and floors are found in Table 2. These numbers represent the materials used in construction of these various exposures. Referring to the excerpts from Table 2, note that each type of construction is represented by a number and a letter. Thus, a "double-pane window" with a "metal frame" is identified as construction number "3C."

Determining Heat-transfer Multipliers

The heat-transfer multiplier (HTM) for each construction number is based on the design temperature difference. For example, for a double-pane window, the construction number 3C has an HTM value of 47.1 at a winter temperature difference of 65°F. A summary of the construction numbers and HTM values for the example is shown in Figure 3-2.

Figure 3-2 Assumed design conditions and construction (heating) (Courtesy, Air Conditioning Contractors of America—ACCA)

		Const. no.	HTM
A.	Determine outdoor design temperature + 6F db (Table 1) Detroit, Mich.		
B.	Select inside design temperature +70°F db		
C.	Design temperature difference: 70° − 6° = 64°F (For convenience, use 65°F.)		
D.	Windows: all rooms—clear glass, double pane, metal frame (no storm); Table 2	3C	47.1
E.	Doors: Metal, fiberglass core, no storm; Table 2	11A	38.4
F.	First-floor walls: basic frame construction, plastic vapor barrier, R-11 insulation, ½-in. asphalt brd. (R1.3) sheathing, and face brick; Table 2	12D	5.2
G.	Ceiling: basic construction, under vented attic, with R-19 insulation; Table 2	16D	3.4
H.	Floor: Hardwood plus R-11 insulation; over enclosed unheated crawl space; Table 2	19B	2.6

Note: Ceilings are 8 ft; all duct work is located in the unheated crawl space and is covered with R-4 insulation (7A, multiplier 0.10).

TABLE 2
Heat Transfer Multipliers (Heating)

No. 3 double-pane window			
		Winter T.D.	
	60	65	70
		–HTM–	
Clear Glass A. Wood frame	33.1	35.8	38.6
B. T.I.M. frame*	36.5	39.6	42.6
C. Metal frame	43.5	(47.1)	50.8

* T.I.M. Thermally improved metal frame

No. 11 metal doors			
		Winter T.D.	
	60	65	70
		–HTM–	
A. Fiberglass core	35.4	(38.4)	41.3
B. Fiberglass core and storm	22.0	23.9	25.7
C. Polystyrene core	28.2	30.6	32.9

(Courtesy, Air Conditioning Contractors of America—ACCA.)

TABLE 2 (cont.)

No. 12 wood frame exterior walls with sheathing and siding or brick, or other exterior finish					
			Winter T.D.		
			60	65	70
	Cav. insul.	Sheathing	–HTM–		
A.	None	½ in. GYPSUM BRD. (R 0.5)	16.3	17.6	19.0
B.	None	½ in. ASPHALT BRD. (R 1.3)	13.0	14.1	15.2
C.	R-11	½ in. GYPSUM BRD. (R 0.5)	5.4	5.8	6.3
D.	R-11	½ in. ASPHALT BRD. (R 1.3	4.8	(5.2)	5.6

No. 16 ceiling under ventilated attic space or unheated room				
		Winter T.D.		
		60	65	70
		–HTM–		
A.	No insulation	35.9	38.9	41.9
B.	R-7 insulation	7.2	7.8	8.4
C.	R-11 insulation	5.3	5.7	6.2
D.	R-19 insulation	3.2	(3.4)	3.7

No. 19 floors over an unheated basement, enclosed crawl space				
		Winter T.D.		
		60	65	80
		–HTM–		
A.	Hardwood floor + no insul.	9.4	10.1	10.9
B.	Hardwood floor + R11 insul.	2.4	(2.6)	2.8
C.	Hardwood floor + R13 insul.	2.3	2.5	2.7

(Courtesy, Air Conditioning Contractors of America—ACCA.)

Recording Construction Numbers

The construction numbers and the HTM values are recorded in the appropriate locations on the data sheet (see Figure 3-3).

Determining Infiltration

For the sample calculation, referring to Table 5, the number of winter air changes per hour for this 1200-ft^2 residence of average construction is 1.0 air changes per hour. Using

				HTM			Entire House		1 FAMILY ROOM		2 BEDROOM	
1	Name of Room						Entire House		1 FAMILY ROOM		2 BEDROOM	
2	Running Ft Exposed Wall						40+30+40+30=140'		20+30+20=70'		15'	
3	Room Dimensions, Ft						40'0" × 30'0"		30'×20'		15'×15'	
4	Ceiling Ht, Ft		Directions Room Faces				8' NEWS		8' NWS		8' N	
	Type of Exposure		Const. No.	HTM Htg	Clg	Area or Length	Btuh Htg	Clg	Area or Length	Btuh Htg	Clg	Area or Length	Btuh Htg	
5	Gross Exposed Walls and Partitions	a	12D			1120			560			120	
		b											
		c											
		d											
6	Windows and Glass Doors (Htg)	a	3C	47.1		95			40			10	
		b											
		c											
		d											
7	Windows and Glass Doors (Clg)	North											
		E & W or NE & NW											
		South or SE & SW											
8	Other Doors		11 A	38.4		40	1536		20	768			
9	Net Exposed Walls and Partitions	a	12 D	5.2		985	5122		500	2600		110	
		b											
		c											
		d											
10	Ceilings	a	16 D	3.4		1200	4080		600	2040		225	
		b											
11	Floors	a	19 B	2.6		1200	3120		600	1560		225	
		b											
12	Infiltration . . . Calc.			84.7		135	11,435		60	5082		10	
13	Sub Total Btuh Loss = 6 + 8 + 9 + 10 + 11 + 12						25,293			12,050			
14	Duct Btuh Loss			10%			2,529			1,205			
15	Total Btuh Loss = 13 + 14						27,822			13,255			
16	People @ 300 and Appliances 1200												
17	Sensible Btuh Gain = 7 + 8 + 9 + 10 + 11 + 12 + 16												
18	Duct Btuh Gain				%								
19	Total Sensible Gain = 17 + 18												

Figure 3-3 Sample of worksheet for manual J load calculation (Courtesy, Air Conditioning Contractors of America—ACCA.)

TABLE 5
INFILTRATION EVALUATION
WINTER AIR CHANGES PER HOUR

Floor Area	900 or less	900–1500
Best	0.4	0.4
Average	1.2	(1.0)
Poor	2.2	1.6

Best, average, and poor categories are based on the quality of the structure. *For example*, *Average* would include a plastic vapor barrier, caulking, weatherstripping, exhaust fans dampered, combustion air from inside, intermittent ignition, and a flue damper.

Procedure A—winter infiltration, HTM calculation.

1. Winter infiltration CFM
   1.0 AC/H × 9600 ft³ × 0.0167 volume
   = 160 ft³/min

2. Winter infiltration Btuh
   1.1 × 160 ft³/min × 65°Winter TD
   = 11,440 Btuh

3. Winter infiltration HTM
   11,440 Btuh ÷ 135 total window and door area
   = 84.7 HTM

Cubic volume of house = floor area × ceiling height In example: 1200 × 8 = 9600 ft³

Procedure A in Table 5, the HTM value for infiltration is 84.7. This value is recorded on the data sheet.

Determining Duct Loss Multiplier

For the example shown, refer to Table 7A; based on supply air temperatures below 120°F and the duct with R-4 insulation located in the crawl space, the duct loss multiplier is 0.10 (10%). This is recorded on the data sheet (see Figure 3-3).

TABLE 7A
DUCT LOSS MULTIPLIERS

Supply air temperatures below 120°F	Duct loss multipliers	
Duct location and insulation value	*Winter design below 15°F*	*Winter design above 15°F*
Enclosed in unheated space Crawl space or basement—none	0.20	0.15
Crawl space or basement—R2	0.15	0.10
Crawl space or basement—R4	(0.10)	0.05
Crawl space or basement—R6	0.05	0.00

(Courtesy, Air Conditioning Contractors of America—ACCA.)

Recording Exposed Areas

The exposed areas for the entire house and individual rooms are recorded on the data sheet (see Figure 3-3).

Multiplying Exposed Areas by HTM Factors

The exposed areas are multiplied by the HTM factors to obtain the heat loss through each exposure. Add the individual exposure losses to obtain a subtotal. Add the duct loss to the subtotal. For the example shown, the total Btuh loss for the entire house is 27,822 Btuh (25,293 + 2529). For one individual room (the family room) the load is 13,255 Btuh (12,050 + 1205). The same procedure applies to the other rooms in the house.

COMPUTER PROGRAMS

A number of computer programs are available for calculating heating and cooling loads. Generally speaking, there are two types:

1. Those that relate directly to the information published by ASHRAE

2. The Right-J Program, which relates directly to *Manual J*, published by ACCA

When using the Right-J Program, it should be determined that the program follows the most recent edition of *Manual J*. A number of important changes have been made in the calculation procedures in recent years. Of primary importance is the calculation of infiltration. Tests have shown that some older types of construction, when compared to newer structures, have high infiltration factors, which can practically double the total load.

The computer programs are fast and accurate, provided that good data is supplied and the operator has sufficient training in operating the computer. It is advisable to compare computer results with manual calculations when initially using the computer programs as a check for possible errors.

The printouts from the computer programs are useful in making presentations or submitting information to building authorities. The summaries indicate not only the final load calculations but also the construction factors used.

Another feature of the computer programs is the ease in making "what-if" (prediction) calculations. For example, it might be of interest to compare various amounts of insulation to determine the most cost-effective thickness to use. This would confirm that the extra first cost is justified based on the savings in operating costs. It is then a simple matter to recalculate the load based on assumed changes in construction factors.

CHAPTER 3 STUDY QUESTIONS

Answers to the study questions are found in the sections of this chapter under the chapter topics indicated.

		CHAPTER TOPIC

1. What is the primary purpose of the heating system?
Overview of heating loads

2. Why is *Manual J* considered a standard of the industry for calculating residential heating loads?
Overview of heating loads

3. Are the outside or inside dimensions of a house used in calculating a heating load?
A typical calculation

4. Which table is used to determine the outside design temperature?
A typical calculation

5. Which table is used to select the construction factors?
A typical calculation

6. Give an example of determining the design temperature difference.
A typical calculation

7. Give an example of selecting the heat transfer multiplier (HTM). How is it used?
A typical calculation

8. What is infiltration and what is its unit of measurement?
A typical calculation

9. What factors are multiplied to determine the heat loss through an exposure?
A typical calculation

10. What is the construction factor number for hardwood floors with no insulation over an unheated basement? Also, what is the HTM factor for a winter design temperature difference of 65°F?
Table 2

4 Evaluating a Heating System

OBJECTIVES

After studying this chapter, the student will be able to:

- Evaluate the furnace selection and the air distribution system for an existing residence

- Determine the input value of fuel used for a heating system

- Measure the air quantity actually being circulated in a forced warm air heating system

DIAGNOSING THE PROBLEM

To diagnose a problem and then decide what is needed to correct it, a service technician must first determine whether the difficulty is a system problem or a mechanical problem. Some typical system problems are:

- Drafts

- Uneven temperature

- Not enough heat

Drafts are currents of relatively cold air that cause discomfort when they come in contact with the body. Drafts may be caused by a downflow of cold air from an outside wall or window.

Uneven temperatures can cause discomfort and are generally due to the following:

1. Different temperatures in a room near the floor and near the ceiling (sometimes called *stratification*) (Figure 4-1)

2. Different temperature in one room compared to another

3. Different temperature on one floor level as compared to another

Uneven room temperatures may be caused by incorrect supply diffuser locations. Cold outside surfaces of a room should be warmed by properly located supply air outlets.

Temperature difference between rooms may be caused by improper balancing of the system due to lack of duct dampers in the branch run to each outlet. Balancing is the process of regulating the flow of air into each room to produce even temperatures.

Not enough heat may be caused by too small a furnace or improper fuel input to the unit to match the heating load of the house.

Some system problems can be solved, or the condition improved, by the service technician. However, some problems are built into the design of the system and can only be corrected by redesign or replacement of major components.

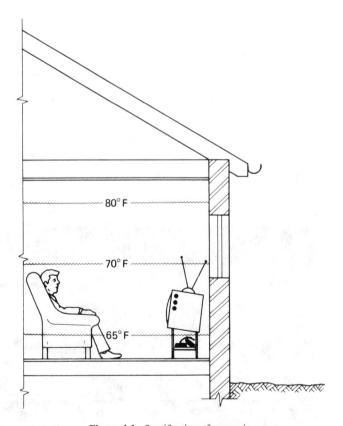

Figure 4-1 Stratification of room air.

EVALUATING THE SYSTEM

The three items that should be considered are the

- Furnace

- Fan

- Air distribution system

Two questions relate to the furnace:

1. Has the proper size been selected?

2. Is the furnace adjusted to produce its rated output?

In Chapter 3 a method was given for determining the heating load of a building. Any losses that occur, such as duct loss or ventilation air, are added to the total room loss to determine the total required heating load. The furnace output rating should be equal to, but not greater than, 15% higher than the total required heating load. If the furnace is too small, it will not heat properly in extreme weather. If it is too large, the "off" cycles will be too long, and the result will be uneven heating.

To determine if a furnace is producing its rated capacity, it is necessary to check the

- Fuel input

- Combustion efficiency

Energy Source: Gas

Many manufacturers void their warranty if the gas input is not adjusted to within 2% of the rated input of the furnace, as shown on the furnace nameplate (see Figure 4-2). This can be easily done by

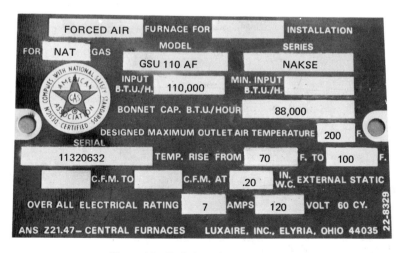

Figure 4-2 Typical gas furnace nameplate.

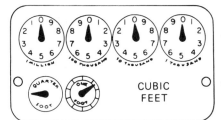

THE DIAL IS MARKED AS TO HOW MUCH GAS IS MEASURED FOR EACH REVOLUTION. USING THE NUMBER OF SECONDS FOR ONE REVOLUTION, AND THE SIZE OF THE TEST DIAL, FIND THE CUBIC FEET OF GAS CONSUMED PER HOUR FROM THE TABLE

CUBIC FEET

SECONDS FOR ONE REV.	SIZE OF TEST DIAL					SECONDS FOR ONE REV.	SIZE OF TEST DIAL				
	¼ CU.FT.	½ CU.FT.	1 CU.FT.	2 CU.FT.	5 CU.FT.		¼ CU.FT.	½ CU.FT.	1 CU.FT.	2 CU.FT.	5 CU.FT.
10	90	180	360	720	1800	36	25	50	100	200	500
11	82	164	327	655	1636	→ 37	–	–	→ 97	195	486
12	75	150	300	600	1500	38	23	47	95	189	474
13	69	138	277	555	1385	39	–	–	92	185	462
14	64	129	257	514	1286	40	22	45	90	180	450
15	60	120	240	480	1200	41	–	–	–	176	439
16	56	113	225	450	1125	42	21	43	86	172	429
17	53	106	212	424	1059	43	–	–	–	167	419
18	50	100	200	400	1000	44	–	41	82	164	409
19	47	95	189	379	947	45	20	40	80	160	400
20	45	90	180	360	900	46	–	–	78	157	391
21	43	86	171	343	857	47	19	38	76	153	383
22	41	82	164	327	818	48	–	–	75	150	375
23	39	78	157	313	783	49	–	–·	–	147	367
24	37	75	150	300	750	50	18	36	72	144	360
25	36	72	144	288	720	51	–	–	–	141	355
26	34	69	138	277	692	52	–	–	69	138	346
27	33	67	133	267	667	53	17	34	–	136	240
28	32	64	129	257	643	54	–	–·	67	133	333
29	31	62	124	248	621	55	–	–	–	131	327
30	30	60	120	240	600	56	16	32	64	129	321
31	–	–	116	232	581	57	–	–	–	126	316
32	28	56	113	225	563	58	–	31	62	124	310
33	–	–	109	218	545	59	–	–	–	122	305
34	26	53	106	212	529	60	15	30	60	120	300
35	–	–	103	206	514						

Figure 4-3 Gas meter measuring dials and table for determining gas input based on dial readings. (Courtesy, Bard Manufacturing Company.)

1. Obtaining the Btu/ft^3 rating of the gas from the local utility*

2. Turning off all other appliances and operating the gas furnace continuously during the test

3. Measuring the length of time it takes for the furnace to consume 1 ft^3 of gas

For example, it if takes 37 s to use 1 ft^3 of gas (using the 1-ft^3 dial on the meter) and the gas rating is 1025 Btu/ft^3, then the input is 1025 Btu/ft^3 × 97 ft^3 = 99,425 Btuh. The 97 is found on the 37-s line in the 1-ft^3 dial column in Figure 4-3. If the furnace is rated at 100,000 Btuh input, the usage would be within requirements.†

* Consult the local gas company for this information.

† Input rating for a gas furnace is given on the furnace nameplate.

Some meters have low input dials other than 1 ft^3. Using the table shown in Figure 4-3 and the method described, a similar check on the gas input can be made. If the input is not correct, it should be changed to the furnace input rating by adjusting the gas-pressure regulating valve or by changing the size of the burner orifices (see the manufacturer's instructions for details.)

Energy Source: Oil

The input rating to an oil furnace can be checked by determining the oil burner nozzle size and measuring the oil pressure.

Nozzles are rated for a given amount of oil flow at 100 pounds per square inch gauge (psig) oil pressure. One gallon of Grade No. 2 oil contains 140,000 Btu. The oil

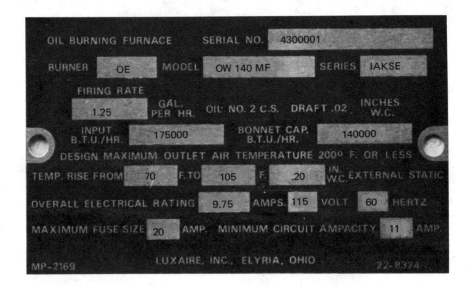

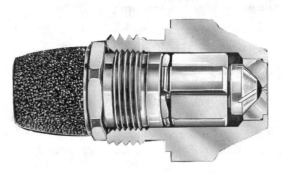

Figure 4-4 Typical oil furnace nameplate and oil burner nozzle (Courtesy, Delavan Corporation.)

burner nozzle is examined and the input flow is read on the nozzle in gallons per hour (gal/h). Thus, a nozzle rated at 0.75 gal/h operating with an oil pressure of 100 pounds per square inch (psi, or lb/in^2.) would produce an input rating of 105,000 Btu (0.75 gal/h × 140,000 Btu). The oil pressure is measured and adjusted, if necessary, to 100 psig within 3%. Figure 4-4 illustrates a typical oil furnace nameplate and oil burner nozzle.

Energy Source: Electricity

For an electric furnace the input is usually rated in watt-hours (Wh) or kilowatt-hours (kWh) (1000 Wh = 1 kWh of electricity consumed). Watts (W) can be converted to Btu by multiplying by 3.4131 (1 W = 3.4131 Btu). For example, if an electric furnace is rated at 30 kWh, the input is 102,393 Btuh (30 kWh × 1000 h/kWh × 3.4131 Btu). Figure 4-5 illustrates a typical electric furnace nameplate.

Efficiency

For both gas and oil furnaces, the output rating is reduced from the input rating by an efficiency factor. However, for an electric furnace, the input is equal to the output since there is no heat loss up the chimney. The general formula is

$$\text{Btuh output} = \text{Btuh input} \times \text{efficiency factor}$$

The output rating of both gas and oil furnaces is shown on the nameplate as a percentage of input. However, the efficiency of the installed furnace is usually lower. A service

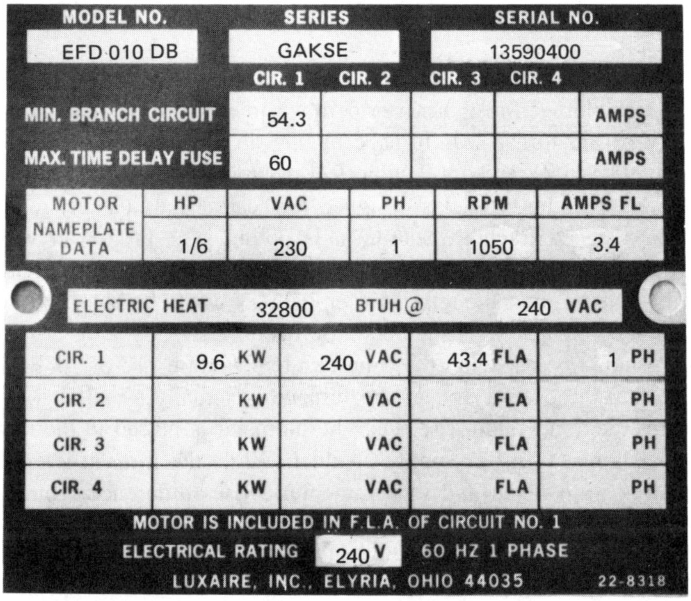

Figure 4-5 Typical electrical furnace nameplate.

technician should perform an efficiency test to determine if the rated efficiency is actually being maintained. The method of determining and adjusting combustion efficiency for both gas and oil furnaces is covered in Chapter 10. In most cases where the combustion efficiency is low, the technician can adjust the fuel burner so that the furnace might again approach the design efficiency. Having measured the efficiency of the furnace, the actual output can be calculated from the formula given. For example, if a gas furnace is operating at 80% efficiency* and has an input of 100,000 Btuh, the output (bonnet capacity) is 80,000 Btuh (100,000 Btuh × 0.80 efficiency). An electric furnace with 30 (kWh) (102,393 Btuh) input operates at 100% efficiency and has an output of 102,393 Btuh (102,393 Btuh × 1.00 efficiency).

It is seldom desirable to select a furnace with a rated output equal to the heat loss of the house. If this were done the furnace could be too small due to system losses or system inefficiency. Other losses can occur that are not accounted for in the heat-loss calculations, and combustion efficiencies may not always be achieved. For these reasons it is good practice to add 10 or 15% to the calculated heat loss to determine the required furnace output.

Fans

The fan produces the movement of air through the furnace, absorbing heat from the heat-exchanger surface and carrying it through the distribution system to the areas to be heated. Discussion of the fan involves.

- Air volume
- Static pressure
- Causes of poor air distribution

Air volume. For the system to operate satisfactorily, the fan must deliver the proper air volume. Most furnaces permit some flexibility (variation) in the air volume capacity of the furnace. A furnace having an output of 80,000 Btuh may be able to produce 800, 1200, and 1600 cubic feet per minute (ft³/min) of air volume, depending on the requirements. Systems designed for heating only usually require less air than do systems designed for both heating and cooling. The proper air volume for heating is usually determined by the required temperature rise. The temperature rise is the supply air temperature minus the return air temperature at the furnace. Systems used for heating only should be capable of a temperature rise of 85°F. Systems designed for heating and cooling should be capable of a minimum temperature rise of 70°F.

To find the quantity of air the furnace is actually circulating, a service technician measures the temperature rise. One thermometer is placed in the return air plenum and the other is placed in the supply air duct. While the furnace is operating continuously the readings are taken and the temperature rise (difference) computed. Thermometer locations for checking temperature rise are shown in Figure 4-6.

For a typical heating-only application, the return air temperature is 65°F and supply

---

* Manufacturer's rating.

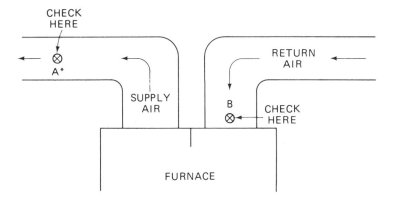

RETURN
AIR

A*

SUPPLY
AIR

B

CHECK
HERE

FURNACE

* CHECK POINT "A" MUST BE FAR ENOUGH DOWNSTREAM
THAT THE THERMOMETER IS NOT EXPOSED TO RADIANT
HEAT FROM THE HEAT EXCHANGER.

Figure 4-6 Thermometer locations for checking temperature rise.

air temperature 150°F, indicating an 85°F temperature rise (150°F − 65°F = 85°F). For a typical heating/cooling system, the return air temperature is 65°F and the supply air temperature is 135°F, indicating a temperature rise of 70°F (135°F − 65°F = 70°F). The air volume circulated is proportionately different for the two types of systems. To determine air volume the following formula is used:

$$\text{ft}^3/\text{min} = \frac{\text{Btuh output of furnace}}{\text{temperature rise (°F)} \times 1.08}$$

Thus, if the temperature rise on an 80,000-Btu output furnace is 85°F, the air volume is

$$\text{ft}^3/\text{min} = \frac{80,000 \text{ Btuh}}{85°\text{F} \times 1.08} = 870$$

If the temperature rise on an 80,000-Btuh output furnace is 70°F, the air volume is

$$\text{ft}^3/\text{min} = \frac{80,000 \text{ Btuh}}{70°\text{F} \times 1.08} = 1058$$

Many furnaces have two-speed fans, with the low speed used for heating and the high speed for cooling. Adjustments in the fan speed can be made on most furnaces to regulate the air volume to meet the requirements of the heating system. This will be discussed further in Chapter 7.

Static pressure.   A manufacturer rates the fan air volume of a furnace to produce each quantity of air at a certain external static pressure. *Static pressure* is the resistance

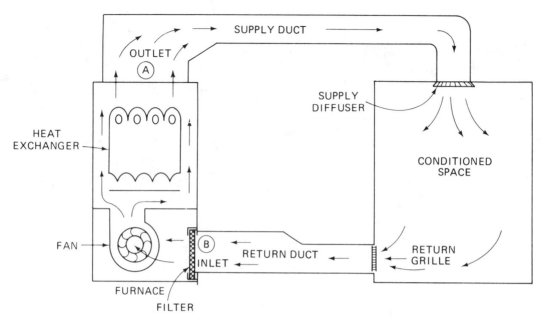

THE EXTERNAL STATIC –

FROM THE OUTLET AT "A" THROUGH THE
SUPPLY DUCT, SUPPLY DIFFUSER, RETURN
GRILLE, AND BACK THROUGH THE RETURN
DUCT TO "B"

THE INTERNAL STATIC –

FROM THE INLET OF THE FURNACE AT "B"
THROUGH THE FILTER, HEAT EXCHANGER
AND FAN TO THE OUTLET AT "A".

Figure 4-7 System external and internal static pressure diagram.

to air flow offered by any component through which the air passes. *External static pressure* is the resistance of all components outside the furnace itself. Thus, if a unit is rated to supply 600 ft^3/min at an external static pressure of 0.20 in., it means that the total resistance offered by supply ducts + return ducts + supply diffusers + return grillers must not exceed 0.20 in. of static pressure. A system external and internal static pressure diagram is shown in Figure 4-7.

Static pressure is measured in inches of water column (W.C.) that the pressure of the fan is capable of raising on a water gauge *manometer* (Figure 4-8). A manometer is an instrument for measuring pressure of gases and vapors.

The pressures in residential systems are small, so an inclined tube manometer is used to increase the accuracy of the readings taken. A manometer indicates the air pressure delivered by the fan above atmospheric pressure.

To illustrate how small these fan readings are, 1 atmosphere 14.7 lb/in.^{2} is equal to 408 in. W.C. Two-tenths of an inch (0.20 in. W.C.) of pressure is 1/2040 atmosphere.

A great deal of care must be taken in designing an air distribution system to stay within the rated external static pressure of the furnace. If the system resistances are too high, the amount of air flow of the furnace is reduced.

All manufacturers' ratings of external static pressure are based on clean filters. Dirty filters can cause reduced air volume and poor heating. A table showing the relationship between increased external static pressure and decreased air volume (ft^3/min) is illustrated in Figure 4-9.

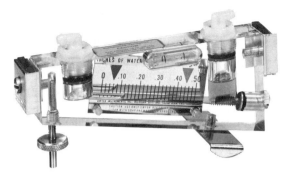

MODEL 170 INCLINED-TYPE PORTABLE
MANOMETER, WITH BUILT-IN LEVELING
AND MAGNETIC CLIPS. RANGE: 0–0.50 IN.
WATER (COURTESY, DWYER INSTRUMENTS, INC.)

SERIES 1222–8–D FLEX-TUBE
U-TUBE MANOMETER, MAGNETIC
MOUNTING CLIPS AND RED
GAUGE OIL INCLUDED.
RANGE: 8-IN. WATER (4–0–4)
(COURTESY, DWYER
INSTRUMENTS, INC.)

MODEL MZF, DRY-TYPE.
SUPPLIED WITH 5-IN. DRAFT
TUBE AND 9 FT OF RUBBER
TUBING. RANGE +0.05 TO 0.25 IN.
WATER (COURTESY, BACHARACH
INSTRUMENT, COMPANY.)

Figure 4-8 Types of manometers.

UPFLOW FURNACES

FURNACE MODEL NO.	FAN SPEED	CFM AIR FLOW AT EXTERNAL STATIC PRESSURE (IN. H_2O)			
		0.20	0.30	0.40	0.50
UPFLOW – (DIRECT DRIVE)					
A	HIGH	600	580	560	540
	MED.	550	520	500	470
	LOW	500	470	440	400
B	HIGH	800	750	700	650
	MED.	720	680	640	600
	LOW	665	630	590	550
C	HIGH	1000	940	870	800
	MED.	850	800	750	700
	LOW	700	670	630	600
D	HIGH	800	750	700	650
	MED.	—	—	—	—
	LOW	710	760	690	540

Figure 4-9 Manufacturer's data showing external static pressures (E.S.P.).

The greater the air volume and static pressure of a furnace, the larger the horsepower of the motor required to deliver the air. Therefore, units used for heat pumps, operating at higher air volumes and higher static pressures, require higher-horsepower motors than do units used for heating only. The speed or revolutions per minute (rev/min) of the fan wheel must often be increased for cooling. The wet cooling coil installed external to the basic furnace has a resistance to the air flow in addition to duct work and grilles. The total external static pressure of a cooling system may be as high as 0.50 in. W.C. static pressure. Following are given two typical performance ratings for a unit that can be applied to either heating only or heating and cooling.

Use	Air volume (cfm)	External static (in. W.C.)	Motor hp
Heating only	700	0.20	⅛
Heating and cooling	800	0.50	¼

Causes of poor air distribution. One of the first jobs of a service technician in evaluating the distribution system is to determine whether it has been designed for heating only or for heating and cooling. If the air volume is found to be too low, it can be caused by one or more of the following:

1. Incorrect fan speed

2. Closed or partially closed dampers

3. Dirty filters

4. Incorrectly sized ducts

5. High-pressure-drop duct fittings

If improper fan speed is the problem, the technician can check on the possibility of speeding it up. This may require a larger motor. The increased speed must be kept within permissible noise levels.

If closed dampers are the problem, adjustments can be made. Dampers are installed for balancing the system (regulating the air flow to each room) (Figure 4-10). Misadjustments should be corrected and, if necessary, the system rebalanced.

If dirty filters are the problem, the owner should be advised of proper preventive maintenance measures.

If duct sizes are the problem, some improvement may be made by speeding up the fan. However, there are limitations on improving this condition without a major redesign.

High-pressure-drop duct fittings are a problem that can often be corrected by minor changes in the duct work. The pressure drop in duct fittings is usually given in terms of the equivalent length of straight duct of the same size having an equal pressure drop.

Evaluating a Heating System   Chap. 4

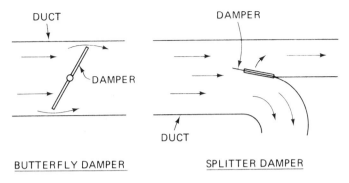

Figure 4-10 Balancing dampers.

Figure 4-11 shows pressure drops in terms of equivalent lengths for various duct fittings. Abrupt turns and restrictions should be avoided whenever possible. Where duct work is placed in an unheated attic, crawl space, or garage, insulated duct work should

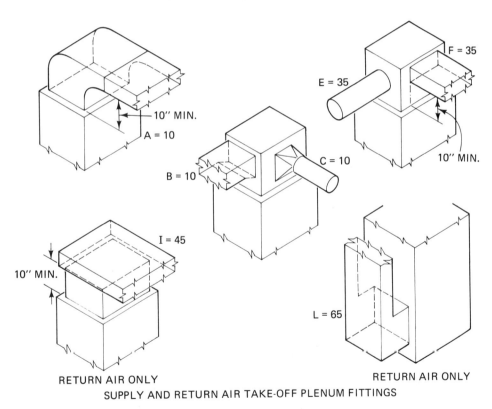

Figure 4-11 Supply and return fittings. (Courtesy, Air Conditioning Contractors of America—ACCA.)

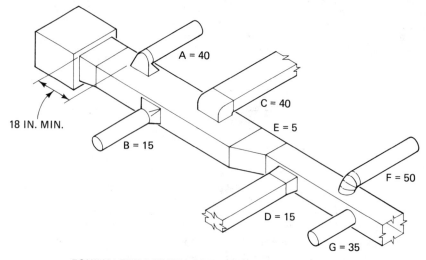

EQUIVALENT LENGTH OF EXTENDED PLENUM FITTINGS

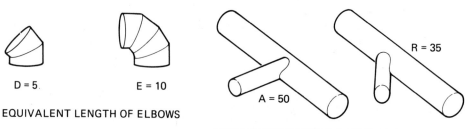

EQUIVALENT LENGTH OF ELBOWS

EQUIVALENT LENGTH ROUND DUCT FITTINGS

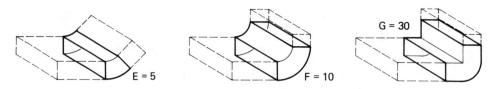

EQUIVALENT LENGTH OF ELBOWS

Figure 4-11 *(cont.)*

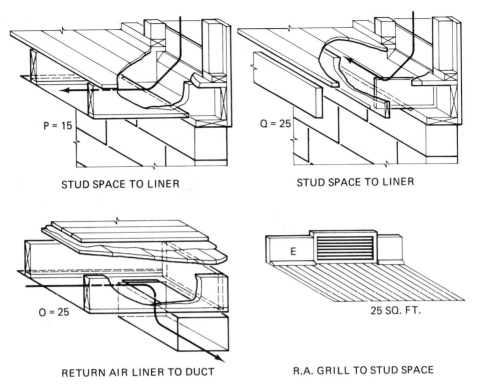

P = 15

STUD SPACE TO LINER

Q = 25

STUD SPACE TO LINER

O = 25

RETURN AIR LINER TO DUCT

E

25 SQ. FT.

R.A. GRILL TO STUD SPACE

EQUIVALENT LENGTH OF RETURN SYSTEM COMPONENTS

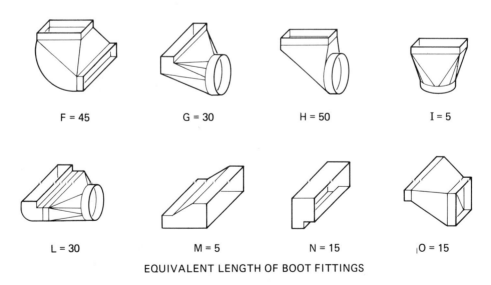

F = 45

G = 30

H = 50

I = 5

L = 30

M = 5

N = 15

O = 15

EQUIVALENT LENGTH OF BOOT FITTINGS

Figure 4-11 *(cont.)*

Evaluating the System

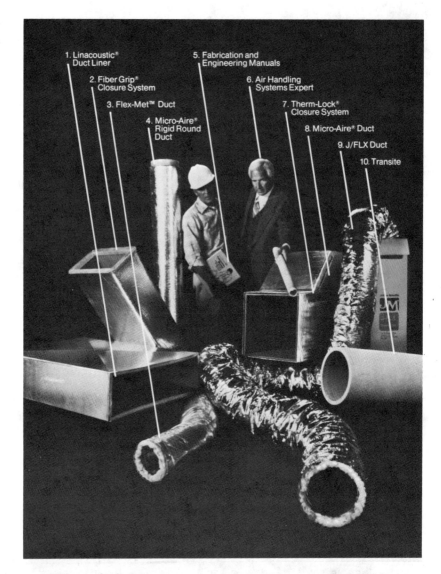

1. Linacoustic® Duct Liner
2. Fiber Grip® Closure System
3. Flex-Met™ Duct
4. Micro-Aire® Rigid Round Duct
5. Fabrication and Engineering Manuals
6. Air Handling Systems Expert
7. Therm-Lock® Closure System
8. Micro-Aire® Duct
9. J/FLX Duct
10. Transite

Figure 4-12 Example of flexible ducts and duct insulation. (Courtesy, Johnsmanville Sales Corporation)

Figure 4-13 Various types of flexible ducts. (Courtesy, Anco Products, Inc.)

be used. Various types of flexible ducts and methods of insulating ducts are illustrated in Figures 4-12 and 4-13.

Supply Air Distribution Systems

In general, there are three types of supply air distribution systems:

1. Radial

2. Perimeter loop

3. Trunk duct and branch

Selection of a system depends upon the house construction and room arrangement. Each system has its advantages for certain types of applications.

Radial. A radial system consists of a number of single pipes running from the furnace to the supply air outlets (Figure 4-14). In these systems the furnace is located near the center of the house so that the various runouts (supply air ducts) will be as nearly equal in length as possible. This system helps to provide warm floors and is used with both crawl-space construction and concrete slab floors.

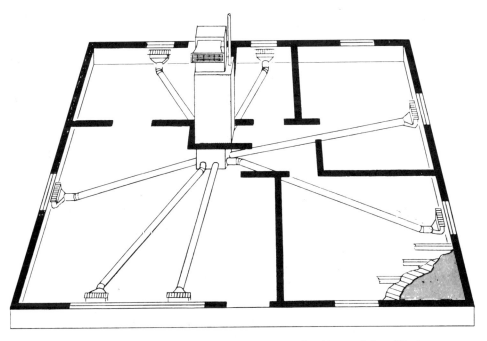

Figure 4-14 Radial supply air distribution system. (Reproduced by permission of Carrier Corporation, copyright Carrier Corporation.)

Evaluating the System

Perimeter loop.   The perimeter loop system (Figure 4-15) is a modification of the radial system. A single duct running along the perimeter (outer edge) of the house supplies air to each supply air diffuser located on the floor above. Radial ducts connect the perimeter loop to the furnace. The runout ducts from the furnace to the loop are larger and fewer than those in the radial system. This system lends itself for use with slab floor construction. The perimeter loop supplies extra heat along the perimeter of the house, warming the floor and heating the exterior walls of the house. The greatest heat loss in a slab floor is near its perimeter.

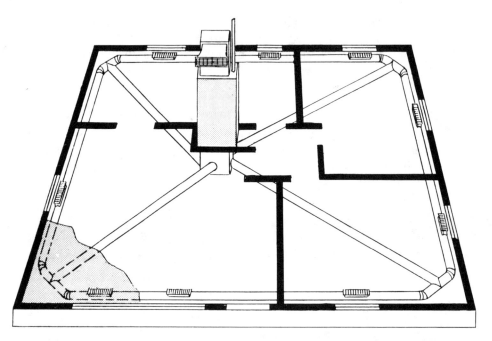

Figure 4-15   Perimeter loop supply air-distribution system. (Reproduced by permission of Carrier Corporation, copyright Carrier Corporation.)

Extended plenum.   The trunk-and-branch system is the most versatile of the system. It permits the furnace to be located in any convenient location in the house. Large ducts carry the air from the furnace to branches or runouts going to individual air outlets. The trunk duct (large duct from furnace) may be the same size throughout its entire length if the length does not exceed 25 ft. This is called an extended plenum (Figure 4-16). On large systems the trunk duct should be reduced in size, after branches remove a portion of the air, so that it tapers toward the end (Figure 4-17). A trunk duct can be used for basement installations or overhead installations of duct work. It can be used for both supply and return systems.

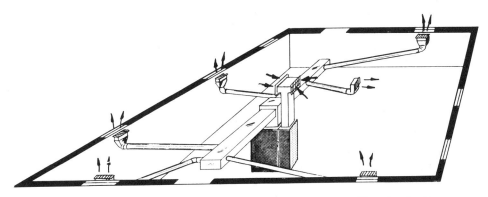

Figure 4-16 Extended plenum air supply distribution system. (Reproduced with permission of Carrier Corporation, copyright Carrier Corporation.)

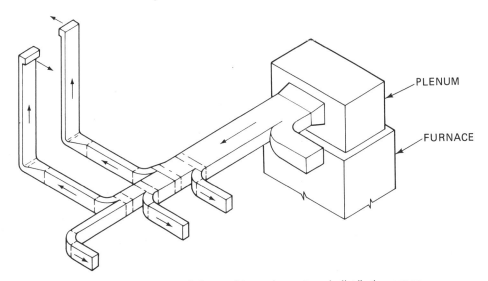

Figure 4-17 Reducing trunk duct used in supply or return air distribution systems.

Diffuser placement. The placement of supply air diffusers, or registers, depends on some extent on the climate of the area in which the house is located. In northern climates, where cold floors can be a problem and where outside exposures must be thoroughly heated, a perimeter location of the supply air diffusers is best. The register can be located in the floor adjacent to each exposed wall or in the baseboard. In many southern climates, where cooling air distribution is more important than heating air distribution, diffusers can be located on an inside wall as high as 6 ft above the floor. In extremely warm climates, the supply air outlet can be placed in the ceiling. Figures

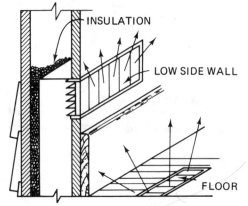

A REGISTERS SET TO DIRECT
AIR UPWARD ALONG THE WALL
AT AS WIDE AN ANGLE AS POSSIBLE

INSULATION

LOW SIDE WALL

FLOOR

FLOOR OR LOW SIDEWALL PERIMETER OUTLETS**A**

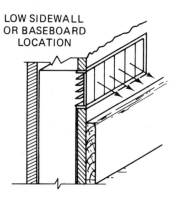

LOW SIDEWALL
OR BASEBOARD
LOCATION

A VERTICAL BARS WITH ADJUSTABLE
DEFLECTION, OR FIXED VERTICAL
BARS WITH DEFLECTION TO RIGHT
AND LEFT NOT EXCEEDING ABOUT
22 DEG. FOR LOW SIDEWALL
LOCATION, THE DEFLECTION FOR
HORIZONTAL, MULTIPLE VANE
REGISTERS SHOULD NOT EXCEED
22 DEG. FOR BASEBOARD LOCATIONS,
THE DEFLECTION FOR HORIZONTAL,
MULTIPLE VANE REGISTERS SHOULD
NOT EXCEED ABOUT 10 DEG.

RECOMMENDED TYPE OF BASEBOARD
AND LOW SIDEWALL INSTALLATION
ON WARM WALL**A**

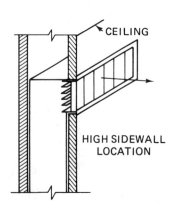

CEILING

HIGH SIDEWALL
LOCATION

A HORIZONTAL VANES, IN BACK OR FRONT,
TO GIVE DOWNWARD DEFLECTIONS NOT TO
EXCEED 15 TO 22 DEG.

RECOMMENDED TYPE OF HIGH SIDEWALL
INSTALLATION ON WARM WALL**A**

Figure 4-18 Placement of air supply distribution outlets. (By permission of *ASHRAE Handbook*.)

GROUP	OUTLET TYPE	OUTLET FLOW PATTERN	SIZE DETERMINED BY
1	CEILING AND HIGH SIDEWALL	HORIZONTAL	MAJOR APPLICATION – HEATING OR COOLING
2	FLOOR REGISTERS, BASEBOARD AND LOW SIDEWALL	VERTICAL, NONSPREADING	MAXIMUM ACCEPTABLE HEATING TEMPERATURE DIFFERENTIAL
3	FLOOR REGISTERS, BASEBOARD AND LOW SIDEWALL	VERTICAL, SPREADING	MINIMUM SUPPLY VELOCITY DIFFERS WITH TYPE AND ACCEPTABLE TEMPERATURE DIFFERENTIAL
4	BASEBOARD AND LOW SIDEWALL	HORIZONTAL	MAXIMUM SUPPLY VELOCITY SHOULD BE LESS THAN 300 FPM

GROUP	MOST EFFECTIVE APPLICATION	PREFERRED LOCATION
1	COOLING	NOT CRITICAL
2	COOLING AND HEATING	NOT CRITICAL
3	HEATING AND COOLING	ALONG EXPOSED PERIMETER
4	HEATING ONLY	LONG OUTLET – PERIMETER, SHORT OUTLET – NOT CRITICAL

Figure 4-19 General characteristics of air supply distribution outlets. (By permission of *ASHRAE Handbook.*)

4-18 and 4-19 show and describe various locations for the placement of air supply distribution outlets. Figure 4-20 shows various types of diffusers, registers, and grilles, some of which are used for supply outlets and some for return inlets.

Return Air Distribution Systems

The return air distribution system is usually of simple construction, having less pressure drop than the supply system. The radial system or the extended plenum system can be used. Where possible, return air is carried in boxed-in (enclosed) joist spaces (Figure 4-21).

Grille placement. In northern climates, where supply air diffusers are located along the perimeter, return air grilles (returns) are usually placed near the baseboard on inside walls. However, since the room temperature is not affected by the location of returns, they may be placed high on the inside walls to prevent drafts. In southern climates, where high inside wall outlets or ceiling diffusers are used, returns can be placed in any convenient location on inside walls. However, short-circuiting of the supply

SUPPLY
REGISTERS
AND GRILLES

SIDEWALL REGISTER

SIDEWALL REGISTER

FLOOR DIFFUSER

BASEBOARD REGISTER

SIDEWALL REGISTER

FLOOR DIFFUSER

BASEBOARD REGISTER

FLOOR DIFFUSER

BASEBOARD DIFFUSER

BASEBOARD REGISTER

BASEBOARD DIFFUSER

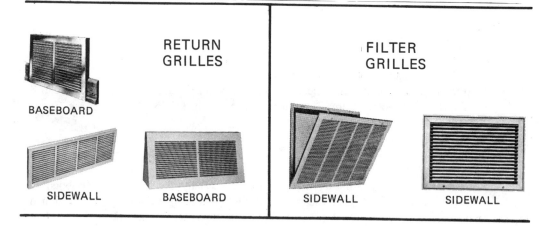

RETURN
GRILLES

FILTER
GRILLES

BASEBOARD

SIDEWALL

BASEBOARD

SIDEWALL

SIDEWALL

Figure 4-20 Various types of diffusers, grilles, and registers. (Courtesy, Hart & Cooley Manufacturing Company.)

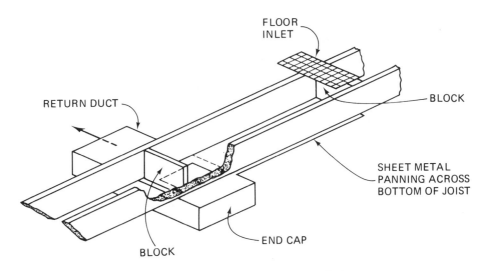

Figure 4-21 Boxed-in joist spaces in return air distribution system.

air directly into the return must be avoided. Whereas supply air outlets (one or more) are placed in every room to be heated, connecting rooms with open doorways can share a common return. Returns are not placed in bathrooms, kitchens, or garages. Air for these rooms must be taken from some other area. The general rule is that the total duct area for the return air system must be equal to the total duct area for the supply air system. Figure 4-22 shows possible locations for the placement of air return grilles in the return air system.

Provision for Cooling

Where cooling as well as heating is supplied from the same outlets, it is necessary to direct the supply air upward for cooling. Cold air is heavier than warm air and tends to puddle (collect near the floor). To raise cold air, baseboard diffusers should have adjustable

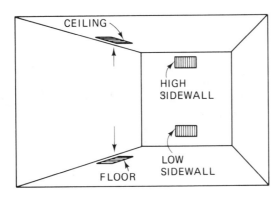

Figure 4-22 Placement of air return grilles in return air distribution system.

Evaluating the System

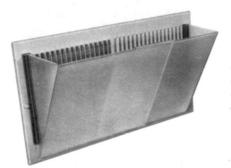

- FITS REGISTERS 9 TO 17 IN.
- SUPER HOLDING POWER MAGNETS
- CLEAR PLASTIC (BLENDS IN)
- HELPS ELIMINATE DRAFTS

Figure 4-23 Air deflector. (Courtesy, Skuttle Manufacturing Company.)

vanes or baffles. This upward movement can be accomplished by using air deflectors (Figure 4-23).

Other Provisions

- Dampers must be provided in each branch supply run from the furnace for balancing the system

BAROMETRIC

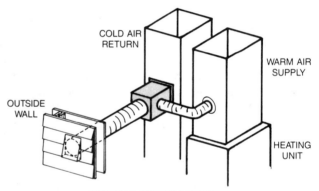

COLD AIR RETURN

WARM AIR SUPPLY

OUTSIDE WALL

HEATING UNIT

TYPICAL INSTALLATION

THERMAL

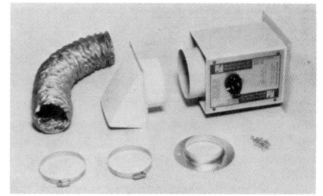

Figure 4-24 Barometric and thermal makeup air controls. (Courtesy, Skuttle Manufacturing Company.)

- All ducts running in unconditioned areas such as attics or garages must be insulated

- Ventilation air should be connected directly to the furnace or return air plenum, not to the intermediate return air duct work

- Outside air must be made available to the furnace for combustion (see Figure 4-24).

CHAPTER 4 STUDY QUESTIONS

The answers to the study questions are found in the sections of this chapter under the chapter topic indicated.

STUDY QUESTIONS	CHAPTER TOPIC
1. What are some of the common problems of residential heating systems from a comfort standpoint?	*Diagnosing the problem*
2. Name three types of uneven temperatures that cause discomfort.	*Diagnosing the problem*
3. Name three parts of the system in which to look for comfort problems.	*Diagnosing the problem*
4. What is the method of determining whether or not a gas furnace is supplied with its rated input?	*Energy source: gas*
5. Which dial on the gas meter is used for timing the rated input of a furnace?	*Energy source: gas*
6. What is the method of rating the flow of oil burner nozzles?	*Energy source: oil*
7. What is the Btu equivalent for 1 W of electricity?	*Energy source: electricity*
8. Give the formula for determining the efficiency of a furnace.	*Efficiency*
9. Give the formula for determining the cubic feet per minute of air circulated.	*Air volume*
10. Define external static pressure in terms of system resistance to the flow of air.	*Static pressure*
11. How is static pressure measured? What units are used?	*Static pressure*
12. How does external static pressure affect the flow of air?	*Static pressure*
13. Is the volume of air required for cooling less than, equal to, or greater than the volume of air required for heating?	*Static pressure*
14. What are the five principal causes of poor air distribution?	*Causes of poor air distribution*

15. Describe the three types of supply air distribution systems.

Supply air distribution systems

16. Define the equivalent length rating of a duct fitting.

Supply air distribution systems

17. What is the best location for return air grilles?

Supply air distribution systems

5 Installation Practice

OBJECTIVES

After studying this chapter, the student will be able to:

- Evaluate the quality of a heating installation in a residence
- Determine the proper wire size and fuse size for electrical circuits
- Determine the proper gas pipe size for a residential gas furnace installation

EVALUATING CONSTRUCTION AND INSTALLATION

When a service technician is called upon to correct a system complaint, there are two areas to be evaluated.

1. **Building construction:** Does the heating system conform to the building requirements?

2. **Furnace installation:** Is the equipment properly installed?

System complaints involve such conditions as drafts, uneven temperatures, cold floors, and other conditions that cause discomfort, even when the equipment may be operating well mechanically. Some of these complaints are due to the design of the system, which cannot be modified without considerable expense. Other system problems can be improved, if not fully corrected, when a service technician understands the cause.

Types of Building Construction

As illustrated in Figure 5-1, the types of building construction that require special treatment for best heating results include:

- Structures with basements

- Structures over crawl spaces

- Concrete slab construction

- Split-level structures

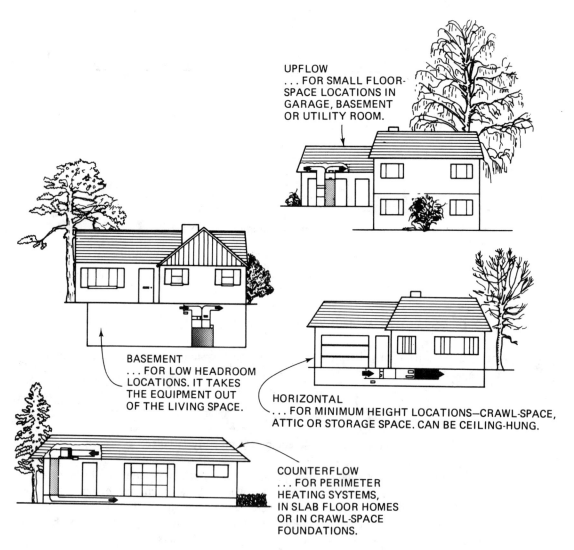

UPFLOW
... FOR SMALL FLOOR-SPACE LOCATIONS IN GARAGE, BASEMENT OR UTILITY ROOM.

BASEMENT
... FOR LOW HEADROOM LOCATIONS. IT TAKES THE EQUIPMENT OUT OF THE LIVING SPACE.

HORIZONTAL
... FOR MINIMUM HEIGHT LOCATIONS—CRAWL-SPACE, ATTIC OR STORAGE SPACE. CAN BE CEILING-HUNG.

COUNTERFLOW
... FOR PERIMETER HEATING SYSTEMS, IN SLAB FLOOR HOMES OR IN CRAWL-SPACE FOUNDATIONS.

Figure 5-1 Types of building construction that require treatment for best heating results.

Structures with basements. These structures should have some heat in the basement to produce warm floors on the level above. This practice should be followed whether or not the basement is finished for a recreation room. The structure should also be designed so that the basement can be properly heated at reasonable cost. The recommended construction for a properly heated basement is shown in Figures 5-2 and 5-3.

The following are desirable construction features of structures with basements:

- Subsoil below floor is well drained.

- A moisture barrier is placed below the floor and between the outside walls and the ground.

- Insulation is placed in the joist around the perimeter of the structure.

- Vaporproof insulating board is applied to the inside basement walls of existing structures and on the outside of new structures.

- Any piping that pierces the vapor barrier should be properly sealed.

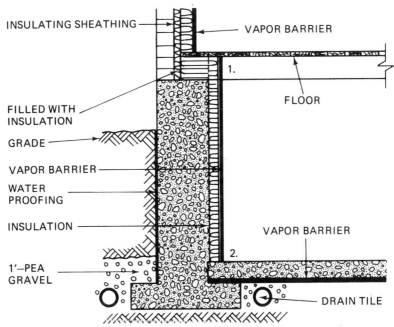

1. CONTINUE VAPOR BARRIER, LAP AND FASTEN,
   TO MAKE COMPLETE WARM-SIDE VAPOR BARRIER

2. CONTINUE VAPOR BARRIER DOWN WALL AND FOLD
   UNDER TO MAKE COMPLETE WARM-SIDE VAPOR BARRIER

Figure 5-2 Application of insulation in basement of existing structure. (Courtesy, The Detroit Edison Company.)

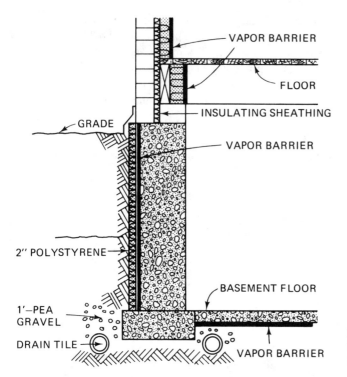

Figure 5-3 Application of insulation in basement of new structure. (Courtesy, The Detroit Edison Company.)

Structures over crawl spaces. It is important that the crawl space be heated in this type of structure. Heating produces warm floors on the level above. The best construction is similar in many ways to basement construction. Where crawl spaces are built above the bare ground a moisture barrier should be used, see Figure 5-4.

The following are features of crawl space construction:

- A moisture barrier is placed over the ground and extended upward a minimum of 6 in. on the side walls.

- The walls are waterproofed on the outside below grade.

- Perimeter joist spaces should be insulated.

- On existing structures insulating should be applied to the inside of the crawl space walls. While on new structures it should be applied to the outside of the walls.

- Ventilation of the crawlspace is provided in summer only.

- Dampers permit adjusting the heat feeding the crawl space area.

Concrete slab construction. It is important to warm the floor in concrete slab construction, particularly around the perimeter where the greatest heat loss occurs. This can be done by placing the heat-distributing ducts in the concrete floor, as shown in Figures 5-6 through 5-9.

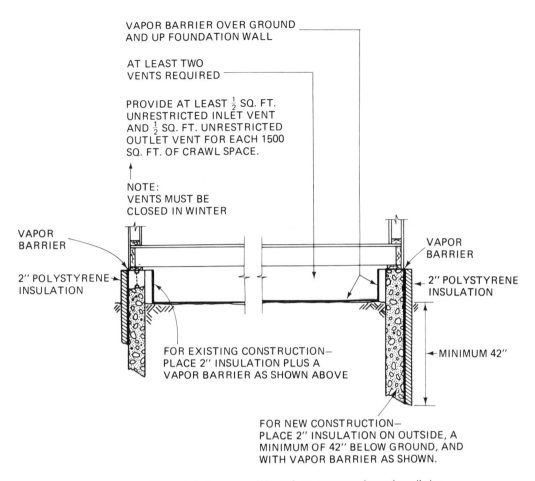

VAPOR BARRIER OVER GROUND
AND UP FOUNDATION WALL

AT LEAST TWO
VENTS REQUIRED

PROVIDE AT LEAST $\frac{1}{2}$ SQ. FT.
UNRESTRICTED INLET VENT
AND $\frac{1}{2}$ SQ. FT. UNRESTRICTED
OUTLET VENT FOR EACH 1500
SQ. FT. OF CRAWL SPACE.

NOTE:
VENTS MUST BE
CLOSED IN WINTER

VAPOR
BARRIER

2" POLYSTYRENE
INSULATION

VAPOR
BARRIER

2" POLYSTYRENE
INSULATION

FOR EXISTING CONSTRUCTION—
PLACE 2" INSULATION PLUS A
VAPOR BARRIER AS SHOWN ABOVE

MINIMUM 42"

FOR NEW CONSTRUCTION—
PLACE 2" INSULATION ON OUTSIDE, A
MINIMUM OF 42" BELOW GROUND, AND
WITH VAPOR BARRIER AS SHOWN.

Figure 5-4 Recommended crawl space construction and ventilation.

Figure 5-5 Concrete slab with perimeter insulation.

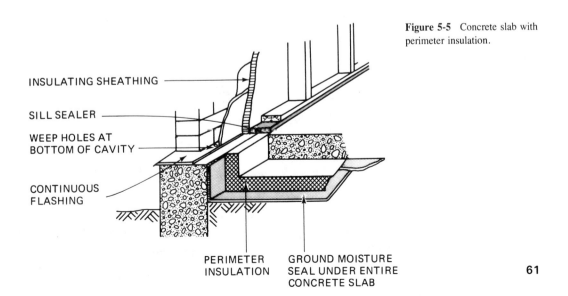

INSULATING SHEATHING

SILL SEALER

WEEP HOLES AT
BOTTOM OF CAVITY

CONTINUOUS
FLASHING

PERIMETER
INSULATION

GROUND MOISTURE
SEAL UNDER ENTIRE
CONCRETE SLAB

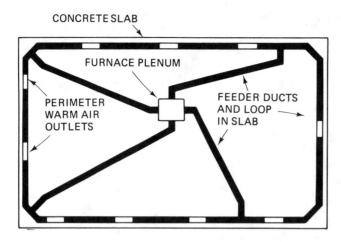

CONCRETE SLAB

FURNACE PLENUM

PERIMETER
WARM AIR
OUTLETS

FEEDER DUCTS
AND LOOP
IN SLAB

Figure 5-6 Perimeter-loop system with feeder and loop ducts in concrete slab (By permission of *ASHRAE Handbook*.)

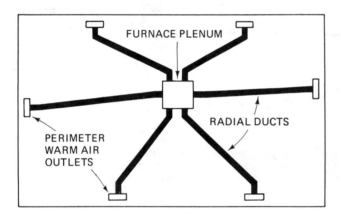

FURNACE PLENUM

PERIMETER
WARM AIR
OUTLETS

RADIAL DUCTS

Figure 5-7 Perimeter-radial system with feeder ducts in concrete slab or crawl space. (By permission of *ASHRAE Handbook*.)

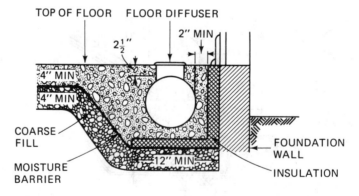

TOP OF FLOOR   FLOOR DIFFUSER

$2\frac{1}{2}''$

2'' MIN

4'' MIN

4'' MIN

COARSE
FILL

MOISTURE
BARRIER

12'' MIN

FOUNDATION
WALL

INSULATION

Figure 5-8 Cross-section of slab construction containing perimeter duct made of one type of material. (By permission of *ASHRAE Handbook*.)

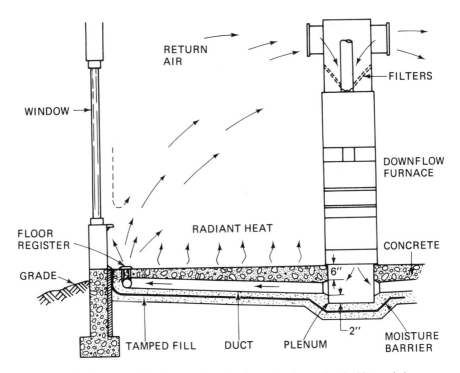

Figure 5-9 Construction of feeder ducts to plenum pit. (Reproduced with permission of Carrier Corporation, copyright Carrier Corporation.)

Some of the items included in this construction and shown in the illustrations are as follows:

- Edge insulation is installed around the perimeter of the slab, as shown in Figure 5-5.

- Ducts embedded in the floor supply perimeter heating (Figures 5-6 through 5-8).

- A concrete pit of proper size is poured below the furnace for the supply air plenum chamber (Figure 5-9).

- A moisture barrier is placed over the ground before the concrete slab is poured.

- Feeder ducts slope downward from the perimeter to the plenum pit.

- Ducts are constructed of waterproof materials with waterproof joints.

- Dampering of individual outlets is provided at the register location.

Split-level structures. This type of construction presents a problem in balancing the heat distribution to provide even heating because each level has its own heat-loss characteristics. Each level must be treated separately from an air distribution and balancing standpoint. Continuous fan operation is strongly recommended. In large structures of this type, a separate unit can be installed for each section.

Evaluating Construction and Installation

Furnace Installation

When a service technician inspects a furnace installation for the first time, it should be determined if minimum standards have been met in the original installation. The owner should be advised of any serious faults that may affect safety and performance. Some installation conditions of importance are

- Clearances from combustible material
- Circulating air supply
- Air for combustion, draft hood dilution, and ventilation
- Vent connections
- Electrical connections
- Gas piping

A service technician should comply with the local codes and regulations that govern installations. If there are no local codes, the equipment should be installed in accordance with the recommendation made by the National Board of Fire Underwriters, the American National Standards Institute (ANSI 2223.1), and the American Standards Association (ASA 221.30).

Clearances from combustible materials. Clearances between the furnace and combustible construction should not be reduced to less than standard unless permissible clearances are indicated on the attached furnace nameplate.
Standard clearances are as follows:

1. Keep 1 in. between combustible material and the top of plenum chamber, 6 in. between sides and rear of unit.
2. Keep 9 in. between combustible material and the draft hood and vent pipe in any direction.
3. Keep 18 in. between combustible material and the front of the unit.

Accessibility clearances take precedence over fire protection clearances (minimum clearances). Figure 5-10 shows recommended minimum clearances in a confined space. Allow at least 24 in. at the front of the furnace if all parts are accessible from the front. Otherwise, allow 24 in. on three sides of the furnace if back must be reached for servicing. When installation is made in a utility room, the door must be of sufficient size to allow replacement of the unit.

Circulating air supply. Circulating air supply may be 100% return air or any combination of fresh outside air and return air. It is recommended that return air plenums be lined with an acoustical duct liner to reduce any possible fan noise. This is particularly important when the distance from the return air grille to the furnace is close.

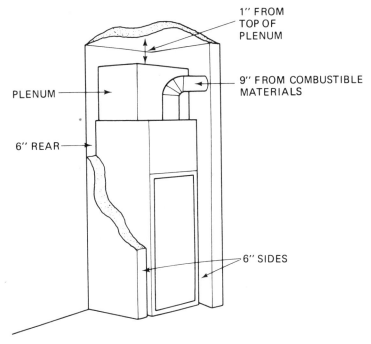

Figure 5-10 Recommended minimum clearances in a confined space.

All duct connections to the furnace must extend outside the furnace closet. Return air must not be taken from the furnace room or closet. Adequate return air duct height must be provided to allow filters to be removed and replaced. All return air must pass through the filter after it enters the return air plenum.

Air for combustion, draft hood dilution, and ventilation. Air for combustion, draft hood dilution, and ventilation differs somewhat for two types of conditions:

1. Furnace in confined space

2. Furnace is unconfined space

Confined space. If furnace is located in a confined space, such as a closet or small room, provisions must be made for supplying combustion and ventilation air (Figures 5-11 and 5-12). Two properly located openings of equal area are required. One opening should be located in the wall, door, or ceiling above the relief opening of the draft diverter. The other opening should be installed in the wall, door, or floor below the combustion air inlet of the furnace. The total free area* of each opening must be at least 1 in. for each 1000 Btuh input. It is recommended that the two permanent openings communicate directly with an additional room(s) of sufficient volume so that the combined volume of all spaces meets the criteria.

* The free area of a grille is the total area of the opening through which the air passes.

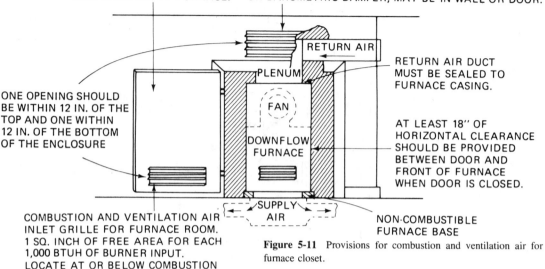

DOOR HEIGHT AND WIDTH SHOULD BE SUFFICIENT TO PROVIDE FOR INSTALLATION AND REMOVAL OF FURNACE.

VENTILATION AIR OUTLET GRILLE FOR FURNACE ROOM, 1 SQ. INCH OF FREE AREA FOR EACH 1,000 BTUH OF INPUT, LOCATED ABOVE DRAFT HOOD OR BAROMETRIC DAMPER, MAY BE IN WALL OR DOOR.

RETURN AIR

PLENUM

RETURN AIR DUCT MUST BE SEALED TO FURNACE CASING.

ONE OPENING SHOULD BE WITHIN 12 IN. OF THE TOP AND ONE WITHIN 12 IN. OF THE BOTTOM OF THE ENCLOSURE

FAN

DOWNFLOW FURNACE

AT LEAST 18″ OF HORIZONTAL CLEARANCE SHOULD BE PROVIDED BETWEEN DOOR AND FRONT OF FURNACE WHEN DOOR IS CLOSED.

COMBUSTION AND VENTILATION AIR INLET GRILLE FOR FURNACE ROOM. 1 SQ. INCH OF FREE AREA FOR EACH 1,000 BTUH OF BURNER INPUT. LOCATE AT OR BELOW COMBUSTION AIR INLET TO FURNACE.

SUPPLY AIR

NON-COMBUSTIBLE FURNACE BASE

Figure 5-11 Provisions for combustion and ventilation air for furnace closet.

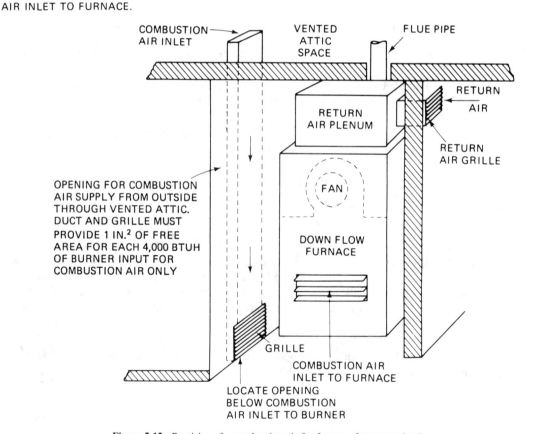

COMBUSTION AIR INLET

VENTED ATTIC SPACE

FLUE PIPE

RETURN AIR

RETURN AIR PLENUM

RETURN AIR GRILLE

OPENING FOR COMBUSTION AIR SUPPLY FROM OUTSIDE THROUGH VENTED ATTIC. DUCT AND GRILLE MUST PROVIDE 1 IN.^{2} OF FREE AREA FOR EACH 4,000 BTUH OF BURNER INPUT FOR COMBUSTION AIR ONLY

FAN

DOWN FLOW FURNACE

GRILLE

COMBUSTION AIR INLET TO FURNACE

LOCATE OPENING BELOW COMBUSTION AIR INLET TO BURNER

Figure 5-12 Provisions for combustion air for furnace, from vented attic space.

In closet installations where space is restricted, it is important to separate properly the incoming air to the furnace used for heating from that which is used for combustion. The openings must communicate directly or by ducts with the outdoors or spaces (crawl or attic) that are open to the outside. A schematic diagram of the air separation is shown in Figure 5-12.

Unconfined space. Air for combustion, draft hood dilution[*], and ventilation must be obtained from the outside or from spaces connected with the outside. If the unconfined space is within a building of unusually tight construction, then a permanent opening or openings, having a total free area of not less than 1 in. per 4000 Btuh of total input rating of all appliances must be provided as specified in ASI = 221.30. These standards are adopted and approved by both the National Fire Protection Association and the National Board of Fire Underwriters, NFPA No. 54.

A direct-vented space heating system vents directly through the outside wall, as shown in Figure 5-13. Directly vented systems draw their combustion air from the outdoors and exhaust the product of combustion in the same manner. In most cases, conditioned air is not used for combustion and makeup air is not required. Direct-vent systems may be mechanically controlled draft or natural draft. Most direct-vent furnaces will have a fan section that can be attached to the return air to aid in air circulation.

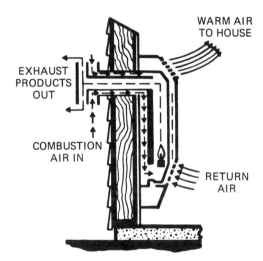

WARM AIR
TO HOUSE

EXHAUST
PRODUCTS
OUT

COMBUSTION
AIR IN

RETURN
AIR

Figure 5-13 Installation of direct-vented room heater. (Used by permission of the copyright holder, American Gas Association.)

Venting. It is important to provide proper venting of flue gases from the standpoint of fire protection as well as for the safety of people in a building. Good practices in venting include the following:

1. A chimney or flue vent outlet must extend above the roof surface and terminate no less than 2 ft above any object within a 10-ft radius or, if an anti-downdraft flue cap is used it is permissible to terminate 2 ft above the roof line, anyplace on the roof. The vent termination should be 1 ft above, or 4 ft away from, any

---

* Dilution air is air that enters a draft hood or draft regulator and mixes with the flue gases.

Evaluating Construction and Installation

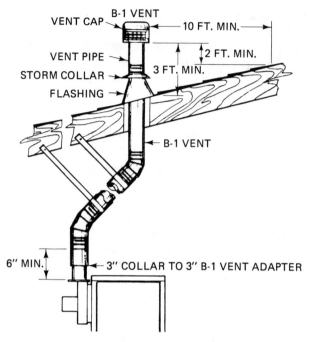

Figure 5-14 Recommendations for installation of type "B-1" vents.

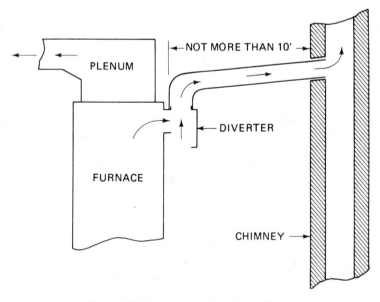

Figure 5-15 Maximum horizontal run of flue.

opening or air inlet to the building. Recommended chimney and flue heights are shown in Figure 5-14.

2. Horizontal runs of flue should maintain a minimum pitch of ¼ in./linear foot and should not exceed 75% of the vertical vent length (Figure 5-15).

3. Support pipes rigidly with hangers or straps.

4. Pipe must be the same size as the flue collar on the unit (Figure 5-16).

5. Run pipe as directly as possible with a minimum number of turns.

6. Do not connect vent piping to a chimney serving an open fireplace.

7. Extend flue pipe through chimney walls flush with the inner face of the chimney lines (Figure 5-17).

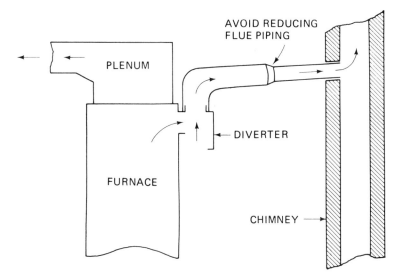

Figure 5-16 Flue pipe sizing.

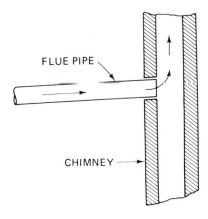

Figure 5-17 Chimney flue connection.

8. When more than one unit is vented into the same flue, the cross-sectional area of the main flue should be equal to the area of the one flue plus one-half the area of the second (Figures 5-18 and 5-19).

9. Observe local ordinances covering vent piping. When local ordinances do not cover the subject, it is recommended that the installer be guided by the *American Gas Association Code Book* NFPA-54

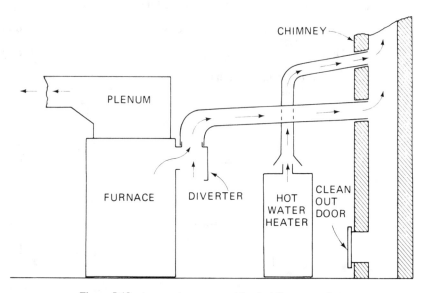

Figure 5-18 Approved arrangement for dual flue connection.

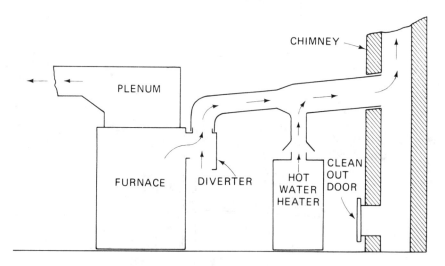

Figure 5-19 Alternate approved arrangement for dual flue connection.

Electrical wiring service.   All electrical wiring and connections should be made in accordance with the National Electric Code and with any local ordinances that may apply. Some of the important items to be observed in providing electrical service are as follows:

1.   A separate 120-V power circuit properly fused should be provided, with a disconnect service readily accessible at the furnace.

2.   The fuse size and the wire size is determined by the National Electric Code. The wire size and fuse size are based on 125% of the nameplate rating full-load amps (A) (FLA). FLA is the manufacturer's running current rating when motor is operated at peak load. The minimum branch circuit from the building service to the furnace should be 14-AWG wire and protected by a 15-Amp circuit breaker or fuse.

3.   All replacement wire used within the combustion area of a furnace should be of the same type and size as the original wire and rated 150 C.

4.   Unless a circuit breaker is used, the fuse should be of the time delay type.

5.   Strain relief connectors should be used at the entrance and exits of junction boxes.

6.   Control circuit wire (for 24 V) should be No. 18 wire with 105 C temperature rating. Low-voltage circuits (24 V) shall not be placed in any enclosure, compartment, or outlet box with line voltage circuits.

7.   Furnace shall be provided with a nameplate, voltage, and amperage ratings. Figure 5-20 shows typical furnace specifications.

Gas connections.   A recommended gas piping arrangement at the furnace is shown in Figure 5-21.

Some of the characteristics of good gas piping are as follows:

1.   Piping should include a vertical section to collect scale and dirt.

2.   A ground joint union should be placed at the connection to the furnace.

3.   A drip leg should be installed at the bottom of the vertical riser.

4.   The manual shutoff valve must be located external to the furnace casing, except where a combination gas valve is used. The manual shutoff is not required with a combination gas valve because the manual shutoff is part of this valve.

5.   Natural gas service pressure from the meter to the furnace is 7 in. W.C. (4.0 oz). At the furnace regulator it is then reduced to 3.5 in. (2.0 oz) to the burners. Liquid petroleum (LP) gas is furnished with a tank pressure regulator to provide 11 in. W.C. (6.3 oz) to the furnace burner.

	NATURAL GAS				
Model No.	NDGK040CF	NDGK050AF	NDGK075AF NDGK075CF	NDGK100AG NDGK100CG	NDGK125AK NDGK125CK
Capacity: Input (Btuh)	40,000	50,000	75,000	100,000	125,000
*Heating capacity (Btuh)	38,000	48,000	70,000	91,000	114,000
**Heating capacity (Btuh) (Ca.)	37,154	46,034	67,648	88,174	108,937
*D.O.E. A.F.U.E. %	94.7	94.8	93.2	91.4	91.1
**C.A. seasonal eff. %	81.8	83.5	84.2	83.4	81.0
Temp. rise (°F)	20–50	20–50	40–70	50–80	35–65
Flue size/type***	2-in./PVC	2-in./PVC	2-in./PVC	2-in./PVC	2-in./PVC
Gas piping size	½ in.	½ in.	½ in.	½ in.	½ in.
Burners (number)	2	2	3	4	5
Electrical data Volts-Ph-Hz.	115/60/1				
F.L.A.	8.0 A	8.0 A	8.0 A	10.8 A	11.1 A
Transformer size (VA)	40				
Filter Size (in.)	(2) 15 × 20 × 1				
Data Type	Washable				
Cooling Max. CFM @ .5 ESP	1300	1200	1230	1380	1965
Capacity Nominal Tons	3	3	3	3½	5
Weight Net (Lbs.)	180	180	190	215	242
Shipping (Lbs.)	202	200	210	240	265

Figure 5-20 Typical furnace specifications.

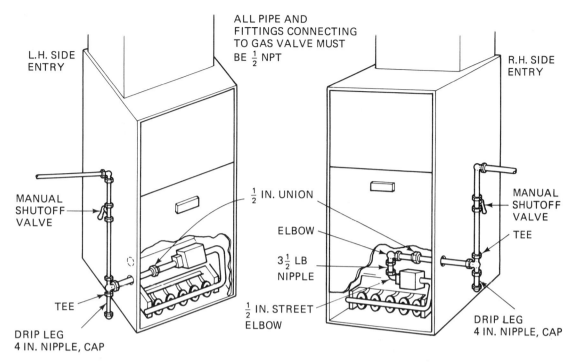

ALL PIPE AND
FITTINGS CONNECTING
TO GAS VALVE MUST
BE $\frac{1}{2}$ NPT

L.H. SIDE
ENTRY

R.H. SIDE
ENTRY

MANUAL
SHUTOFF
VALVE

$\frac{1}{2}$ IN. UNION

MANUAL
SHUTOFF
VALVE

ELBOW

TEE

$3\frac{1}{2}$ LB
NIPPLE

TEE

$\frac{1}{2}$ IN. STREET
ELBOW

DRIP LEG
4 IN. NIPPLE, CAP

DRIP LEG
4 IN. NIPPLE, CAP

Figure 5-21 Recommended gas piping arrangement.

Natural Gas Pipe Sizing

Adequate gas supply must be provided to the gas furnace. The installation contractor is usually responsible for providing piping from the gas source to the equipment. Therefore, if other gas appliances are used in the building, the entire gas piping layout must be examined from the gas meter to each piece of equipment to determine the proper gas piping sizes for the systems.

It may also be advisable, if additional gas requirements are being added to an existing building, to be certain that the gas meter supplied is adequate. This can be done by advising the gas company of the total connected load. The utility company will provide the necessary service at the meter.

General procedures.   The procedure for determining the proper gas piping sizes from the meter is as follows:

1.   Sketch a layout of the actual location of the gas piping from the meter to each gas appliance. Indicate on the sketch the length of each section of the piping diagram. Indicate on the sketch the Btuh input required for each gas appliance.

Evaluating Construction and Installation

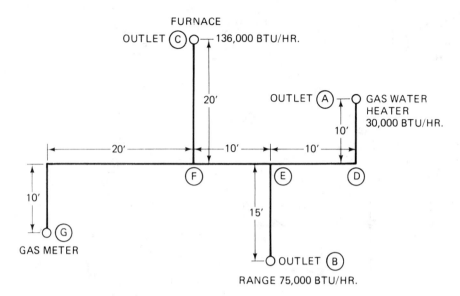

FURNACE

OUTLET (C) ◯—— 136,000 BTU/HR.

OUTLET (A) ◯ GAS WATER HEATER 30,000 BTU/HR.

20'

10'

20'

10'

10'

(F)

(E)

(D)

10'

15'

(G) GAS METER

◯ OUTLET (B)

RANGE 75,000 BTU/HR.

Figure 5-22 Typical gas piping layout.

See Figure 5-22 for an example. Note in this diagram that there are three appliances on the system

2. Convert the Btuh input of each gas appliance to cubic feet per hour by dividing the Btuh input by the Btu/ft^3 rating of the gas used. The example shown uses natural gas with a rating of 1000 Btu/ft^3. Thus, for the appliances shown in Figure 5-22 the cubic feet of gas used for each appliance is as follows:

Outlet	Appliance	Btuh input	Natural gas (ft^3/h)
A	Water heater	30,000	30
B	Range	75,000	75
C	Furnace	136,000	136

3. Determine the amount of gas required in cubic feet per hour for each section of the piping system, as shown on the layout

4. Using the appropriate figure (Figures 5-23, 5-24, 5-27, 5-29, and 5-30), select and record the proper pipe sizes

Most residential gas piping systems are sized using Figure 5-23 because most natural gas is delivered from the meter at a pressure of 0.5 psig and a specific gravity of $\frac{6}{10}$ (0.6). The specific gravity refers to the relative weight of 1 ft^3 of the gas as compared to an equal quantity of air.

In using Figure 5-23, the maximum length of pipe to the appliance or the greatest distance from the meter is used for sizing the entire piping system. Thus, in Figure

SAMPLE PROBLEM STEPS

Nominal Iron Pipe Size, Inches	Length of Pipe, Feet													
	10	20	30	40	50	60	70	80	90	100	125	150	175	200
1/4	32	22	18	15	14	12	11	11	10	9	8	8	7	6
3/4	72	49	40	34	30	27	25	23	22	21	18	17	15	14
1/2	132	92	73	63	56	50	46	43	40	38	34	31	28	26
3/4	278	190	152	130	115	105	96	90	84	79	72	64	59	55
1	520	350	285	245	215	195	180	170	160	150	130	120	110	100
1 1/4	1,050	730	590	500	440	400	370	350	320	305	275	250	225	210
1 1/2	1,600	1,100	890	760	670	610	560	530	490	460	410	380	350	320
2	3,050	2,100	1,650	1,450	1,270	1,150	1,050	990	930	870	780	710	650	610
2 1/2	4,800	3,300	2,700	2,300	2,000	1,850	1,700	1,600	1,500	1,400	1,250	1,130	1,050	980
3	8,500	5,900	4,700	4,100	3,600	3,250	3,000	2,800	2,600	2,500	2,200	2,000	1,850	1,700
4	17,500	12,000	9,700	8,300	7,400	6,800	6,200	5,800	5,400	5,100	4,500	4,100	3,800	3,500

Steps indicated: 2, 3 → 1/2 row; 4, 5 → 3/4 row; 6 → 1 row; 7 → 1 1/4 row. Column 60 circled.

* For specific gravity figure, check your local utility company.

Figure 5-23 Maximum capacity of pipe in cubic feet of gas per hour for gas pressures of 0.5 psig or less and a pressure drop of 0.3-in. W.C. (based on a 0.60 specific gravity gas). (Used by permission of the copyright holder, American Gas Association.)

5-22 the length of pipe to outlet (A) is 60 ft, and this number is used for all pipe sizes. Using the data above with the piping layout in Figure 5-22 and Figure 5-23, the pipe sizes are determined as follows:

1. Since 60 ft is the greatest distance from the meter, point *A* to point *G* (10 ft + 10 ft + 10 ft + 20 ft + 10 ft), the 60 "length of pipe" line is used in Figure 5-23.

2. Staying on the 60 "length of pipe" line, move down the column until the cubic feet per hour of the gas carried in *AD* (30) is covered. A ½-in. pipe, which can carry up to 50 ft³/h, is used

3. *DE* carries the same 30 ft³/h, so it is also ½ in.

4. *BE* carries 75 ft³/h, so it requires ¾-in. pipe, which carries up to 105 ft³/h.

5. *EF* carries 105 (30 + 75) ft³/h, so it is also ¾ in.

6. *CF* carries 136 ft³/h, so it requires 1-in. pipe, which carries up to 195 ft³/h.

7. FG carries 241 (136 + 105) ft³/h, so it requires 1¼-in. pipe, which carries up to 400 ft³/h.

Pipe section	Total-ft³/h natural gas carried in section	Iron pipe size (in.)
AD	30	½
DE	30	½
BE	75	¾
EF	105 (30 + 75)	¾
CF	136	1
FG	241 (136 + 105)	1¼

When using specific gravities other than 0.60, use Figure 5-24. For example, assume that the natural gas has a specific gravity of 0.75. From Figure 5-24 the multiplier would be 0.90. This multiplier would be used to redetermine the cubic feet per hour of gas handled by each part of the piping system.

When the 0.90 multiplier is applied to the previous example, the results are as follows:

Pipe section	ft³/h determined in example	ft³/h using multiplier of 0.90	Iron pipe size (in.)
AD	30	27 (0.90 × 30)	½
DE	30	27 (0.90 × 30)	½
BE	75	68 (0.90 × 75)	¾
EF	105	94 (0.90 × 105)	¾
CF	136	122 (0.90 × 136)	1
FG	241	217 (0.90 × 241)	1¼

Specific gravity	Multiplier		Specific gravity	Multiplier
.35	1.31		1.00	.78
.40	1.23		1.10	.74
.45	1.16		1.20	.71
.50	1.10		1.30	.68
.55	1.04		1.40	.66
.60	1.00		1.50	.63
.65	.96		1.60	.61
.70	.93		1.70	.59
(.75)	(.90)		1.80	.58
.80	.87		1.90	.56
.85	.84		2.00	.55
.90	.82		2.10	.54

Figure 5-24 Multipliers to be used only with Figures 5-23 and 5-25 when applying different specific gravity factors. (Used by permission of the copyright holder, American Gas Association.)

Commercial/industrial sizing. The volume of gas to be provided must be determined directly from the manufacturer's input ratings for the equipment being installed. In industrial gas pipe sizing, the measured length and the equivalent length of fittings and valves are used to arrive at the total equivalent length (TEL), which is then used for sizing the pipe. See Figure 5-25 and the example given.

Note: The "equivalent length" given for a fitting or gas cock is the resistance to flow that could be experienced in a section of straight pipe the same size. In the example the resistance to flow of the $\frac{3}{4}$-in. 90 ell is 2.06 ft which is equal to the resistance to flow in 2.06 ft of $\frac{3}{4}$-in. straight pipe (as found in Figure 5-25).

EQUIVALENT LENGTH OF STRAIGHT PIPE								
SCREWED FITTING		$\frac{1}{2}$	$\frac{3}{4}$	1	$1\frac{1}{4}$	$1\frac{1}{2}$	2	$2\frac{1}{2}$	3
90 ELL		1.55	2.06	2.62	3.45	4.02	5.17	6.16	7.67
45 ELL		0.73	0.96	1.22	1.61	1.88	2.41	2.88	3.58
TEE		3.10	4.12	5.24	6.90	8.04	10.3	12.3	15.3
GAS COCK		0.36	0.48	0.61	0.81	0.94	1.21	1.44	1.79

Figure 5-25 Equivalent lengths in feet, computed on the inside diameter of schedule 40 steel pipe.

Evaluating Construction and Installation

Sample piping problem. Using Figure 5-25 and the layout (Figure 5-26), the calculation for the TEL would be as follows, using the ¾-in. steel pipe.

$$
\begin{array}{lll}
\text{Measured length} & = 38 & \text{ft} \\
\text{Fittings} & = 8.10 \text{ ft} \leftarrow \begin{bmatrix} 4.12 \\ 2.06 \\ .96 \\ .96 \end{bmatrix} \\
\text{Gas cock} & = \underline{0.48 \text{ ft}} \\
\\
\text{TEL} & = 46.50 \text{ ft}
\end{array}
$$

SAMPLE PIPING PROBLEM

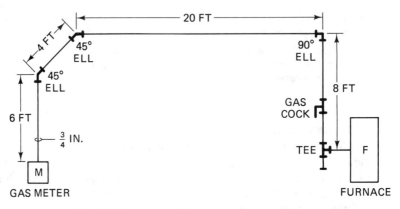

Figure 5-26 Sample piping layout—gas meter to furnace.

The simplified method for sizing gas piping for commercial and industrial applications is described next:

1. Measure the length of pipe from the gas meter to the most remote outlet. This is the only measurement necessary. To find the TEL, simply add 50% to the measured length.

2. Determine the Btuh required for each piece of equipment. Divide these figures by the heating value of the gas. For example:

$$
\frac{\text{Btuh}}{\text{heating value}} = \text{ft}^3/\text{h} \qquad \frac{75,000}{1,000} = 75 \text{ ft}^3/\text{h}
$$

3. Determine the volume (ft³/h) of gas that each section of the piping will carry.

4. Use the measured length of pipe and volume of gas flow in each section and outlet. Use Figure 5-27 for sizing.

Sample piping problem. Determine the necessary pipe size for each section and outlet of Figure 5-28. The natural gas has a specific gravity of 0.6 and a heating value

Nominal Iron Pipe Size Inches	Total Equivalent Length of Pipe in Feet										
	50	100	150	200	250	300	400	500	1000	1500	2000
1	284	195	157	134	119	108	92	82	56	45	39
1¼	583	400	322	275	244	221	189	168	115	93	79
1½	873	600	482	412	386	331	283	251	173	139	119
2	1681	1156	928	794	704	638	546	484	333	267	229
2½	2680	1842	1479	1266	1122	1017	870	771	530	426	364
3	4738	3256	2615	2238	1983	1797	1538	1363	937	752	644
3½	6937	4767	3828	3277	2904	2631	2252	1996	1372	1102	943
	9663	6641	5333	4565	4046	3666	3137	2780	1911	1535	1313
	17482	12015	9649	8258	7319	6632	5676	5030	3457	2776	2376
	28308	19456	15624	13372	11851	10738	9190	8145	5598	4496	3848
	58161	39974	52100	27474	24350	22062	18883	16735	11502	9237	7905
	105636	72603	58303	49900	44225	40071	34296	30396	20891	16776	14358
	167236	114940	92301	78998	70014	63438	54295	48120	33073	26559	22731

Figure 5-27 Pipe sizing table for pressures under 1 lb; approximate capacity of pipes of different diameters and lengths in cubic feet per hour with pressure drop of 0.5 in. W.C. and 0.6 specific gravity. (Used by permission of the copyright holder, American Gas Association.)

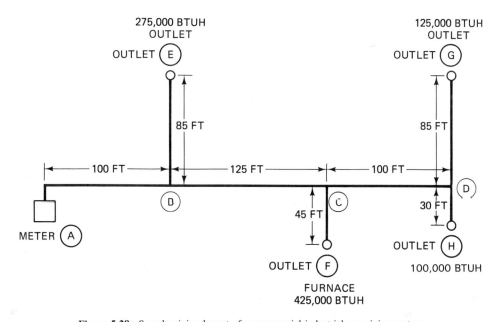

Figure 5-28 Sample piping layout of a commercial-industrial gas piping system.

of 1000 Btu/ft³. Gas pressure is 8 in. W.C. with a maximum allowable pressure drop of 0.5 in. W.C. in the piping.

1. The measured length of the piping from the meter (*A*) to the most remote outlet (*G*) is 100 ft + 125 ft + 100 ft + 85 ft = 410 ft.

2. Increase the measured length by 50%: 410 ft + 205 ft = 615 ft. The value 615 ft is then the TEL that is used to determine the pipe sizes from Figure 5-26.

3. When the calculated TEL falls between two columns in Figure 5-27, the larger TEL is used. In this case 615 ft falls between 500 and 1000; therefore, the 1000 column is used.

Main sections	Btuh	Flow in section ft³/h	Nominal iron pipe size (in.)
AB	925,000	925	3
BC		925 − 275 = 650	3
CD		650 − 425 = 225	2

Branches	Btuh	Flow in Branch ft³/h	Nominal iron pipe size (in.)
BE	275,000	275	2
CF	425,000	425	2½
DH	100,000	100	1¼
DG	125,000	125	1½

Liquid Petroleum Gas Pipe Sizing

Liquid petroleum gas is popular in areas where natural gas is in short supply. Trailers and recreation vehicles (RVs) use liquid petroleum (LP) gas for refrigeration as well as

Nominal (I.D.) Iron Pipe Size, Inches	Length of Pipe, Feet											
	10	20	30	40	50	60	70	80	90	100	125	150
½	275	189	152	129	114	103	96	89	83	78	69	63
¾	567	393	315	267	237	217	196	185	173	162	146	132
1	1071	732	590	504	448	409	378	346	322	307	275	252
1¼	2205	1496	1212	1039	913	834	771	724	677	630	567	511
1½	3307	2299	1858	1559	1417	1275	1181	1086	1023	976	866	787
2	6221	4331	3465	2992	2646	2394	2205	2047	1921	1811	1606	1496

Figure 5-29 Maximum capacity of pipe in thousands of Btuh of undiluted liquefied petroleum gases (at 11 in. W.C. inlet pressure, based on a pressure drop of 0.5 in. W.C.). (Used by permission of the copyright holder, American Gas Association.)

Outside Diameter, Inch	Length of Tubing, Feet									
	10	20	30	40	50	60	70	80	90	100
3/8	39	26	21	19	—	—	—	—	—	—
1/2	92	62	50	41	37	35	31	29	27	26
5/8	199	131	107	90	79	72	67	62	59	55
3/4	329	216	181	145	131	121	112	104	95	90
7/8	501	346	277	233	198	187	164	155	146	138

Figure 5-30 Maximum capacity of semirigid tubing in thousands of Btuh of undiluted liquefied petroleum gases (at 11 in. W.C. inlet pressure, based on a pressure drop of 0.5 in. W.C.). (Used by permission of the copyright holder, American Gas Association.)

heating. Figure 5-29 and 5-30 are used to calculate the pipe or tubing sizes necessary to supply LP gas to the furnace.

REVIEW PROBLEM

Using the sketch in Figure 5-31, assume the following loads:

Outlet A	50,000
Outlet B	60,000
Outlet C	150,000

Determine the pipe sizes for natural gas using a pressure drop of 0.3 in. W.C. and 0.60 specific gravity gas.

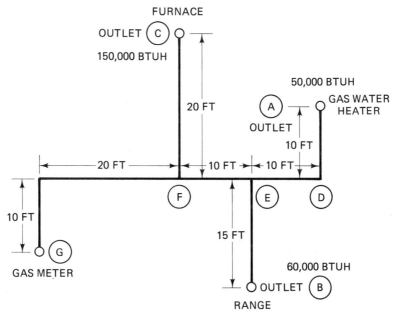

Figure 5-31 Gas piping layout from Figure 5-22 with new loads.

CHAPTER 5 STUDY QUESTIONS

The answers to the study questions are found in the sections of this chapter under the chapter topic indicated.

STUDY QUESTIONS	CHAPTER TOPIC
1. Name four general types of residential building construction.	*Types of building construction*
2. What are the desirable basement, crawl space, and concrete slab construction features?	*Types of building construction*
3. Describe the three types of air distribution systems for slab-type construction.	*Concrete slab construction*
4. Name three rules that apply to clearances from combustible materials.	*Clearances from combustible materials*
5. Name one important rule in supplying air for combustion.	*Air for combustion, draft hood dilution, and ventilation*
6. Name five (of the nine) rules for venting.	*Venting*
7. State two important rules for providing electric wiring service.	*Electrical wiring service*
8. Name three (of the five) items of recommended practice for reconnecting gas to the furnace.	*Gas connections*
9. Briefly describe the procedure for determining the proper gas piping sizes from the meter to the various gas appliances.	*Gas pipe sizing*
10. What is the natural gas pressure usually delivered from the meter?	*Gas pipe sizing*
11. What is the specific gravity of natural gas in most areas?	*Natural gas pipe sizing*
12. What design gas pipe pressure drop is considered good practice for residential gas piping?	*Natural gas pipe sizing*
13. What additional factors are considered in sizing gas piping for commercial and industrial users?	*Commercial/industrial piping*
14. What is the gas pressure delivered to the piping for LP gas?	*Liquid petroleum gas pipe sizing*
15. What is the pressure drop used for sizing the piping using LP gas?	*Liquid petroleum gas pipe sizing*
16. Crawl-space ventilation is provided during what period of the year?	*Structures over crawl spaces*
17. What is the principal problem on a split-level house?	*Split-level structures*
18. For industrial gas piping, what measurements are included in "equivalent length"?	*Commercial/industrial*

19. If the furnace is placed in a confined space, what special provisions need to be made?

20. In a house of tight construction, how much open area for outside air must be provided?

6 Combustion and Fuels

After studying this chapter, the student will be able to:

- Compare the heating qualities of various fuels
- Determine the conditions necessary for efficient utilization of fuels
- Use combustion test instruments
- Evaluate the results of combustion testing
- Determine the changes that must be made to reach maximum combustion efficiency

COMBUSTION

Combustion is the chemical process in which oxygen is combined rapidly with a fuel to release the stored energy in the form of heat. There are three conditions necessary for combustion to take place:

1. **Fuel:** Consisting of a combination of carbon and hydrogen
2. **Heat:** Sufficient to raise the temperature of the fuel to ignition (burning) point
3. **Oxygen:** From the air, combined with the elements in the fuel

Figure 6-1 illustrates the conditions necessary for combustion.

The fuel can be gas (such as natural gas), liquid (such as fuel oil), or solid (such as coal). Two elements all fuels have in common are hydrogen and carbon.

Fuel must be heated to burn. For example, a pilot burner (small flame) can be used to ignite gas burners; electric ignition (an electric spark) is used to ignite oil; and, usually, a wood-burning fire is used to ignite coal. An example of a pilot burner and spark igniter is shown in Figure 6-2.

Air containing oxygen must be present for burning of fuel to take place. As an example, a burning candle can be extinguished by placing a glass jar around it to enclose it (Figure 6-3). The candle goes out when it no longer has oxygen to burn.

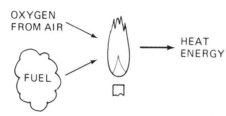

Figure 6-1 Conditions necessary for combustion.

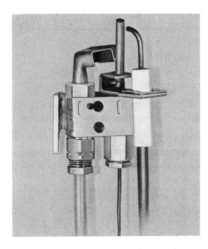

Figure 6-2 Example of pilot burner and spark igniter. (Courtesy, White-Rodgers, Division of Emerson Electric Company.)

Figure 6-3 Candle flame extinguished by lack of oxygen.

Combustion

TYPES OF COMBUSTION

There are two types of combustion: complete combustion and incomplete combustion. Complete combustion must be obtained in all fuel-burning devices. Incomplete combustion is dangerous.

Complete combustion results when carbon combines with oxygen to form carbon dioxide (CO_2), which is nontoxic and can be readily exhausted to the atmosphere. The hydrogen combines with oxygen to form water vapor (H_2O), which also can be harmlessly exhausted to the atmosphere.

Incomplete combustion results when a lack of sufficient oxygen causes the formation of undesirable products, including:

- Carbon monoxide (CO)

- Pure carbon or soot (C)

- Aldehyde, a colorless volatile liquid with a strong unpleasant odor (CH_3CHO)

Both carbon monoxide and aldehyde are toxic and poisonous. Soot causes coating of the heating surface of the furnace and reduces heat transfer (useful heat). Thus, the heating service technician must so adjust the fuel-burning device to produce complete combustion of the fuel.

During complete combustion the fuel combines with oxygen in the air to produce carbon dioxide and water vapor:

$$CH_4 + O_2 \rightarrow CO_2 + 2H_2O$$

Caution: Sufficient air must be provided for proper combustion to take place to prevent the dangers of incomplete combustion.

Air consists of about 21% oxygen and 79% nitrogen by volume (Figure 6-4). The nitrogen in the air dilutes the oxygen, which otherwise would be too concentrated to breathe in its pure form. Nitrogen is an *inert* chemical. The inert quality in a chemical

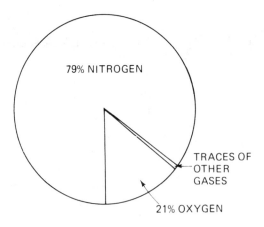

79% NITROGEN

TRACES OF OTHER GASES

21% OXYGEN

Figure 6-4 Chemical composition of air.

means that it remains in a pure state without combining with other chemicals under ordinary conditions. For example, in a furnace when nitrogen is heated to temperatures higher than 2000°F, it does not react with the elements of the fuel. It enters the furnace with the combustion air and leaves through the chimney as pure nitrogen.

Flue Gases

The flue gases of a furnace operating to produce complete combustion contain:

- Carbon dioxide

- Water vapor

- Nitrogen

- Excess air

Carbon dioxide and water vapor are the products of complete combustion. Nitrogen remains after oxygen in the combustion air is consumed by the fuel. Excess air is supplied to the fuel-burning device to guard against the possibility of producing incomplete combustion. Normally, furnaces are adjusted to use 5 to 50% excess air. The effect of the amount of excess air on the CO_2 in the flue gases is shown in Figure 6-5.

APPROXIMATE MAXIMUM CO_2 VALUES FOR VARIOUS FUELS WITH DIFFERENT PERCENTAGES OF EXCESS AIR

TYPE OF FUEL	MAXIMUM THEORETICAL CO_2 PERCENT	PERCENT CO_2 AT GIVEN EXCESS AIR VALUES		
		20%	40%	60%
GASEOUS FUELS				
NATURAL GAS	12.1	9.9	8.4	7.3
PROPANE GAS (COMMERCIAL)	13.9	11.4	9.6	8.4
BUTANE GAS (COMMERCIAL)	14.1	11.6	9.8	8.5
MIXED GAS (NATURAL AND				
CARBURETED WATER GAS)	11.2	12.5	10.5	9.1
CARBURETED WATER GAS	17.2	14.2	12.1	10.6
COKE OVEN GAS	11.2	9.2	7.8	6.8
LIQUID FUELS				
NO. 1 AND 2 FUEL OIL	15.0	12.3	10.5	9.1
NO. 6 FUEL OIL	16.5	13.6	11.6	10.1
SOLID FUELS				
BITUMINOUS COAL	18.2	15.1	12.9	11.3
ANTHRACITE	20.2	16.8	14.4	12.6
COKE	21.0	17.5	15.0	13.0

Figure 6-5 The effect of excess air on the CO_2 in the flue gases. (By permission of *ASHRAE Handbook*.)

Types of Combustion

NO.	CITY	HEAT VALUE, BTU/CU FT	SPECIFIC GRAVITY
1	ABILENE, TEX.	1121	0.710
2	AKRON, OHIO	1037	0.600
3	ALBUQUERQUE, N.M.	1120	0.646
4	ATLANTA, GA.	1031	0.604
5	BALTIMORE, MD.	1051	0.590
6	BIRMINGHAM, ALA.	1024	0.599
7	BOSTON, MASS.	1057	0.604
8	BROOKLYN, N.Y.	1049	0.595
9	BUTTE, MONT.	1000	0.610
10	CANTON, OHIO	1037	0.600
11	CHEYENNE, WYO.	1060	0.610
12	CINCINNATI, OHIO	1031	0.591
13	CLEVELAND, OHIO	1037	0.600
14	COLUMBUS, OHIO	1028	0.597
15	DALLAS, TEX.	1093	0.641
16	DENVER, COLO.	1011	0.659
17	DES MOINES, IOWA	1012	0.669
18	DETROIT, MICH.	1016	0.616
19	EL PASO, TEX.	1082	0.630
20	FT. WORTH, TEX.	1115	0.649
21	HOUSTON, TEX.‡	1031	0.623
22	KANSAS CITY, MO.	945	0.695
23	LITTLE ROCK, ARK.	1035	0.590
24	LOS ANGELES, CALIF.	1084	0.638
25	LOUISVILLE, KY.	1034	0.506
26	MEMPHIS, TENN.	1044	0.608
27	MILWAUKEE, WIS.	1051	0.627
28	NEW ORLEANS, LA.	1072	0.612
29	NEW YORK CITY	1049	0.595
30	OKLAHOMA CITY, OKLA.	1080	0.615
31	OMAHA, NEB.	1020	0.669
32	PARKERSBURG, W. VA.	1049	0.592
33	PHOENIX, ARIZ.	1071	0.633
34	PITTSBURGH, PA.	1051	0.595
35	PROVIDENCE, R.I.	1057	0.601
36	PROVO, UTAH	1032	0.605
37	PUEBLO, COLO.	980	0.706
38	RAPID CITY, S.D.	1077	0.607
39	ST. LOUIS, MO.	–	–
40	SALT LAKE CITY, UTAH	1082	0.614
41	SAN DIEGO, CALIF.	1079	0.643
42	SAN FRANCISCO, CALIF.	1086	0.624
43	TOLEDO, OHIO	1028	0.597
44	TULSA, OKLA.	1086	0.630
45	WACO, TEX.	1042	0.607
46	WASHINGTON, D.C.	1042	0.586
47	WICHITA, KAN.	1051	0.690
48	YOUNGSTOWN, OHIO	1037	0.600

*Average analyses obtained from the operating utility company (a) supplying the city; the supply may vary considerably from these data — especially where more than one pipeline supplies the city. Also, as new supplies may be received from other sources, the analyses may change.

Figure 6-6 The Btu ratings for units of natural gas. (By permission of *ASHRAE Handbook*.)

Heating Values

Each fuel when burned is capable of producing a given amount of heat, depending on the constitutents of the fuel. This information is useful in determining the heating capacity of a furnace. If the heating value of a unit of fuel produces a given amount of Btu, and the number of units of fuel burned per hour is known, the input rating of the furnace can be calculated. The Btu ratings for units of natural gas are shown in Figure 6-6. The specific gravity and heating value of fuel oil is shown in Figure 6-7, and the approximate Btu ratings for coal are shown in Figure 6-8.

EXAMPLE: An oil furnace burning No. 2 fuel oil uses 0.75 gal/h. What is the input rating of the furnace?

SOLUTION: The heating value of No. 2 oil from Figure 6-7 is between 141,800 and 137,000 Btu/gal. To simplify calculations, rating is rounded to 140,000 Btu/gal. Therefore, the input rating of the furnace would be

$$140,000 \text{ Btu/gal} \times 0.75 \text{ usage rate} = 105,000 \text{ Btuh input}$$

GRADE NO.	GRAVITY, API	WEIGHT, LB PER GALLON	HEATING VALUE, BTU PER GALLON
1	38–45	6.95 –6.675	137,000–132,900
2	30–38	7.296–6.960	141,800–137,000
4	20–28	7.787–7.396	148,100–143,100
5L	17–22	7.94 –7.686	150,000–146,800
5H	14–18	8.08 –7.89	152,000–149,400
6	8–15	8.448–8.053	155,900–151,300

(API AMERICAN PETROLEUM INSTITUTE RATING)

Figure 6-7 Typical gravity and heating values for standard grades of fuel oil. (By permission of *ASHRAE Handbook*.)

RANK	BTU PER LB AS RECEIVED
ANTHRACITE	12,700
SEMIANTHRACITE	13,600
LOW-VOLATILE BITUMINOUS	14,350
MEDIUM-VOLATILE BITUMINOUS	14,000
HIGH-VOLATILE BITUMINOUS A	13,800
HIGH VOLATILE BITUMINOUS B	12,500
HIGH-VOLATILE BITUMINOUS C	11,000
SUBBITUMINOUS B	9,000
SUBBITUMINOUS C	8,500
LIGNITE	6,900

Figure 6-8 Approximate Btu ratings for various types of coal. (By permission of *ASHRAE Handbook*.)

Figure 6-9 Units of measurement for gas, oil, and coal.

Note: The Btu ratings for gas are given in Btu/ft^3, for oil in Btu/gal, and for coal in Btu/lb. The units used differ for each fuel because of the form in which they are delivered (Figure 6-9).

Losses and Efficiencies

When fuel is burned in a furnace, a certain amount of heat is lost in the hot gases that rise through the chimney. Although this function is necessary for disposal of the products of combustion, the loss should be minimized to allow the furnace to operate at its highest efficiency. Air entering the furnace at room temperature, or lower, is heated to fuel gas temperatures. These temperatures range from 350°F to 600°F, depending on the design of the furnace and its adjustment by a service technician.

If the amount of heat lost is 20%, the efficiency of the furnace would be 80%. Figure 6-20 shows the calculation of the efficiency based on knowing the temperature and the carbon dioxide content of the flue gases.

Knowing the efficiency of the furnace makes it possible for a heating service technician to calculate the output of the furnace. The following formula is used:

$$\text{Btuh input} \times \% \text{ efficiency} = \text{Btu output}$$

EXAMPLE: The input of an oil furnace is 105,000 Btuh. Its efficiency is 80%. What is its output?

SOLUTION: 105,000 Btu × 0.80 efficiency = 84,000 Btuh output

Types of Flames

Basically, there are two types of flames: yellow and blue (Figure 6-10). Pressure-type oil burners burn with a yellow flame. Modern Bunsen-type gas burners burn with a blue flame. The difference is due mainly to the manner in which air is mixed with the fuel.

A yellow flame is produced when gas is burned by igniting fuel gushing from an open end of a gas pipe, such as may be seen in fixtures used for ornamental decoration.

A blue flame is produced when approximately 50% of the air requirement is mixed with the gas prior to ignition. This is called primary air. A Bunsen-type burner uses this arrangement. The balance of air, called *secondary air*, is supplied during combustion to the exterior of the flame. Air adjustments are discussed in Chapter 8.

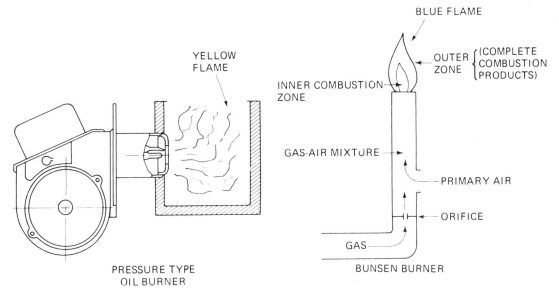

YELLOW FLAME

PRESSURE TYPE
OIL BURNER

BLUE FLAME

OUTER ZONE { (COMPLETE COMBUSTION PRODUCTS)

INNER COMBUSTION ZONE

GAS-AIR MIXTURE

PRIMARY AIR

ORIFICE

GAS

BUNSEN BURNER

Figure 6-10 Types of flames produced by pressure type oil burner and Bunsen burner. [Courtesy, Robertshaw Control Company (Bunsen Burner.)]

Improper gas flames are the result of inefficient or incomplete combustion and can be caused by:

- An excess supply of primary air

- A lack of secondary air

- The impingement of the flame on a cool surface (Figure 6-11)

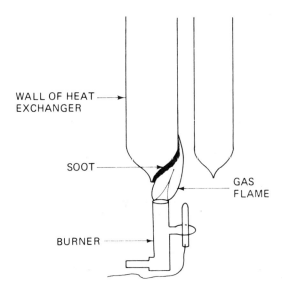

WALL OF HEAT EXCHANGER

SOOT

GAS FLAME

BURNER

Figure 6-11 Soot caused by impingement of flame on cool wall of heat exchanger.

Types of Combustion

FUELS

Fuels are available in three forms: gases, liquids, and solids. Gases include natural gas and liquid petroleum; fuel oils are rated by grades 1, 2, 4, 5, and 6; and coals are of various types, mainly anthracite and bituminous. Each fuel has its own individual Btu heat content per unit and its own desirable or undesirable characteristics. The fuel selection is usually based on availability, price, and type of application.

Types and Properties of Gaseous Fuels

There are three types of gaseous fuels. They are:

- Natural gas
- Manufactured gas
- Liquid petroleum (LP)

Natural gas comes from the earth in the form of gas and often accumulates in the upper part of oil wells. Manufactured gases are combustible gases, usually produced from solid or liquid fuel and used mainly for industrial processes. LP is by-product of the oil refining process. It is so named because it is stored in liquid form. However, LP is vaporized when burned.

Natural gas.   Natural gas is nearly odorless and colorless. Therefore, an odorant, such as a mercaptan (any of various compounds containing sulfur and having a disagreeable odor), is added so that a leak can be sensed. The content of gases differs somewhat according to locality. It is recommended that information be obtained from the local gas company relative to the specific gravity and the Btu/ft^3 content of the gas available.

The specific gravity affects piping sizes. *Specific gravity* is the ratio of the weight of a given volume of substance to an equal volume of air or water at a given temperature and pressure. Thus, gas with a specific gravity of 0.60 weighs $\frac{6}{10}$ or $\frac{3}{5}$ as much as air for an equal volume.

The Btu/ft^3 content of gas varies from 900 to 1200, depending on the locality, but it is usually in the range of 1000 to 1050 Btu/ft^3.

The chief constituent of natural gas is methane. Commonly called marsh gas, methane is a gaseous hydrocarbon that is a product of decomposition of organic matter in marshes or mines or of the carbonization of coal. Natural gas is comprised of from 55 to 95% methane combined with other hydrocarbon gas.

Manufactured gas.   Manufactured gas is produced from coal, oil, and other hydrocarbons. It is comparatively low in Btu/ft^3, usually in the range of 500 to 600. It is not considered an economical space-heating fuel.

Liquid petroleum.   There are two types of liquid petroleum: propane and butane. Propane is the more useful of the two as a space heating fuel since it boils at $-40°$F and therefore can be readily vaporized for heating in a northern climate. Butane boils at about 32°F.

Propane has a heating value of 21,560 Btu/lb or about 2500 Btu/ft^3. Butane has a heating value of 21,180 Btu/lb or about 3200 Btu/ft^3. When LP gas is used as a heating fuel, the equipment must be designed to use this type of gas. When ordering equipment, the purchaser must indicate which type of gaseous fuel is being used. Conversion kits are available to convert natural gas furnaces to LP gas when necessary. It is important to follow the manufacturer's instructions with great care.

Note: Propane and butane vapors are generally considered more dangerous than those of natural gas, since they have higher specific gravities (propane 1.52, butane 2.01). Because the vapor is heavier it tends to accumulate near the floor, thereby increasing the danger of an explosion upon ignition.

Types and Properties of Fuel Oils

Fuel oils are rated according to their Btu/lb content and API gravity (shown in Figure 6-7). The API gravity is an index selected by the American Petroleum Institute. There are six grades of oil: Nos. 1, 2, 4, 5 (light), 5 (heavy), and 6. Note that the lighter-weight oils have a higher API gravity.

Grade No. 1: A light-grade distillate prepared for vaporizing-type oil burners

Grade No. 2: A heavier distillate than Grade No. 1 and is manufactured for domestic pressure-type oil burners

Grade No. 4: Light residue or heavy distillate. It is produced for pressure-type commercial oil burners using a higher pressure than domestic burners.

Grade No. 5 (light): A residual-type fuel of medium weight. It is used for commercial-type burners that are specially designed for its use.

Grade No. 5 (heavy): A residual-type fuel for commercial oil burners. It usually requires preheating.

Grade No. 6: Also called Bunker C; a heavy residue used for commercial burners. It requires preheating in the tank to permit pumping, and additional preheating at the burner to permit atomization (breaking up into fine particles).

Types and Properties of Coals

There are four different types of coal: anthracite, bituminous, subbituminous, and lignite. Coal is constituted principally of carbon with the better grades having as much at 80% carbon. The types vary not only in Btu/lb but also in their burning and handling qualities.

Anthracite. Anthracite is a clean, hard coal. It burns with an almost smokeless short flame. It is difficult to ignite but burns freely when started. It is noncaking, leaving a fine ash that does not clog grates and ash removal equipment.

Bituminous.   Bituminous coals include a wide range of coals varying from high grade in the east to low grade in the west. It is more brittle than anthracite coal and readily breaks up into small pieces for grading and screening. The length of the flame is long, but varies for different grades. Unless burning is carefully controlled, much smoke and soot can result.

Subbituminous.   This coal has a high moisture content and tends to break up when dry. It can ignite spontaneously when stored. It ignites easily and burns with a medium flame. It is desirable for its noncaking characteristic and because it forms little soot and smoke.

Lignite.   Lignite coal has a woody consistency, is high in moisture content and low in heating value, and is clean to handle. Lignite has a greater tendency to break up when dry than does subbituminous coal. Because of its high moisture content, it is difficult to ignite. It is noncaking and forms little smoke and soot.

EFFICIENCY OF OPERATION

Combustion is a chemical reaction resulting in the production of a flame. The fuels used for heating consist chiefly of carbon. In combustion, carbon and oxygen are combined to produce heat. Instruments are used to measure how well the equipment performs the process of combustion. The heating service technician makes whatever adjustments are necessary to produce the most efficient operation.

The products of combustion that leave the oil-heating unit through the flue are

- Carbon dioxide (CO_2)
- Carbon monoxide (CO)
- Oxygen (O)
- Nitrogen (N)
- Water vapor (H_2O)

A description of the products of combustion is shown in Figure 6-12.

The measurement of the CO_2 in the flue gases is an indication of the amount of air used by the fuel-burning equipment. It is desirable to have a high CO_2 measurement, as this indicates a hot fire. The maximum CO_2 measurement for oil with no excess air is 15.6%; for natural gas, 11.8%. However, it is not practical with field-installed equipment to reach these high CO_2 readings. In practice, oil furnaces should have a CO_2 reading of between 10 and 12%; natural gas furnaces should read between $8\frac{1}{4}$ and $9\frac{1}{2}$%.

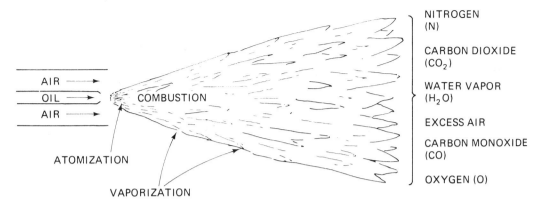

AIR →
OIL →
AIR →

COMBUSTION

ATOMIZATION

VAPORIZATION

NITROGEN
(N)

CARBON DIOXIDE
(CO_2)

WATER VAPOR
(H_2O)

EXCESS AIR

CARBON MONOXIDE
(CO)

OXYGEN (O)

Figure 6-12 Products of combustion.

The CO_2 in the flue gases is the indicator used (along with stack temperature) to measure the efficiency of combustion.

INSTRUMENTS USED IN TESTING

Instruments used for combustion testing are available from a number of manufacturers. While the illustrations for the instruments described below have been provided by specific companies, instruments that perform similar functions can be obtained from various other manufacturers.

The instruments and their functions are:

- **Draft Gauge:** used for measuring draft (Figure 6-13)

Figure 6-13 Draft gauge model MZF, dry type, range +0.05 to +0.25 in. water, supplied with 5-in. draft tube and 9 ft of rubber tubing. (Courtesy, Bacharach Instrument Company.)

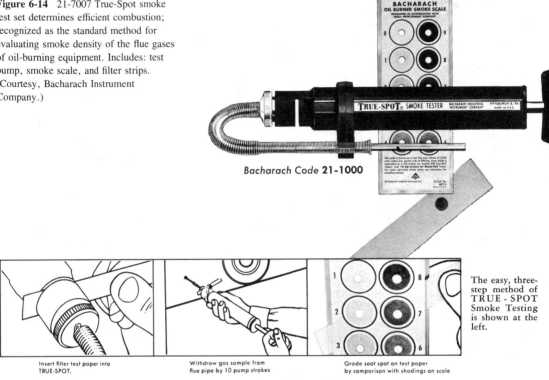

Figure 6-14 21-7007 True-Spot smoke test set determines efficient combustion; recognized as the standard method for evaluating smoke density of the flue gases of oil-burning equipment. Includes: test pump, smoke scale, and filter strips. (Courtesy, Bacharach Instrument Company.)

Bacharach Code **21-1000**

The easy, three-step method of TRUE - SPOT Smoke Testing is shown at the left.

Insert filter test paper into TRUE-SPOT.

Withdraw gas sample from flue pipe by 10 pump strokes

Grade soot spot on test paper by comparison with shadings on scale

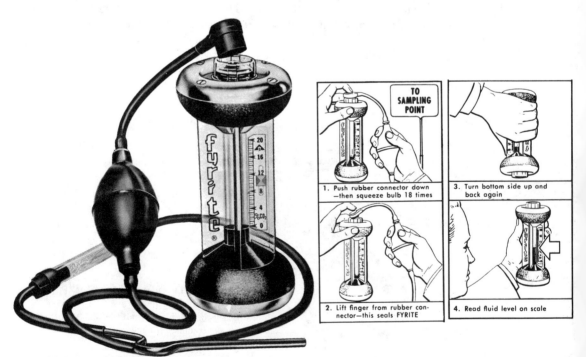

TO SAMPLING POINT

1. Push rubber connector down —then squeeze bulb 18 times

2. Lift finger from rubber connector—this seals FYRITE

3. Turn bottom side up and back again

4. Read fluid level on scale

Figure 6-15 Fyrite gas analyzers, available for measuring carbon dioxide or oxygen, can be exposed to temperatures from $-30°$ to $150°F$, and gases up to $850°F$ may be tested. Kit 10-5001 CO_2 (range 0–20%) and Kit 10-5012 O_2 (range 0–21%). Case is included. (Courtesy, Bacharach Instrument Company.)

- **True-Spot Smoke Tester:** used for determining smoke scale (Figure 6-14)

- **Flue Gas Analyzer:** used for testing CO_2 content (Figure 6-15)

- **Stack Thermometer:** used for determining stack temperature (Figure 6-16)

Complete combustion kits (Figure 6-17) are available with many of the items listed above. The location of the various parts of the heating plant equipment, and sample holes for testing, are shown in Figure 6-18.

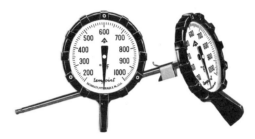

Figure 6-16 Tempoint dial thermometer, bimetal type, accurate from $-40°$ to $+1000°F$. Designed to read stack temperatures, recalibration possible. (Courtesy, Bacharach Instrument Company.)

Combustion testing kit for gas oil and coal-fired installations; includes: CO_2 indicator, draft gauge 0 to .25″ W.C., smoke gauge pump, smoke chart, stack thermometer, combustion efficiency slide rule, portable magnehelic gauge with 4″ dial 0 to .25″ W.C. and 300–2000 FPM, carrying case and operating instructions. (Courtesy, Dwyer Instruments, Inc.)

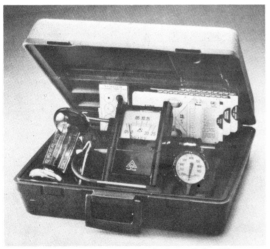

Oil burner combustion testing kit; includes fyrite CO_2 indicator, true spot smoke tester, fire efficiency finder/stack loss sliderule, dial thermometer, MZF draft gauge, draftrite draft gauge and carrying case. Gas burner combustion kits are also available. (Courtesy, Bacharach Instrument Company)

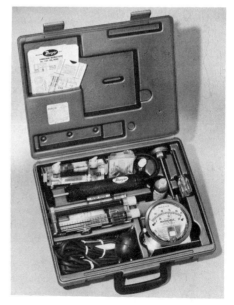

Figure 6-17 Combustion testing kits.

Instruments Used in Testing

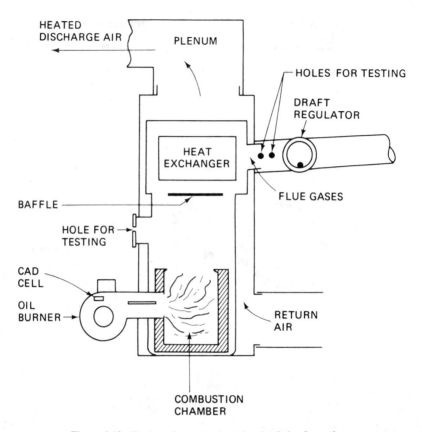

Figure 6-18 Heating plant equipment showing holes for testing.

TESTING PROCEDURES

Tests should be made in the following order:

1. Draft measurement

2. CO_2 content

3. Stack temperature

4. Smoke sample

The equipment should be run for a minimum of 5 to 10 min before testing to stabilize operating conditions. A record should be kept both before adjustments are made and after the tests.

Draft Test

The draft gauge reads in inches of water column. For example, a reading of 0.02 in. W.C. means 2 hundredths of an inch of water column.

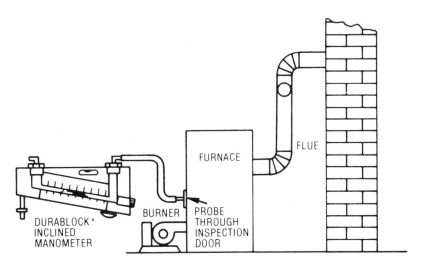

Figure 6-19 Using a draft gauge to adjust for efficient combustion. (Courtesy, Dwyer Instruments, Inc.)

Always calibrate the instrument before using it. Place the instrument on a level surface and adjust the indicator needle to read zero.

Drill a $\frac{1}{4}$-in. hole in the fire box door (Figure 6-19) and two $\frac{1}{4}$-in. holes in the flue at the point just after it leaves the heat exchanger. The holes in the flue must be placed between the heat exchanger and the draft regulator on an oil furnace, and between the heat exchanger and the draft diverter on a gas furnace. One of the two holes in the flue is used for the stack thermometer; the other is used for the CO_2 and smoke tests.

Occasionally, an additional $\frac{1}{4}$-in. hole is drilled in the flue pipe near the chimney to measure chimney draft. This is normally used only when it is necessary to troubleshoot draft problems.

The draft should always be negative when measured with the draft gauge, since the flue gases are moving away from the furnace. The draft-over-the-fire, measured at the firebox door, should be -0.01 to -0.02 in. W.C. The difference between the draft reading in the flue at the furnace outlet, and the draft-over-the-fire reading indicates the heat-exchanger leakage.

Smoke Test

The burner flame should not produce excessive smoke. Smoke causes soot (carbon) to collect on the surfaces of the heat exchanger, reducing its heat-transfer rate. A soot deposit of $\frac{1}{8}$ in. can cause a reduction of 10% in the rate of heat absorption.

Measurement of smoke is performed by using a smoke tester. A sample is collected by pumping 2200 cm^3 (10 full strokes with the sampling pump) through a 0.38-cm^2 area filter paper. The color of the sample filter paper spot is compared to a standard graduated smoke scale (Figure 6-14). Spot zero (0) is white and indicates no smoke. Spot number 9 is darkest and represents the most extreme smoke condition. Between zero and 9 the scale has 10 different grades. It is most desirable to produce smoke at a scale of number

Testing Procedures

1 or number 2 but not zero. Older style or conversion units could read as high as number 4. Zero indicates excess air supply to the burner and low efficiency. Readings higher than number 2 indicate the production of excessive carbon and soot. Normally, this test is performed only on oil-burning equipment.

Carbon Dioxide Test

An analyzer for CO_2 uses potassium hydroxide (KOH), a chemical that has the property of being able to absorb large quantities of CO_2. A known volume of flue gas is run into the tester. Since KOH will absorb only CO_2, the reduction in volume of the flue gas is an indication of the amount of CO_2 absorbed by the KOH solution.

Instructions for using the tester shown in Figure 6-15 are as follows:

1. Set the instrument to zero by adjusting the sliding scale to the level of the fluid in the tube.

2. Insert sample tube in flue opening. Place rubber connector on top of instrument and depress to open valve. Collapse bulb 18 times to fill instrument with flue gas and to release valve.

3. Tip instrument over and back twice and hold at 45-degree angle for 5 s.

4. Hold instrument upright and read CO_2 content on scale. Release pressure by opening valve when test is complete.

Stack Temperature

A stack thermometer is used to determine stack temperature. Insert thermometer in flue hole as shown in Figure 6-18. Operate burner unit until the temperature rise, as read on the thermometer, is no more than 3°F/min (indicating stability); then read the final stack temperature.

COMBUSTION EFFICIENCY

Combustion efficiency, expressed in percentage, is a measure of the useful heat produced in the fuel compared to the amount of fuel available. Thus, a furnace that operates at 80% efficiency is one that loses 20% of the fuel value in the heat that goes out through the chimney. High-efficiency furnaces have an operating efficiency of up to 96%.

A combustion efficiency slide rule is a useful tool (Figure 6-20). After determining the stack (flue) temperature and CO_2 content, and by using the appropriate slide on the rule, the combustion efficiency can be determined.

Note that combustion efficiency is based on net stack temperature. Net stack temperature is the reading taken on the stack thermometer minus the room temperature (the temperature of the air entering the furnace).

For example, assume that the net stack temperature for an oil burner is found to be 500°F and the CO_2 content is determined as 9%. Using the slide rule, move the large

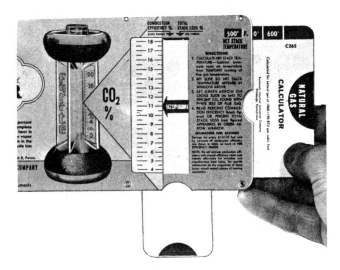

Figure 6-20 Combustion efficiency slide rule. (Courtesy, Bacharach Instrument Company.)

slide to the right so that 500 appears in the small window at the upper right marked "net stack temperature." Then move the small vertical slide until the arrow points to reading 9 on the CO_2 scale. Through the window in the arrow, read the figures 80 (black) and 20 (red). This means that the combustion efficiency is 80% and the stack loss is 20%. The table in Figure 6-21 shows, for example, how increasing the combustion efficiency from 80% to 85% would save $5.90 of every $100 of fuel cost.

FROM AN ORIGINAL EFFICIENCY OF	TO AN INCREASED COMBUSTION EFFICIENCY OF:							
	55%	60%	65%	70%	75%	80%	85%	90%
50%	9.10	16.70	23.10	28.60	33.30	37.50	41.20	44.40
55%	–	8.30	15.40	21.50	26.70	31.20	35.30	38.90
60%	–	–	7.70	14.30	20.00	25.00	29.40	33.30
65%	–	–	–	7.10	13.30	18.80	23.50	27.80
70%	–	–	–	–	6.70	12.50	17.60	22.20
75%	–	–	–	–	–	6.30	11.80	16.70
80%	–	–	–	–	–	–	5.90	11.10
85%	–	–	–	–	–	–	–	5.60

Figure 6-21 Fuel saved by increasing efficiency. (Courtesy, R. W. Beckett Corporation.)

Combustion Efficiency

ANALYSIS AND ADJUSTMENTS

Usually, the original tests are made after routine maintenance has been performed. The combustion tests indicate the condition of the equipment and point to further service or adjustments that may be necessary.

Oil-Burning Equipment

On oil-burning equipment, adjustments are made in the air supply to the burner. Air is reduced to maintain a smoke test within the number 1 to number 2 limits while providing the highest possible CO_2 content in the flue gases.

If an efficiency rating of 75% or better cannot be obtained as a result of adjustments in the air supply, further service on the burner is required.

Listed below are some common causes of low CO_2 content and smoky fires (Figure 6-22).

1. Incorrect air supply

2. Combustion chamber air leaks

3. Improper operation of draft regulator

4. Insufficient draft

5. Burner "on" periods too short

6. Oil does not conform to burner requirements

7. Air-handling parts defective or incorrectly adjusted

8. Firebox cracked

9. Spray angle of nozzle unsuitable

10. Nozzle worn, clogged, or incorrect type

11. Gallons/hour rate too high for size of combustion chamber

12. Ignition delay due to defective stack control

13. Nozzle spray or capacity unsuited to type of burner

14. Oil pressure to nozzle improperly adjusted

15. Nozzle loose or not centered

16. Electrodes dirty, loose, or incorrectly set

17. Cutoff valve leaks

18. Rotary burner motor running under speed

Some conditions that produce poor efficiency, such as those indicated below, can be determined by visual inspection.

1. Improper fan delivery or incorrect air shutter opening.

2. Furnace or boiler has excessive air leaks.

3. Draft regulator is improperly installed or sticking.

4. Draft is insufficient due to defective flue or insufficient height of chimney.

5. Burner "on" periods are too short.

6. Oil does not conform to burner requirements.

7. Air handling parts defective or incorrectly adjusted.

8. Firebox is cracked or of improper refractory material.

9. Spray angle of nozzle unsuited to air pattern of burner or shape of firebox.

10. Nozzle is worn, clogged or of incorrect type.

11. Gph. rate is too high for size of combustion chamber.

12. Ignition is delayed due to defective stack control.

13. Nozzle spray or capacity unsuited to the particular type of burner being used.

14. Oil pressure to nozzle improperly adjusted causing poor spray characteristics.

15. Nozzle is loose or not centered.

16. Electrodes are dirty, loose or incorrectly set.

17. Cut-off valve leaks, allowing after-drip of fuel oil.

18. Rotary burner motor is running underspeed.

Figure 6-22 Common causes of low CO_2 content and smoky fires. (Courtesy, Bacharach Instrument Company.)

Analysis and Adjustments

1. Check burner shutdown. A flame should last no longer than 2 s after burner shuts down.

2. Check the flame. It should be symmetrically shaped and centered in the combustion chamber. It should not strike the walls or floor of the combustion chamber.

3. Check for air leaks. There should be no leakage around burner tube where it enters the combustion chamber.

4. Check the burner operating period. Burning periods of less than 5 min duration usually do not produce efficient operation.

Gas-Burning Equipment

On gas-burning equipment, the primary air is reduced by adjusting the air shutter to provide a blue flame. The secondary air is a fixed quantity on most furnaces. However, inspection should be made to determine if the secondary air restrictor has become loose or, perhaps, removed. Correction should be made, if required.

If the flame does not adjust properly to produce a blue flame, and an efficiency rating of 75% or better cannot be obtained, further service is required.

Some causes of poor efficiency are:

1. **Too Much Excess Air:** It may be necessary to place a restrictor in the flue pipe to reduce the draft. The method of flue restrictor placement is shown in Figure 6-23.

There should be a neutral point in all gas furnaces. Also, there should be a slight positive pressure in the top of the heat exchanger and a slight negative pressure near the bottom. The neutral point should be in a location slightly above the fire (observation) door.

2. **Unclean Burner Ports:** To clean burner ports, remove lint and dirt.

3. **Insufficient Gas Pressure:** The draft diverter should be checked with the burner in operation. Air should be moving into the opening, thus indicated a negative pressure at the inlet. This can be verified by holding a lighted match at the opening.

4. **Improper Gas Pressure:** The gas pressure should be $3\frac{1}{2}$ in. W.C. at the manifold for natural gas. Check the gas meter for input into the furnace. It should read the same as the input indicated on the furnace nameplate. If the gas pressure reads between 3 and 4 in. W.C. and still does not produce the rated input, the orifice should be cleaned or replaced with one of proper size. For LP the gas pressure should be 11 in. W.C. at the manifold on the furnace.

5. **Check the "On" and "Off" Periods of the Furnace:** "On" periods of less than 5 min are too brief to produce high efficiency.

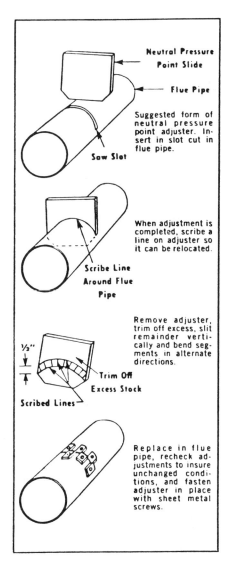

Figure 6-23 Flue restrictor placement. (Courtesy, Bacharach Instrument Company.)

CHAPTER 6 STUDY QUESTIONS

The answers to the study questions are found in the sections of this chapter under the chapter topic indicated.

STUDY QUESTIONS	CHAPTER TOPIC
1. What type of process is combustion? Describe the action that takes place.	*Combustion*
2. What are the three conditions necessary for combustion?	*Combustion*

3. What action takes place during complete combustion? What chemicals are combined and what are the products? — *Types of combustion*

4. What is the cause of incomplete combustion? What are the products formed? — *Types of combustion*

5. What is the percent of oxygen in the air? — *Types of combustion*

6. What is the range of heating values for natural gas, fuel oil, and coal? — *Heating values*

7. What is the maximum efficiency for natural gas and oil fuels? — *Losses and efficiencies*

8. What is the proper color for an oil flame? A gas flame? — *Types of flames*

9. Should the draft-over-the-fire, for an oil burner, be positive, negative, or neutral? — *Draft test*

10. Using a draft regulator, with an oil furnace, what is the proper draft measurement over-the-fire? — *Draft test*

11. In testing for CO_2 in the flue gas with a potassium hydroxide analyzer, how many times should the bulb be collapsed? — *Carbon dioxide test*

12. What should be the combustion efficiency on a standard oil-burning furnace? — *Combustion efficiency*

13. What dollar savings for every $100 of fuel cost would be saved in increasing the efficiency from 60% to 80%? — *Combustion efficiency*

14. Name ten conditions that can cause an oil burner to produce a low CO_2 and a smoky fire. — *Oil burning equipment*

15. Name three conditions that can cause a gas burner to operate at low efficiency. — *Gas burning equipment*

7 Parts Common to All Furnaces

OBJECTIVES

After studying this chapter, the student will be able to:

- Identify the various components of forced warm air heating furnaces

- Adjust the speed of a furnace fan

- Provide proper service and maintenance for common parts of a heating system

HOW A FURNACE OPERATES

A warm air furnace is a device for providing space heating. Fuel, a form of energy, is converted into heat and distributed to various parts of a structure.

Fuel-burning furnaces provide heat by combustion of the fuel within a heat exchanger. Air is passed over the outside surface of the heat exchanger, transferring the heat from the fuel to the air. In a fuel-burning furnace, the products of combustion are exhausted to the atmosphere through the flue passages connected to the heat exchanger.

In an electric furnace, air passes directly over the electrically heated elements without the use of a heat exchanger, since no products of combustion are formed.

A forced-air furnace uses a fan to propel the air over the heat exchanger and to circulate the air through the distribution system. A furnace is considered to be a residential type when its input is less than 250,000 Btuh.

BASIC COMPONENTS

There are seven basic components of a forced warm air furnace:

1. Heat exchanger

2. Fuel-burning device

3. Cabinet or enclosure

4. Fan and motor

5. Air filters

6. Humidifier

7. Controls

The fuel-burning device, item 2, is discussed in Chapter 8. The controls, item 7, are discussed in Chapters 16 through 19.

Gravity-type warm air furnaces include all the components just listed with the exception of the fan and motor and air filters. The basic components of a gravity warm air heating system are shown in Figure 7-1. The gravity furnace is so named because air is circulated over the heat exchanger and through the distribution system by the force of gravity. Air heated by the furnace becomes lighter and rises. The movement of air is caused by the colder (heavier) air replacing the heated air, creating continuous movement as long as heat is applied. Gravity furnaces for residential heating have been replaced to a great extent by the forced air design.

GRAVITY WARM-AIR HEATING SYSTEM

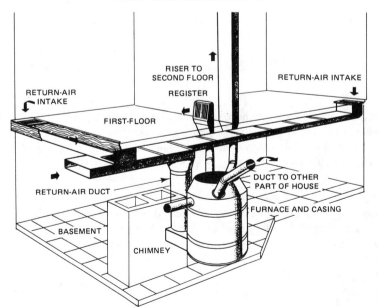

Figure 7-1 Basic components of a gravity warm air heating system. (Courtesy, Small Homes Council—Building Research Council, University of Illinois.)

ARRANGEMENT OF COMPONENTS

Four different designs of forced-air furnaces are in common use, each requiring a different arrangement of the basic components. The four designs are

1. Horizontal

2. Upflow or highboy

3. Lowboy

4. Downflow or counterflow

The *horizontal* furnace is used in attic spaces or crawl spaces where the height of the furnace must be kept as low as possible (Figures 7-2 and 7-3). Air enters at one end

BLOWER   FLUE CONNECTION

R.A.
INLET
AND
FILTER

HEAT EXCHANGER

BURNER AND
CONTROLS

WARM
AIR
OUTLET

Figure 7-2 Horizontal forced warm air furnace. (By permission of *ASHRAE Handbook.*)

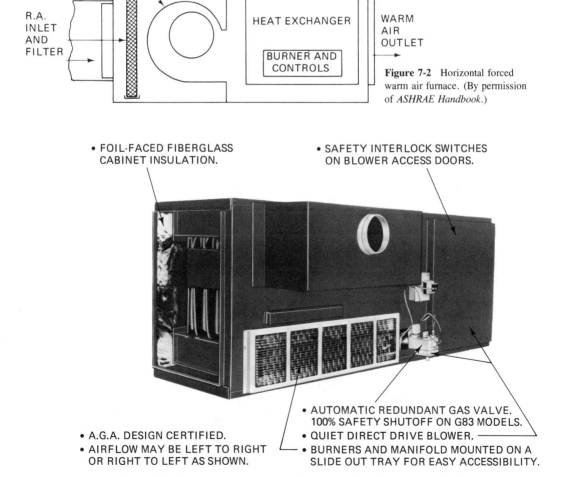

• FOIL-FACED FIBERGLASS
  CABINET INSULATION.

• SAFETY INTERLOCK SWITCHES
  ON BLOWER ACCESS DOORS.

• AUTOMATIC REDUNDANT GAS VALVE.
  100% SAFETY SHUTOFF ON G83 MODELS.

• A.G.A. DESIGN CERTIFIED.
• AIRFLOW MAY BE LEFT TO RIGHT
  OR RIGHT TO LEFT AS SHOWN.

• QUIET DIRECT DRIVE BLOWER.
• BURNERS AND MANIFOLD MOUNTED ON A
  SLIDE OUT TRAY FOR EASY ACCESSIBILITY.

Figure 7-3 Horizontal forced warm air furnace, gas-fired. (Courtesy, Magic Chef Air Conditioning.)

PARTS IDENTIFICATION

1. FLUE CONNECTION.
2. BURNER ACCESS PANEL. LIFT UP AND OUT TO REMOVE.
3. FAN AND LIMIT CONTROL.
4. WIRING MAKE-UP BOX.
5. MAIN GAS VALVE.
6. PILOT BURNER.
7. MAIN BURNERS.
8. FILTER.
9. FAN MOTOR.
10. FAN AND FILTER ACCESS PANEL. LIFT UP AND OUT TO REMOVE.
11. DURACURVE HEAT EXCHANGER.
12. DIRECT DRIVE FAN.

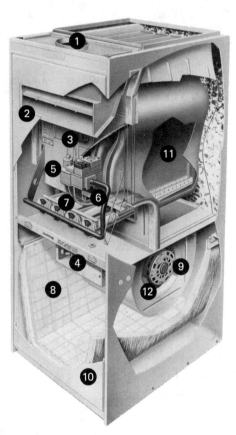

Figure 7-4 Upflow (highboy) forced warm air furnace, gas-fired. (Courtesy, Lennox Industries, Inc.)

① AIR CONDITIONER   ② ELECTRONIC AIR CLEANER

①A HEAT PUMP   ③ HUMIDIFIER

Figure 7-5 Installed upflow warm air furnace, gas-fired, including air conditioner, air cleaner, flue vent damper, and humidifier. (Reproduced with permission of Carrier Corporation.)

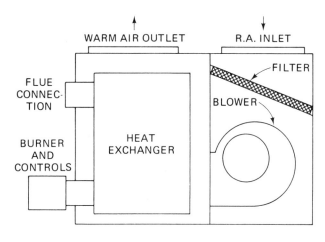

Figure 7-6 Lowboy forced warm air furnace. (By permission of ASHRAE Handbook.)

of the unit through the fan compartment and is forced horizontally over the heat exchanger, exiting at the opposite end.

The *upflow*, or *highboy*, design is used in the basement or a first-floor equipment room where floor space is at a premium (Figures 7-4 and 7-5). The fan is located below the heat exchanger. Air enters at the bottom or lower sides of the unit and leaves at the top through a warm air plenum.

The *lowboy* furnace occupies more floor space and is lower in height than the upflow design, making it ideally suited for basement installation (Figure 7-6). The fan is placed alongside the heat exchanger. A return air plenum is built above the fan compartment. A supply air plenum is built above the heat-exchanger compartment.

The *downflow* or *counterflow* design is used in houses having an under-the-floor type of distribution system (Figure 7-7). The fan is located above the heat exchanger. The

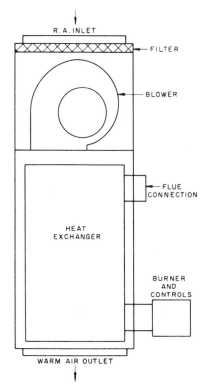

Figure 7-7 Downflow (counterflow) forced warm air furnace. (By permission of ASHRAE Handbook.)

return air plenum is connected to the top of the unit. The supply air plenum is connected to the bottom of the unit.

DESCRIPTION OF COMPONENTS

Although forced warm air furnaces differ in their fuel-burning equipment and many of the controls required for operation, many other components are the same or similar. These components vary somewhat, depending upon the size of the furnace and the arrangement of parts, but basically they have characteristics and functions in common. Components of a typical gas-fired forced warm air furnace are shown in Figure 7-8.

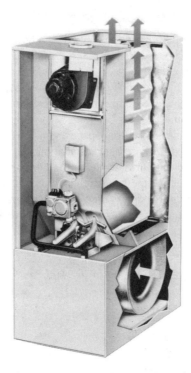

Figure 7-8 Components of a typical gas-fired, upflow forced warm air furnace. (Reprinted with permission of the Dealer Products Group of The Trane Company, a division of American Standard, Inc.)

Heat Exchanger

The heat exchanger is the part of the furnace where combustion takes place using gas, oil, or coal as fuel. The heat exchanger is usually made of cold-rolled, low-carbon steel with welded seams. There are two general types of heat exchangers:

1. Individual section

2. Cylindrical

The individual section. This type of heat exchanger has a number of separate heat exchangers (Figure 7-9). Each section has individual burners (fuel-burning devices).

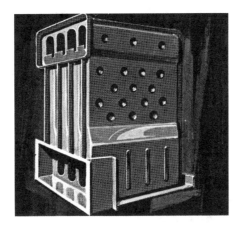

Figure 7-9 Individual section heat exchanger. (Courtesy, General Electric Company.)

These sections are joined together at the bottom so that a common pilot can light all burners. The sections are joined together at the top so that flue gases are directed to a common flue. The individual section type of heat exchanger is used only on gas-burning equipment.

The cylindrical. This type of heat exchanger has a single combustion chamber and uses a single-port fuel-burning device (Figure 7-10). The cylindrical type of heat exchanger is used on gas, coal, and oil units.

Many heat exchangers for coal, gas, and oil have two types of surfaces:

1. Primary

2. Secondary

The primary surface is in contact with or in direct sight of the flame and is located where the greatest heat occurs. The secondary surface follows the primary surface in the path between the burner and the flue and is used to extract as much heat as possible from the flue gases before the products of combustion are taken out through the flue to the chimney.

The fuel used by the furnace has a definite relation to the amount of chimney draft required. Coal, because of the high resistance of its fuel bed, requires a relatively high

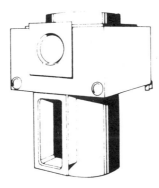

Figure 7-10 Cylindrical heat exchanger.

Description of Components

113

draft. Oil requires a relatively low draft. Gas requires a balanced draft, which is effective only when the furnace is providing heat.

Cabinet

Cabinets for forced warm air furnaces serve many functions. They provide

- An attractive exterior

- Insulation in the area around the heat exchanger

- Mounting facilities for controls, fan and motor, filters, and other items which they enclose

- Access panels for parts requiring service

- Connections for the supply and return air duct

- An airtight enclosure for air to travel over the heat exchanger

Cabinets for gas and oil furnaces are usually rectangular in shape and have a baked-enamel finish. Cabinets are insulated on the interior with aluminum-backed mineral wool, fiberglas, or a metal liner so that the surface will not be too hot to the touch. Insulation also makes it possible to place flammable material in contact with the cabinet without danger of fire.

The trend now is to furnish complete units so that a minimum amount of assembly time is required for installation. Usually, only duct and service connections need be made by the installer. Knockouts (readily accessible openings) are provided for gas and electric connections. The bolts used for holding the unit in place during shipment are also used for leveling the unit during installation. On highboy units, return air openings in the fan compartment can be cut in the cabinet sides or bottom to fit installation requirements.

Fans and Motors

Much of the successful performance of a heating system depends upon the proper operation of the fan and fan motors. The fan moves air through the system, obtaining it from return air and outside air, and forces it over the heat exchanger and through the supply distribution system to the space to be heated.

Fans used are the centrifugal type with forward curved blades (Figure 7-11). Air enters through both ends of the wheel (double inlet) and is pumped or compressed (the buildup of air pressure) at the outlet. Fans and motors must be the proper size to deliver the required amount of air against the total resistance produced by the system. Depending upon the quantity of air moved and the resistance of the system, a motor of the proper size is selected.

It is usually necessary to make some adjustment of the air quantities at the time of installation, because the resistance of the system cannot be fully determined beforehand. Generally, the higher the speed of the fan the greater the cubic-foot-per-minute output, thereby requiring more power and often a higher-horsepower motor.

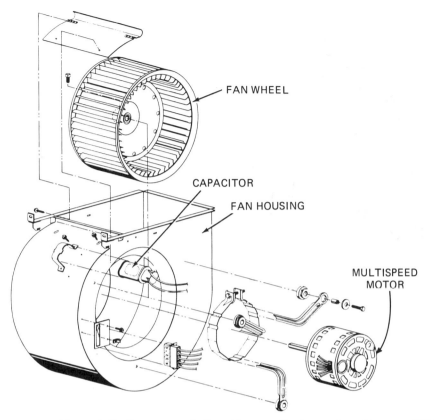

FAN WHEEL

CAPACITOR

FAN HOUSING

MULTISPEED
MOTOR

Figure 7-11 Components of direct-drive centrifugal type fan. (Courtesy, BDP Company.)

Types of fans. Two types of fan motor arrangements are used:

1.   Belt-drive

2.   Direct-drive

The *belt-drive* arrangement uses a fixed pulley on the fan shaft and a variable-pitch pulley on the motor shaft (Figure 7-12). The speed of the fan is directly proportional to the ratio of the pulley diameters. The following equation is used:

$$\begin{array}{c}\text{speed of fan,}\\ \text{revolutions per}\\ \text{minute (rev/min)}\end{array} = \frac{\begin{array}{c}\text{diameter of the motor}\\ \text{pulley, inches}\end{array}}{\begin{array}{c}\text{diameter of the fan}\\ \text{pulley, inches}\end{array}} \times \begin{array}{c}\text{rev/min}\\ \text{of the motor}\end{array}$$

EXAMPLE: What is the fan speed using a 3-in. motor pulley, a 9-in. fan pulley, and an 1800 rev/min motor?

Description of Components

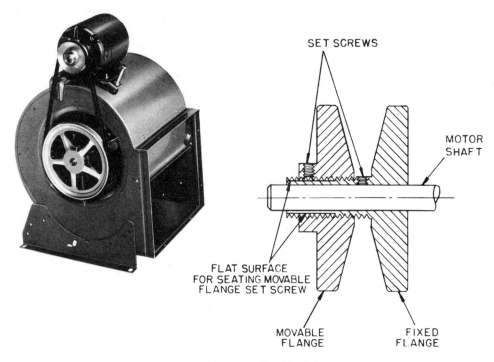

SET SCREWS

MOTOR SHAFT

FLAT SURFACE
FOR SEATING MOVABLE
FLANGE SET SCREW

MOVABLE
FLANGE

FIXED
FLANGE

Figure 7-12 Belt-drive centrifugal fan with adjustable pitch motor pulley. [Courtesy, Lau Division, Phillips Industries, Inc. (Fan and Motor.)]

SOLUTION

$$\text{rev/min of fan} = \frac{3 \text{ in.}}{9 \text{ in.}} \times 1800 = 600$$

The diameter of a variable-pitch pulley can be changed by adjusting the position of the outer flange of the pulley. This arrangement permits adjustment of the speed up to 30%. For changes greater than this, a different pulley must be used.

On the belt-drive arrangement, provision is made for regulating the belt tension and isolating the motor from the metal housing. The belt tension should be sufficient to prevent slippage. The motor mounts (usually rubber) provide isolation to prevent sound transmission.

The amperage draw of the motor is an indication of the amount of loading of the motor. The maximum loading is indicated on the motor nameplate as full-load amperes (FLA). If the FLA are exceeded, a larger motor must be used. Additional information on measuring amperage draw is given in Chapter 14. If the motor is not drawing its full capacity in FLA, it is an indication that the motor is underloaded. This may be caused by the additional resistance of dirty filters.

The *direct-drive* arrangement has the fan mounted on an extension of the motor shaft. Fan speeds can be changed only by altering the motor speed, which is accomplished

(a)

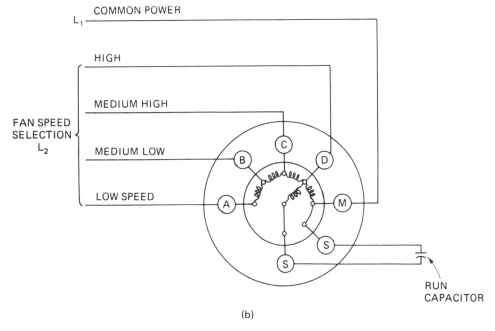

(b)

Figure 7-13 Tap-wound motor used for altering speed of direct-drive centrifugal fan. (Courtesy, Lau Division, Phillips Industries, Inc.)

by the use of extra windings on the motor, sometimes called a *tap-wound*, or *multispeed*, motor (Figure 7-13).

A tap-wound motor has a series of connections, each providing a different speed. Often one speed is selected for heating and another speed is selected for cooling.

Air Filters

Air filters are located on the suction side of a fan. They serve to remove fumes and smoke as well as undesirable airborne particles such as lint, fly ash, dust, pollen, fungus, spores, and bacteria.

The desirability of air filters in a forced warm air heating system in relation to human comfort and the three types of filters used are discussed in Chapter 2. Air filters are also beneficial to health and cleanliness.

Both the disposable and permanent types of air filters remove particles down to 10 μm. The electronic type removes particles down from 10 μm to 0.1 μm.

Disposable types of air filters are usually made of fibrous material and, in the average residence, are normally effective for 3 to 4 months. Some disposable types of air filters have an electrostatic quality. The friction of the air stream through them creates a small charge of electricity which attracts particles. Air filters must be cleaned or replaced periodically to maintain unit efficiency.

Permanent types of air filters are usually made of polyurethane or metal mesh. These filters can be washed and reused. Some require a special adhesive coating to maintain their dust holding capacity.

Electronic air filters create a strong, direct current, electrical field. A charge is applied to the airborne particles and they are collected on a plate with the opposite charge. The collected particles are removed by washing the filter.

Humidifiers and Humidistats

Humidifiers are used to add moisture to indoor air. The amount of moisture required depends upon

- The outside temperatures

- The house construction

- The amount of relative humidity that the interior of the house will withstand without condensation problems

It is desirable to maintain 30% to 50% relative humidity. Too little humidity may cause furniture to crack. Too much humidity can cause condensation problems. From a comfort and health standpoint, a range as wide as 20% to 60% relative humidity is acceptable.

The colder the outside temperature, the greater the need for humidification. The amount of moisture the air will hold depends upon its temperature. The colder the outside air, the less moisture it contains. Air from the outside enters the house through infiltration. When outside air is warmed, its relative humidity is lowered unless moisture is added by humidification (Figure 7-14).

For example, air at 20°F and 60% relative humidity contains 8 grains of moisture

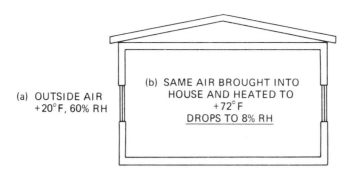

(a) OUTSIDE AIR
+20°F, 60% RH

(b) SAME AIR BROUGHT INTO
HOUSE AND HEATED TO
+72°F
DROPS TO 8% RH

INDOOR RELATIVE HUMIDITY TABLE

OUTDOOR RELATIVE HUMIDITY						
100%	6	9	14	21	31	46
80%	5	7	11	17	25	37
60%	3	5	(8%)	13	19	28
40%	2	4	6	8	12	18
20%	1	2	3	4	6	10
	0°	10°	20°	30°	40°	50°

OUTDOOR TEMPERATURE

THE ABOVE CHART SHOWS WHAT HAPPENS TO THE HUMIDITY IN YOUR HOME
WHEN YOU HEAT COLD WINTER AIR TO 72° ROOM TEMPERATURE. EXAMPLE:
WHEN OUTDOOR TEMPERATURE IS 20° AND OUTDOOR RELATIVE HUMIDITY
IS 60%, INDOOR RELATIVE HUMIDITY DROPS TO ONLY 8%. YOU NEED 30% TO
45% FOR COMFORT.

Figure 7-14 The effect of temperature on relative humidity. (Courtesy, Humid-Aire Corporation.)

per pound of air. When air is heated to 72°F, it can hold 118 grains of moisture per pound. Thus, to maintain 50% relative humidity in a 72°F house, the grains of moisture per pound must be increased to 59 ($118 \div 2 = 59$). One pound of air entering a house from the outside will require the addition of 51 grains of moisture ($59 - 8 = 51$). The amount of infiltration depends upon the tightness of the windows and doors and other parts of the construction.

It is impractical in most buildings to maintain high relative humidity when the outside temperature is low. Condensation forms on the inside of the window when the surface temperature reaches the dew point temperature of the air. The *dew point temperature* is the temperature at which moisture begins to condense when the air temperature is lowered.

Types of Humidistats. It is desirable to control the amount of humidity in the house by the use of a humidistat. A *humidistat* is a device that regulates the "on" and

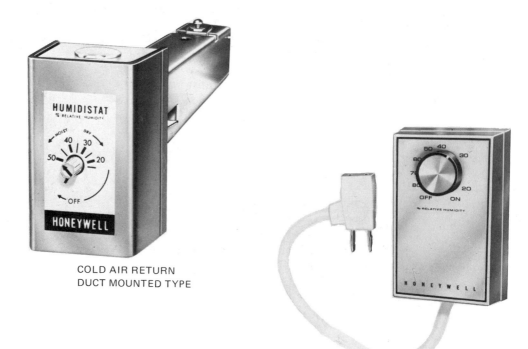

COLD AIR RETURN
DUCT MOUNTED TYPE

WALL MOUNTED TYPE

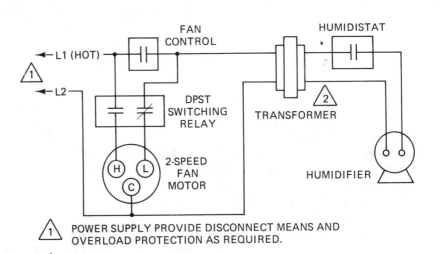

POWER SUPPLY PROVIDE DISCONNECT MEANS AND
OVERLOAD PROTECTION AS REQUIRED.

24-V WIRING.

Figure 7-15 Two types of humidistats and a typical wiring diagram.
(Courtesy, Honeywell Inc.)

"off" periods of humidification (Figure 7-15). The setting of a humidistat can be changed to comply with changing outside temperatures.

Types of humidifiers. There are three general types of humidifiers:

1. Evaporative

2. Atomizing

3. Vaporizing

There are also three types of evaporative humidifiers:

1. Plate

2. Rotating drum or plate

3. Fan-powered

The *plate* type of evaporative humidifier (Figure 7-16) has a series of porous plates mounted in a rack. The lower section of the plates extends down into the water that is contained in the pan. A float valve regulates the supply of water to maintain a constant level in the pan. The pan and plates are mounted in the warm air plenum.

The *rotating drum* type of evaporative humidifier (Figure 7-17) has a slowly revolving drum covered with a polyurethane pad partially submerged in water. As the drum rotates, it absorbs water. The water level in the pan is maintained by a float valve. The humidifier is mounted on the side of the return air plenum. Air from the supply plenum is ducted into the side of the humidifier. The air passes over the wetted surface, absorbs moisture, then goes into the return air plenum.

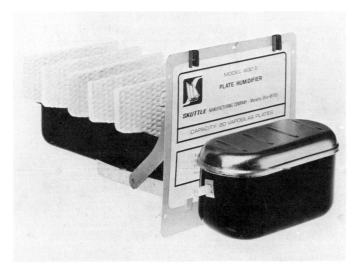

Figure 7-16 Plate-type evaporative humidifier. (Courtesy, Skuttle Manufacturing Company.)

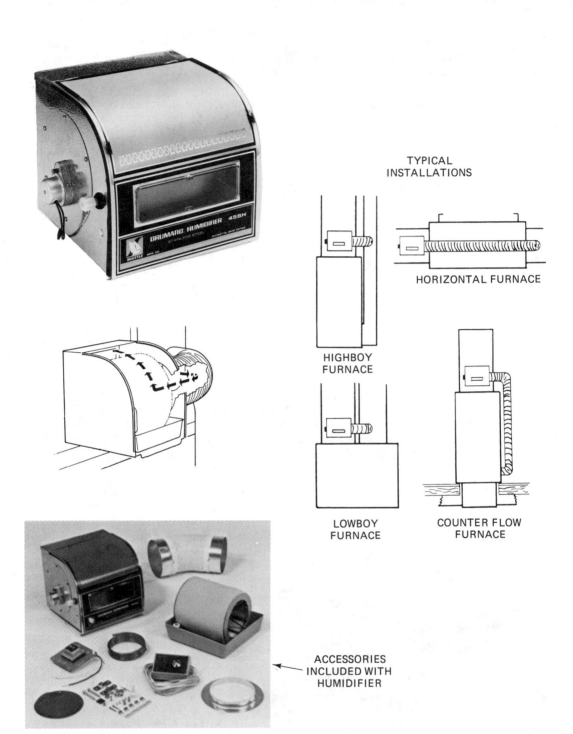

TYPICAL INSTALLATIONS

HORIZONTAL FURNACE

HIGHBOY FURNACE

LOWBOY FURNACE

COUNTER FLOW FURNACE

ACCESSORIES INCLUDED WITH HUMIDIFIER

Figure 7-17 Rotating drum-type evaporative humidifier. (Courtesy, Skuttle Manufacturing Company.)

Parts Common to All Furnaces   Chap. 7

The *rotating plate*–type evaporative humidifier (Figure 7-18) is similar to the drum type in that the water-absorbing material revolves. However, this type is normally mounted on the underside of the main warm air supply duct.

The *fan-powered*-type evaporative humidifier (Figure 7-19) is mounted on the supply air plenum. Air is drawn in by the fan, forced over the wetted core, and delivered back into the supply air plenum. The water flow over the core is controlled by a water valve. A humidistat is used to turn the humidifier on and off, controlling both the fan and the

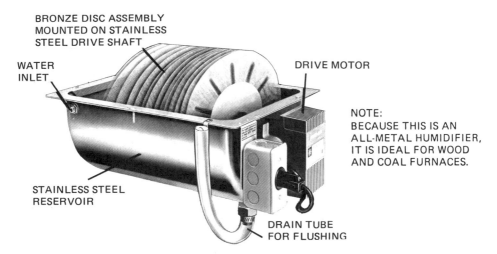

Figure 7-18 Rotating plate-type evaporative humidifier. (Courtesy, Humid-Aire Corporation.)

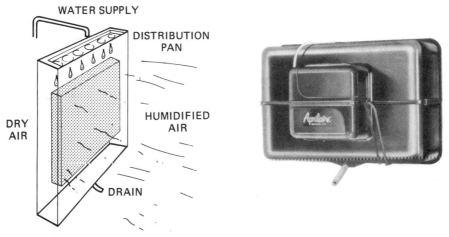

Figure 7-19 Fan-powered-type evaporative humidifier. (Courtesy, Research Products Corporation.)

Description of Components

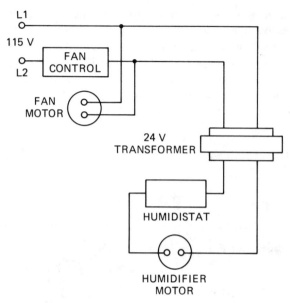

Figure 7-20 Wiring diagram for system with single-speed motor. (Courtesy, Skuttle Manufacturing Company.)

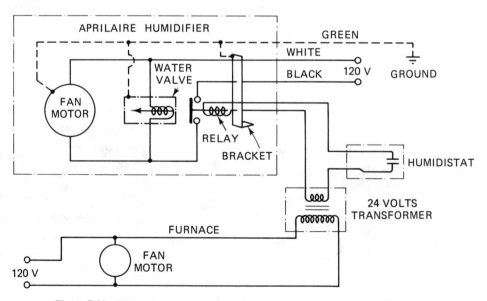

Figure 7-21 Wiring diagram for fan-powered-type evaporative humidifier. (Courtesy, Research Products Corporation.)

water valve. The control system is set up so that the humidifier can operate only when the furnace fan is running. Wiring diagrams are shown in Figures 7-20 and 7-21.

This centrifugal atomizing type of humidifier (Figure 7-22) consists of a copper enclosure that contains a rapidly rotating disc (3250 rev/min) that throws water against the "vapor-maker" comb centrifugally, which atomizes the water into minute particles. Primary air enters under the disc, picks up the atomized water and introduces it into the space or duct where surrounding air absorbs it. This model uses an air intake from the duct and its own heavy-duty fan to move the water vapor back into the duct. The model shown has a capacity of 3 lb/hr on the supply side.

The *vaporizing* type of humidifier (Figure 7-23) uses an electrical heating element immersed in a water reservoir to evaporate moisture into the furnace supply air plenum.

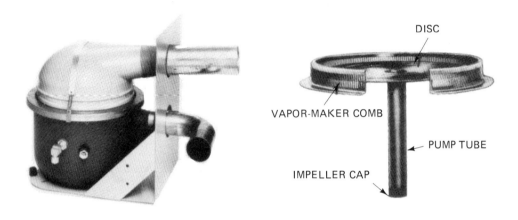

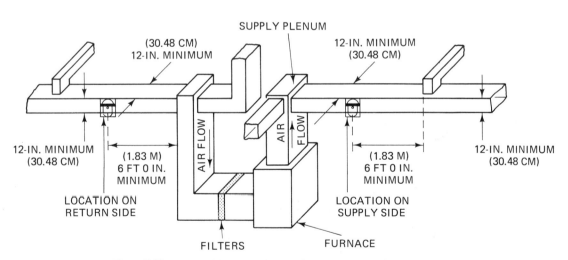

Figure 7-22 The atomizing type of humidifier. (Courtesy, Walton Laboratories.)

HEAT PUMP AND ELECTRIC FORCED AIR FURNACE HUMIDIFIERS

DESIGNED SPECIFICALLY FOR MAXIMUM EFFICIENCY ON THESE SPECIAL SYSTEMS.

INSTALLS ANYWHERE ON THE SYSTEM —

BECAUSE THIS HUMIDIFIER HAS ITS OWN HEAT SOURCE, IT CAN BE MOUNTED IN THE "COLD AIR" RETURN SECTION, AS WELL AS IN THE "HOT AIR" SUPPLY. OFTEN, THE "RETURN" PLENUM IS MORE CONVENIENT BECAUSE THERE ARE NO AIR CONDITIONING COILS TO INTERFERE. THIS UNIT REQUIRES A HUMIDISTAT CONTROL. THIS CONTROL MAY BE ROOM MOUNTED, OR IN THE RETURN AIR SECTION OF THE SYSTEM.

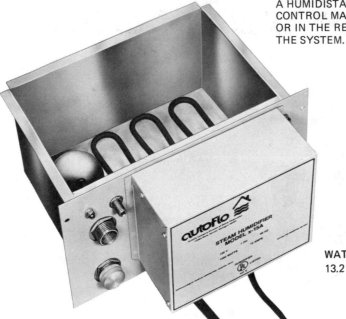

WATER VAPOR OUTPUT:
13.2 TO 19.1 GAL PER DAY

HERE IS HOW IT WORKS!

THIS IS A HIGH CAPACITY HUMIDIFIER FOR TODAY'S HEAT PUMP AND ELECTRIC FURNACES . . . WHERE LOW AIR TEMPERATURES DO NOT PROVIDE ENOUGH HEAT FOR AN EVAPORATIVE TYPE HUMIDIFIER TO FUNCTION PROPERLY.

THE STAINLESS STEEL RESERVOIR IS INSTALLED IN THE RETURN OR SUPPLY PLENUM, OR DUCT. THE CONTROLS ARE IN A COMPACT MODULE ON THE EXTERIOR PANEL, WHERE ALL ELECTRICAL AND WATER CONNECTIONS ARE MADE. A REMOTE HUMIDISTAT TURNS ON AN INCALOY HEAT ELEMENT TO HEAT THE WATER IN THE RESERVOIR. WHEN THE WATER REACHES 170°F., THE FURNACE FAN IS TURNED ON TO DISTRIBUTE THE PURE STEAM THROUGHOUT THE HOME. WHEN THE SELECTED HUMIDITY IS REACHED, THE HEAT ELEMENT TURNS OFF. WHEN THE WATER COOLS, THE FAN CONTROL TURNS OFF.

Figure 7-23 Vaporizing type of humidifier. (Courtesy, Autoflo, a division of Masco Corporation.)

A constant level of water is maintained in the reservoir. These humidifiers can operate even though the furnace is not supplying heat. The humidistat not only starts the water heater but also turns on the furnace fan if it is not running.

Note: Problems can arise in the use of humidifiers when the water hardness (mineral content) is too great. Typical water hardness from major U.S. cities is shown in Figure 7-24. An accessory-type water treatment unit can be added to both spray-type and drum-

FUNDAMENTALLY, ONLY DISTILLED WATER OR RAIN WATER CAUGHT BEFORE IT REACHES THE GROUND IS FREE FROM MINERALS. WATER FROM WELLS, LAKES, RIVERS ALL CONTAIN VARYING AMOUNTS OF MINERALS IN SOLUTION. THESE MINERALS ARE PICKED UP AS WATER MOVES THROUGH OR ACROSS WATER-SOLUBLE PORTIONS OF THE EARTH'S SURFACE. IN MANY CASES, THE LEVEL OF THESE MINERALS IS SUFFICIENTLY HIGH TO MAKE WATER-CONDITIONING EQUIPMENT NECESSARY TO REMOVE THE OBJECTIONABLE MINERALS FOR NORMAL DOMESTIC USE.

IT IS COMMON KNOWLEDGE THAT WATER EVAPORATED FROM A TEA-KETTLE LEAVES A RESIDUE KNOWN AS LIME. SINCE EVAPORATION OF WATER IS THE ONLY WAY TO CREATE AND DISTRIBUTE WATER VAPOR INTO THE AIR PRESENT IN HOMES, IT IS APPARENT THAT MINERAL RESIDUE RESULTING FROM EVAPORATION PRESENTS A PROBLEM.

WATER HARDNESS VARIES IN DIFFER-ENT LOCALITIES. DRINKING WATER CONTAINS SOME HARDNESS — CONSIS-TING PRIMARILY OF CALCIUM CARBONATE AND/OR MAGNESIUM CARBONATE. THIS HARDNESS IS EXPRESSED IN GRAINS PER GALLON:

CLASS OF HARDNESS	GRAINS HARDNESS PER GALLON	% FIGURES IN U.S.
LOW	3–10	30
AVERAGE	10–25	55
HIGH	25–50	15

IF A GALLON OF WATER OF AVERAGE HARDNESS IS EVAPORATED, A RESIDUE OF 20 GRAINS REMAINS. IF 100 GALLONS OF 20 GRAIN HARDNESS WATER ARE EVAPORATED TO PROVIDE HUMIDITY, APPROXIMATELY 1/3 LB OF SOLIDS WILL BE LEFT.

CITY WATER DATA

STATE AND CITY	SOURCE OF SUPPLY	MAXIMUM WATER TEMP. °F	HARDNESS PPM
CALIFORNIA			
FRESNO	W	72	87
LOS ANGELES	WS	79	195
SACRAMENTO	S	83	76
SAN FRANCISCO	S	66	181
FLORIDA			
JACKSONVILLE	WS	90	305
MIAMI	W	82	78
ILLINOIS			
CHICAGO	S	73	125
PEORIA	W	67	386
SPRINGFIELD	S	84	164
MAINE			
PORTLAND	S	70	12
MICHIGAN			
DETROIT	S	78	100
MUSKEGON	S	71	153
NEW YORK			
ALBANY	S	70	42
BUFFALO	S	76	118
NEW YORK	WS	73	30
TEXAS			
DALLAS	WS	87	75
EL PASO	W	88	160
HOUSTON	W	89	120
SAN ANTONIO	W	78	221
WASHINGTON			
SPOKANE	W	55	147

S = Surface: river, reservoir, lake
W = Well

FOR YOUR LOCAL FIGURES CALL YOUR WATER BOARD.

Figure 7-24 Typical water hardness for major U.S. cities. (Courtesy, The Trane Company.)

type humidifiers when the water hardness is more than 10 grains of dissolved mineral particles per gallon. A kit is available for testing the hardness of water.

MAINTENANCE AND SERVICE

Air-Flow Adjustment

For heating, the volume of air handled by the fan should be adjusted to maintain an air temperature rise through the furnace of 85°F (or the air temperature rise indicated on the nameplate).

Adjustments vary according to the type of fan drive as follows:

- Changes in fan speed for belt-driven fans are made by altering the position of the adjustable motor pulley flanges. Opening up the flanges decreases the speed of the fan. Closing the flange opening increases the speed of the fan.

- The motor speed of a direct-drive (tap-wound) motor is adjusted by changing the motor leads. Different speeds use different motor leads. Consult the wiring diagram for the connections necessary to increase or decrease fan speed.

Caution: Increasing the fan speed will increase the power required to drive the fan. Check the amperage draw of the motor to be certain that it is within nameplate amperage. Too high an amperage can cause overheating, overload dropout, or motor damage.

Lubrication

For proper lubrication refer to the manufacturer's instructions, if available. Check first to see if the fan or motor has sealed bearings, in which case no lubrication is required. If a unit does not have sealed bearings, the following information is useful:

- Some fan bearings are grease-type with screw-on caps. These require No. 2 consistency neutral mineral grease. A full cap should be screwed down one revolution for every 6 months (mo) of operation.

- Other fan bearings have cups with a spring cap. Lubricate at start-up and every 6 mo, with SAE No. 10 nondetergent oil. Add oil slowly to saturate the wick and packing.

- Belt-driven motors generally use SAE No. 10 oil at the beginning of operation and every 6 mo thereafter.

- Direct-drive motors are usually prelubricated with the lubrication lasting about 3 years (y). After this period of time, add oil slowly to each bearing using about 3 drops of SAE No. 10 oil.

Fan Shaft End Play

Inspect fan for excessive shaft end play. Normal end play on units with sleeve bearings is $\frac{1}{32}$ to $\frac{1}{16}$ in. If adjustment is necessary, reposition the thrust collar, which is located on the shaft next to the bearing.

Pulley Alignment

Use a straightedge along both motor and fan pulleys. Move pulleys on shafts or adjust motor mount to attain proper alignment (Figure 7-25).

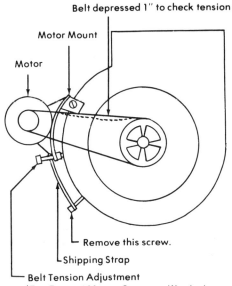

Belt depressed 1″ to check tension

Motor Mount

Motor

Remove this screw.

Shipping Strap

Belt Tension Adjustment
(For Fan and Motor, Courtesy, Westinghouse Electric Corporation, Heating and Cooling Division).

Always re-adjust belt tension after adjusting motor pulley so that it is not loose enough to cause slippage nor tight enough to cause bearing wear. To adjust tension, remove the screw which fastens the shipping strap to the blower housing (the entire strap may be removed if desired.) Adjust tension by means of the bolt in the motor tail piece. A properly adjusted belt can be deflected approximately one inch with moderate pressure of the hand.

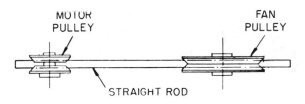

MOTOR PULLEY

FAN PULLEY

STRAIGHT ROD

CHECKING PULLEY ALIGNMENT

Figure 7-25 Checking pulley alignment and belt tension. [Reprinted with permission of Carrier Corporation, Copyright Carrier Corporation (Pulley Alignment.)]

Belt Tension

Adjust belt tension just tight enough to prevent slippage (Figure 7-25). Allow belt to be depressed 1 in. minimum.

Heat Exchangers

Inspect flue passages for soot collection on the heat exchangers. The accumulation of soot can be caused by defective equipment or improper burner adjustment. After the cause is determined and corrected, clean the passages with a brush (Figure 7-26). Remove draft hood and burner assembly for access to flue passages, heat exchangers, and flue baffles.

Humidifiers

Refer to manufacturers' instructions for maintaining humidifiers. Each type has specific service requirements. While in use, humidifiers require inspection once a month. Periodic cleaning to remove minerals is important. The frequency of cleaning depends upon the mineral content of the water being supplied to the unit. When a humidifier is not in use, it should be thoroughly cleaned, and the evaporative media pad replaced, the water shut off, and the float assembly cleaned and adjusted. Water is turned on again when the humidifier is put back into service.

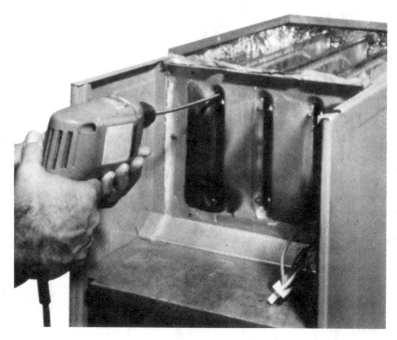

Figure 7-26 Cleaning flue passages in furnace heat exchanger. (Courtesy, Bryant Air Conditioning.)

CHAPTER 7 STUDY QUESTIONS

The answers to the study questions are found in the sections of this chapter under the chapter topic indicated.

STUDY QUESTIONS	CHAPTER TOPIC
1. What parts of a forced-air furnace are not included in a gravity furnace?	*Basic components*
2. What are the four different configurations of parts available on forced warm air furnaces?	*Arrangement of components*
3. Where is the fan located in respect to the heat exchanger on each type of furnace?	*Arrangement of components*
4. Describe the two types of heat exchangers on standard furnaces.	*Heat exchanger*
5. What material is used to construct the standard heat exchanger?	*Heat exchanger*
6. What type of furnace uses individual section–type heat exchangers?	*Heat exchanger*
7. What type of fuel requires the greatest chimney draft?	*Heat exchanger*
8. What are the two types of fan-motor arrangements	*Fans and motors*
9. What type of fans are used on forced warm air furnaces?	*Fans and motors*
10. If a motor has a 3-in. pulley and the blower a 12-in. pulley, using a motor operating at 1200 rev/min, what is the speed of the fan?	*Types of fans*
11. How much can the fan speed be adjusted with a variable-pitch motor pulley?	*Types of fans*
12. Describe the various types of air filters.	*Air filters*
13. How is the inside humidity requirement affected by the outside temperature?	*Humidifiers and humidistats*
14. Describe the construction of various types of humidistats.	*Types of humidistats*
15. Describe the various types of humidifiers.	*Types of humidifiers*
16. What are the three types of evaporative humidifiers?	*Types of humidifiers*
17. What water hardness requires an accessory-type water treatment unit?	*Types of humidifiers*
18. Name at least five types of maintenance required for furnaces.	*Maintenance and service*

8 Components of Gas-Burning Furnaces

OBJECTIVES

After studying this chapter, the student will be able to:

- Identify the components of a gas-burning assembly
- Adjust a gas burner for best performance
- Provide service and maintenance for a gas burner assembly

GAS-BURNING ASSEMBLY

The function of a gas-burning assembly is to produce a proper fire at the base of the heat exchanger. To do this, the assembly must

- Control and regulate the flow of gas
- Assure the proper mixture of gas with air
- Ignite the gas under safe conditions

To accomplish these actions, a gas burner assembly consists of four major parts or sections. These parts are the

1. Gas valve
2. Safety pilot

3. Manifold and orifice

4. Gas burners and adjustment

An illustration of a complete gas burner manifold assembly is shown in Figure 8-1.

Gas Valve

The gas valve section consists of a number of parts, with each performing a different function. On older units, these operations were entirely separate. On more modern units, these parts are all contained in a combination gas valve (CGV), and include:

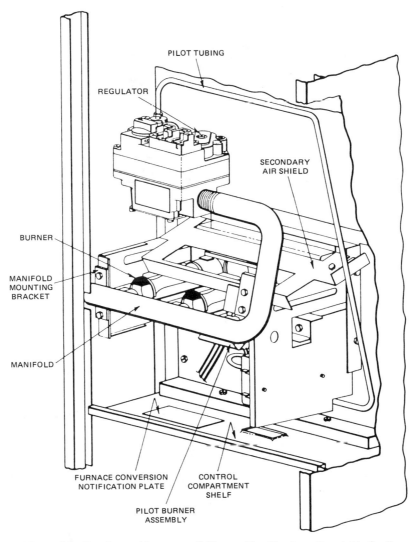

Figure 8-1 Complete gas burner manifold assembly. (Courtesy, Bryant Air Conditioning.)

Gas-Burning Assembly

- Hand shutoff valve

- Pressure reducing valve

- Safety shutoff equipment

- Operator or automatic gas valve

Figure 8-2 shows the separate parts of the gas valve section installed along the manifold, sometimes called a *gas regulator train*. Figure 8-3 shows the combination valve (CGV) that includes these separate parts, each of which is replaceable if trouble should develop.

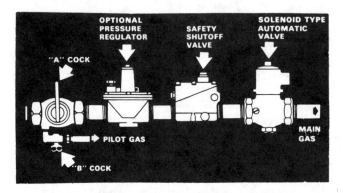

Figure 8-2 Older style gas manifold showing separate components. (Courtesy, Honeywell Inc.)

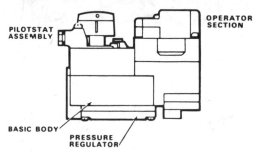

Figure 8-3 Combination gas valve (CGV). (Courtesy, Honeywell Inc.)

Hand shutoff valves.   Referring to Figure 8-2, note that the main shutoff valve or gas cock is composed of two parts, an A cock and a B cock. The A cock is used to manually turn the main gas supply on and off. The B cock is used to turn the gas supply to the pilot on and off manually.

These gate or ball-type valves are open when the handle is parallel to the length of the pipe and closed when the handle is perpendicular to the length of the pipe. They should be either on or off and not placed in an intermediate position. If it is desirable to regulate the supply of gas, it should be done by adjusting the pressure regulator.

Pressure-reducing valve.   The pressure-reducing valve, or pressure regulator, decreases the gas pressure supplied from the utility meter at approximately 7 in. W.C. to $3\frac{1}{2}$ in. W.C. The regulator maintains a constant gas pressure at the furnace to provide a constant input of gas to the furnace. On an LP system the regulator is supplied at the tank and, therefore, an additional regulator is not necessary at the furnace.

As shown in Figure 8-4, the spring exerts a downward pressure on the diaphragm, which is connected to the gas valve. The spring pressure tends to open the valve. When the gas starts to flow through the valve, the downstream pressure of the gas creates an upward pressure on the diaphragm tending to close it. Thus, the spring pressure and the downstream gas pressure oppose each other and must equal each other for the pressure to remain in equilibrium. To adjust the gas pressure, the cap is removed and the spring tension is adjusted. Also note that the vent maintains atmospheric pressure on the top of the diaphragm.

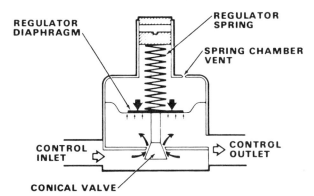

Figure 8-4 Pressure-reducing valve and its operation. (Courtesy, Honeywell Inc.)

Safety shutoff equipment.   The safety shutoff equipment consists of a

- Pilot burner

- Thermocouple or thermopile

- Pilotstat power unit

The pilot burner and the thermocouple or thermopile are assembled into one unit as shown in Figures 8-12, 8-13, and 8-14. This unit is placed near the main gas burner. The thermocouple is connected to the pilotstat power unit. The pilotstat power unit may be located in the CGV or installed as a separate unit in the gas regulation train, as shown in Figure 8-2.

The pilot burner has two functions:

1. It directs the pilot flame for proper ignition of the main burner flame.

2. It holds the thermocouple or thermopile in correct position with relation to the pilot flame.

The thermocouple or thermopile extends into the pilot flame and generates sufficient voltage to hold in the pilotstat. The thermopile generates additional voltage, which also operates the main gas valve.

The pilotstat power unit is held in by the voltage generated by the thermocouple. If the voltage is insufficient, indicating a poor or nonexistent pilot light, the power unit drops out, shutting off the main gas supply. These units are of two types: one that shuts off the gas supply to the main burner only, and the other that shuts off the supply of gas to both the pilot and the main burner. Units burning LP gas always require 100% shutoff.

The Principle of the Thermocouple. Two dissimilar metal wires are welded together at the ends to form a thermocouple (Figure 8-5). When one junction is heated and the other remains relatively cool, an electrical current is generated which flows through the wires. The voltage generated is used to operate the pilotstat power unit.

The Thermopile. The thermopile is a number of thermocouples connected in series (Figure 8-6). One thermocouple may generate 25 to 30 millivolts (mV). A thermopile may generate as high as 750 or 800 mV (1000 mV equals 1 V).

The Power Unit. The power unit is energized by the voltage generated by the thermocouple or thermopile. This voltage operates through an electromagnet. The voltage generated is sufficient to hold in the plunger against the pressure of the spring. The position of the plunger against the electromagnet must be manually set. If the thermo-

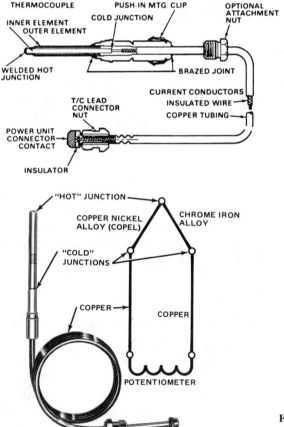

Figure 8-5 Basic themocouple construction. (Courtesy, Honeywell Inc.)

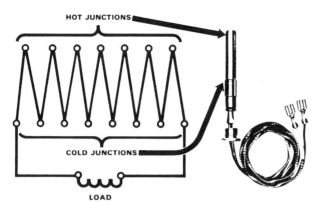

Figure 8-6 Basic thermopile construction. (Courtesy, Honeywell Inc.)

couple voltage drops due to a poor or nonexistent pilot, the plunger is released by the spring. This action either causes the plunger itself to block the flow of gas or operates an electrical switch that shuts off the supply of gas. The plunger must be manually reset when the proper pilot is restored. Figure 8-7 shows the pilotstat mechanism installed in a CGV.

Operator-controlled automatic gas valve. The main function of the operator is to control the gas flow. Some operators control the gas flow directly; some regulate the pressure on a diaphragm, which, in turn, regulates the gas flow. The various types of operators are:

- Solenoid
- Diaphragm

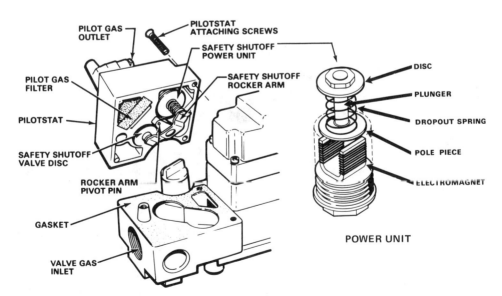

Figure 8-7 Pilotstat mechanism in a CGV. (Courtesy, Honeywell Inc.)

Gas-Burning Assembly

- Bimetal

- Bulb

Solenoid Valve Operators. These units (Figure 8-8) employ electromagnetic force to operate the valve plunger. When the thermostat calls for heat, the plunger is raised, opening the gas valve. These valves are often filled with oil to eliminate noise and to serve as lubrication.

Diaphragm Valve Operators. On these operators (Figure 8-9) gas is used to control the pressure above and below the diaphragm. The diaphragm is attached to the valve. To close the valve, gas pressure is released above the diaphragm. With equal pressure

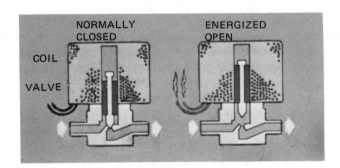

Figure 8-8 Solenoid valve operator. (Courtesy, Honeywell Inc.)

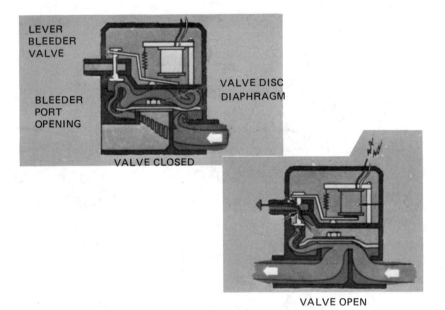

Figure 8-9 Magnetic diaphragm valve operator. (Reprinted with permission of Carrier Corporation, Copyright Carrier Corporation.)

Components of Gas-Burning Furnaces   Chap. 8

above and below the diaphragm, the weight of the valve closes it. To open the valve, the supply of gas is cut off above the diaphragm and gas pressure is vented to atmosphere. The pressure of the gas below the diaphragm opens the valve. These valves also can be filled with oil.

Bimetal Operators.   Bimetal operators (Figure 8-10) have a high-resistance wire wrapped around the blade. When the thermostat calls for heat, current is supplied to the wire, causing it to heat and warp the blade. This warping action opens the valve. The valve action is slow, and therefore this valve is sometimes referred to as a *delayed-action valve*.

Bulb-Type Operators.   Bulb-type operators (Figure 8-11) use the expansion of a liquid-filled bulb to provide the operating force. A snap-action disk is also incorporated to speed up the opening and closing action.

Safety Pilot

The function of the safety pilot is to provide an ignition flame for the main burner and to heat the thermocouple to provide safe operation.

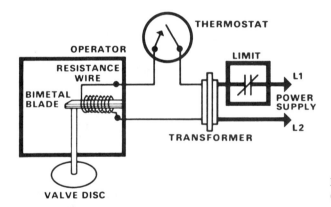

Figure 8-10 Bimetal-type valve operator. (Courtesy, Honeywell Inc.)

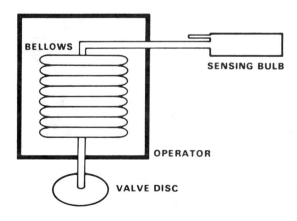

Figure 8-11 Bulb-type valve operator. (Courtesy, Honeywell Inc.)

Gas-Burning Assembly

Pilot burner. There are two types of pilot burners:

1. Primary-aerated

2. Non-primary-aerated

On the *primary-aerated pilot* (Figure 8-12), the air is mixed with the gas before it

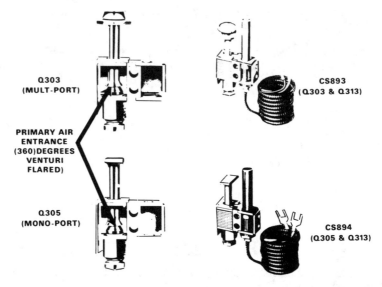

Figure 8-12 Primary-aerated pilot designs. (Courtesy, Honeywell Inc.)

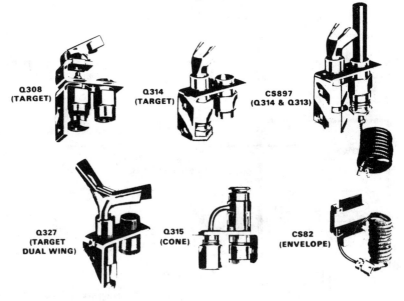

Figure 8-13 Non-primary-aerated pilot designs. (Courtesy, Honeywell Inc.)

enters the pilot burner. The disadvantage of this is that dirt and lint tend to clog the screened air opening. The air opening must be periodically cleaned.

On the *non-primary-aerated pilot* (Figure 8-13), the gas is supplied directly to the pilot, without the addition of primary air. All the necessary air is supplied as secondary air. This eliminates the need for cleaning the air passages.

Pilot burner orifice.   The orifice is the part that controls the supply of gas to the burner. The drilled opening permits a small stream of gas to enter the burner. The amount that enters is dependent upon the size of the drilled hole and the manifold pressure. Some cleaning of this opening may be required. This can be done by blowing air through the orifice or by using a suitable nonoily solvent.

Pilot flame.   The pilot flame should envelope the thermocouple $\frac{3}{8}$ to $\frac{1}{2}$ in. at its top, as shown in Figure 8-14. The gas pressure at the pilot is the same as in the burner manifold, $3\frac{1}{2}$ to 4 in. of water column for natural gas; 11 in for LP gas. Too high a pressure decreases the life of the thermocouple. Too low a pressure provides unsatisfactory heating of the thermocouple tip. Poor flame conditions are shown in Figure 8-15.

3/8 TO 1/2 INCH

ADJUST PILOT FLOW ADJUSTMENT SCREW TO GIVE A SOFT, STEADY FLAME ENVELOPING 3/8 TO 1/2 INCH OF THE TIP OF THE THERMOCOUPLE OR GENERATOR.

Figure 8-14 Pilot flame adjustment. (Courtesy, Honeywell Inc.)

FLAME TYPES	POSSIBLE CAUSES	FLAME TYPES	POSSIBLE CAUSES
LIGHT BLUE / YELLOW / LAZY YELLOW FLAME	1 DIRTY LINT SCREEN OR PRIMARY AIR OPENING 2 STARVING DUE TO EXCESSIVE INPUT TO MAIN BURNER 3 ORIFICE TOO LARGE	NOISY LIFTING BLOWING FLAME	HIGH GAS PRESSURE
WAVING BLUE FLAME	1 EXCESSIVE DRAFT AT PILOT LOCATION 2 RECIRCULATING PRODUCTS OF COMBUSTION	HARD SHARP FLAME	1 CHARACTERISTIC OF MANUFACTURED, BUTANE AIR, AND PROPANE AIR 2 ORIFICE TOO SMALL
SMALL BLUE FLAME	1 ADJUSTING SCREW CLOSED OFF 2 LOW GAS SUPPLY PRESSURE 3 CLOGGED PILOT BURNER ORIFICE 4 IMPROPER ORIFICE (TOO SMALL) 5 CLOGGED PILOT LINE FILTER	3/8 TO 1/2 / NORMAL FLAME	PROPER INSTALLATION

Figure 8-15 Poor pilot flame conditions. (Courtesy, Honeywell Inc.)

Gas-Burning Assembly

Manifold and Orifice

The manifold delivers gas equally to all the burners. It connects the supply of gas from the gas valve to the burners. It is usually made of $\frac{1}{2}$- to 1-in. pipe. Connections can be made either to the right or left, depending on the design, as shown in Figure 8-16.

The orifice used for the main burners is similar to the pilot orifice, only larger. The drilled opening permits a fast stream of raw gas to enter the burner. The orifice is sized to permit the proper flow of gas. Items to be considered in sizing the orifice are

- Type of gas

- Pressure in manifold

- Input of gas required for each burner

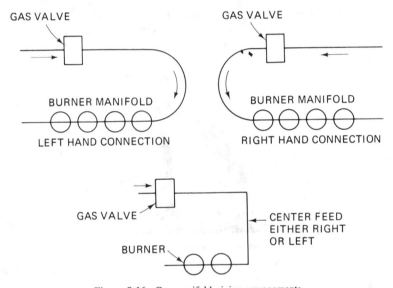

Figure 8-16 Gas manifold piping arrangements.

Gas Burners and Adjustment

Primary and secondary air.   Most gas burners require that some air be mixed with the gas before combustion. This air is called primary air (Figure 8-17). Primary air constitutes approximately one-half of the total air required for combustion. Too much primary air causes the flame to lift off the burner surface. Too little primary air causes a yellow flame.

Air that is supplied to the burner at the time of combustion is called secondary air (Figure 8-18). Too little secondary air causes the formation of carbon monoxide. To be certain that enough secondary air is provided, most units operate on an excess of secondary air. An excess of about 50% is considered good practice. To produce a good flame it is essential to maintain the proper ratio between primary and secondary air.

Components of Gas-Burning Furnaces   Chap. 8

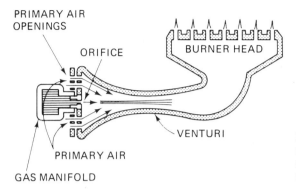

Figure 8-17 Primary air to gas burner. (Reprinted with permission of Carrier Corporation, Copyright Carrier Corporation.)

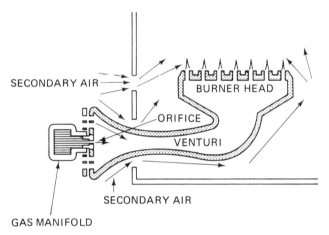

Figure 8-18 Secondary air to gas burner. (Reprinted with permission of Carrier Corporation, Copyright Carrier Corporation.)

The venturi. In a multiport burner, gas is delivered into a venturi (mixing tube) creating a high gas velocity. The increase in gas velocity creates a sucking action, which causes the primary air to enter the tube and mix with the raw gas.

Crossover ignitors. The crossover or carryover ignitor is a projection on each burner near the first few ports that permits the burner that lights first to pass flame to the other burners. There is a baffle, as shown in Figure 8-21, which directs gas to the first few ports of the burner to assure the proper supply of fuel to the area of the ignitor.

Note: Burners that fail to light properly can cause rollout, a dangerous condition where flame emerges into the vestibule.

Draft diverter. The draft diverter (Fig. 8-19) is designed to provide a balanced draft (slightly negative) over the flame in a gas fired furnace. The bottom of the diverter is open to allow air from the furnace room to blend with the products of combustion. In case of blockage or downdraft in the chimney, the flue gases vent to the area around the furnace.

Note: The American Gas Association (AGA) requires a rigid test to be certain that under these conditions complete combustion occurs and there is no danger of suffocation of the flame.

Gas-Burning Assembly

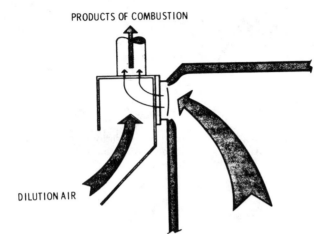

PRODUCTS OF COMBUSTION

DILUTION AIR

Figure 8-19 Draft diverter. (Reprinted with permission of Carrier Corporation, Copyright Carrier Corporation.)

Types of burners. There are four types of burners, classified according to the type of burner head:

1. Single-port or inshot

2. Drilled port

3. Slotted port

4. Ribbon

Single-Port or Inshot. The single-port burner (Figure 8-20) is the simplest type. The outlet is an extension of the burner tube. The flame is directed toward a metal plate that spreads the flame. Although the burner is relatively troublefree, it is noisy and less efficient than the other types.

Drilled-Port. The drilled-port burner is usually made of cast iron with a series of small drilled holes. The size of the hole varies for different types of gas.

Slotted-Port. The slotted-port burner (Figure 8-21) is similar to the drilled port burner, but in place of holes, it uses elongated slots. It has the advantage of being able to burn different types of gas without change of slot size. It is also less susceptible to clogging with lint.

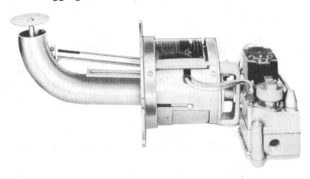

Figure 8-20 Single-port, or upshot, burner. (Courtesy, Adams Manufacturing Company.)

Components of Gas-Burning Furnaces   Chap. 8

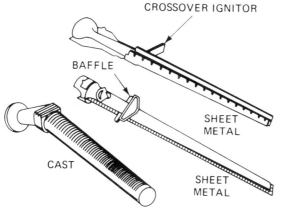

CROSSOVER IGNITOR

BAFFLE

CAST

SHEET
METAL

SHEET
METAL

Figure 8-21 Slotted-port burners. (Reprinted with permission of Carrier Corporation, Copyright Carrier Corporation.)

Ribbon.   The ribbon burner has a continuous opening down each side and, when it is lit, the flame has the appearance of a ribbon. The burner itself is made either of cast iron or fabricated metal. The ribbon insert is usually corrugated stainless steel.

MAINTENANCE AND SERVICE

The main items requiring service on gas-burning equipment are

- Gas burner assembly
- Pilot assembly
- Automatic gas valve

After the equipment is in use for a period of time, each of these items may require service, depending on the conditions of the installation.

Gas Burner Assembly

Problems that can arise include

- Flashback
- Carbon on the burners
- Dirty air mixture
- Noise of ignition
- Gas flames lifting from ports
- Appearance of yellow tips in flames

When the velocity of the gas-air mixture is reduced below a certain speed, the flame will flash back through the ports. This is undesirable and must be corrected. The solution

Maintenance and Service

is to close the primary air shutter as much as possible and still maintain a clear blue flame (Figure 8-22).

Burners that become clogged with carbon due to flashback conditions must be cleared in order not to interfere with the proper flow of gas.

If the burner flame becomes soft and yellow-tipped, it is an indication that cleaning is required. Items requiring cleaning are the shutter opening, venturi, and the burner head itself. In some cases these can be cleaned with the suction of a vacuum cleaner. In other cases, a thin, long-handled brush may be used to thoroughly reach the inside of the mixing tube.

Noise of ignition is usually caused by delayed or faulty ignition. Conditions that must be checked and corrected, if necessary, are location of the pilot, poor flame travel, or poor distribution of the flame on the burner itself.

Lifting flames are usually caused by too high a gas pressure or improper primary air adjustment. The gas pressure for natural gas at the manifold should be 3.5 in. W.C. Primary air should be adjusted to provide a blue flame.

The appearance of yellow tips on the flame indicate incomplete combustion, which can cause sooting of the heat exchanger. The following items should be checked and corrected, if necessary:

(a) **Gas Pressure:**   Should be 3.5 in. W.C. for natural gas.

(b) **Clogged Orifices:**   Inspect and clean if required.

(c) **Air Adjustment:**   Use minimum primary air required for blue flame.

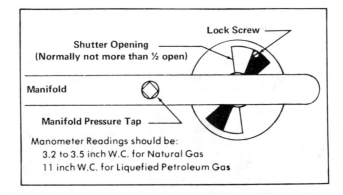

PRIMARY AIR ADJUSTMENT
To adjust primary air supply, turn main gas supply **ON** and operate unit for 15 to 20 minutes. Then loosen set screw and rotate shutter on burner bell. Open shutter until the yellow tips just disappear. Lock shutter in position by tightening set screw. Turn main gas supply **OFF**, let cool completely, and re-check operation and flame characteristics from a cold start.

Figure 8-22 Primary air and its adjustment.

(d) **Alignment:** Gas stream should move down center of venturi tube.

(e) **Flues:** Air passages must not be clogged.

(f) **Air Leaks:** Air from fan or strong outside air current can cause yellow flame.

Pilot Assembly

Pilot problems can be caused by

- Clogged air openings
- Dirty pilot filters
- Clogged orifice
- Defective thermocouples

Dirt and lint in the air opening are the most common problems. Cleaning solves these problems.

Pilots for manufactured gases use pilot filters. The cartridge must be replaced periodically.

Occasionally, it is necessary to clean the pilot orifice, which may become clogged from an accumulation of dirt, lint, carbon, or condensation in the lines.

If the pilot flame does not adequately heat the thermocouple, not enough dc voltage will be generated and the electromagnet will not energize sufficiently to permit the opening of the automatic gas valve. The thermocouple can be checked, as shown in Figure 14-4.

Automatic Gas Valve

Most gas valves are of the diaphragm type with an electromagnetic or heat motor-operated controller. The two principal problems that can occur with gas valves are

1. The valve will not open.
2. Gas leakage through the valve.

First, the pilot must be checked to be certain that the proper power is being produced by the thermocouple. If the gas valve will not open after following the lighting procedure shown on the nameplate, proceed as follows.

Check to determine if power is available at the valve. If power is available, connect and disconnect the power and listen for a muffled click which indicates that the lever arm is being actuated. Check to be sure that the vent above the diaphragm is open. If the valve still does not operate, replace the entire operator or valve top assembly.

If gas continues to leak through the valve outlet or the vent opening after the valve is deenergized, the entire valve head assembly should be replaced.

CHAPTER 8 STUDY QUESTIONS

The answers to the study questions are found in the sections of this chapter under the chapter topic indicated.

STUDY QUESTIONS	*CHAPTER TOPICS*
1. What are the functions of the gas burner assembly and what are its component parts?	*Gas-burning assembly*
2. On the modern gas valve, there are two shutoff cocks. For what are they used?	*Hand shutoff valves.*
3. What is the proper natural gas pressure leaving the gas valve?	*Pressure reducing valve*
4. What are the component parts of the safety shutoff equipment?	*Safety shutoff equipment*
5. What are the functions of the pilot burner?	*Safety shutoff equipment*
6. How much voltage does the thermocouple generate?	*Safety shutoff equipment*
7. What does CGV represent?	*Safety shutoff equipment*
8. What type of valve operator has a delayed action feature?	*Operator controlled automatic gas valve*
9. Describe the operation of the two types of pilot burners.	*Pilot burners*
10. What type of valve requires 100% shutoff?	*Safety shutoff equipment*
11. What is the function of the power unit?	*Safety shutoff equipment*
12. Describe a proper pilot flame.	*Pilot flame*
13. What factors are considered in sizing the main burner orifice?	*Manifold and orifice*
14. Describe what is meant by primary and secondary main burner air.	*Primary and secondary air*
15. What is the purpose of the venturi?	*The venturi*
16. What is the function of the draft diverter?	*Draft diverter*
17. Name and describe the various types of main gas burners.	*Types of burners*
18. Describe the service required for gas-burning equipment.	*Maintenance and service*
19. Describe the various problems that can arise on the gas burner assembly, pilot assembly, and automatic gas valve.	*Maintenance and service*

9 Components of Oil-Burning Furnaces

OBJECTIVES

After studying this chapter, the student will be able to:

- Identify the components of an oil burner

- Adjust an oil burner for best performance

- Provide service and maintenance for an oil burner

OIL-BURNING UNITS

Oil must be vaporized to burn. There are two ways to vaporize oil:

1. **By Heat Alone:** For example, oil can be vaporized by heating an iron pot containing oil and igniting it with a flame or spark.

2. **By Atomization and Heating:** Oil is vaporized by forcing it under pressure through an orifice, causing it to break up into small droplets. The atomized oil is then ignited by an electric spark.

TYPES OF BURNERS

There are four types of oil burners:

Type	Method of vaporizing oil
1. Pot	Heating
2. Rotary	Atomizing
3. Low pressure	Atomizing
4. High pressure	Atomizing

Pot-Type

In a pot-type oil burner (Figure 9-1), oil enters near the bottom of an open pot. The oil is ignited by a pilot flame or by electric ignition. The starting flame heats a plate in the lower portion of the pot, which then serves to vaporize oil and mix it with combustion air. The flame increases in size, heating not only the plate but the sides of the chamber. The high fire consumes enough vaporized oil for the full capacity of the burner.

Under low-fire conditions, such as on startup, the pot-type burner forms carbon in the pot, which tends to clog the air passages. The pot burner also is sensitive to changes in draft conditions, affecting combustion. These problems in operation have restricted its use.

Horizontal-Rotary

A horizontal-rotary-type oil burner (Figure 9-2) uses centrifugal force to atomize the oil. Oil is fed into a rapidly rotating cup located in the center of the burner. The oil is thereby forced through an orifice, throwing the atomized oil toward the furnace walls. Forced air for combustion is mixed with the atomized oil.

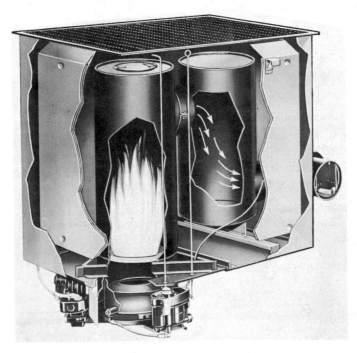

Figure 9-1 Pot-type oil burner. (Courtesy, Shell Oil Company.)

Components of Oil-Burning Furnaces   Chap. 9

Figure 9-2 Horizontal-rotary-type oil burner. (Courtesy, Shell Oil Company.)

The mixture is usually ignited at the base of the heat exchanger by an electric spark. The flame rises along the outside surface of the heat exchanger, evenly heating its surface.

This type of burner has excellent combustion efficiency. However, it requires considerable maintenance. The amount of service required by the horizontal type of burner has limited its residential use. A vertical model is in common use for commercial- and industrial-size burners.

Low-Pressure

In a low-pressure gun-type burner (Figure 9-3), oil and primary air are mixed prior to being forced through an orifice or nozzle. A pressure of 1 to 15 psig on the mixture, plus the action of the orifice, causes the atomization of the oil. Secondary air is drawn

Figure 9-3 Low-pressure gun-type oil burner. (Reproduced by permission of Carrier Corporation, Copyright Carrier Corporation.)

Types of Burners

151

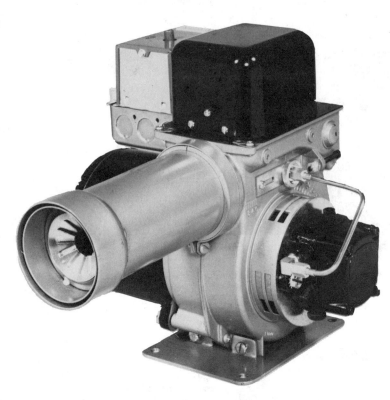

Figure 9-4 High-pressure gun-type oil burner. (Courtesy, the Carlin Company.)

into the spray mixture after it is released from the nozzle. Electric spark ignition is used to light the combustible mixture.

Although the low-pressure-type burner has achieved some success, it has been replaced to a great extent by the high-pressure burner. Higher pressure produces better atomization and high efficiencies.

High-Pressure

A high-pressure gun-type burner (Figure 9-4) forces oil at 100 psig pressure through the nozzle, breaking the oil into fine, mistlike droplets. The atomized oil spray creates a low-pressure area into which the combustion air flows. Combustion air is supplied by a fan through vanes, creating turbulence and complete mixing action.

The high-pressure gun-type burner is the most popular domestic burner. It is simple in construction, relatively easy to maintain, and efficient in operation. Therefore, the balance of this unit concentrates exclusively on providing information relative to the high-pressure burner.

HIGH-PRESSURE BURNER COMPONENTS

The high-pressure oil burner is actually an assembled unit. The component parts are made by a few well-known manufacturers. The parts are mass-produced, low in cost, and readily available for servicing requirements. The component parts of the high-pressure burner are shown in Figure 9-5.

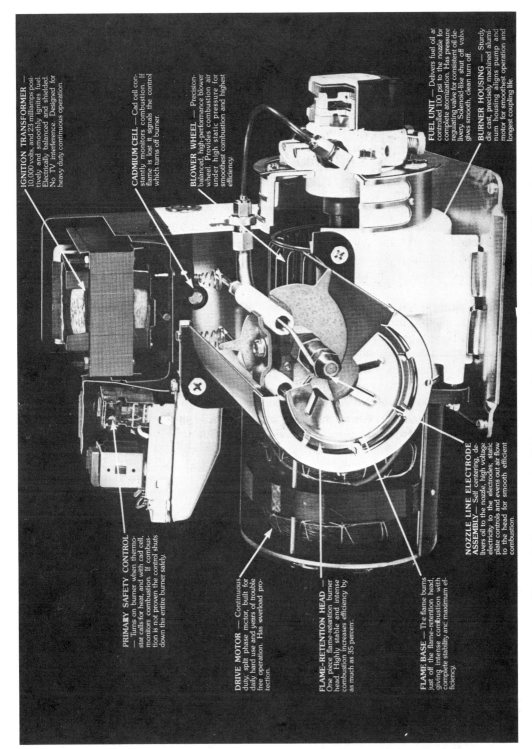

IGNITION TRANSFORMER — 10,000 volts and 23 milliamps positively and smoothly ignites fuel. Electrically balanced and shielded. No TV interference. Designed for heavy duty continuous operation.

CADMIUM CELL — Cad cell constantly monitors combustion. If flame is lost it signals the control which turns off burner.

BLOWER WHEEL — Precision-balanced, high-performance blower wheel. Provides combustion air under high static pressure for smoothest combustion and highest efficiency.

FUEL UNIT — Delivers fuel oil at controlled 100 psi to the nozzle for complete atomization. Has pressure regulating valve for consistent oil delivery. Solenoid-like shut off valve gives smooth, clean turn off.

BURNER HOUSING — Sturdy die cast, precisely machined aluminum housing aligns pump and motor for smoothest operation and longest coupling life.

PRIMARY SAFETY CONTROL — Turns on burner when thermostat calls for heat, and with cad cell, monitors combustion. If combustion is not proven the control shuts down the entire burner safely.

DRIVE MOTOR — Continuous duty, split phase motor, built for daily hard use and years of trouble free operation. Has overload protection.

FLAME-RETENTION HEAD — One piece flame-retention burner head. Highly stable and intense combustion increases efficiency by as much as 35 percent.

FLAME BASE — The flame burns just off the flame-retention head, giving intense combustion with complete stability and maximum efficiency.

NOZZLE LINE ELECTRODE ASSEMBLY — Self centering, delivers oil to the nozzle, high voltage electricity to the electrodes; static plate controls and evens out air flow to the head for smooth efficient combustion.

Figure 9-5 Component parts of high-pressure oil burner. (Courtesy, R. W. Beckett Corporation.)

153

Power Assembly

The power assembly consists of the motor, fan, and fuel pump. The nozzle assembly consists of the nozzle, the electrodes, and parts related to the oil/air mixing action. The ignition system consists of the transformer and electrical parts.

The motor drives the fan and fuel pump. The fan forces air through the blast tube to provide combustion air for the atomized oil. The fuel pump draws oil from the storage tank and delivers it to the nozzle.

The oil-air mixture is ignited by an electric spark formed between two properly positioned electrodes in the nozzle assembly. The spark is created by a transformer that increases the 120-V primary power supply to 10,000-V secondary supply to form a low-current spark arc.

Fuel pumps. All fuel pumps are of the rotary type using cams, gears, or a combination of both. The principal parts of the fuel pump in addition to the gears are: the shaft seal, the pressure-regulating valve, and the automatic cutoff valve.

The shaft seal is necessary, since the pump is driven by an external source of power.

The pressure-regulating valve has an adjustable spring that permits regulation of the oil pressure. The pump actually delivers more oil than the burner can use. The excess oil is dumped back into the supply line or returns to the tank. All pumps also have an adjustment screw for regulating the pressure of the oil delivered to the nozzle.

The automatic cutoff valve stops the flow of oil as soon as the pressure drops. Thus, when the burner is stopped, the oil is quickly cut off to the nozzle to prevent oil dripping into the combustion chamber.

Fuel oil pumps are designed for single-stage (Figure 9-6) or two-stage operation (Figure 9-7). The single-stage unit is used where the supply of oil is above the burner and the oil flows to the pump by gravity. The two-stage unit is used where the storage tank is below the burner. The first stage is used to draw the oil to the pump. The second stage is used to provide the pressure required by the nozzle. The suction on the pump should not exceed a 15-in. vacuum.

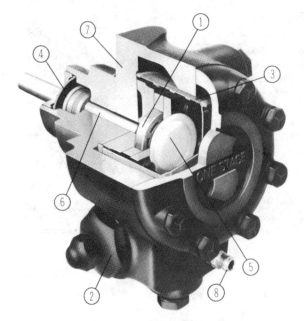

Figure 9-6 Single-stage oil pump. (Courtesy, Sundstrand Hydraulics, Inc.)

1. GEARS
2. CUTOFF VALVE
3. STRAINER
4. SHAFT SEAL
5. ANTI-HUM DEVICE
6. SHAFT BEARING
7. BODY
8. BLEED VALVE

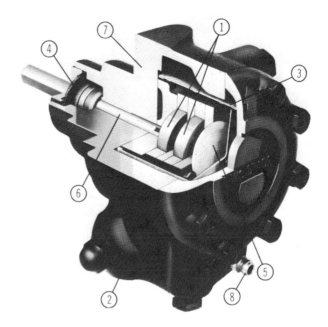

1. GEARS
2. CUTOFF VALVE
3. STRAINER
4. SHAFT SEAL
5. ANTI-HUM DEVICE
6. SHAFT BEARING
7. BODY
8. BLEED VALVE

Figure 9-7 Two-stage oil pump. (Courtesy, Sundstrand Hydraulics, Inc.)

Piping connections to the fuel pump are of two types: single-pipe and two-pipe. In the single-pipe system there is only one pipe from the storage tank to the burner. Plug B must be removed from the pump so that the unused oil can return to the low-pressure side of the pump. On the two-pipe system, two pipes are run from the storage tank to the burner. One carries supply oil and the other return oil. Plug B must be left in place and plug A removed so that unused oil can return to the storage tank. The bleed plug is used on a single-pipe system to remove the air from the line (Figure 9-8).

Various pump models are made by a number of manufacturers. Some pumps have clockwise rotation; some have counterclockwise rotation. It is important when changing a pump to use an identical replacement, since oil pumps vary in the location of connections, as shown in Figure 9-9. Always refer to the manufacturer's information and specification sheets for connection details.

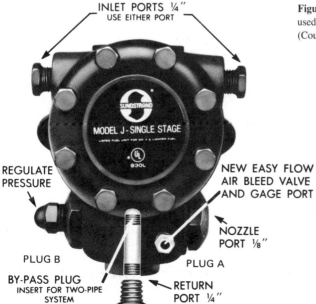

INLET PORTS ¼"
USE EITHER PORT

MODEL J - SINGLE STAGE

REGULATE PRESSURE

NEW EASY FLOW
AIR BLEED VALVE
AND GAGE PORT

NOZZLE
PORT ⅛"

PLUG B

PLUG A

BY-PASS PLUG
INSERT FOR TWO-PIPE
SYSTEM

RETURN
PORT ¼"

Figure 9-8 Connections showing plugs A and B used to convert a single-pipe to a two-pipe system. (Courtesy, Sundstrand Hydraulics, Inc.)

155

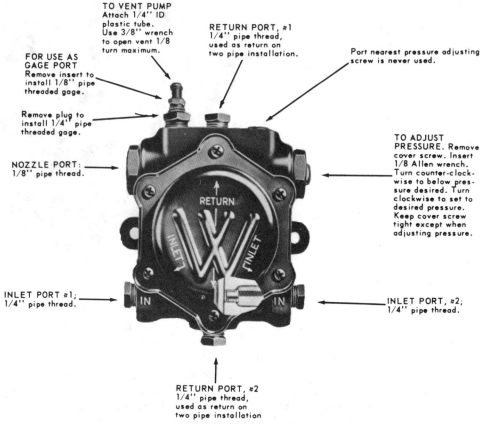

TO VENT PUMP
Attach 1/4'' ID plastic tube. Use 3/8'' wrench to open vent 1/8 turn maximum.

RETURN PORT, #1
1/4'' pipe thread, used as return on two pipe installation.

Port nearest pressure adjusting screw is never used.

FOR USE AS GAGE PORT
Remove insert to install 1/8'' pipe threaded gage.

Remove plug to install 1/4'' pipe threaded gage.

NOZZLE PORT:
1/8'' pipe thread.

RETURN

INLET

INLET

TO ADJUST PRESSURE. Remove cover screw. Insert 1/8 Allen wrench. Turn counter-clockwise to below pressure desired. Turn clockwise to set to desired pressure. Keep cover screw tight except when adjusting pressure.

INLET PORT #1;
1/4'' pipe thread.

IN

IN

INLET PORT, #2;
1/4'' pipe thread.

RETURN PORT, #2
1/4'' pipe thread, used as return on two pipe installation

NOTE: For maximum performance INLET VACUUM, when measured at unused INLET PORT, should not exceed 10'' Hg on single stage pumps, and 15'' Hg on two stage pumps.

SINGLE PIPE INSTALLATION

Recommended only when bottom of tank is above fuel unit, unless pump code ends in 15.
1. Remove BYPASS PLUG if installed, through IN-LET PORT #2.
2. Connect inlet line to preferred INLET PORT.
3. Plug all unused ports securely.
4. Start burner and bleed all air from the system by opening VENT PLUG. Close VENT securely when oil flow in-tube is clear.

TWO-PIPE INSTALLATION

1. Insert BYPASS PLUG if not installed, through INLET PORT #2.
2. Connect inlet line to preferred INLET PORT.
3. Connect return line to preferred RETURN PORT.
4. Plug all unused ports securely.
5. Start burner. Two stage pumps will self-vent. If single stage and code ends in 3 or 4, bleed all air from system by opening VENT PLUG. Close VENT securely when oil flow in tube is clear.

Figure 9-9 Oil pump showing connection locations. (Courtesy, Webster Electric Company, Inc.)

TEST PROCEDURE FOR OIL PUMPS

A simplified test procedure for oil burner pumps is shown in Figure 9-10. Note that the connections shown are for a specific model pump. However, similar connections can be made to other models by referring to the manufacturer's connection details on the specification sheets.

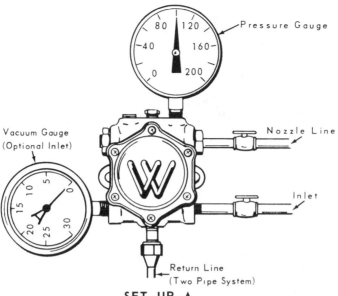

SET-UP-A

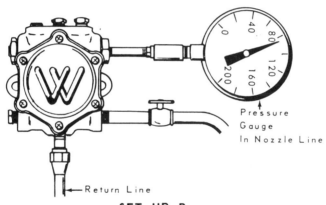

SET-UP-B

Test All Units With By-Pass Installed For Two Pipe System

Delivery and Vacuum Test - - Set-Up A Above
1. Set pressure adjusting screw to required pressure.
2. Measure nozzle delivery at set pressure.
3. Close inlet valve to check vacuum.

Cut Off Test - - Set-Up B Above
1. Set pressure at 100 PSI.
2. Shut off motor. Pressure should hold at between 75 and 90 PSI. If pressure drops to 0 PSI cut off leaks.

Figure 9-10 Test procedure for oil burner pump. (Courtesy, Webster Electric Company, Inc.)

Test Procedure for Oil Pumps

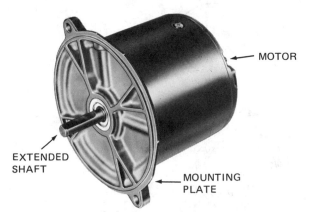

EXTENDED SHAFT

MOTOR

MOUNTING PLATE

Figure 9-11 Oil burner motor. (Courtesy, Essex Group, Controls Division, Steveco Products, Inc.)

Motor. The motor supplies power to rotate the pump and fan. Usually, a split-phase motor (with a start and run winding) is used (Figure 9-11). This type of motor provides enough torque (starting power) to move the connected components. In the event a motor fails, it must be replaced by substituting one with the same horsepower, direction of rotation, mounting dimension, revolutions per minute, shaft length, and shaft diameter.

Multiblade fan and air shutters. The multiblade (squirrel cage) centrifugal fan delivers air for combustion. It is enclosed within the fan housing. The inlet to the fan has an adjustable opening so that the amount of air volume handled by the fan can be manually controlled. The outlet of the fan delivers the combustion air through the blast tube of the burner (see Figure 9-5).

Shaft coupling. The shaft coupling connects the motor to the fuel pump (Figure 9-12). This coupling

- Provides alignment between the pump and motor shafts
- Absorbs noise that may be created by the rotating parts
- Is strongly constructed to endure the starting and stopping action of the motor

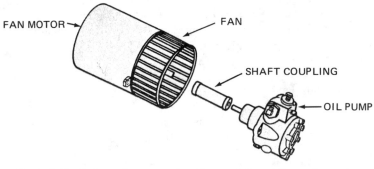

FAN MOTOR

FAN

SHAFT COUPLING

OIL PUMP

Figure 9-12 Shaft coupling. (Reproduced by permission of Carrier Corporation, Copyright Carrier Corporation.)

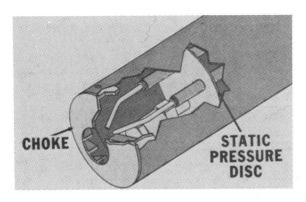

Figure 9-13 Static disc, choke, and swirl valves. (Reproduced by permission of Carrier Corporation, Copyright Carrier Corporation.)

Static disc choke and swirl vanes. As shown in Figure 9-13 the static disc, which is located in the center of the draft tube, causes the air from the fan to build up velocity at the inside surface of the tube. The choke is located at the end of the tube and restricts the area, thus further increasing the air velocity. The swirl vanes located near the choke give turbulence to the leaving air, which assists the mixing action.

Nozzle Assembly

The nozzle assembly consists of the oil feed line, the nozzle, electrodes, and transformer connections (Figure 9-14). This assembly serves to position the electrodes in respect to the nozzle opening, and provides a mounting for the high potential electrical leads from the transformer. The assembly is located near the end of the blast tube.

Electrode position. The correct position of the electrodes is shown in Figure 9-15. The electrodes must be located out of the oil spray, but close enough for the spark to arc into the spray. The spark gap between the electrodes is important. If the electrodes are not centered on the nozzle orifice, the flame will be one-sided and cause carbon to form on the nozzle.

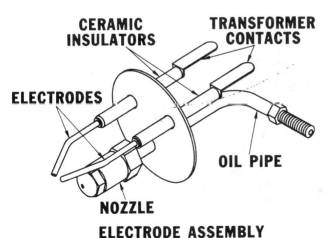

Figure 9-14 Nozzle assembly. (Reproduced by permission of Carrier Corporation, Copyright Carrier Corporation.)

Test Procedure for Oil Pumps

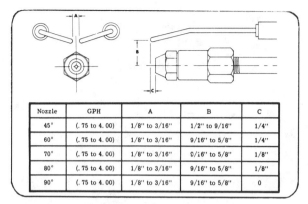

Nozzle	GPH	A	B	C
45°	(.75 to 4.00)	1/8" to 3/16"	1/2" to 9/16"	1/4"
60°	(.75 to 4.00)	1/8" to 3/16"	9/16" to 5/8"	1/4"
70°	(.75 to 4.00)	1/8" to 3/16"	0/16" to 5/8"	1/8"
80°	(.75 to 4.00)	1/8" to 3/16"	9/16" to 5/8"	1/8"
90°	(.75 to 4.00)	1/8" to 3/16"	9/16" to 5/8"	0

Recommended Electrode Settings. NOTE: Above 4.00 GPH, it may be advisable to increase dimension C by ⅛" to insure smooth starting. When using double adapters: (1) Twin ignition is the safest and is recommended, with settings same as above. (2) With single ignition, use the same A and B dimensions as above, but add ¼" to dimension C. Locate the electrode gap on a line midway between the two nozzles.

Figure 9-15 Electrode positioning. (Courtesy, Delavan Corporation.)

Nozzle. A nozzle construction is shown in Figure 9-16. The purpose of the nozzle is to prepare the oil for mixing with the air. The process is called *atomization*.

Oil first enters the strainer. The strainer has a mesh that is finer in size than the nozzle orifice so as to catch solid particles that could clog the nozzle.

From the strainer, the oil enters slots that direct the oil to the swirl chamber. The swirl chamber gives the oil a rotary motion when it enters the nozzle orifice, thus shaping the spray pattern. The nozzle orifice increases the velocity of the oil. The oil leaves in the form of a mist or spray and mixes with the air from the blast tube. Because of the fine tolerances of the nozzle construction, servicing is usually impractical. A defective or dirty nozzle is normally replaced.

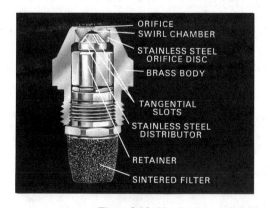

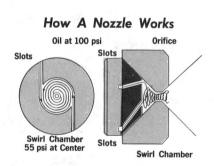

Figure 9-16 Nozzle construction. (Courtesy, Delavan Corporation.)

Spray patterns. The requirements for nozzles vary with the type of application. Nozzles are supplied with two variations: the shape of the spray and the angle between the sides of the spray.

There are three spray shapes, as shown in Figure 9-17: hollow (H), semihollow (SH), and solid (S). The hollow and the semihollow are most popular on domestic burners because they provide better efficiencies when used with modern combustion chambers.

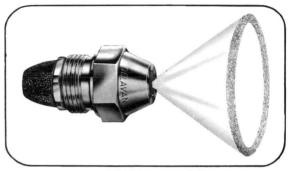

HOLLOW CONE (H)

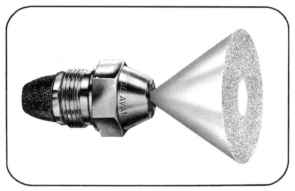

SEMI—HOLLOW CONE (SH)

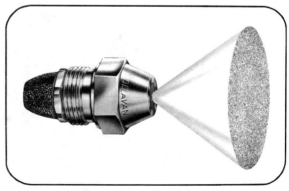

SOLID CONE (S)

Figure 9-17 Spray patterns. (Courtesy, Delavan Corporation.)

Test Procedure for Oil Pumps

161

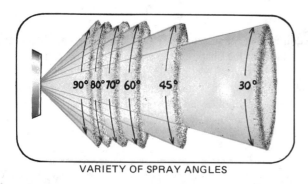

VARIETY OF SPRAY ANGLES

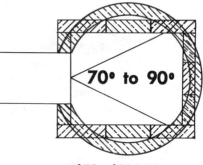

70° TO 90° FOR ROUND
OR SQUARE CHAMBERS

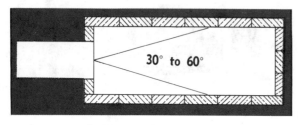

30° TO 60° FOR LONG
NARROW CHAMBERS

Figure 9-18 Relationship of spray angle to combustion chamber shape. (Courtesy, Delavan Corporation.)

The angle of the spray must correspond to the type of combustion chamber (Figure 9-18). An angle of 70° to 90° is usually best for square or round chambers. An angle of 30° to 60° is best for long, narrow chambers.

Ignition system. All high-pressure burners have electric ignition. The power is supplied by a step-up transformer connected to two electrodes. A transfomer is shown in Figure 9-19. The transformer supplies high voltage, which causes a spark to jump between the two electrodes. The force of the air in the blast tube causes the spark to arc (or bend) into the oil-air mixture, igniting it.

Figure 9-19 Transformer. (Courtesy, Webster Electric Company, Inc.)

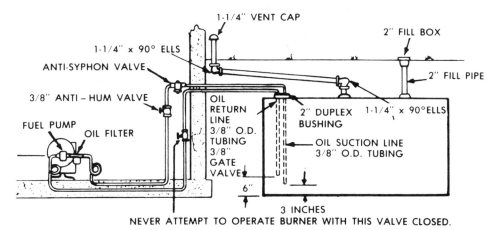

NEVER ATTEMPT TO OPERATE BURNER WITH THIS VALVE CLOSED.

TWO STAGE PUMP (2 PIPE)

DISTANCE TANK BOTTOM BELOW PUMP (FEET)	MAX. RUN LENGTH (FT.) INCLUDES LIFT		DISTANCE TANK BOTTOM BELOW PUMP (FEET)	MAX. RUN LENGTH (FT.) INCLUDES LIFT	
	3/8" O.D. TUBING	1/2" O.D. TUBING		3/8" O.D. TUBING	1/2" O.D. TUBING
1	65	100	9	45	100
2	63	100	10	42	100
3	60	100	11	40	100
4	58	100	12	37	100
5	55	100	13	35	100
6	53	100	14	32	100
7	50	100	15	30	100
8	48	100	16	27	100

Figure 9-20 Outside underground tank installation. (Courtesy, Heil-Quaker.)

Ceramic insulators surround the electrodes where they are close to metal parts. Insulators also serve to position the electrodes.

The transformer* increases the voltage from 120 V to 10,000 V but reduces the amperage (current flow) to about 20 mA. This low amperage is relatively harmless and reduces wear on the electrode tips.

Oil Storage and Piping

Most cities have rules and regulations governing the installation and piping of oil tanks to which the installation mechanic must adhere.

There are two tank locations:

1. Outside (underground)
2. Inside (usually in the basement)

An outside tank can be 550, 1000, or 1500 gal in capacity. An inside tank usually has a capacity of 275 gal. Tanks must be approved by Underwriters Laboratories (UL).

Outside underground tank. As shown in Figure 9-20, an outside underground tank should be installed at least 2 ft below the surface. The fill pipe should be 2 in.

* Because of its high voltage, caution should be used in checking the transformer.

international pipe size (IPS) and the vent pipe 1¼ in. IPS. The vent pipe must be of a greater height than the fill pipe. The bottom of the tank should slope away from the end having the suction connection. A slope of 3 in. in its length is adequate. Piping connections to the tank should use swing connections to prevent breaking the pipe when movement occurs. Oil suction and return lines are usually made of ⅜-in outside diameter (OD) copper tubing, positioned within 3 in. of the bottom of the tank.

A UL-approved suction line filter should be used. A globe valve should be installed between the tank and the filter. A check valve should be installed in the suction line at the pump to keep the line filled at all times. A suitable oil level gauge should be installed. The tank should be painted with at least two coats of tar or asphaltum paint.

Inside tank.   An inside tank installation is shown in Figure 9-21. Many of the regulations and installation conditions for inside tanks are the same as those for outside tanks. The fill pipe should be 2 in. IPS and the vent pipe, 1¼ in. IPS. An oil level gauge

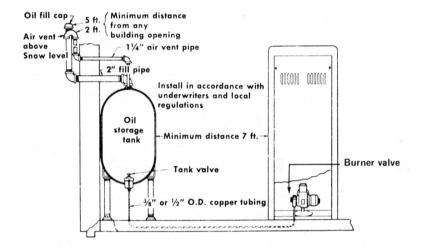

FUEL-UNIT BELOW TANK, ONE-PIPE SYSTEM

Firing rates for this type installation do not normally exceed 1-1/2 G.P.H. A head of oil up to 20 feet may be maintained, if necessary. Under these circumstances maximum length of suction line should not exceed 140 feet.

Any increase in firing rates or reduction in head pressures would necessitate a corresponding reduction in maximum length of the supply line.

NOTE: In pressurized suction lines the pressure should never exceed 10 psi – preferably less.

Figure 9-21 Inside tank installation. (Courtesy, Webster Electric Company, Inc.)

should be installed. The oil piping is usually $\frac{3}{8}$-in. OD copper tubing. A filter should be installed in the oil suction lines.

Inside tank installation varies in some ways from outside tank installation. The slope for the tank bottom should be about 1 in. and directed toward the oil suction connection. Two globe-type shutoff valves should be used, one at the tank and one at the burner. The valve at the tank should be a fuse type. The oil line between the tank and the burner should be buried in concrete. The tank should be at least 7 ft from the burner.

ACCESSORIES

Two important accessories are the combustion chamber and the draft regulator. The combustion chamber is placed in the lower portion of the heat exchanger, surrounding the flame on all sides with the exception of the top. A barometric damper is used as a draft regulator. The draft regulator is placed in the flue pipe between the furnace and the chimney.

Combustion Chambers

The purpose of a combustion chamber is to protect the heat exchanger and to provide reflected heat to the burning oil. The reflected heat warms the tips of the flame, assuring complete combustion.

No part of the flame should touch the surface of the combustion chamber. If the combustible mixture does touch, the surface will be cooled and incomplete combustion will result. It is essential that the chamber fit the flame. The nozzle must be located at the proper height above the floor. The bottom area of the combustion chamber is usually 80 in.^{2}/gal for nozzles between 0.75 and 3.00 gal/min, 90 in.^{2}/gal for nozzles between 3.50 and 6.00 gal/min, and 100 in.^{2}/gal for nozzles 6.50 gal/min and higher.

Three types of material are generally used for combustion chambers:

1. Metal (usually stainless steel)

2. Insulating firebrick

3. Molded ceramic

Metal is used in factory-built, self-contained furnaces and is used without backfill (material in space between chamber and heat exchanger). Insulated firebrick is used for conversion burners to fit almost any type of heat-exchanger shape, and uses fiberglass-type backfill. The molded ceramic chamber is prefabricated to the proper shape and size and uses fiberglass-type backfill (Figure 9-22).

Draft Regulators

A draft regulator maintains a constant draft over the fire, usually 0.01 to 0.03 in. W.C. Too high a draft causes undue loss of heat through the chimney. Too little draft causes incomplete combustion.

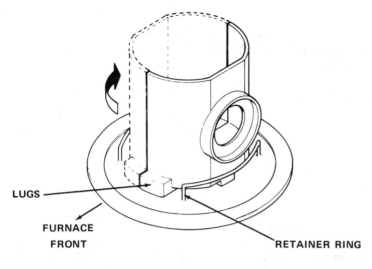

LUGS

FURNACE
FRONT

RETAINER RING

Figure 9-22 Molded ceramic combustion chamber. (Courtesy, Luxaire, Inc.)

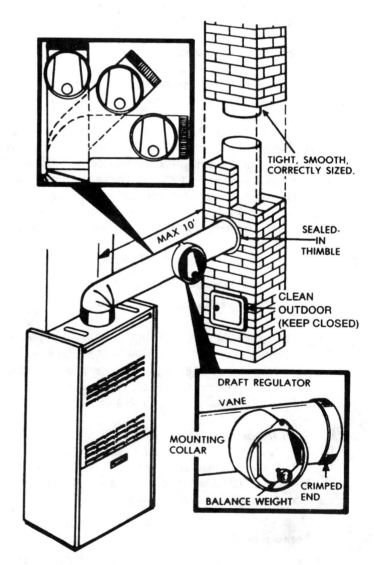

TIGHT, SMOOTH, CORRECTLY SIZED.

MAX 10'

SEALED-IN THIMBLE

CLEAN OUTDOOR (KEEP CLOSED)

DRAFT REGULATOR

VANE

MOUNTING COLLAR

CRIMPED END

BALANCE WEIGHT

Figure 9-23 Application of draft regulator. (Courtesy, Heil-Quaker.)

166

A draft regulator (Figure 9-23) consists of a small door in the side of the flue pipe. The door is hinged near the center and controlled by adjustable weights. Basement air is admitted to the flue pipe as required to maintain a proper draft over the fire.

MAINTENANCE AND SERVICE

Annual maintenance of oil burner equipment is essential to good operation. Service procedures are outlined below. See Figure 9-24.

Burner Assembly

1. Clean fan blades, fan housing, and screen.

2. Oil motor with a few drops of SAE No. 10 oil.

3. Clean pump strainer.

4. Adjust oil pressure to 100 psig.

5. Check oil pressure cutoff.

6. Conduct combustion test and adjust air to burner for best efficiency.

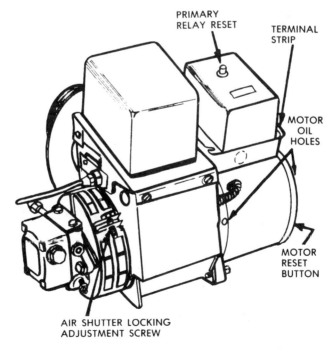

Figure 9-24 Oil burner. (Courtesy, Heil-Quaker.)

Maintenance and Service

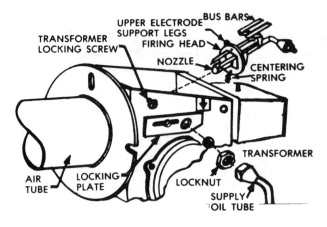

Figure 9-25 Removing oil burner nozzle assembly. (Courtesy, Heil-Quaker.)

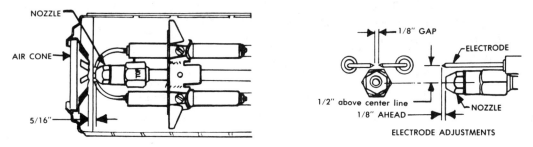

Figure 9-26 Nozzle position and electrode adjustment. (Courtesy, Heil-Quaker.)

Nozzle Assembly

See Figures 9-25 and 9-26.

1. Replace nozzle.

2. Clean nozzle assembly.

3. Check ceramic insulators for hairline cracks and replace, if necessary.

4. Check location of electrodes and adjust, if necessary.

5. Replace cartridges in oil line strainers.

Ignition System and Controls

1. Test transformer spark. The spark should jump $\frac{1}{2}$ in. or better and can be checked with a screw driver with an insulated handle, as shown in Figure 9-27.

2. Clean thermostat contacts.

3. Clean control elements that may become contaminated with soot, especially those that protrude into furnace or flue pipe.

4. Check system electrically.

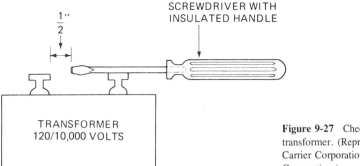

SCREWDRIVER WITH
INSULATED HANDLE

TRANSFORMER
120/10,000 VOLTS

Figure 9-27 Checking the ignition transformer. (Reproduced by permission of Carrier Corporation, Copyright Carrier Corporation.)

Furnace (Figure 9-28)

1. Clean combustion chamber and flue passages

2. Clean furnace fan blades

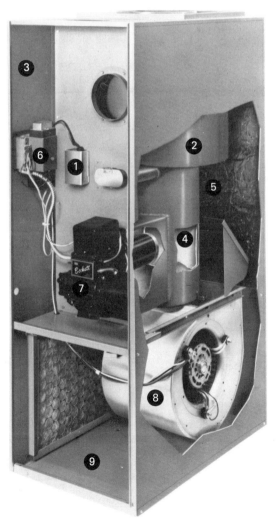

1. FAN SWITCH
2. HEAT EXCHANGER
3. CABINET
4. COMBUSTION CHAMBER
5. HEAVY INSULATION
6. RELAY
7. OIL BURNER
8. FAN
9. DUSTPROOF BASE PAN

Figure 9-28 Components of a typical forced warm air furnace, oil-fired. (Courtesy, Magic Chef Air Conditioning.)

3. Oil fan motor

4. Replace air filter

After this work is completed, run the furnace through a complete cycle and check all safety controls (Chapter 18). Clean up exterior of furnace and area around furnace.

Caution: If the unit runs out of oil or if there is an air leak in the lines, the fuel pump can become air-bound and not pump oil. To correct this, the air must be bled from the pump and replaced with oil. On a one-pipe system, this is done by loosening or removing the plug on the port opposite the intake. Start the furnace and run until oil flows out of the opening; then turn it off and replace the plug. The system can then be put back into operation. A two-pipe pump is considered to be self-priming. However, if it does fail to prime, follow the procedure just described.

CHAPTER 9 STUDY QUESTIONS

The answer to the study questions are found in the sections of this chapter under the chapter topic indicated.

STUDY QUESTIONS	CHAPTER TOPIC
1. How is oil vaporized on a pressure operated gun-type oil burner?	*Oil-burning units*
2. Name and describe four types of oil burners. Which is the most popular?	*Types of burners*
3. On a high-pressure oil burner, is the air mixed with the oil before or after passing through the nozzle?	*High-pressure burner components*
4. Are the electrodes that ignite the oil located in or out of the oil spray?	*Electrode position*
5. Describe the application of single- and two-stage oil pumps.	*Fuel pumps*
6. What is the type of motor used on a gun-type oil burner?	*Motor*
7. What is the purpose of the nozzle on an oil burner?	*Nozzle*
8. What governs the shape of flame used on the oil burner?	*Spray patterns*
9. What is the normal capacity of an inside oil tank?	*Oil storage and piping*
10. What size of copper tubing is used to connect the oil burner?	*Inside tank*
11. What are the maintenance and service requirements of an oil burner?	*Maintenance and service*
12. What action is necessary in case the burner runs out of oil and fails to start?	*Maintenance and service*

10 High-Efficiency Furnaces

OBJECTIVES

After studying this chapter, the student will be able to:

- Describe the different types of high-efficiency furnaces

- Read a wiring diagram for a high-efficiency furnace and determine the sequence of operations

- Troubleshoot service problems and determine corrective action

CHARACTERISTICS OF HIGH EFFICIENCY FURNACES

The energy crisis has encouraged manufacturers of gas furnaces to design equipment that exceeds the usual 80% efficiency. These new ratings are given in percent A.F.U.E. (annual fuel utilization efficiency) calculated in accordance with Department of Energy test procedures.

The ability of these high-efficiency (H.E.) furnaces to achieve better performance is based on two qualities:

1. **Lower Fuel Gas Temperature:** The furnaces extract more heat from the flue gas by lowering its temperature and bringing it nearer to ambient temperature before exhausting the flue gas.

2. **Condensation of the Water Vapor in the Flue Gas:** Condensation results

in the recovery of the latent heat of vaporization. Almost 1000 Btu's are released per pound of water condensed.

Components common to the various designs include the following:

1. **Induced Draft Fan:** This fan mechanically propels the flue gas through the heat exchanger passages. However, the induced draft fan serves only as a purge device on the Pulse™ furnace and is used only in the precombustion and postcombustion cycles.

2. **Secondary Heat Exchanger Surface:** Such a surface permits removing more heat from the flue gases than the normal primary heat exchanger. The basic heating surface reduces the flue gas temperature to around 500°F, and the secondary surface brings it down to around 150°F or lower.

3. **The Condensate Drain:** This drain is required to remove the products of combustion that condense at the lower flue gas temperatures. This condensate consists mainly of water vapor, but can contain other substances, due to impurities in the gas, and can be corrosive. Therefore, it must be handled properly in order to prevent damage caused by improper piping or to an inadequate disposal arrangement.

4. **Flue Pipe Design.** Due to the lower temperature and the reduced volume of flue gas, such materials as PVC plastic piping can be used for the vent stack. This feature has an advantage in the application of the equipment, simplifying the structural requirements.

One possible disadvantage of the H.E. furnaces may be their limited capacities. Most of these units do not exceed 115,000 Btuh output. However, due to the improved construction of most homes and the practice of more accurate furnace sizing, the smaller-capacity furnaces are adequate for many larger homes. The use of two furnaces is usually a good solution where more capacity is required.

TYPES OF DESIGNS

Generally speaking, the industry has created three distinctive designs of H.E. furnaces. All these designs have A.F.U.E. ratings in excess of 90%, meaning that the ratio of output to input is in the range of 90% to 97%. These designs include the following:

1. The recuperative design

2. The Pulse™ design

3. The heat transfer module design

The Recuperative Design

An illustration of a typical recuperative design is shown in Figure 10-1. The figure lists the various components. Referring to the figure, this furnace operates as follows:

Natural gas (or LP) is metered through a redundant gas valve (1) and is burned using monoport inshot burners (2), and combustion takes place in the lower portion of the primary heat exchangers (3). The hot gases then pass into a collection chamber and through a stainless steel duct into a secondary heat exchanger (4). This heat exchanger has stainless steel tubes with turbulators and exterior aluminum fins. Combustion gases are drawn through the secondary heat exchanger by an induced draft fan (5) and exhausted to the vent stack (6). Moisture condenses out of the flue gas and is collected in the drain assembly (7) and directed to the floor drain.

The multispeed direct-drive fan (8) delivers return air first over the secondary heating surface (4) and then over the primary surface (3) to the plenum outlet.

1. REDUNDANT GAS VALVE
2. MONOPORT INSHOT BURNERS
3. ALUMINIZED, PRIMARY HEAT EXCHANGER
4. SECONDARY CONDENSING HEAT EXCHANGER
5. INDUCED DRAFT FAN
6. PVC VENT OUTLET
7. CONDENSATE DRAIN TRAP
8. MULTISPEED DIRECT-DRIVE MOTOR

Figure 10-1 Exposed view of recuperative-type H.E. gas-fired furnace. (Courtesy, Bryant Air Conditioning.)

Types of Designs

Figure 10-2 Cutaway view of recuperative-type H.E. gas-fired furnace. (Reprinted with permission of the Dealer Products Group of The Trane Company, a division of American Standard, Inc.)

Electronic ignition eliminates the need for a continuous pilot. The cabinet is insulated with fiberglass.

Another illustration of a recuperative design is shown in Figure 10-2.

The Pulse™ Design

An illustration of the essential parts of the Pulse™ combustion unit is shown in Figure 10-3. Combustion takes place in a finned, cast-iron chamber. Note in the lower part of this chamber the gas intake, the air intake, the spark plug ignition, and the flame sensor. At the time of initial combustion the spark plug ignites the gas-air mixture. The pressure in the chamber following combustion closes the gas and air intakes. The pressure buildup also forces the hot gases out of the combustion chamber, through the tail pipe, into the heat exchanger exhaust decoupler, and into the heat exchanger coil. As the chamber empties after combustion, its pressure becomes negative, drawing in a new supply of gas and air for the next pulse of combustion. The flame remnants of the previous combustion ignite the new gas/air mixtures and the cycle continues. Once combustion is started the purge fan and the spark ignitor are shut off. These pulse cycles occur about 60 to 70 times a second.

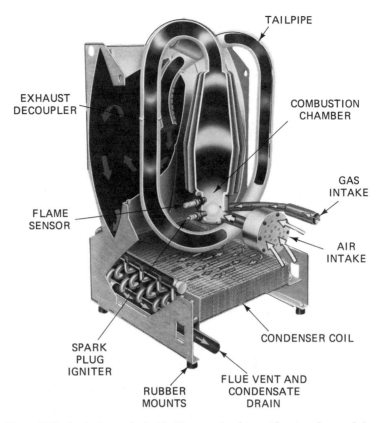

Figure 10-3 Spark plug method of igniting gas-air mixture. (Courtesy, Lennox Industries, Inc.)

The sequence of operation of the Purge™ furnace is as follows:

When the room thermostat calls for heat it initiates the operation of the purge fan which runs for 34 s. This is followed by the turning on of the ignition and the opening of the gas valve. The flame sensor provides proof of ignition and de-energizes the purge fan and spark ignition. The furnace fan automatically starts 30 to 45 s after combustion ignition.

When the thermostat is satisfied, the gas valve closes and the purge fan is turned *on* for 34 s. The furnace fan continues to operate until the temperature in the plenum reaches 90°F. In case the flame is lost before the thermostat is satisfied, the flame sensor will try to reignite the gas-air mixture three or five times before locking out. Should there be either a loss of intake gas or air, the furnace will automatically shut down.

Note that combustion air is piped with the same PVC-type pipe as used for the exhaust gases. The range of the condensate liquid is from a pH of 4.0 to 6.0, which permits it to be drained into city sewers or septic tanks. The combustion mixture of gas and air are preset at the factory, and no field adjustments are necessary.

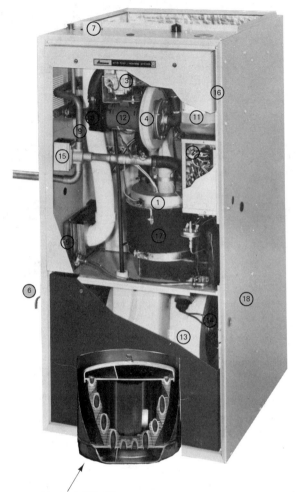

CUTAWAY VIEW OF
HEAT TRANSFER MODULE

1. HEAT TRANSFER MODULE
2. SOLID STATE ELECTRONIC CONTROLS
3. NEGATIVE PRESSURE GAS VALVE
4. COMBUSTION AIR FAN
5. RECUPERATIVE COIL
6. CONDENSATE DRAIN
7. EXHAUST PIPE
8. SOLUTION PUMP
9. SOLUTION TUBING

10. HEATING COIL
11. RESERVE LIQUID BANK
12. COMBINATION MOTOR
13. TURBO-BLADED AIR FAN
14. DIRECT DRIVE FAN MOTOR
15. DIVERTER VALVE
16. STEEL CABINET
17. INSULATION
18. ELECTRODE POSITION POINT

Figure 10-4 Exposed view of H.E. furnace, showing cutaway of the heat-transfer module. (Courtesy, Amana Refrigeration, Inc.)

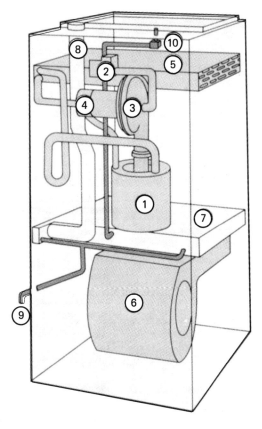

1. CERAMIC IGNITOR	6. AIR FAN
2. GAS VALVE	7. RECUPERATIVE COIL
3. COMBUSTION AIR FAN	8. PVC VENT PIPE
4. SOLUTION PUMP	9. CONDENSATE DRAIN
5. HEATING COIL	10. WATER VALVE

Figure 10-5 Diagrammatic internal view of H.E. furnace. (Courtesy, Amana Refrigeration, Inc.)

The Heat-Transfer Module (HTM™) Design

Figure 10-4 illustrates a cutaway view of the heat transfer module–designed furnace and gives a list of the various components. Figure 10-5 is a diagrammatic view of the interior of the furnace, which is useful in explaining the operation of the equipment.

Referring to Figure 10-5 on a call for heat by the room thermostat, a ceramic ignitor inside the HTM™ (1) is activated and reaches a temperature of 2500°F. The gas valve (2) opens and the combustion fan (3) is started, mixing gas and air, delivering the fuel to the HTM™ unit. As the mixture passes over the hot ignitor, combustion begins transferring heat through hundreds of steel fins to the glycol-water solution in the HTM™ unit. A solution pump (4) circulates the solution from the module to the heating coil (5) and back to the HTM™ in a closed circuit. As the coil is heated, the furnace fan (6) delivers air over the finned surface, transferring the heat to the air distribution system.

The ignitor also acts as a safety device. If combustion does not ocurr in 15 s, the gas valve is automatically closed. As the solution expands, the increased volume is stored in an expansion tank. In case the temperature of the liquid is excessive, the gas valve is also automatically closed.

Flue gas leaves the furnace at about 300°F and is circulated through the recuperative coil (7). This coil transfers heat to the return air before it enters the heating coil. Exhaust gases leave the recuperative coil at about 115°F, causing the moisture to condense. Exhaust gases leave through the vent stack (8). Condensate is removed from the furnace through the drain (9). Since the condensate consists of a mild acid, at the end of the heating cycle the recuperate coil is flushed by opening a water valve (10).

Another feature of this furnace, with the HTM™, is its ability to heat domestic hot water. The hot water accessory is shown connected in Figure 10-6. The diverter valve

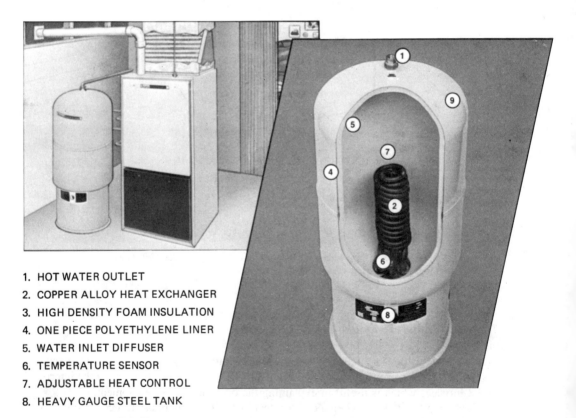

1. HOT WATER OUTLET
2. COPPER ALLOY HEAT EXCHANGER
3. HIGH DENSITY FOAM INSULATION
4. ONE PIECE POLYETHYLENE LINER
5. WATER INLET DIFFUSER
6. TEMPERATURE SENSOR
7. ADJUSTABLE HEAT CONTROL
8. HEAVY GAUGE STEEL TANK

Figure 10-6 Domestic hot-water heater accessory, installed with energy-efficient furnace. (Courtesy, Amana Refrigeration, Inc.)

High-Efficiency Furnaces   Chap. 10

shown in Figure 10-4 can direct the glycol-water solution from the HTM unit to the water heater automatically to maintain domestic hot water at a selected temperature. This heater is an accessory that can be added in the field. It has the capacity to heat 126 gal/h of water. The water heater should be installed with a water softener or phosphate treatment system to control mineral deposits.

WIRING DIAGRAMS

In this section, types of diagrams are shown as follows:

1. All-electric controls

2. Electric controls with some printed circuits (solid-state)

Both of these systems shown are for recuperative-type units.

All-Electric Controls

A number of controls are included in these diagrams that are not common to standard furnaces. These controls are described as follows:

1. **Fan Door Switch:** This control prevents operation of the furnace when the fan door is open.

2. **Ignitor:** This control generates a spark to ignite the gas pilot. The type used for natural gas varies somewhat from the one used for LP gas.

3. **Mercury Flame Sensor:** This device senses the presence of the pilot flame and will permit the main gas valve to open in 30 to 45 s.

4. **Pressure Differential Switch:** This is a safety control and prevents the gas valve from opening unless the induced draft fan is delivering sufficient combustion air through the heat exchanger.

5. **Thermal Limit:** This is a safety control located in the burner cover. The circuit breaks at 333°F.

All these five controls are used in the wiring diagrams shown in Figures 10-7 through 10-10.

Sequence of operation. On a call for heating by the room thermostat, the induced draft fan is turned on (Figure 10-7). This is accomplished by connecting the R and W terminals in the thermostat, energizing the R1 relay, and closing the circuit to the induced draft fan motor. The pilot valve is not energized until the induced draft fan creates sufficient pressure in the pressure differential switch to close.

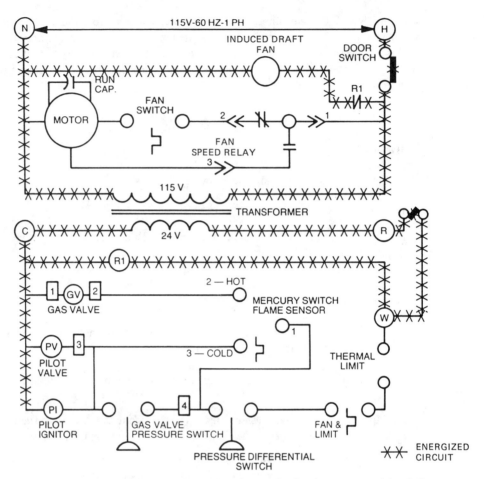

Figure 10-7 Wiring diagram for reclaimer furnace showing thermostat energizing draft fan motor. (Reprinted with permission of the Dealer Products Group of The Trane Company, a division of American Standard, Inc.)

On start-up the contacts in the thermal-limit switch and the high-limit switch are closed (Figure 10-8). By closing the contacts in the differential switch the mercury-flame-sensor switch completes a circuit from positions 1 to 3, energizing the pilot gas valve and the ignitor. The pilot ignites and the ignitor is turned off.

Within 45 to 60 s after the pilot is lighted, the mercury flame sensor moves to complete the circuit between positions 1 and 2 and opens the main gas valve (Figure 10-9). The pilot remains lighted through the contacts on the gas pressure switch.

The fan switch energizes the furnace fan motor when the bonnet temperature reaches 130°F (Figure 10-10).

Service problems. Service problems that can occur include the following most commonly encountered:

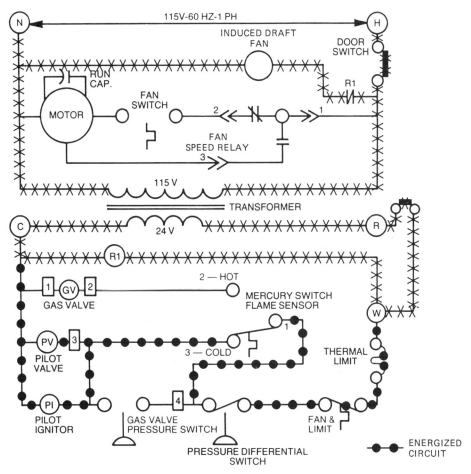

Figure 10-8 Wiring diagram for reclaimer furnace showing pilot gas valve and igniter energized. (Reprinted with permission of the Dealer Products Group of The Trane Company, a division of American Standard, Inc.)

1. Induced draft, fan running: no spark.

2. Induced draft, fan running, pressure differential switch closed: no spark.

3. Spark will not shut off after pilot flame is established.

4. Pilot flame: main burner will not light.

5. Pilot lights and then goes off when main gas valve opens.

No Spark: Induced Draft, Fan Running. Place a jumper across the pressure differential switch temporarily contacts. If spark occurs, remove vent pipe from top of furnace. Turn gas off.

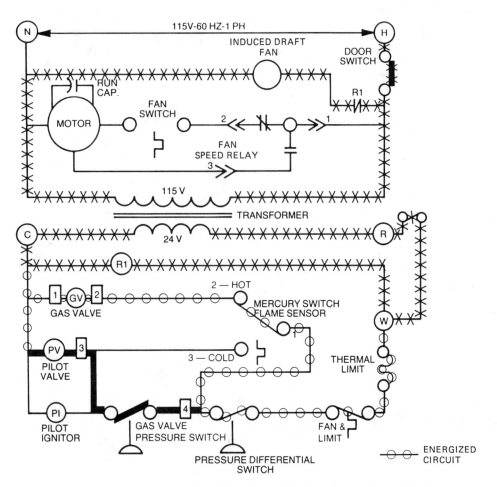

Figure 10-9 Wiring diagram for reclaimer furnace showing main gas valve energized. (Reprinted with permission of the Dealer Products Group of The Trane Company, a division of American Standard, Inc.)

1. Disconnect hose from induced draft fan and push wire through hole to induced draft fan wheel. If line is open, connect draft gauge to pressure differential switch.

2. Operate the furnace. If the draft exceeds 0.60 in. W.C., the induced draft fan is working satisfactorily.

3. Slowly block off the vent discharge on top of the furnace. If the switch opens within ±0.05 of the pressure required by the furnace, the switch is satisfactory. If not, replace the switch.

If the switch is functioning properly, the problem is probably in the external vent. Find the problem and correct it.

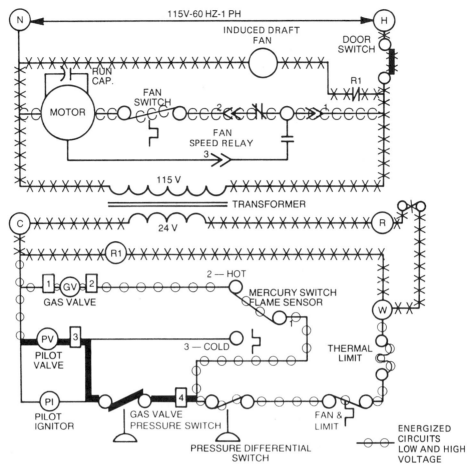

Figure 10-10 Wiring diagram for reclaimer furnace showing air fan energized. (Reprinted with permission of the Dealer Products Group of The Trane Company, a division of American Standard, Inc.)

No Spark: Induced Draft Fan Running, Pressure-Differential Switch Closed.

1. Check to see that 24 V is available across the ignitor terminals. If not, check for the open circuit:
   (a) In thermal limit
   (b) In limit switch
   (c) In auxiliary limit switch
   Mercury flame sensor should have a closed circuit between terminals 1 and 3. If the circuit is open, replace the flame sensor.

2. Disconnect ignitor. Suppy 24 V to terminals. If there's no spark, replace the ignitor.

Spark Will Not Shut Off After Pilot Flame is Established.

1. Make sure the electrode tip is in the pilot flame.

2. Ensure that the ignitor is grounded to the furnace chassis.

3. If the spark still continues, replace the ignitor.

Pilot Flame, But Main Burner Will Not Ignite.

1. Verify that the main gas valve is in the on position.

2. Check to see that the pilot flame covers ½ in. of the mercury-flame-sensor element.

3. Shut off the furnace for 1 min and turn it back on through the thermostat. Within 45 s after the pilot ignites, the gas valve should open. Temporarily place a jumper across terminals 1 to 3 on the mercury flame sensor.
    a. If the main gas valve opens, the flame sensor is defective and should be replaced.
    b. If the main gas valve does not open it is defective and should be replaced.

Pilot Flame Goes Out When Main Gas Valve Opens. Check the natural gas pressure. It should be 5 in. W.C. or greater.

1. If the gas pressure is low, adjust the regulator.

2. If the gas pressure stays above the minimum, the gas pressure switch is defective and must be replaced.

Electric Controls Some with Printed Circuits

A typical wiring diagram for this system is shown in Figure 10-11. There are two solid-state control boards:

1. The flame control module

2. The printed circuit (P.C.) board

The chief difference in this design is the use of a hot-surface ignitor that directly ignites the main gas burner. The unit has no gas pilot.

The sequence of operation is as follows (See Figure 10-11). On a call for heating, a circuit is completed through the P.C. board and the induced draft fan is started. Pressure switch 1 closes, energizing the flame-control module. The silicone carbide ignitor is energized, and in 45 s the main gas valve opens. The flame sensor confirms the ignition, and in 7 s the ignitor is de-energized. After approximately 80 s, with a wind velocity less than 20 mi/h against the vent termination, pressure switch 2 opens, placing the induced draft fan on low speed. The cut-in point of the furnace fan is usually 120°F, and the cut-out point is 90°F.

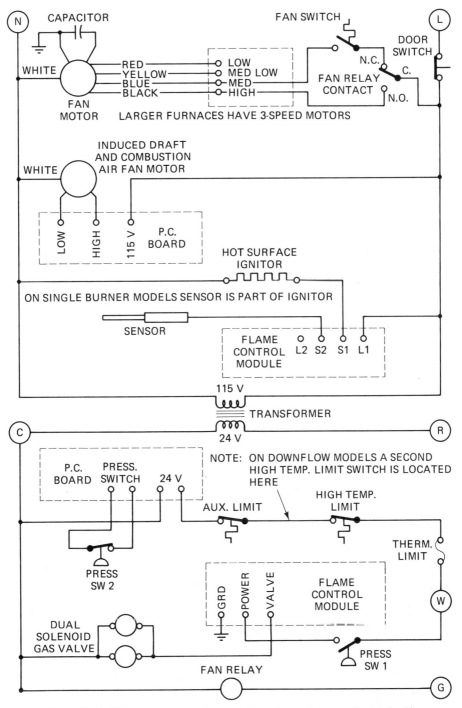

Figure 10-11 Wiring for printed circuit model reclaimer furnace. (Reprinted with permission of the Dealer Products Group of The Trane Company, a division of American Standard, Inc.)

Wiring Diagrams

AIR FOR COMBUSTION

This section describes the use of PVC and stainless steel pipe and fittings used on HE furnaces to convey combustion air, provide venting, and run condensate drains.

Details for this information are shown in the following diagrams:

Figure	Description
10-12	Air for combustion
10-13	Vertical and horizontal venting*
10-14	PVC venting through floor, ceiling, and roof*
10-15	Venting through masonry chimneys*
10-16	Venting through combustible and noncombustible walls*
10-17	Condensate drains

*The arrangement of vent fittings must conform to the National Fuel Gas Code, ANSI: 2223.1.

Figure 10-12 shows typical PVC piping for the combustion-air supply for a HE gas furnace. Generally speaking, for HE furnaces (40,000 to 120,000 Btu/h input), the PVC size for combustion air is 2-in. (2⅜-in. OD) schedule 40 PVC for pipe and fittings. It is important to use only approved PVC solvent cement.

The operation of exhaust fans, ventilation systems, or clothes dryers may create conditions requiring special attention to avoid unsatisfactory operation of installed gas-burning equipment.

In especially cold climates, it is possible that use of openings in outside walls may result in overventilation or excessive cooling of the utility room or other confined-space

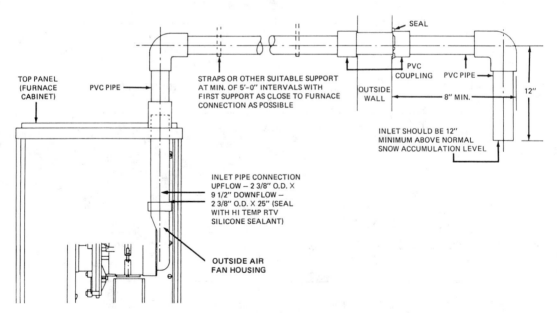

Figure 10-12 Air piping for combustion. (Reprinted with permission of the Dealer Products Group of The Trane Company, a division of American Standard, Inc.)

furnace locations. Under certain conditions, this might introduce the hazard of freezing water lines or water heaters. In this case, a supply air duct should be used to heat this space.

The outside air fan is not designed to support the weight of the inlet pipe. To avoid damage to the fan, support must be provided, as illustrated in Figure 10-12.

A grille or coarse screen must be placed over the openings to prevent blockage by leaves or other debris. Manufacturers specifications must also be checked for specific recommendations relating to sizing. Louvers and grilles that are not in a fixed position must be interlocked with the equipment so that they are opened automatically when the equipment operates.

HORIZONTAL AND VERTICAL VENTING

The horizontal pipe should be supported every 3 ft, with the first support as close to the furnace as possible (Figure 10-13a). The induced draft fan and/or furnace cabinet should not support the weight of the flue pipes.

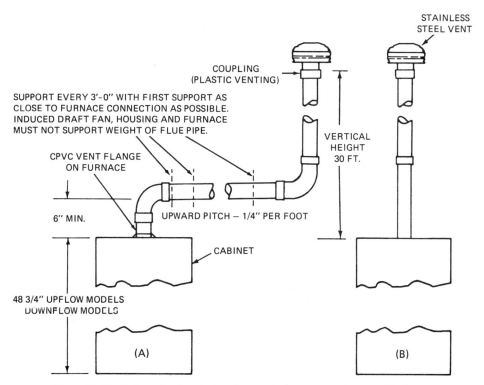

Figure 10-13 Horizontal and vertical venting. (a) Supports and pitch required for horizontal vent section. (b) Direct vertical venting through roof. (Reprinted with permission of the Dealer Products Group of The Trane Company, a division of American Standard, Inc.)

Figure 10-13b shows a vertical stack directly off the top of the furnace. Here, also, adequate supports need to be provided so that the induced draft fan does not support the weight of the flue pipe.

The maximum height of the flue discharge above the furnace should be 30 ft.

For most HE furnaces the unit system is assembled from 3-in. schedule 40 PVC pipe and fittings. The AGA has a certified that the design of flues for recuperative furnaces shall have a minimum of 1 in. clearance from combustible materials with a single wall vent pipe.

It is important to seal the joints between the flange, pipe, coupling, and metal panel with high temperature RTV silicon sealant (Figure 10-14).

Although the vent pipe can be PVC, the vent cap is stainless steel as shown in Figure 10-14c. The applicable fittings for venting through the roof are metalvent, metalbestos, and the equivalent.

A galvanized fire-stop should be fabricated with a $3\frac{7}{8}$-in.-diameter hole in the support flange, as shown in Figure 10-14b.

Figure 10-15 shows two conditions: (A) PVC venting only through an unused

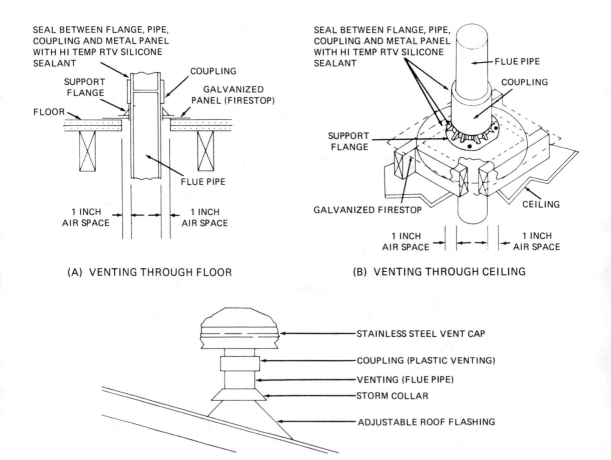

(A) VENTING THROUGH FLOOR

(B) VENTING THROUGH CEILING

(C) VENTING THROUGH ROOF

Figure 10-14 PVC venting through floor, ceiling, and roof. (Reprinted with permission of the Dealer Products Group of The Trane Company, a division of American Standard, Inc.)

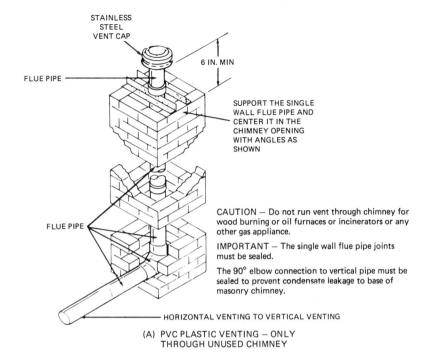

STAINLESS STEEL VENT CAP

FLUE PIPE

6 IN. MIN

SUPPORT THE SINGLE WALL FLUE PIPE AND CENTER IT IN THE CHIMNEY OPENING WITH ANGLES AS SHOWN

FLUE PIPE

CAUTION — Do not run vent through chimney for wood burning or oil furnaces or incinerators or any other gas appliance.

IMPORTANT — The single wall flue pipe joints must be sealed.

The 90° elbow connection to vertical pipe must be sealed to prevent condensate leakage to base of masonry chimney.

HORIZONTAL VENTING TO VERTICAL VENTING

(A) PVC PLASTIC VENTING — ONLY THROUGH UNUSED CHIMNEY

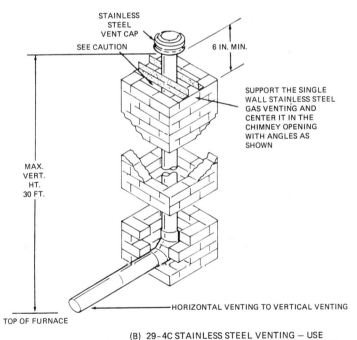

STAINLESS STEEL VENT CAP

SEE CAUTION

6 IN. MIN.

SUPPORT THE SINGLE WALL STAINLESS STEEL GAS VENTING AND CENTER IT IN THE CHIMNEY OPENING WITH ANGLES AS SHOWN

MAX. VERT. HT. 30 FT.

HORIZONTAL VENTING TO VERTICAL VENTING

TOP OF FURNACE

(B) 29-4C STAINLESS STEEL VENTING — USE THROUGH CHIMNEY THAT VENTS ANOTHER GAS APPLIANCE

Figure 10-15 Venting through masonry chimneys. (Reprinted with permission of the Dealer Products Group of The Trane Company, a division of American Standard, Inc.)

Horizontal and Vertical Venting

189

chimney and (B) stainless steel venting using a chimney that vents other gas appliances. Vents for HE furnaces should not be run through chimneys used for wood burning, oil furnaces, or incinerators. Stainless steel should be used if the chimney is used for other gas appliances.

If the remaining free area between a single wall flue pipe and the masonry chimney is to be used for other gas appliances, venting areas must be sufficient to vent the additional appliances (Figure 10-15b). Each appliance must be connected to the chimney with a separate entry opening.

All single wall flue pipe joints must be sealed.

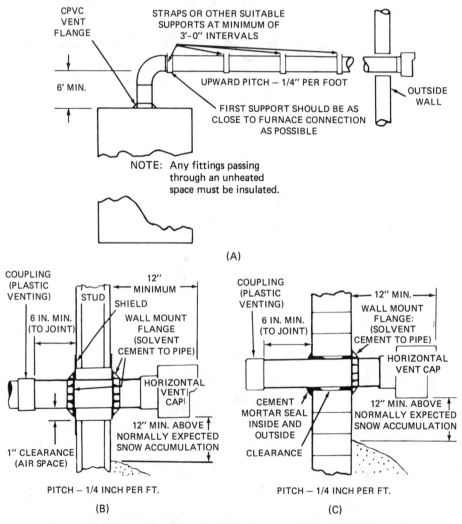

Figure 10-16 Venting through walls. (a) Horizontal pitch required. (b) Installation through combustible walls. (c) Installation through noncombustible walls. (Reprinted with permission of the Dealer Products Group of The Trane Company, a division of American Standard, Inc.)

High-Efficiency Furnaces   Chap. 10

Venting Through Walls

Figure 10-16a shows the ¼ in.-per-foot upward pitch of the vent pipe to the outside wall. Figure 10-16b shows the vent construction requirements through a combustible wall. The shield must be 24-gauge galvanized or aluminum sheet metal with minimum dimensions of 12 in. by 12 in.

The vent construction through a noncombustible wall is shown in Figure 10-16c. The hole through the wall must be large enough to maintain the required vent pitch. All wall-mount flanges and shields must be properly sealed.

Location of the vent cap. The vent cap must be 12 in. above the normally expected snow level. It must be 7 in. above grade if it is adjacent to public walkways. The cap must be 4 in. horizontally away from any door or window and 6 in. away from any building.

CONDENSATE DRAINS

Typical condensate drain connections are shown in Figure 10-17. The recommended size is ½-in. inside diameter (ID) or ⅝-in. OD. CPVC pipe and fittings, with joints sealed with CPVC solvent cement. Connections must be made to an open drain.

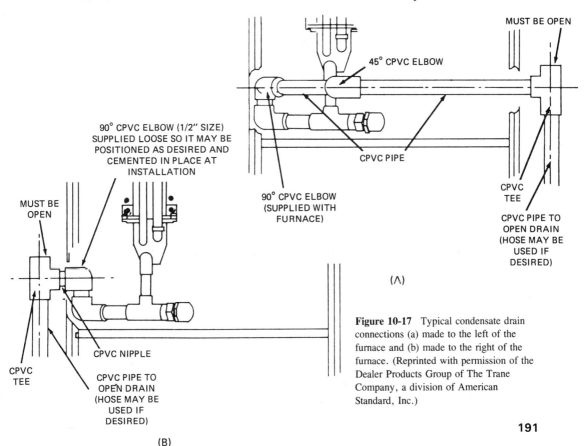

MUST BE OPEN

45° CPVC ELBOW

90° CPVC ELBOW (1/2" SIZE) SUPPLIED LOOSE SO IT MAY BE POSITIONED AS DESIRED AND CEMENTED IN PLACE AT INSTALLATION

CPVC PIPE

90° CPVC ELBOW (SUPPLIED WITH FURNACE)

CPVC TEE

CPVC PIPE TO OPEN DRAIN (HOSE MAY BE USED IF DESIRED)

MUST BE OPEN

(A)

CPVC NIPPLE

CPVC TEE

CPVC PIPE TO OPEN DRAIN (HOSE MAY BE USED IF DESIRED)

(B)

Figure 10-17 Typical condensate drain connections (a) made to the left of the furnace and (b) made to the right of the furnace. (Reprinted with permission of the Dealer Products Group of The Trane Company, a division of American Standard, Inc.)

191

Drops of condensate may form on the inside of the vent pipe as it passes through cooler areas. This will flow by gravity into the vent collar on the induced draft fan outlet, which then drains into the condensate drain connections.

Stainless Steel Pipe and Fittings

All stainless steel fittings must be installed with the male ends in direction of flow.

All horizontal stainless steel sections must be positioned with the seam on top.

All horizontal sections must be pitched upward in the direction of flow a minimum of $\frac{1}{4}$ in./ft.

All horizontal sections must be supported at a minimum of every 3 ft.

All joints must be fastened, sealed, and tested for leaks. Seal all joints with high-temperature silicone sealant.

All joints must be secured with three screws (stainless steel). Do not place any screws at the bottom of a horizontal joint; otherwise, leakage may occur at this point.

All the information contained in these installation instructions is based on industry standards; however, final approval is controlled by local ordinances.

CHAPTER 10 STUDY QUESTIONS

The answers to the study questions are found in the sections of this chapter under the chapter topic indicated.

STUDY QUESTIONS	CHAPTER TOPIC
1. What are the characteristics of a high-efficiency furnace that contribute to the additional capacity?	*Characteristics*
2. What is meant by annual fuel utilization efficiency (A.F.U.E.)?	*Types of design*
3. Name and describe the three types of designs.	*Types of design*
4. How much heat is dissipated for every pound of water condensed?	*Characteristics*
5. What is the efficiency range of the high-efficiency gas furnaces?	*Characteristics*
6. What is the normal number of pulses per second for a pulse-type furnace?	*Pulse™ design*
7. What is the pH range for the condensed liquid in a high efficiency furnace?	*Pulse™ design*
8. On the heat-transfer module design, what is the temperature of the ceramic ignitor?	*Heat-transfer module design*

9. If combustion does not occur, how many seconds are required for the gas to shut off on the HTM™ design.

Heat transfer module design

10. What is the temperature of the exhaust gases on the recuperative design?

Characteristics

11. Describe five controls that are unique on the high-efficiency furnaces?

All-electric controls

12. Describe the control sequence for a high-efficiency reclaimer furnace.

Sequence of operation

13. Name three common service problems and their solutions.

Service problems

14. Describe the piping used for combustion air.

Air for combustion

15. Describe the piping used for venting.

Venting through walls

16. Describe the piping used for condensate drains.

Condensate drains

11 Heat Pumps

OBJECTIVES

After studying this chapter, the student will be able to:

- Describe the different types of heat pumps
- Explain the operation of a heat pump
- Read a wiring diagram for a heat pump control system
- Troubleshoot a defective heat pump system

CHARACTERISTICS

The heat pump system is a modification of a cooling system, using the refrigeration cycle not only to cool the building but also to heat it electrically. Electrical heating using resistance-type elements is usually prohibitive from an operative cost standpoint. However, the heat pump uses a heat-transfer principal to greatly improve electrical heating efficiency. Using strictly resistance heat, a watt of electricity is converted into 3.4 Btu of heat. Using the heat pump under most favorable conditions, 1 W of power can produce 12 or 13 Btu.

TYPES OF HEAT PUMPS

The heat pump is a mechanical device used to transfer heat from a "heat source" and discharge it to a "heat sink." Heat is absorbed from one medium, added to the heat of

194

compression (produced by the refrigeration compressor), and rejected to a second medium (usually air).

There are two types of heat pumps in common usage: the air-to-air and the water-to-air designs. The air-to-air type uses air both as a heat source and as a heat sink. The water-to-air type uses water for the heat source and air for the heat sink. The air-to-air design is more frequently used due to easier accessibility of air as compared to water.

The two types of heat pumps are similar in that they both utilize the refrigeration cycle to transfer or move heat from one area to another. There are, however, some important differences. For one thing, the air-to-air heat pump uses an outdoor heat exchanger (a finned tube coil) to pick up heat for the heating cycle. Under certain conditions this coil requires defrosting. On the water-to-air heat pump the heat source is a constant or near-constant-temperature water supply, always above freezing temperatures, which does not require a defrost cycle.

A second important difference is the use of supplementary heat. On the air-to-air design, as the outside temperature drops and the need for heat is increased, supplementary heat must be added. On the water-to-air system with a constant-temperature supply of water available, the heating capacity is not affected by the outside temperature. Supplementary heat is added only when the normal heating capacity of the unit is insufficient to handle the load. Since the unit is usually selected based on its cooling capacity, it is not considered good practice to oversize the unit more than approximately 20% to handle heating. Thus, under extreme weather conditions, supplementary heat is required.

THE REFRIGERATION CYCLE

The refrigeration cycle is shown in Figure 11-1. Starting with the compressor, high-temperature–high-pressure refrigerant vapor is delivered to the condenser. The vapor is

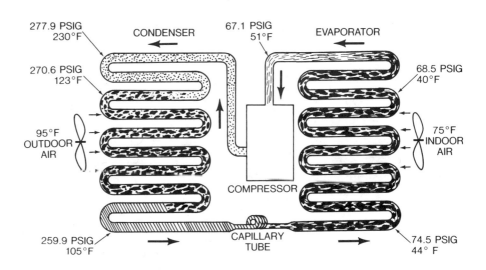

Figure 11-1 Typical refrigeration cycle used for cooling. (Reprinted with permission of the Dealer Product Group of The Trane Company, a division of American Standard, Inc.)

cooled by air (for an all-air system), changing the vapor into liquid refrigerant. The liquid is then passed through an orifice (metering device) attached to the inlet side of the evaporator, reducing its temperature and pressure and permitting it to boil and absorb heat. The low-temperature–low-pressure refrigerant vapor then flows back to the compressor and the cycle is repeated.

Heat is exchanged in three places: in the condenser, where heat is dissipated, in the evaporator, where heat is absorbed, and in the compressor, where electrical energy from the motor and compression cycle are converted into heat and added to the refrigerant.

The heat produced by the compressor is added to the heat absorbed by the evaporator and is exhausted to the outside air. The heat absorbed by the evaporator causes the indoor air to be cooled.

Using the refrigeration cycle as a heat pump, the position of the two coils is reversed. The condenser is placed inside the building to heat the air, and the evaporator is placed in the outdoor air to absorb heat. Needless to say, it is not practical physically to alter the position of these coils in changing from cooling to heating. To accomplish the same thing, a reversing valve is used in the heat pump, as shown in Figure 11-2.

With the reversing valve in the position shown in Figure 11-2a, the cycle cools the indoor air. With the reversing valve in the position shown in Figure 11-2b, the cycle heats the indoor air. Note the arrangement at the bottom of the drawing for reversing the direction of refrigerant flow through the metering devices when changing from cooling to heating. Two metering devices are used, one for cooling and one for heating. A check valve in parallel with each metering device functions to direct the flow through the metering device being used, bypassing the unused metering device.

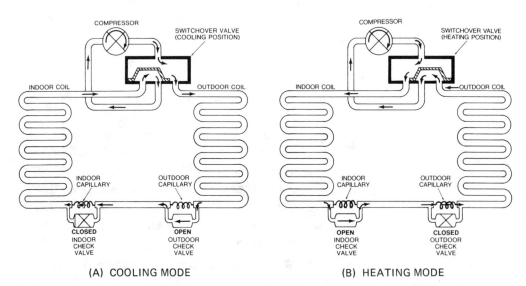

Figure 11-2 Basic heat pump circuits. (Reprinted with permission of the Dealer Products Group of The Trane Company, a division of American Standard, Inc.)

THE DEFROST CYCLE

Another necessary element in the air-to-air heat pump design is the defrost arrangement for the outside coil. There are times during heating when the refrigerant temperature in the outdoor coil is below freezing temperatures and ice forms on the coil, restricting the air flow. To prevent inefficient heating as a result of this condition, the outdoor coil is automatically defrosted when necessary.

One way to control the defrost cycle is to use a Dwyer defrost arrangement, as shown in Figure 11-3. The control system must accomplish two functions to initiate the defrost cycle:

1. The temperature of the refrigerant must be below 32°F.

2. The coil must be sufficiently frosted to restrict the air flow 70% to 90%.

Position B in Figure 11-3 shows the defrost termination switch open, indicating the refrigerant temperature is above 32°F. Position A shows the vacuum-operated switch contacts open, indicating the coil is not iced up sufficiently to require defrost.

Position C shows the defrost termination switch closed, indicating the refrigerant temperature is below 32°F. Position D shows the vacuum-operated switch contacts closed, indicating the need for defrosting the coil.

Based on the two switches (positions C and D) in defrost, the reversing valve automatically places the cycle in the cooling mode (Figure 11-2a), supplying hot gas

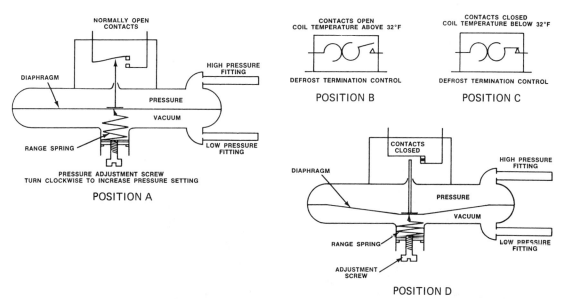

Figure 11-3 Dwyer defrost system's mechanical operation. (Reprinted with permission of the Dealter Products Group of The Trane Company, a division of American Standard, Inc.)

from the compressor to the outside coil and defrosting it. The defrost cycle continues until the refrigerant temperature reaches 55°F, opening the defrost termination switch (position B) and automatically placing the system back in the heating mode (Figure 11-2b).

SUPPLEMENTARY HEAT

The air-to-air heat pump is most effective in absorbing heat from the outdoor air when it is relatively warm outside. For example, on a typical 5-horsepower (hp) unit, the relationship of watts input, total Btu output, and outside air temperature are as follows, based on an outdoor condition of 70% relative humidity and indoor temperature at 70°F:

Outdoor Temperature (°F)	Compressor Motor (watts input)	Total Output (Btuh)
60	4,520	57,100
50	4,060	50,100
47*	3,920	48,000
40	3,570	40,800
30	3,200	32,900
20	2,960	27,500
17*	2,890	25,900
10	2,670	22,500
0	2,360	17,600
−10	2,045	12,700
−20	1,735	7,800

* Department of Energy (DOE) standard test points

The heat pump produces more heat even at −20°F (7800 Btuh) than resistance heating (1735 W × 3.4 = 5899 Btuh). Thus, the control system continues to operate the heat pump even at low outside temperatures.

Since the amount of heat required by a building increases as the outside temperature

SINGLE-PACKAGE UNIT
(LEFT REAR PORTION)

LOW VOLTAGE
JUNCTION
BOX   CONTACTOR

FAN
RELAY

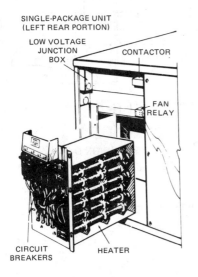

CIRCUIT
BREAKERS   HEATER

Figure 11-4 Electric strip heater package used for supplementary heat. (Courtesy, Heil-Quaker Corporation.)

becomes lower, supplementary heat must be added. This additional heat could come from a gas furnace or an electric strip heater. The electric source is more common. Figure 11-4 shows an electric strip heater package being inserted into a packaged heat pump. The heating element is compact and can be installed without a chimney, thus simplifying installation. Heat pumps are more popular in the warmer climates, since less supplementary heat needs to be added.

THE AIR-TO-AIR SYSTEM

Many of the items included in this section, such as certain rating definitions, the calculations for supply air temperature rise, the type of thermostat used, the refrigeration piping, and details of condensate drains, also apply to the water-to-air heat pump. For sake of completeness these sections can be referred to in studying the water-to-air systems.

There are two principal arrangements of equipment available:

1. The split system

2. The single package

The split system requires two or more components. Figure 11-5 shows the equipment for a three-component split system.

INDOOR SECTION

OUTDOOR SECTION

Figure 11-5 Components of split-system heat pumps. (Courtesy, Carrier Corporation.)

199

COMPRESSOR SECTION

As shown in Figure 11-6, the furnace section is inside the building and consists mainly of a circulation fan, a heat-transfer coil, a supplementary heat source, and an air filter. The compressor section is also placed indoors for weather protection, possibly in

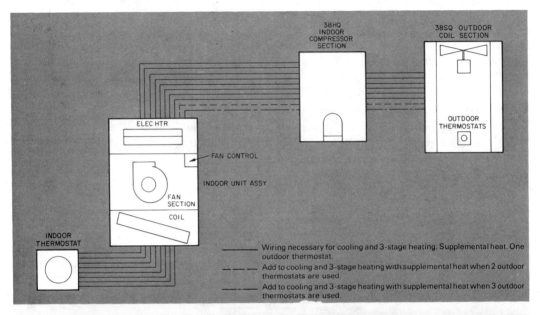

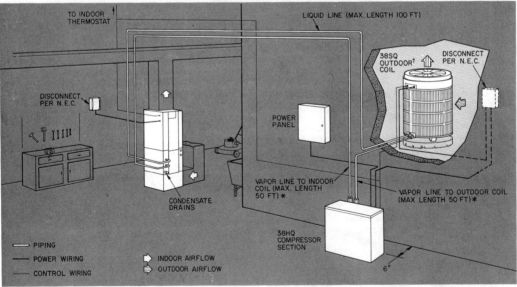

*Standard accessory tubing package may be used. Vapor line must be sectioned at compressor unit.
†Allow 1'-6" minimum distance between unit and building for service.
NOTE: Wiring and piping are general guides only. They are not intended for a specific installation.

Figure 11-6 Location of components of split-system heat pumps, including schematic of piping and wiring. (Courtesy, Carrier Corporation.)

a garage to reduce noise disturbance. The outdoor section consists of a heat-transfer coil and a fan for either dissipating heat for cooling or picking up heat for heating.

A typical single-package system is shown in Figure 11-7. All components are housed in a single enclosure, which is installed outside the building, as shown in Figure 11-9. Where this arrangement can be applied, it reduces field labor.

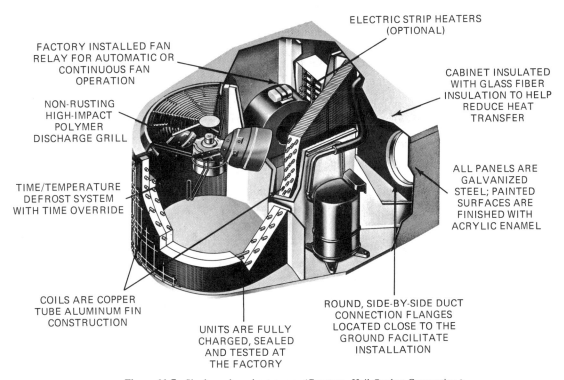

ELECTRIC STRIP HEATERS (OPTIONAL)

FACTORY INSTALLED FAN RELAY FOR AUTOMATIC OR CONTINUOUS FAN OPERATION

NON-RUSTING HIGH-IMPACT POLYMER DISCHARGE GRILL

CABINET INSULATED WITH GLASS FIBER INSULATION TO HELP REDUCE HEAT TRANSFER

TIME/TEMPERATURE DEFROST SYSTEM WITH TIME OVERRIDE

ALL PANELS ARE GALVANIZED STEEL; PAINTED SURFACES ARE FINISHED WITH ACRYLIC ENAMEL

COILS ARE COPPER TUBE ALUMINUM FIN CONSTRUCTION

UNITS ARE FULLY CHARGED, SEALED AND TESTED AT THE FACTORY

ROUND, SIDE-BY-SIDE DUCT CONNECTION FLANGES LOCATED CLOSE TO THE GROUND FACILITATE INSTALLATION

Figure 11-7 Single package heat pump. (Courtesy, Heil-Quaker Corporation.)

Ratings

Figure 11-8 shows typical heat-pump performance data. Ratings are based on Air Conditioning and Refrigeration Institute (ARI) standards. Standards and terms for rating heat pumps are as follows:

1. **Cooling Standard:** 80°F db, 67°F wb temperature of the air entering indoors and 95°F db air entering outdoor unit.

2. **Hi-Temp Heating Standard:** 70°F db temperature of air entering indoors and 47°F db, 43°F wb air entering outdoor unit.

3. **Lo-Temp Heating Standard:** 70°F db temperature of air entering indoors and 17°F db, 15°F wb air entering outdoor unit.

4. **Coefficient of Performance (C.O.P.):** A rating given to heat pumps equivalent to the ratio of output over input. Output is in Btuh and input is converted to Btuh by multiplying watts input by 3.413 Btu per watt. For example, the C.O.P. for a nominal 2-hp unit, operating with 47°F air entering the outdoor coil, is as follows:

$$\text{C.O.P.} = \frac{25{,}200 \text{ Btuh}}{2450 \text{ watts} \times 3.4 \text{ Btu/watt}}$$

$$\text{C.O.P.} = 3.02$$

5. **Heating Season Performance Factor (HSPF):** A ratio of heat output in Btu to watts input.

6. **Seasonal Energy Efficient Ratio (SEER):** Applied to the cooling performance and is also a ratio of Btu output to watts input.

7. **Sound Rating Number (SRN):** A noise-level rating (decibels)

8. **Total Capacity (T.C.):** Thousands of Btuh.

9. **Units Rated with Accessory Liquid Line Solenoid (w/lls)**

10. **Cubic Feet per Minute (ft³/min):** the air volume rating of the indoor fan.

All ratings are based on ARI Standard 240 and Department of Energy (DOE) test procedures at 450 ft³/min indoor air volume per ton (12,000 Btuh) cooling capacity with 25 ft of connecting refrigerant lines.

| | | | | | ARI Standard Ratings (1-Ph) | | | | | | |
| | | | | | Cooling | | Hi-Temp Heat | | Lo-Temp Heat | | |
Nominal Tons	Indoor Compressor Section	Outdoor Section	Indoor Fan Section	CFM	TC	SEER w/lls	TC	C.O.P.	TC	C.O.P.	HSPF
2.0	IC-024	OS-940	IF-024	850	23.8	9.80	25.2	2.90	15.3	2.05	7.65
2.5	IC-030	OS-940	IF-030	1025	27.6	9.55	29.6	2.90	18.0	2.05	7.55
3.0	IC-036	OS-940	IF-036	1175	32.4	9.85	34.0	2.95	20.0	2.00	7.65

Figure 11-8 Typical heat pump performance data.

Indoor-Air-Temperature Rise

Referring to Figure 11-8, note that at top performance the largest unit shown, with 47°F outside air, delivers 34,000 Btu using 1175 ft³/min. To determine the temperature rise (TR) on heating, the following formula is applied:

$$Btu = ft^3/min \times 1.08 \times TR$$

$$TR = \frac{34,000}{1175 \times 1.08} = 27°F$$

Based on a return air temperature of 70°F, the delivered air is 97°F (70°F + 27°F). Thus, a heat pump delivers relatively low-temperature air compared to a conventional furnace. This fact is important to keep in mind when designing the distribution system. Otherwise, discomfort can be the result.

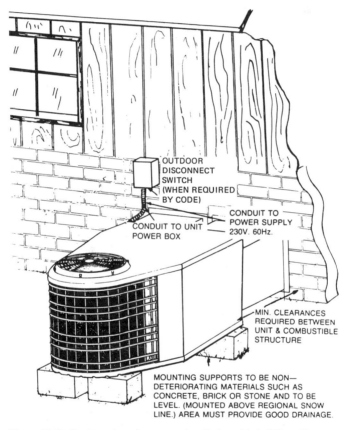

OUTDOOR
DISCONNECT
SWITCH
(WHEN REQUIRED
BY CODE)

CONDUIT TO
POWER SUPPLY
230V. 60Hz.

CONDUIT TO UNIT
POWER BOX

MIN. CLEARANCES
REQUIRED BETWEEN
UNIT & COMBUSTIBLE
STRUCTURE

MOUNTING SUPPORTS TO BE NON—
DETERIORATING MATERIALS SUCH AS
CONCRETE, BRICK OR STONE AND TO BE
LEVEL. (MOUNTED ABOVE REGIONAL SNOW
LINE.) AREA MUST PROVIDE GOOD DRAINAGE.

Figure 11-9 Single package heat pump installed outside building. (Courtesy, Heil-Quaker Corporation.)

Dual Compressor Systems

Certain manufacturers produce units with two compressors. This has the advantage on the heating cycle of providing increased heat at lower outside temperatures when it is

INTEGRATED HEATING CAPACITIES* (At First Stage — one compressor operating)

Indoor Compr Section 38HQ	Outdoor Coil Section* 38SQ	Indoor Fan Coil	Temperature of Air Entering Outdoor Coil (Edb F)													
			27		32		37		42		47		57		67	
			Cap.	kW	Cap.	kW	Cap.	kW	Cap.	kW	Cap.	kW	Cap.	kW	Cap.	kW
227	940	40AQ036	18.5	2.8	21.0	2.9	23.7	3.0	26.7	3.1	30.3	3.2	38.1	3.5	46.5	3.7

INTEGRATED HEATING CAPACITIES* (At Second Stage — both compressors operating)

Indoor Compr Section 38HQ	Outdoor Coil Section* 38SQ	Indoor Fan Coil	Temperature of Air Entering Outdoor Coil (Edb F)													
			-13		-3		7		17		27		32		37	
			Cap.	kW	Cap.	kW	Cap.	kW	Cap.	kW	Cap.	kW	Cap.	kW	Cap.	kW
227	940	40AQ036	15.8	3.4	20.0	3.8	24.3	4.1	28.6	4.5	33.9	4.8	36.3	5.1	38.7	5.3

Cap — Capacity (1000 Btuh), includes fan motor heat and deduction for thermal line losses of 15 ft of piping exposed to outdoor conditions.

kW — Power input includes compressor motor power input, indoor and outdoor fan motor input.

* Integrated Heating Capacities — Values shown reflect a capacity reduction at those outdoor air temperatures at which frost forms on outdoor coil.

NOTE: Heating ratings shown in table are without accessory electric heater and are based on 70 F db air entering indoor coil, 85% rh air entering outdoor coil, and ARI-rated cfm. See Heating Capacity Correction Factors table, in the manufacturer's literature, to calculate heating capacity and power input at other cfm's and indoor coil entering air temperature.

Figure 11-10 Typical heating capacities for dual compressor heat pump. (Courtesy, Carrier Corporation.)

most needed. Figure 11-10 shows the heating performance of a typical dual compressor system with one and two compressors operating.

As shown in Figure 11-10, the heating capacity at 27°F entering-outdoor-air temperature is 18.5 MBh (18,500 Btuh) with one compressor and 33.9 MBh (33,900 Btuh) with two compressors.

Locating the Outdoor Coil Sections

The outdoor coil section must be installed free of obstructions to permit full air flow to and from the heat exchanger, illustrated in Figure 11-11. It should not be closer than 30 in. from a wall or 48 in. from a roof overhang. It should be mounted on a base separate from the structure of the building to isolate any vibration.

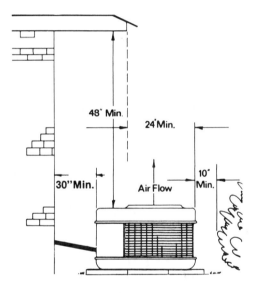

Figure 11-11 Typical outdoor coil section location. (Courtesy, Addison Products Company & Knight Energy Institute.)

Heat-Pump Thermostat

The heat-pump thermostat differs from the normal furnace thermostat in that it has an emergency heat position. This is used to operate the supplementary heat manually when the heat pump requires service.

Hold-Back Thermostat

A hold-back thermostat is provided to restrict the use of supplementary heat. This is usually set at 26°F to prevent the supplementary heat from being used until the outside temperature drops below this point.

The Air-to-Air System

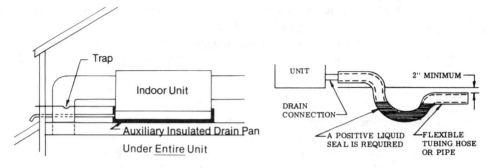

Figure 11-12 Typical condensate drain trap installation. (Courtesy, Addison Products Company & Knight Energy Institute.)

The Condensate Drain

The inside coil section must be provided with a condensate drain. The drain pan must be level or sloping slightly toward the drain connection. The flow is actuated by gravity and must be trapped, as shown in Figure 11-12.

Refrigerant Piping Connections

It is good practice to use precharged tubing for the refrigerant lines with special couplings, as shown in Figure 11-13. If the condensing unit is below the inside coil, the lines should slope towards the outside unit, as shown in Figure 11-14. If the condensing unit is above the inside coil, the suction line should be trapped, as shown in Figure 11-15.

The suction accumulator.　A suction accumulator (Figure 11-16) is often placed in the suction line between the evaporator and the compressor. This device traps liquid refrigerant that may damage the compressor. The liquid gradually evaporates in the accumulator and enters the compressor as a vapor. Any trapped oil is allowed to enter the suction line slowly through a metering orifice located in the lower portion of the U tube.

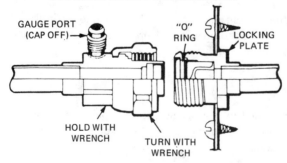

Figure 11-13 Precharged refrigerant line coupling. (Addison Products Company & Knight Energy Institute.)

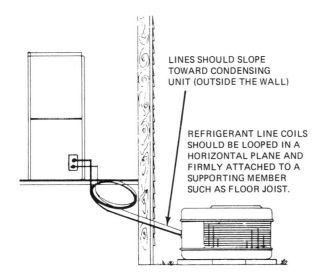

LINES SHOULD SLOPE
TOWARD CONDENSING
UNIT (OUTSIDE THE WALL)

REFRIGERANT LINE COILS
SHOULD BE LOOPED IN A
HORIZONTAL PLANE AND
FIRMLY ATTACHED TO A
SUPPORTING MEMBER
SUCH AS FLOOR JOIST.

Figure 11-14 Refrigerant lines connected to outdoor unit located below indoor unit. (Addison Products Company & Knight Energy Institute.)

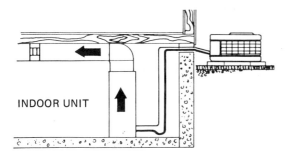

INDOOR UNIT

Figure 11-15 Vertical discharge piping. Note trap in suction line below indoor unit and pipe sloping outdoor unit. (Courtesy, Addison Products & Knight Energy Institute.)

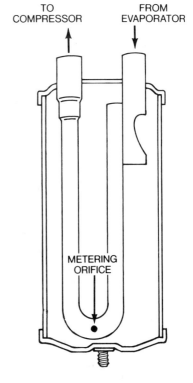

TO COMPRESSOR

FROM EVAPORATOR

METERING ORIFICE

Figure 11-16 Suction line accumulator. (Reprinted with permission of the Dealer Products Group of The Trane Company, a division of American Standard, Inc.)

The Air-to-Air System

Refrigerant metering devices.   As shown in Figure 11-2, the heat pump uses two metering devices, one for the cooling cycle and one for the heating cycle. There are two types of metering devices used by various manufacturers: the capillary tube (see Figure 11-2) and the thermostatic expansion valve, or TEV (see Figure 11-17). The TEV has a sensing bulb on the suction line that controls the flow of refrigerant. Under ideal conditions it provides complete evaporation of the liquid before the refrigerant enters the compressor.

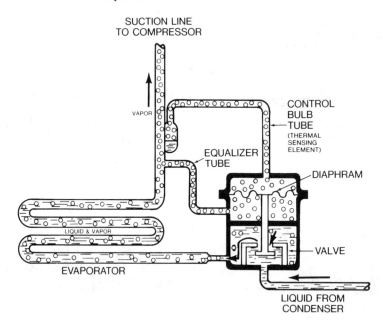

Figure 11-17 Thermostatic expansion valve. (Reprinted with permission of the Dealer Products Group of The Trane Company, a division of American Standard, Inc.)

In the *emergency heating mode*, when the outdoor temperature falls below 26°F, supplementary heat is supplied in stages to meet the requirements of the thermostat. The heat-pump portion of the unit, consisting of the compressor, outdoor fan, and reversing valve, is inoperative. The heat is supplied by electric strip heaters.

In the *defrost mode*, the compressor, the outdoor fan, and the indoor fan are in operation in the same manner as in the cooling mode. This is done to supply heat to the outdoor coil and defrost it. The air pressure drop, the refrigerant temperature, and time are all factors in controlling the defrost cycle on a demand basis.

Wiring Diagrams and Sequence of Operation

The wiring diagrams shown in this section are strictly electrical (not solid-state). Some manufacturers have effectively used solid-state controls. These will be described later. Since the majority of heat pump service problems are electrical, a thorough understanding of the electrical system is essential.

The cooling mode.   The wiring diagram for a typical heat pump, operated in the cooling mode, is shown in Figure 11-18. The thermostat is shown in the lower left, the indoor unit is on the right (top and bottom), and the outdoor unit is at the upper left.

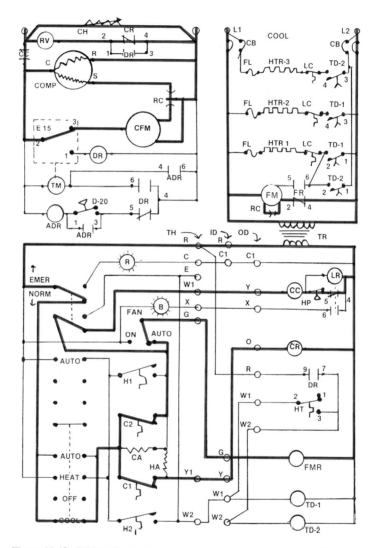

Figure 11-18 Wiring diagram for a typical heat pump, cooling mode. (Courtesy, Addison Products Company & Knight Energy Institute.)

KEY TO SYMBOLS

ADR	Auxiliary Defrost Relay	E15	Defrost Control
FM	Fan Motor	FL	Fuse Link
FMR	Fan Motor Relay	HA	Heating Anticipator
FR	Fan Relay (Contacts)	HP	High Pressure Control
B	Blue "Check" Light	HTR	Heater, Auxiliary Electric
CA	Cooling Anticipator	HT	Holdback Thermostat
CB	Circuit Breaker	H1	1st Stage Heating
CC	Compressor Contactor	H2	2nd Stage Heating
CFM	Condenser Fan Motor	LC	Limit Control
CH	Crankcase Heat	LR	Lockout Relay
CR	Cooling Relay	R	Red "Emerg" Heat Light
C1	1st Stage Cooling	RC	Run Capacitor
C2	2nd Stage Cooling	RV	Reversing Valve
DR	Defrost Relay	TD	Time Delay Relay
D-20	Pressure Switch—Defrost	TM	Time Motor (Part of E15)
		TR	Control Transformer

Figure 11-19 Key to symbols used in wiring diagrams. (Courtesy, Addison Products Company & Knight Energy Institute.)

The key to the symbols is shown in Figure 11-19. In Figure 11-18 the energized circuits for cooling are highlighted.

When the system switch on the thermostat is set to cooling, the fan switch is set on auto, and the room temperature is above the thermostat setting, three low-voltage circuits are made:

1. The circuit to the cooling relay (CR)

2. The circuit to the fan motor relay (FMR)

3. The circuit to the compressor contactor (CC)

The CR relay energizes the reversing valve in the outdoor unit. The FMR relay starts the indoor fan at high speed. The CC contactor starts the compressor and outdoor fan. The cooling cycle is in operation.

The heating mode. When the system switch on the thermostat is set to heating, the fan switch is set on the auto position, and the room temperature is below the thermostat setting, two low-voltage circuits are made (see Figure 11-20):

1. The circuit to the fan motor relay (FMR)

2. The circuit to the compressor contactor (CC)

The system operates just as it did on cooling, *except the reversing valve is de-energized*.

With the heat pump operating and if the room temperature continues to drop 1° or 2° below the thermostat setting, the second-stage heating (the supplementary heat) is

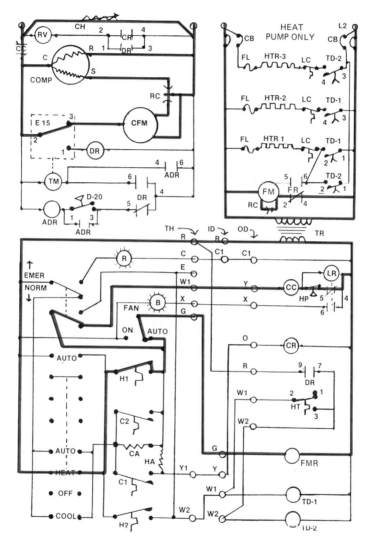

Figure 11-20 Wiring diagram for typical heat pump, first-stage heating (heat pump only). (Courtesy, Addison Products Company & Knight Energy Institute.)

The Air-to-Air System

activated. When the secondary heat contacts (*H2*) are made in the room thermostat, the following sequence takes place (see Figure 11-21):

1. The first time-delay relay (TD-1) is energized, closing the circuit in the indoor unit to two or more electric strip heaters.

2. If the outdoor temperature measured on the hold-back thermostat (HT) is below 26°F, a circuit is made to the second time-delay relay (TD-2). This closes the circuit to the remaining electric strip heaters. The unit now is in maximum heat position.

In the emergency heating mode, the heat pump is inoperative and the system is manually switched to emergency heat, as shown in Figure 11-22. Three low-voltage circuits are energized:

1. The fan motor relay (FMR)

2. The first time-delay relay (TD-1)

3. The *red* light, indicating emergency heat is on

The inside fan is operated by the FMR relay. The heater elements are energized through the TD-1 relay and the TD-2 relay if the outside temperature is below 26°F.

The defrost mode. In the defrost mode the system is primarily in the cooling cycle (see Figure 11-23). The only difference is that the indoor fan is operating, and part of the resistance heat is turned on to offset the cooling effect. The *demand defrost control system* is used to assure defrosting only when necessary. The defrost initiation is a function of

1. The air pressure drop across the outdoor coil

2. The refrigerant coil temperature

3. The defrost time (not to exceed 10 min)

There are four controls used to initiate and terminate the defrost cycle:

1. The pressure switch (D-20)

2. The auxiliary defrost relay (ADR)

3. The defrost relay (DR)

4. The defrost control (E-15), as shown in wiring diagram (Figure 11-23).

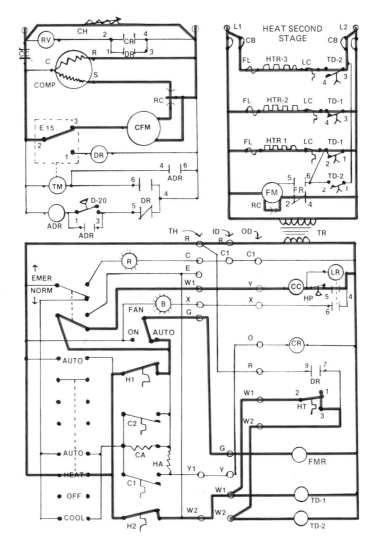

Figure 11-21 Wiring diagram for typical heat pump, second-stage heating. (Courtesy, Addison Products Company & Knight Energy Institute.)

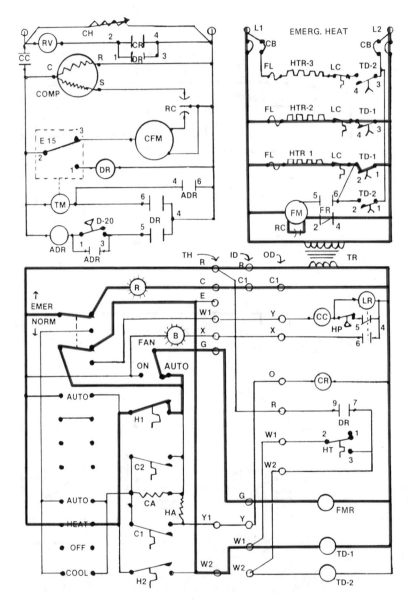

Figure 11-22 Wiring diagram for typical heat pump, emergency heat. (Courtesy, Addison Products Company & Knight Energy Institute.)

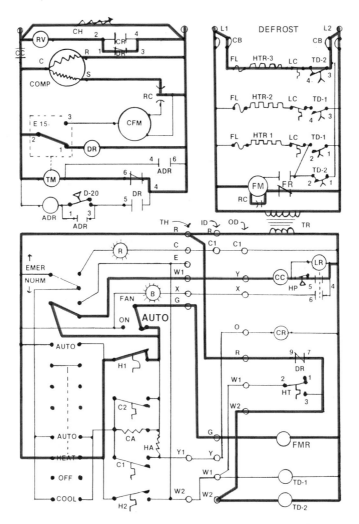

Figure 11-23 Wiring diagram for typical heat pump, defrost mode. (Courtesy, Addison Products Company & Knight Energy Institute.)

The *D-20 demand-defrost pressure switch*, shown in Figure 11-24, senses the air pressure difference across the indoor coil. If the pressure difference is between 0.4 in. and 0.7 in. (W.C.)*, the switch is closed.

The *ADR*, shown in Figure 11-25, is a magnet relay with a 208/240 V holding coil and two normally open (NO) switches. When the coil is energized, a circuit is completed between terminals 1 and 3 and another circuit between 4 and 6.

The *defrost relay*, shown in Figure 11-26, has three normally closed (NC) switches and three (NO) switches.

* As read on a water manometer.

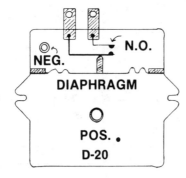

Figure 11-24 Demand-defrost pressure switch for heat pump defrost system. (Courtesy, Addison Products Company & Knight Energy Institute.)

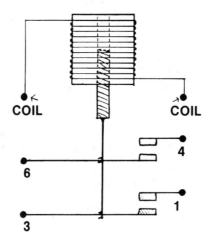

Figure 11-25 Auxiliary defrost relay for heat pump defrost system. (Courtesy, Addison Products Company & Knight Energy Institute.)

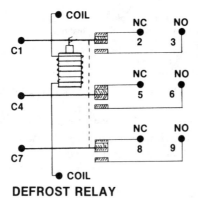

Figure 11-26 Defrost relay for heat pump defrost system. (Courtesy, Addison Products Company & Knight Energy Institute.)

The *E-15 defrost control*, shown in Figure 11-27, is a single-pole double-throw switch (SPDT). The switch is activated by two forces, one from the movement of pressure cam A and the other by the pressure arm C created by the temperature sensor. During the normal cycle, the switch is held closed by these two forces. In order for the switch to open, both of these forces must be removed from pressure arm B. The cam is moved by a timing motor and reaches a low point every 15 min. The force exerted by pressure arm C is removed when the coil temperature reaches 26°F as sensed by the temperature sensing bulb.

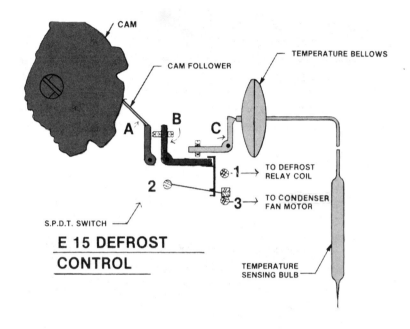

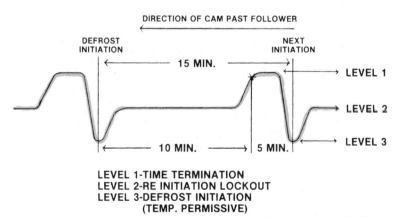

LEVEL 1-TIME TERMINATION
LEVEL 2-RE INITIATION LOCKOUT
LEVEL 3-DEFROST INITIATION
(TEMP. PERMISSIVE)

Figure 11-27 Diagram shows the operating cam configuration and sequence for the E-15 defrost control. (Courtesy, Addison Products Company & Knight Energy Institute.)

The Air-to-Air System

The first indication of the need for defrost is by the D-20 pressure switch closing, caused by a buildup of frost on the outdoor coil. This energizes the ADR, closing two switches (see Figure 11-28):

1. Energizing the timer motor (TM)

2. Forming a holding circuit to keep the ADR energized in case the D-20 opens prematurely

Assuming the pressure drop is caused by frost, the timer cam advances to the low point, and the coil temperature reaches 26°F, the defrost timer (E-15) switch opens, turning off the outdoor condenser fan motor (CFM) and energizing the defrost relay (DR). This causes the following action, as shown in Figure 11-29.

1. The reversing valve (RV) is energized

2. The ADR is de-energized

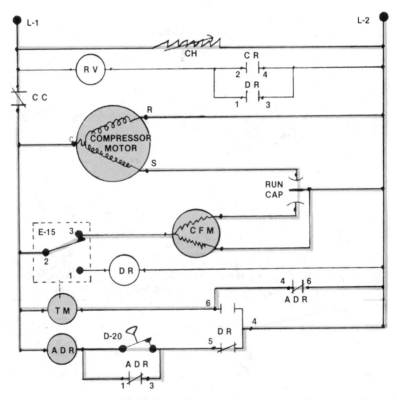

Figure 11-28 Diagram shows the defrost control sequence when the pressure drops across the outdoor coil. (Courtesy, Addison Products Company & Knight Energy Institute.)

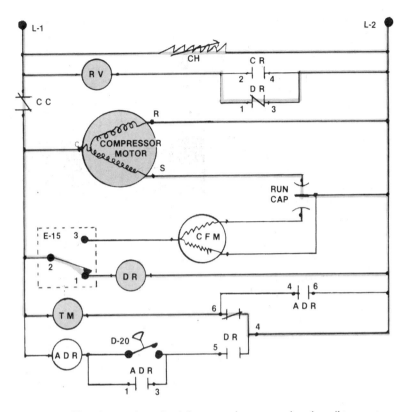

Figure 11-29 Diagram shows the defrost control sequence when the coil temperature drops to 26°F or lower. (Courtesy, Addison Products Company & Knight Energy Institute.)

3. A circuit is formed to continue energizing the TM

4. The second-stage heater (HTR-3) is turned on through the time-delay relay (TD-2), as shown in Figure 11-23.

When the outdoor coil temperature reaches 55°F or the timer cam advances to the high point (a maximum of 10 min defrost), the defrost cycle is terminated and the E-15 switch returns the system to normal operation.

Refrigeration System Servicing

A useful method of diagnosing refrigeration service problems is to refer to Figure 11-30. This chart lists the more frequent problems and suggested solutions. The same methods used for evacuating, leak testing, and refrigerant charging air-conditioning systems are also used to service heat pumps. Remember that a heat pump must have proper air flow and proper refrigerant charge.

* As read on a water manometer.

The Air-to-Air System

Problem		Suction Pressure	Head Pressure	Superheat	Compressor Amperage	Temp. Diff. Over Indoor Coil	Possible Solutions
Low Refrigerant Charge		LOW	LOW	HIGH	LOW	LOW	Possible icing of evaporator. Repair leak, evacuate and Charge by Weight.
RESTRICTION		LOW	LOW	HIGH	LOW	LOW	Most Restrictions occur in strainer. Possible icing of evaporator.
Low Air Flow Over Indoor Coil	Heating	HIGH	HIGH	LOW	HIGH	HIGH	Cause: Dirty Filter; Dirty Blower Wheel; Duct to small. Supply outlets closed.
	Cooling	LOW	LOW	LOW	LOW	HIGH	
Low Air Flow Over Outdoor Coil	Heating	LOW	LOW	LOW	LOW	LOW	Cause: Dirty Coil - Bad Fan Motor - Fan Blade - Ice on coil - air blocked by building, etc.
	Cooling	HIGH	HIGH	LOW	HIGH	LOW	
Leaking Check Valve Heating or Cooling Mode		HIGH	HIGH	LOW	HIGH	LOW	Switch System to opposite Mode. If conditions correct themselves this proves check valve was leaking.
Compressor running but not pumping		HIGH	LOW	HIGH OR NONE	LOW	LOW	If not pumping at all suction and head pressure will be equal and no refrigeration.
Reversing Valve Leaking or Stuck Mid Position		HIGH	LOW	HIGH OR NONE	LOW	LOW	All four lines of reversing valve will be hot.
Unit Not Defrosting		LOW	LOW	LOW	LOW	LOW	Outdoor Coil will be iced over. Check Refrigerant Charge, defrost controls.

Figure 11-30 Heat pump service problems and possible solutions. (Courtesy, Addison Products Company & Knight Energy Institute.)

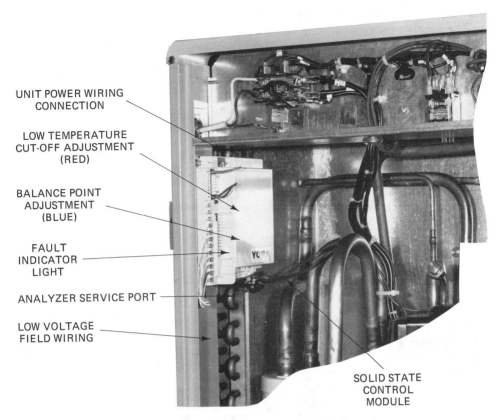

UNIT POWER WIRING
CONNECTION

LOW TEMPERATURE
CUT-OFF ADJUSTMENT
(RED)

BALANCE POINT
ADJUSTMENT
(BLUE)

FAULT
INDICATOR
LIGHT

ANALYZER SERVICE PORT

LOW VOLTAGE
FIELD WIRING

SOLID STATE
CONTROL
MODULE

Figure 11-31 Location of the solid-state control module in the outdoor compressor unit or a heat pump system. (Courtesy, York Corporation.)

Solid-state control. A solid-state control module is used by certain manufacturers to replace some of the standard electrical or mechanical controls. A typical control system of this type is shown in Figure 11-31. This logic module responds to the demand signal of the thermostat, examines the input from four sensors ("outdoor," "discharge," "defrost," and "liquid"), and determines when the heat pump or the supplementary heaters shall operate.

Balance point adjustment. The location of the balance-point adjustment is shown in Figure 11-31. The balance point is the lowest ambient temperature at which the heat pump can operate without the use of supplementary heat. The balance point is set by the local contractor based on

1. Outdoor design temperature

2. Building heat loss

3. Unit capacity

The Air-to-Air System

Low ambient cutoff adjustment. Figure 11-31 shows the location of the low ambient cutoff adjustment. This is the minimum outside temperature at which it is no longer economical to operate the heat pump. Below this temperature all heating is performed by the secondary heat source. This setting is supplied by the manufacturer at $-10°F$, but it can be adjusted upward by the contractor.

The service analyzer. The service analyzer, shown in Figure 11-32, is used by the serviceperson to determine any malfunction in the operation of the heat pump. The analyzer indicates the service problem by a fault code:

Fault Code	Failure Mode
2	Discharge pressure reaches approximately 400 psig
3	Discharge temperature reaches approximately 275°F
4	Discharge temperature did not reach approximately 90°F within 1 hr of compressor operation
5	Defrost failure
7	Outdoor temperature sensor failure
8	Liquid line temperature sensor failure
9	Bonnet sensor shorted

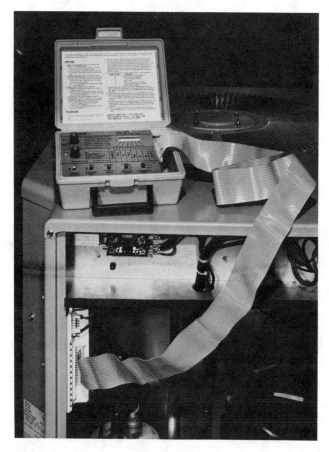

Figure 11-32 Service analyzer attached to solid-state control module in outdoor compressor unit. (Courtesy, York Corporation.)

WATER-TO-AIR SYSTEMS

Water-to-air heat pump systems use a water-to-refrigerant heat exchanger on the water side and an air-to-refrigerant heat exchanger on the air side. The water-to-refrigerant coil is usually on the coaxial type (tube-in-tube), located inside the building. There are two types of piping arrangements: the open-loop system and the closed-loop system.

On the open-loop system, water is continuously supplied at the rate of 1 to 5 gal/min per ton from a deep well, lake, or river. A common source consists of drawing well water through the heat pump and then discharging it into a lake, river, or disposal well, as shown in Figure 11-33. This is an excellent system for areas where plentiful, high-quality ground water can be obtained inexpensively. The coefficient of performance is usually 3.00 or better and is not affected by outdoor air temperature.

On the closed-loop system, water is circulated through a coil buried in the earth. Coils are placed in trenches 4 to 6 ft deep (Figure 11-34). Since the earth's temperature

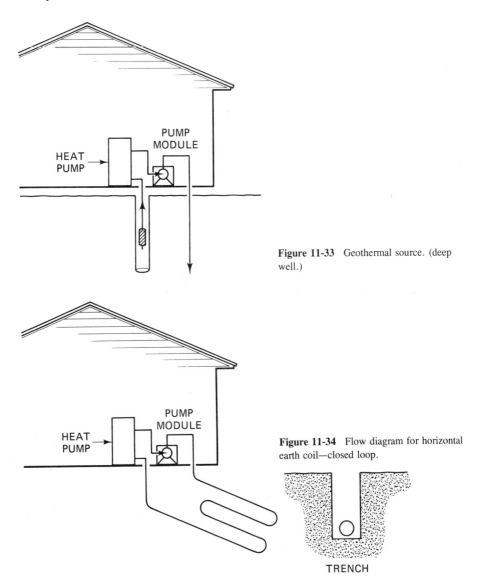

Figure 11-33 Geothermal source. (deep well.)

Figure 11-34 Flow diagram for horizontal earth coil—closed loop.

TRENCH

will decrease as heat is removed, the coefficient of performance is reduced during operation. Thus, the closed-loop system is not as efficient as the open-loop system and requires longer piping. If temperature below freezing may be encountered, an antifreeze solution must be used.

A flow diagram for the cooling cycle is shown in Figure 11-35; for the heating cycle, in Figure 11-36. Water valves are used to furnish more precise water flow for both heating and cooling. On cooling, the valve controls compressor-discharge pressure. On heating, the valve controls compressor-suction pressure. Note that the thermal expansion valve used is capable of controlling refrigerant flow in both directions.

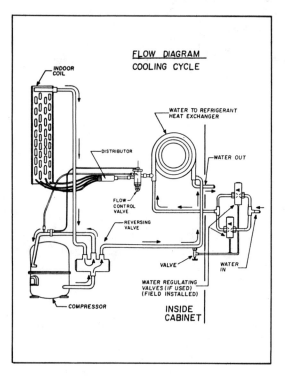

Figure 11-35 Flow diagram for well water system: cooling cycle. (Courtesy, WeatherKing, Inc.)

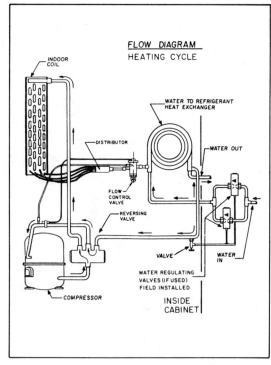

Figure 11-36 Flow diagram for well water system: heating cycle. (Courtesy, Weather-King, Inc.)

Performance Data

Figure 11-37 shows typical performance data for both heating and cooling on the closed-loop system. The capacity of the unit is dependent both on the entering water temperature (EWT) and the water flow in gallons per minute. Ratings for heat absorbed by the condenser (QA) and heat rejected by the condenser (QR) are given in MBh. Note the standard conditions on which these ratings are based. Figure 11-38 shows typical performance data on both heating and cooling for the open-loop system.

COOL

EWT	GPM	LWT	QR	PS	PD
45	2	75	29.8	69-75	151-166
	3	65	30.5	67-73	137-151
	4	60	30.8	67-73	130-144
55	2	84	29.0	70-76	168-185
	3	75	29.6	70-76	156-171
	4	70	29.9	69-75	148-163
65	3	84	28.7	71-77	176-193
	4	79	29.0	70-76	168-185
	5	77	29.1	70-76	166-182
75	3	94	27.9	73-79	199-217
	5	86	28.3	71-77	187-205
	7	83	28.4	71-77	184-202
85	4	99	27.2	74-81	217-236
	6	94	27.5	74-81	211-229
	8	92	27.5	73-79	208-226

At standard rated air flow and 80 / 67 air entering cooling coil.

Depending upon return air conditions air flow temperature drops should be from 14° to 20°.

HEAT

EWT	GPM	LWT	QA	PS	PD
45	6	40	14.5	52-57	208-226
	8	41	15.0	53-59	211-229
	10	42	15.1	55-60	214-233
55	4	47	16.5	60-65	220-239
	6	49	17.3	64-70	226-245
	8	51	17.7	65-72	230-250
65	4	56	18.8	71-77	236-256
	6	58	19.9	74-81	243-263
	8	60	20.3	78-84	246-267
75	3	61	20.5	81-87	250-272
	4	64	21.6	84-91	256-278
	5	66	22.2	87-93	260-282

NOTE 1 - At standard rated air flow and 70°F return air
NOTE 2 - Indoor air temperature difference in heating °F = 25 to 40°F depending on water temperature, GPM and air flow.

Figure 11-37 Performance data, water-source heat pump, closed-loop. (Courtesy, WeatherKing, Inc.)

E.W.T.	GPM	BTUH TOTAL	BTUH SENS.	WATTS	EER W/OUT PUMP	EER WITH PUMP	HEAT REJ.
45	2.0	24800	16700	1730	14.3	13.4	29800
	3.0	25700	17100	1660	15.5	14.0	30500
	4.0	26100	17300	1630	16.0	14.0	30800
50	2.0	24200	16500	1770	13.7	12.8	29300
	3.0	25100	16900	1710	14.7	13.3	30000
	4.0	25500	17000	1670	15.3	13.4	30300
55	2.0	23700	16300	1820	13.0	12.2	29000
	3.0	24500	16600	1750	14.0	12.7	29600
	4.0	24900	16800	1720	14.5	12.7	29900
00	3.0	23900	16400	1800	13.3	12.1	29100
	4.0	24300	10500	1770	13.7	12.1	29400
	5.0	24500	16600	1750	14.0	12.0	29600
65	3.0	23300	16100	1850	12.6	11.5	28700
	4.0	23700	16300	1820	13.0	11.5	29000
	5.0	23900	16400	1790	13.4	11.4	29100
70	•3.0	22700	15900	1900	11.9	10.9	28300
	5.0	23300	16100	1840	12.7	10.9	28700
	7.0	23600	16300	1820	13.0	10.5	28900
75	3.0	22100	15600	1950	11.3	10.4	27900
	5.0	22700	15900	1900	11.9	10.3	28300
	7.0	22900	16000	1880	12.2	10.0	28400

EWT	GPM	BTUH TOTAL	WATTS	COP W/OUT PUMP	HEAT OF ABSORP.
25	6	13500	1480	2.7	9300
	8	13800	1490	2.7	9600
	10	14000	1500	2.7	9800
30	•6	15000	1550	2.8	10500
	8	15300	1570	2.9	10800
	10	15500	1580	2.9	11000
35	6	16400	1620	3.0	11800
	8	16800	1640	3.0	12100
	10	17100	1660	3.0	12300
40	6	18000	1700	3.1	13100
	8	18400	1720	3.1	13500
	10	18700	1740	3.2	13700

Figure 11-38 Performance data, water-source heat pump, open-loop. (Courtesy, WeatherKing, Inc.)

Water-to-Air Systems

Water Piping

Figure 11-39 shows a typical ground-loop piping system. Gate valves and unions should be used on each side of components requiring removal for service. The expansion tank must be large enough to handle the change in volume of the liquid due to temperature variations. A relief valve is required by local codes. A purge valve located at the highest point of the system is convenient for removing air during charging. The circulating pump must be adequate to supply the required gallons per minute against the total pressure drop of the system.

Figure 11-40 shows a typical open-loop piping arrangement. The water regulating valves (I) (J) are included for groundwater temperatures below 70°F. Valves (A) and (B) are isolation valves. Valve (B) is a globe or ball valve, which can be used for balancing. Valves (C) and (D) are used for maintenance for flushing the system when required.

Figure 11-41 shows a schematic diagram of a typical heat-recovery arrangement to provide domestic hot water. A typical hot water exchanger with pump is shown in Figure 11-42.

Knowing the water quality is important in determining the treatment required. Corrosion, scale formations, biological growths, and suspended solids can present real

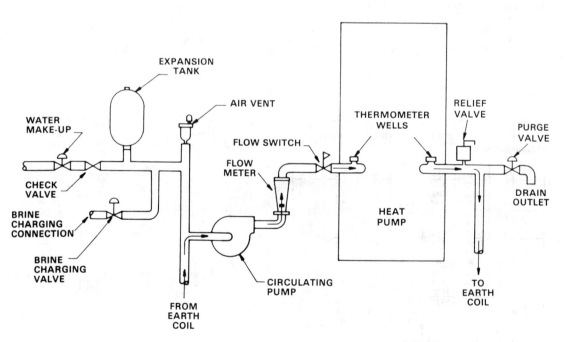

Figure 11-39 Typical ground-loop heat pump piping system.

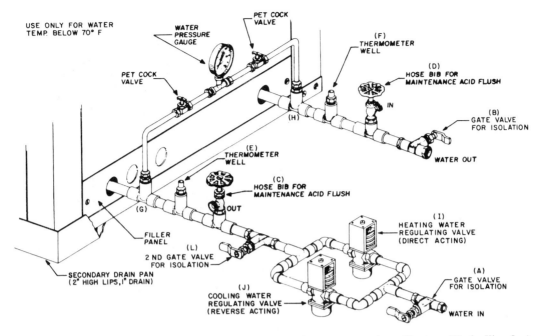

Figure 11-40 Typical piping connections to water-source heat pump, open-loop. (Courtesy, WeatherKing, Inc.)

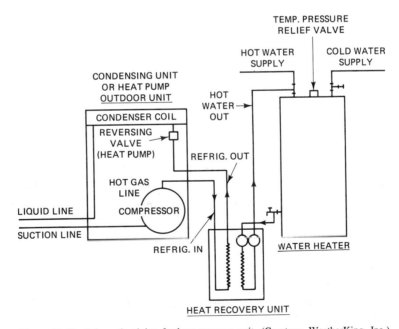

Figure 11-41 Schematic piping for heat recovery unit. (Courtesy, WeatherKing, Inc.)

Water-to-Air Systems

1. HEAT EXCHANGER
2. WATER PUMP
3. DISCHARGE (HOT GAS) THERMOSTAT
4. WATER LINE THERMOSTAT
5. SECONDARY SAFETY THERMOSTAT
6. INTERNAL FUSE
7. DISCONNECT SWITCH
8. CAN MOUNT VERTICAL OR HORIZONTAL
9. FREEZE PROTECTION THERMOSTAT
10. AIR BLEED PORT
11. REFRIGERANT PORT

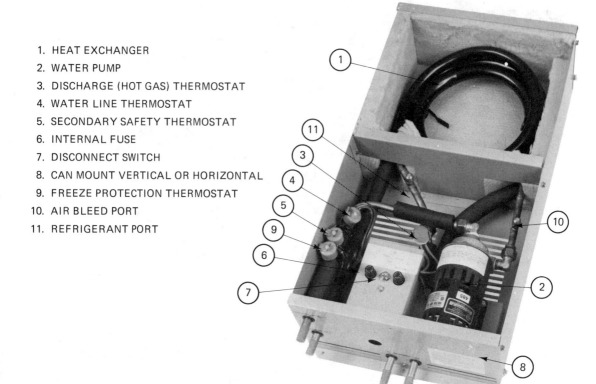

Figure 11-42 Domestic hot water heat exchanger. (Courtesy, Bard Manufacturing Co.)

problems. For single-water-source units, manufacturers usually supply a cupronickel condenser, since some types of corrosion attack all copper tubes.

For a single-source system on small installations, it is advisable to use an inexpensive filter that can be periodically cleaned. For a multiple-unit system on a larger building with a closed-loop recirculating water system, an automatic chemical treatment arrangement should be considered. Each system must be considered individually on its own merits.

Wiring Diagram

A typical wiring diagram is shown in Figure 11-43. The lockout relay is used as a safety control trip to prevent the compressor from short cycling. The defrost relay controls the reversing valve.

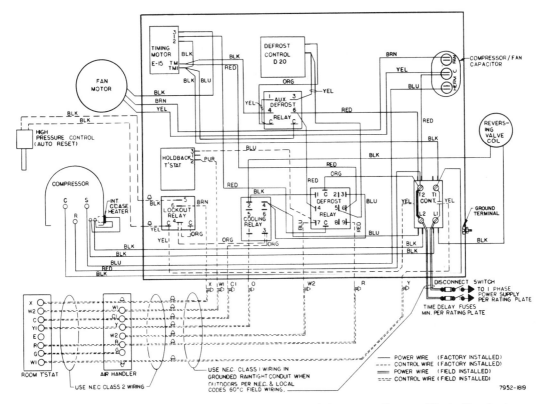

Figure 11-43 Typical wiring diagram for a water-to-air heat pump. (Courtesy, WeatherKing, Inc.)

CHAPTER 11 STUDY QUESTIONS

The answers to the study questions are found in the sections of this chapter under the chapter topic indicated.

STUDY QUESTIONS	*CHAPTER TOPICS*
1. How many Btu's are converted into heat per watt of input by a heat pump?	*Characteristics*
2. Describe the two types of heat pumps used for residential applications.	*Types of heat pumps*
3. Describe how the refrigeration cycle operates during the heat pump mode.	*The refrigeration cycle*
4. Why is the defrost cycle necessary?	*The defrost cycle*
5. When is supplementary heat used?	*Supplementary heat*

6. For the air-to-air system, what is the difference between a single package and a split system?

The air-to-air system

7. What are the conditions for a high-temperature and low-temperature rating?

Ratings

8. How is the air temperature rise determined for a heat pump?

Indoor air temperature rise

9. For a typical 5-hp air-to-air heat pump with outside temperature of 47°F, what would be the output?

Supplementary heat

10. At what refrigerant temperature is the defrost cycle usually terminating?

The defrost cycle

11. How many Btu's are converted into heat by 1 W of resistance heat?

Characteristics

12. Which type of heat pump is most commonly used for residential application?

The air-to-air system

13. What does C.O.P. mean?

Ratings

14. What is the advantage of a dual compressor unit?

Dual compressor systems

15. Where should the outdoor coil section be located?

Locating outdoor coil sections

16. How does a heat pump thermostat differ from a standard heating thermostat?

Heat pump thermostat

17. How is precharged tubing used for heat pump applications?

Refrigerant piping connections

18. Describe the control sequence for the heating mode.

The heating mode

19. Describe the control sequence for the defrost mode.

The defrost mode

20. What is meant by balance point adjustment?

Balance point adjustment

21. How is a service analyzer used?

The service analyzer

22. Describe the operation of a water-to-air heat pump.

Water-to-air systems

23. What is the difference between an open-loop and a closed-loop system?

Water-to-air systems

24. How can heat recovery be used for domestic hot water?

Water piping

12 Basic Electricity and Electrical Symbols

OBJECTIVES

After studying this chapter, the student will be able to:

- Identify the basic electrical symbols used in wiring diagrams for electrical load devices

- Determine the types of circuits used to connect electrical loads

ELECTRICAL TERMS

A knowledge of certain electrical terms is necessary in working with electrical power. Most power used for warm air heating systems is alternating current. Some of the common terms used in describing alternating current are:

Volts: A measure of electromotive force (EMF) or pressure being supplied to cause the electrical current to flow

Amperes: A measure of the flow of current (electrons) through a conductor

Ohms (Ω):   A measure of the resistance to current flow through a conductor

Watts: A measure of power consumed by an electrical load

Power Factor: The resulting fraction obtained by dividing watts by the product of volts times amperes

Ohm's Law

Ohm's law is used to predict the behavior of electrical current in an electrical circuit. Simply stated,

$$E = IR$$

where: E = electromotive force EMF, volts

I = intensity of current, amperes

R = resistance, ohms

Ohm's law can be stated in three ways (Figure 12-1). An example of the use of Ohm's law is shown in Figure 12-2. Given E = 120 V and R = 10 Ω. $I = E/R$, the current flow in the circuit, is 12 A:

$$I = \frac{120 \text{ V}}{10 \text{ } \Omega} = 12 \text{ A}$$

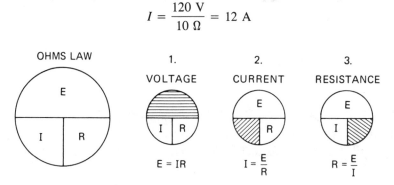

Figure 12-1 Ohm's law.

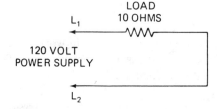

Figure 12-2 Simple electrical circuit.

A voltmeter can be used to measure the voltage between L_1 and L_2. An ohmmeter can be used to measure the resistance of the load, but should be used *only when the power is turned off.* An ammeter can be used to measure amperes.

Series Circuits

A series circuit is one in which each resistance is wired end-to-end like a string of box cars on a train. In a series circuit the amperage stays the same throughout the circuit.

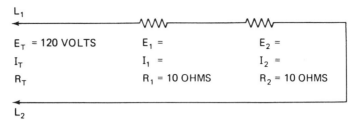

Figure 12-3 Series circuit.

The voltage is divided between the various loads. The total resistance of the circuit is the sum of the various resistances in the circuit. Thus, using Figure 12-3,

$$E_T = E_1 + E_2$$

$$I_T = I_1 = I_2$$

$$R_T = R_1 + R_2$$

Given $E_T = 120$, $R_1 = 10$, $R_2 = 10$, then

1. $R_T = R_1 + R_2 = 10 + 10 = 20\ \Omega$

2. $I_T = \dfrac{E_T}{R_T}$ (Ohm's law) $= \dfrac{120}{20} = 6\ A$

3. $I_T = I_1 = I_2 = 6\ A$

4. $E_1 = I_1 \times R_1 = 10 \times 6 = 60\ V$

5. $E_2 = I_2 \times R_2 = 10 \times 6 = 60\ V$

Parallel Circuits

In a parallel circuit each load provides a separate path for electricity, and each path may have different current flowing through it. The amount is determined by the resistance of the load. The voltages for each load are the same. The total current is the sum of the individual load currents. The reciprocal of the total resistance is equal to the sum of the reciprocals of the individual resistances. Thus, using Figure 12-4

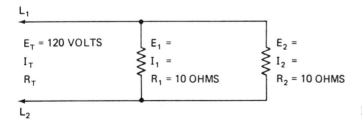

Figure 12-4 Parallel circuit.

Electrical Terms

$$E_T = E_1 = E_2$$

$$I_T = I_1 + I_2$$

$$\frac{1}{R_T} = \frac{1}{R_1} + \frac{1}{R_2}$$

or, for two resistances,

$$R_T = \frac{R_1 \times R_2}{R_1 + R_2}$$

Given $E_T = 120$, $R_1 = 10$, $R_2 = 10$, then

1. $E_T = E_1 = E_2 = 120$ V

2. $I_1 = \dfrac{E_1}{R_1}$ (Ohm's law) $= \dfrac{120}{10} = 12$ A

3. $I_2 = \dfrac{E_2}{R_2} = \dfrac{120}{10} = 12$ A

4. $I_T = I_1 + I_2 = 12 + 12 = 24$ A

5. $R_T = \dfrac{E_T}{I_T} = \dfrac{120}{24} = 5\Omega$

   or

   $$R_T = \frac{R_1 \times R_2}{R_1 + R_2} = \frac{10 \times 10}{10 + 10} = \frac{100}{20} = 5 \ \Omega$$

Electrical potential.   *Electrical potential* is the force that produces the flow of electricity. It is similar to the action of a pump in a water system which causes the flow of water. The battery in a flashlight is a source of electrical potential. The unit of electrical potential is a *volt*. Volts are measured with a voltmeter.

Resistance.   *Resistance* is the pressure exerted by the conductor in restricting the flow of current. In a water system, the flow would be limited by the size of the pipe. In an electrical system, the flow of current is limited by the size of the conducting wire or by the electrical devices in the circuit. Resistance in an electrical circuit can be a means of converting electrical energy to other forms of energy, such as heat, light, or mechanical work. The unit of resistance is the *ohm*. Ohms are measured with an ohmmeter.

Power.   *Power* is the use of energy to do work. An electrical power company charges its customers for the amount of energy used. The unit of power is the *watt*. Watts are measured with a wattmeter.

Electromagnetic action.   *Magnetic action* is the force exerted by a magnet (Figure

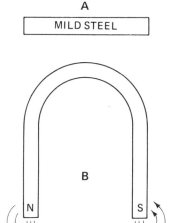

Figure 12-5 Magnetic action.

12-5). A magnet has two poles: north and south. Like poles repel while unlike poles attract. The force of a magnet is dependent on its strength and the distance between the magnet and the metal it is affecting.

Current. *Current* is a term used in electricity to describe the rate of electrical flow. Electricity is believed to be the movement of *electrons*, small electrically charged particles, through a *conductor*. A conductor is a type of metal through which electricity will flow under certain conditions. These conditions will be described later in the unit. Current flow is measured in amperes with an electrical instrument called an ammeter.

There are two types of electric current: *direct current* and *alternating current*. In *direct current* (dc), the electrons move through the conductor in only one direction. This is the type of current produced by a battery. In *alternating current* (ac), the electrons move first in one direction and then in the other, alternating their movement usually 60 times per second [called 60 cycles or 60 hertz (Hz)]. Alternating current is the type available for residential use and is supplied by an electric power company.

Electromagnetic action is the force exerted by the magnetic field of a magnet (Figure 12-6). Current flowing through a conductor creates a magnetic field around the conductor. This action is extremely useful in construction of electrical devices.

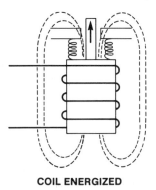

COIL ENERGIZED

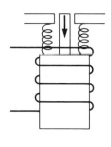

COIL DE-ENERGIZED

Figure 12-6 Electromagnetic action.
(Courtesy, I-T-E Electrical Products.)

Electrical Terms

If an insulated conductor is coiled and alternating current is passed through it, two important effects are produced:

1. A magnetic effect with directional force is produced in the field inside the coil. This force can move a separate metal plunger. The resultant action is called the *solenoid effect*. A solenoid is shown in Figure 12-7.

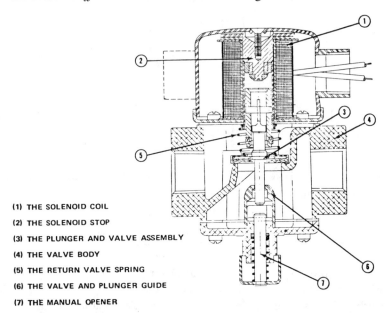

(1) THE SOLENOID COIL

(2) THE SOLENOID STOP

(3) THE PLUNGER AND VALVE ASSEMBLY

(4) THE VALVE BODY

(5) THE RETURN VALVE SPRING

(6) THE VALVE AND PLUNGER GUIDE

(7) THE MANUAL OPENER

Figure 12-7 Solenoid valve. (Courtesy, Robertshaw Controls Company.)

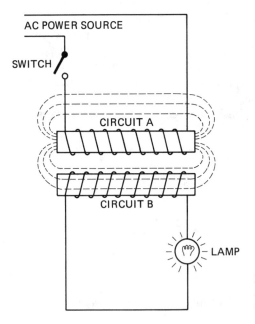

Figure 12-8 A flow of current in circuit A induces a flow of current in B by electromagnetic induction.

2. A magnetic field effect can transfer current to a nearby circuit, causing current to flow. This is called *electromagnetic induction* (Figure 12-8).

The solenoid effect is used to operate switches and valves. The electromagnetic induction effect is used to operate motors and transformers.

Capacitance. *Capacitance* is the charging and discharging ability of an electrical device, called a *capacitor*, to store electricity. Capacitors are made up of a series of conductor surfaces separated by insulation (Figure 12-9). The unit of capacitance is the *farad* (F). Most capacitors for furnace motors are used to increase the starting power of the motor. These capacitors are rated in microfarads (μF).

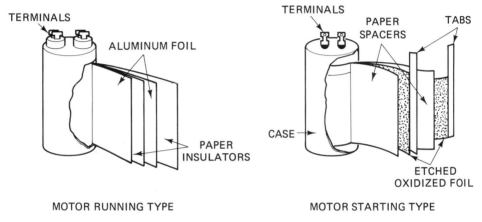

MOTOR RUNNING TYPE   MOTOR STARTING TYPE

Figure 12-9 Capacitors. (Courtesy, Sprague Electric Co.)

CIRCUITS

Electrical devices are used in a *circuit* to perform various functions. A circuit is an electrical system that provides a

- Source of power
- Path for power to follow
- Place for power to be used (load)

An electrical circuit is shown in Figure 12-10.

The source of power can be a battery that stores direct current or a connection to a power company's generator that supplies alternating current. The path is a continuous electrical conductor (such as copper wire) that connects the power supply to the load and from the load back to the power supply. The load is a type of electrical resistance that converts power to other forms of energy such as heat, light, or mechanical work.

A switch can be inserted into the circuit to connect (make) or disconnect (break) the

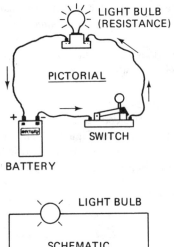

LIGHT BULB (RESISTANCE)

PICTORIAL

BATTERY

SWITCH

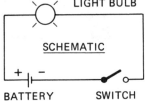

LIGHT BULB

SCHEMATIC

BATTERY   SWITCH

Figure 12-10 An electrical circuit.

flow of current as desired, to control the operation of the load. Thus, a light switch is used to turn a light on and off by making or breaking its connection to the power supply.

A single-phase power supply, such as that used for heating equipment, always consists of two wires. For 120-V ac power, one wire is called *hot* (usually black) and the other wire is called *neutral* (usually white). The hot wire can be found by using a test light attached to two wire leads (Figure 12-11). Touch one lead to the hot wire and the other

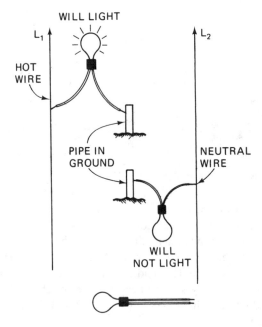

WILL LIGHT

L_1

HOT WIRE

L_2

PIPE IN GROUND

NEUTRAL WIRE

WILL NOT LIGHT

Figure 12-11 Use of test light.

Basic Electricity and Electrical Symbols   Chap. 12

to ground (a metal pipe inserted in the ground) and the bulb will light. Touch one lead to the neutral wire and the other to the ground and the bulb will not light.

In a circuit using ac power, the assumption is made that power moves from the hot wire through the load to the neutral wire (although the current does alternate). This assumption is made only to simplify tracing circuits and locating switches.

Caution: Switches are always placed between the hot wire and the load; not between the load and the neutral wire. Thus, when the switch is open (disconnecting the circuit) it is safe to work on the load. If the switch were on the neutral side of the load touching the load it could complete the circuit to ground. This dangerous condition could cause current to flow through a person's body with serious or fatal results.

A circuit consists of a source of electrical current, a path for it to follow, and a place for it to go (electrical load). Switches are inserted in the path of the current to control its flow either manually or automatically. Electrical devices are connected in circuits to produce a specific resultant action, such as operating a fan motor or a firing device on a furnace.

There are two basic types of circuits: series and parallel. Electrical devices can be connected in either of these ways, or in a combination of both.

Referring to Figure 12-12, using 120-V alternating current as a power source, the two wires are termed L_1 (hot) and L_2 (neutral). The hot wire is usually black and the neutral wire is usually white. Most 120-V installations include a third wire (color coded green) for the earth ground. These systems require a three-prong plug and outlet.

The fuse inserted in the hot side of the line is usually incorporated in the switching device known as a *fused disconnect*. Where the load is in some type of residence, a thermal fuse is used. In case of a shorted circuit or overload, the fuse melts and automatically disconnects the power. Where the type of load is a motor, a time-delay fuse is used.

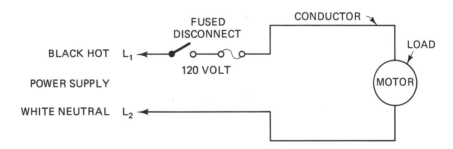

Figure 12-12 A typical electrical circuit, including a source of power, a path for the current to flow in, and a load.

ELECTRICAL DEVICES

Electrical devices are chiefly of two types (Figure 12-13):

1. Loads

2. Switches

Electrical Devices   **239**

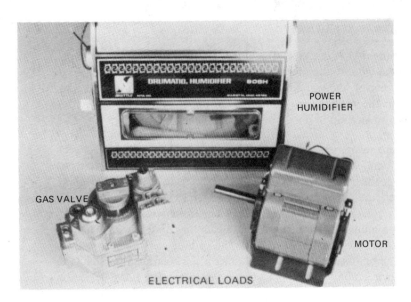

Figure 12-13 Loads and switches.

Loads have resistance and consume power. Loads usually transform power into some other form of energy. Examples of loads are motors, resistance heaters, and lights.

Switches are used to connect loads to the power supply or to disconnect them when they are not required.

Loads and Symbols

The common loads used on heating equipment are described next, along with the symbol used to represent them in the schematic wiring diagram.

Motors. The electrical motor is usually considered the most important load device in the electrical system. It can be represented in two ways: by a large circle or by the internal wiring (Figure 12-14).

To better understand the electrical motor application, refer to the legend on the wiring diagram. The symbol may represent a fan motor, an oil burner motor, or an

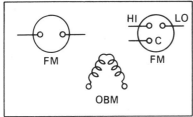

LEGEND

FM = FAN MOTOR
FM = FAN MOTOR, MULTIPLE SPEED
OBM = OIL BURNER MOTOR

Figure 12-14 Electric motor and symbols. (Courtesy, Essex Group, Controls Division, Steveco Products, Inc.)

automatic humidifier motor. When current flows through the motor, the motor should run.

Solenoids. The second most important device is the solenoid (Figure 12-15). When the current flows through the solenoid (coil of wire), magnetism is created. The

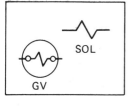

LEGEND

SOL = SOLENOID (RELAY COIL)
GV = SOLENOID (GAS VALVE)

Figure 12-15 Solenoid and symbols.

solenoid is a device designed to harness and use magnetism. It is most frequently used to open and close switches. It is also used to open and close valves.

It is common practice to use letters under the symbol to abbreviate the name of the device and to provide reference to the legend. For example, GV under the symbol would be shown in the legend to mean gas valve.

Relays. A relay is a useful application of a solenoid. By flowing current through the solenoid coil, one or more mechanically operated switches can be opened or closed. The solenoid coil is located in one circuit, while the switches are usually in separate circuits.

The relay is identified by the symbols shown in Figure 12-16 and 12-17. There are at least two parts to the relay: the coil and the switch (or switches). The switch may be in one part of the diagram and the coil in another. The two symbols are identified as belonging to the same electrical device by the letters above them.

When the switch has a diagonal line across it, it is a closed switch; without the diagonal line, the switch is open. All wiring diagrams show relay switches in their normal position, the position when no current is applied to the solenoid coil. Thus, in a diagram, where no current is flowing through the coil, the open switches are called *normally open* and the closed switches are called *normally closed*. When current is applied to the coil, all of the related switches change position (Figure 12-17).

There are several types of relays used in heating work. They differ in the number of NO and NC switches.

Resistance heaters. Another form of load device commonly used is the resistance heater. In the resistance heater, electricity is converted to heat. Heat in an electric furnace is produced by electricity. Heat is also used to control switches. The higher the resistance, the greater the amount of heat that is produced. The symbols for a resistance heater is a zigzag line (Figure 12-18). A letter is used under the heater symbol to designate its use as indicated in the legend.

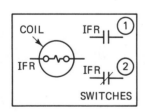

IFR = INDOOR FAN RELAY

Figure 12-16 Indoor fan relay switch and symbols, switch 1 open and switch 2 closed. (Courtesy, Essex Group, Controls Division, Steveco Products, Inc.)

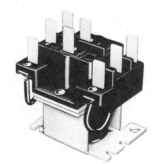

RELAY SWITCH

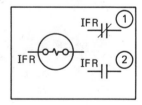

IFR = INDOOR FAN RELAY

Figure 12-17 Indoor fan relay switch and symbols, switch 2 open and switch 1 closed. (Courtesy, Essex Group, Controls Division, Steveco Products, Inc.)

LEGEND

RH = RESISTANCE HEATER

Figure 12-18 Resistance heater and symbols.

Heat relays. The symbols and letters for a heat relay are shown in Figure 12-19. In heating circuits, particularly for electric heating, resistance heaters are used to operate switches. The advantage of this type of relay is that it provides a time delay in operating the switch.

When current is supplied to the heater, it heats up a bimetal element located in another circuit. Bimetal elements are made by bonding together two pieces of metal that expand at different rates. As the bimetal heats its shape is changed, thereby closing or opening a switch.

Lights. Lights are a type of load. They have resistance to current flow. A signal light is often used to indicate an electrical condition that cannot otherwise be readily

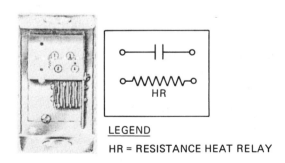

LEGEND

HR = RESISTANCE HEAT RELAY

Figure 12-19 Heat relay and symbols. (Courtesy, Honeywell Inc.)

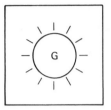

LEGEND

G = GREEN LIGHT

Figure 12-20 Light and symbol.

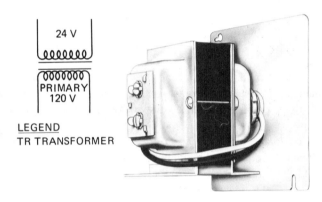

LEGEND
TR TRANSFORMER

Figure 12-21 Transformer and symbol.
(Courtesy, Essex Group, Controls
Division, Steveco Products, Inc.)

observed. The color of the light is often indicated by a letter on the symbol (Figure 12-20).

Transformers. In heating systems, it is often desirable to use two or more different voltages to operate the system. The fan must run on line voltage (usually 120 V), but the thermostat circuit (control circuit) can often best be run on low voltage (24 V). A transformer is used to change from one voltage to another. The legend and symbols for transformers are shown in Figure 12-21.

ELECTRICAL SWITCHES AND THEIR SYMBOLS

Loads perform many functions. However, switches perform only one: to start and stop the flow of electricity.

Electrical switches are classified according to the force used to operate them: manual, magnetic (solenoid), heat, light, or moisture.

The terms normally open and normally closed refer to the position of the switch with no operating force applied. All wiring diagrams show the position of the switches when the operating solenoid (relay coil) or mechanism is de-energized.

A thermostat is assumed to be an N.O. switch. A cooling thermostat makes (closes) an electrical circuit upon a rise in temperature.

A heating limit switch is considered an N.C. switch since it is normally closed when the system is in operation, and opens only when excessively high temperatures are reached in the furnace.

It is important to identify the type of force that operates a switch. Only then can its normal position be accurately determined.

The simplest type of switch is one that makes (closes) or breaks (opens) a single electrical circuit. Other switches make or break several circuits. The switching action is described by:

- Number of poles (number of electrical circuits through the switch)

- The throw (number of places for the electrical current to go)

The following abbreviations are often used to designate the types of switching action.

SPST: Single-pole single-throw
SPDT: Single-pole double-throw
DPST: Double-pole single-throw
DPDT: Double-pole double-throw

These designations and their symbols are shown in Figure 12-22.

The common types of switches used for heating equipment controls are described, together with the symbols used to represent them.

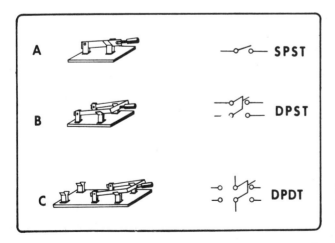

Figure 12-22 Designations and symbols for switching actions. (Reproduced by permission of Carrier Corporation, copyright Carrier Corporation.)

Electrical Switches and Their Symbols

Manual Switches

Manual switches are operated by hand, and are usually used to disconnect the power supply when equipment is shut down for extended periods of time. For example, a room air conditioner is turned off when summer days are cool, or at the end of the cooling season.

Disconnect switches used on heating units are manual switches used to disconnect the power supply to the unit when servicing is required (Figure 12-23). These switches may also have fuses (heat-operated switches), which will be described later.

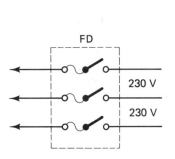 

Figure 12-23 Fused safety switch and symbol.

Manual switches are used when it is undesirable to operate the equipment automatically. For example, a bathroom heater can have a manual switch, thus providing extra bathroom heat only when needed.

Room thermostats normally have two switches, so that the occupant has the choice of operating the system on heating or cooling, or turning the unit off. The switch is marked "heat-off-cool." A manual fan switch is also provided to permit the choice of fan operation, continuously or automatically. This switch is marked "on-auto." The fan can be run in the summer for ventilation and air movement without operating the unit on cooling. The switches are located on the subbase of the thermostat.

Magnetic Switches

Magnetic or solenoid switches are electrically operated switches using the force of the magnetic effect to operate the switch. To produce the required amount of power to operate the switch, the wire is coiled, creating a strong magnetic effect on a metal core.

Magnetic or solenoid switches have various names, depending upon their use. Among these are relays (Figure 12-24), contactors (Figure 12-25) and starters (Figure 12-26).

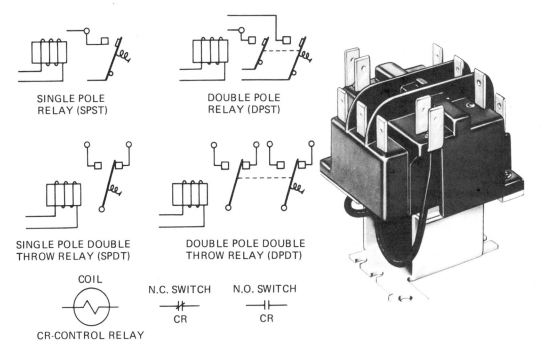

SINGLE POLE
RELAY (SPST)

DOUBLE POLE
RELAY (DPST)

SINGLE POLE DOUBLE
THROW RELAY (SPDT)

DOUBLE POLE DOUBLE
THROW RELAY (DPDT)

COIL

N.C. SWITCH
CR

N.O. SWITCH
CR

CR-CONTROL RELAY

Figure 12-24 Relay switch, symbols, and switching action. (Courtesy, Essex Group, Controls Division, Steveco Products, Inc.)

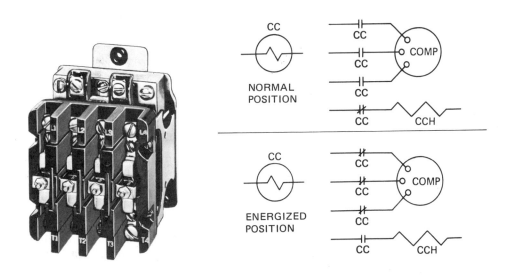

CC

NORMAL
POSITION

CC
CC
COMP
CC
CC
CCH

CC

ENERGIZED
POSITION

CC
CC
COMP
CC
CC
CCH

Figure 12-25 Contactor switch and symbol. (Courtesy, Essex Group, Controls Division, Steveco Products, Inc.)

Electrical Switches and Their Symbols

247

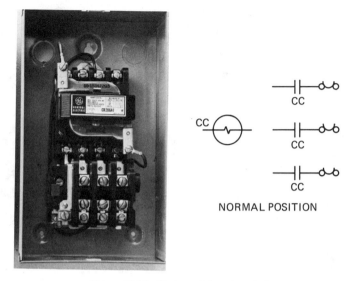

Figure 12-26 Starter switch and symbol.

Relays were described earlier in this chapter. Contactors are relatively large electric relays used to start motors. Starters are also relatively large relays that include overload (excess current) protection. The National Electric Code specifies whether a motor requires a manual, contactor, or starter switch.

Solenoid switches may also be used to operate valves which regulate the flow of a fluid (liquid or vapor). An example of this type of valve is the gas valve, described in Chapter 8.

Some types of overloads can also be described as magnetic-type switches. An overload device protects a motor against excess current flow. Normal amounts of current will not energize the solenoid, but excess amounts of current will. When the solenoid is energized, it trips a mechanically interlocked switch that cuts off the power to the motor.

Heat-Operated Switches

There are many types of heat-operated switches. In all cases, heat is the force that operates the switch. These switches include thermostats, fan and limit controls, heat relays, fuses, overloads, and circuit breakers.

Thermostats. A heating thermostat (Figure 12-27) *makes* (closes) on a drop in room temperature. The intensity of heat reacts on the bimetal, changing its shape, which in turn actuates a switch. The thermostat is usually shown as an NO switch. Thermostats are discussed in Chapter 16.

Fan and limit controls. Fan and limit controls (Figure 12-28) have a bimetal sensing element that protrudes into the warm air passage of a furnace. The fan control

Basic Electricity and Electrical Symbols   Chap. 12

CIRCUIT MAKES ON
TEMPERATURE DROP
FOR HEATING

Figure 12-27 Thermostat switch and symbol. (Courtesy, Honeywell Inc.)

Figure 12-28 Combination fan and limit control switch and symbol.

makes on a rise in temperature. It is considered to be an NO switch because with the furnace shut down, the fan control will have an open switch.

The limit control protects the furnace against excessively high air temperatures, turning off the firing devices when a predetermined temperature is reached. The limit control is diagrammed as an NC switch.

HR

Figure 12-29   Heat relay switch and symbol. (Courtesy, Honeywell Inc.)

Heat relays.   Heat relays (Figure 12-29) are similar to magnetic or solenoid relays in function. However, the mechanical action takes place as a result of heat produced in an electric resistance. When the resistance coil is energized, heat is produced. This heat is applied to one or more bimetal elements. As the bimetal elements expand, they either break an electrical circuit or make an electrical circuit.

The heat relay is a delayed-action switch. This means that the switch requires some amount of time to change position. Depending on the construction, the time delay may be 15s, 30s, 45s, or more. This feature permits staging or sequencing loads (turning loads on automatically at different times). Since the inrush current to a load when first turned on is usually many times greater than its running current, sequencing is important. Sequencing permits using a smaller power service to the appliance. A sequencer is used on an electric furnace to turn on the electric heating elements in steps.

Fuses.   Fuses (Figure 12-30) are placed in an electrical circuit to cut off the flow of current when there is an overload or a short. An *overload* is current in excess of the circuit design. A *short* is a direct connection between the two wires of a power supply without having the current pass through a load. In either case, the fuse will heat and melt, breaking the circuit continuity and stopping the flow of current. Where the fault is overcurrent, the melting of the fuse takes place slowly. Where the fault is a short, the melting of the fuse takes place quickly.

Some circuits require a time-delay fuse. An example is a motor circuit. The inrush of current in starting (a fraction of a second) is so great that an ordinary fuse would "blow" before the motor reached running speed. This initial motor current is called *locked rotor amperes* (LRA). The running amperes or *full-load amperes* (FLA) is much less. Because of the special design of delayed-action fuses, they may be selected on the basis of FLA.

According to the National Electric Code, fuses and wiring can be sized on the basis of 125% of FLA.

Overloads.   Overloads (Figure 12-31) can be constructed in many ways. All overloads are designed to stop the flow of current when safe limits are exceeded. Overloads differ from fuses in that they do not have one-time usage as does a fuse. When a fuse

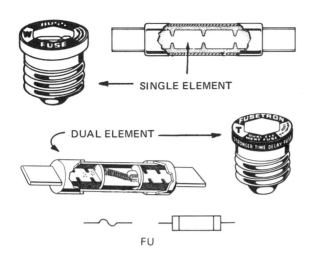

SINGLE ELEMENT

DUAL ELEMENT

FU

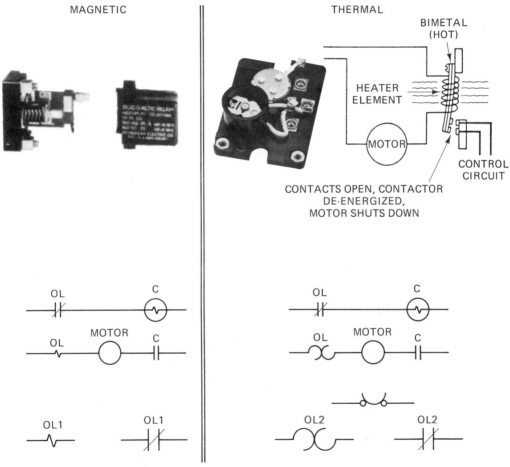

Figure 12-31 Overload switches and symbols. (Courtesy, Motors & Armatures, Inc.)

Electrical Switches and Their Symbols

melts, it must be replaced to return the circuit to operation. When an overload senses excess current, a switch is opened, breaking the flow of current. Some of these switches are automatically reset when the current returns to normal, others must be manually reset. An overload is considered an NC switch, since it is closed when no current is flowing through the circuit and during normal operation of the equipment.

Circuit breakers. The main power circuit to a heating furnace must be protected against excess current flow by a fuse or a circuit breaker (Figure 12-32). Either one of these switches will disconnect the power supply if the equipment draws excess current. The circuit breaker is a type of overload device placed in the power supply, which will "trip" (open the circuit) in the event of excessive current flow. When the fault is corrected, the circuit breaker can be manually reset to restore the circuit to its original condition.

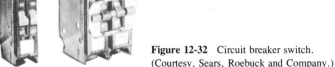

Figure 12-32 Circuit breaker switch.
(Courtesy, Sears, Roebuck and Company.)

Light-Operated Switches

Some switches are activated by light. An example is the cad cell used on the primary control of an oil burner. *Cad cell* refers to a cadmium sulfate sensing element. In the presence of light, the electrical resistance of a cad cell is about 1000 Ω; in darkness, its resistance is about 100,000 Ω. The cad cell is located on the draft tube of an oil burner and senses the presence (or proof) of a flame. If the cad cell is in darkness, there is no flame; if the cad cell is lighted, the flame is proof that the burner has been started by the ignition system. It therefore acts as a safety device.

In the electrical circuit the cad cell is placed in series with a relay coil. If the cad cell does not sense adequate light from the flame the relay will not be energized. If the cad cell senses the flame, its resistance is reduced and the relay is energized, which allows the burner to continue running.

Moisture-Operated Switches

The presence of moisture in the air can be used to operate a switch. Certain materials, including human hair and nylon, expand when moist and contract when dry. These two materials are used to sense the relative humidity in the air. The change in the length of a strand of hair or nylon can be used to operate a suitable switch. The switch will turn a humidifier on or off to maintain the desired relative humidity in a space.

Electrical Diagrams

The greatest advances in the design and use of forced warm air heating equipment came after the invention of automatic control systems. It was then no longer necessary to operate the equipment manually. Automatic controls regulate the furnace to maintain the desired temperature conditions. Forced air heating owes its very beginning to the use of electricity to drive the fan motor.

A wiring diagram describes an electrical system. There are generally two types of diagrams for warm air heating units:

1.   Connection

2.   Schematic

A connection diagram shows the electrical devices in much the same way that they are actually positioned on the equipment (Figure 12-33). Lines are connected to the electrical terminals to show the paths the electric current will follow.

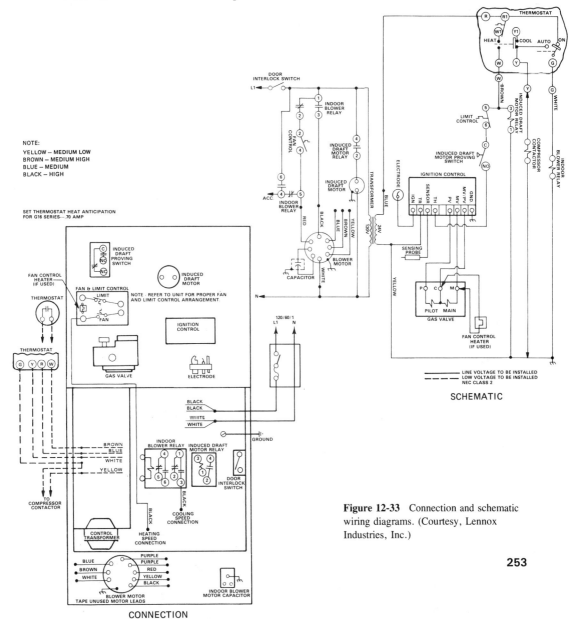

Figure 12-33   Connection and schematic wiring diagrams. (Courtesy, Lennox Industries, Inc.)

The schematic diagram (Figure 12-33) uses symbols to represent the electrical devices. The arrangement of the symbols in the diagram, using ladder-type connecting lines, indicates how the system works. It shows the sequence of operation. This diagram is essential to the service technician in troubleshooting problems in heating systems.

CHAPTER 12 STUDY QUESTIONS

The answers to the study questions are found in the sections of this chapter under the chapter topic indicated.

STUDY QUESTIONS	CHAPTER TOPIC
1. Define volts, amperes, ohms, and watts.	*Electrical terms*
2. State Ohm's law and give an example of its use.	*Ohm's law*
3. How does a series circuit differ from a parallel circuit?	*Series circuits, parallel circuits*
4. State the formulas for series and parallel circuits.	*Series circuits, parallel circuits*
5. Describe how a solenoid coil uses electromagnetic action.	*Electromagnetic action*
6. How are capacitors rated?	*Capacitance*
7. What is an electrical circuit?	*Circuits*
8. How do loads differ from switches?	*Electrical devices*
9. Give the electrical symbols for motors, heaters, solenoids, relays, lights, and transformers.	*Loads and symbols*
10. How does a relay operate?	*Relays*
11. What does SPST, SPDT, DPST and DPDT mean?	*Electrical switches and their symbols*
12. Give the symbol for normally closed switch, normally open switch, thermostat, fan and limit control, fuse, overload, and capacitor.	*Electrical switches and their symbols*
13. How does the symbol for a heating thermostat differ from the symbol for a cooling thermostat?	*Electrical switches and their symbols*
14. What is the difference between a connection and a schematic wiring diagram?	*Electrical diagrams*

13 Schematic Wiring Diagrams

OBJECTIVES

After studying this chapter, the student will be able to:

- Read and construct a schematic electrical wiring diagram

PURPOSE OF A SCHEMATIC

A schematic wiring diagram (schematic) consists of a group of lines and electrical symbols arranged in ladder form to represent the individual circuits controlling or operating a unit. The lines represent the connecting wires. The electrical symbols represent loads or switches. The rungs of the ladder represent individual electrical circuits. The unit can be an electrical-mechanical device such as a furnace.

UNDERSTANDING A SCHEMATIC

To understand a schematic diagram, a student must know:

- The purpose of each electrical component
- Exactly how the unit operates, both mechanically and electrically
- The sequence of operation of each electrical component

Sequence refers to the condition where the operation of one electrical component follows another to produce a final result. It represents the order of events as they occur in a system of electrical controls.

All electrical systems must be wired by making connections to power and to each electrical device. A schematic diagram is important to assist a service technician in wiring the equipment, locating connections for testing circuits, and in analyzing the operation of the control system. Occasionally, however, a schematic diagram may be unavailable, so it is essential that a service technician be able to construct one.

Following is the legend to the schematic diagrams used in this chapter.

CR	Control relay
FC	Fan control
FD	Fused disconnect
FM	Fan motor
FR	Fan relay
FS	Fan switch
GV	Gas valve
IFR	Indoor fan relay
L	Limit
LA	Limit auxiliary
L_1, L_2	Power supply
N.C.	Normally closed
N.O.	Normally open
T	Thermostat
TR	Transformer
Y,R,G,W	Terminals of thermostat

SCHEMATIC CONSTRUCTION

Connection and schematic wiring diagrams are shown in Figures 13-1 and 13-2.

To draw a schematic and to separate the individual circuits on the unit itself, a service technician must be able to trace (or follow) the wiring of each individual circuit. The method of tracing a circuit is as follows:

1. Start at one side of the power supply (L_1), go through the resistance (load), and return to the other side of the power supply (L_2). This is a *complete circuit*.

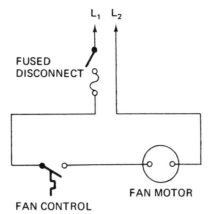

FUSED
DISCONNECT

FAN CONTROL

FAN MOTOR

Figure 13-1 Connection wiring diagram.

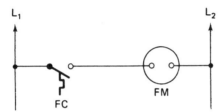

FC

FM

Figure 13-2 Schematic wiring diagram.

2. If a technician starts at L_1 and goes through the resistance and cannot reach L_2 or returns back to L_1, this is an *open circuit.*

3. If a technician starts at L_1 and reaches L_2 without passing through a resistance (load), this is a *short circuit.*

Rules for Drawing: Vertical Style

(a) Use letters on each symbol to represent the name of the component.

(b) The names of all components represented by letters should be listed in the legend.

(c) When using a 120-V-ac power supply,* show the hot line (L_1) on the left side and the neutral line (L_2) on the right side of the diagram.

(d) When using a 120-V power supply, the switches must be placed on the hot side (L_1) of the load.

(e) Relay coils and their switches (Figure 13-3) should be marked with the same (matching) symbol letters.

(f) Numbers can be used to show wiring connections to controls or terminals.

---

* In 208, 230, 240, or 440-V single-phase circuits, there are two hot wires and no neutral wire. In these circuits switches can be placed on either side of the load.

Schematic Construction

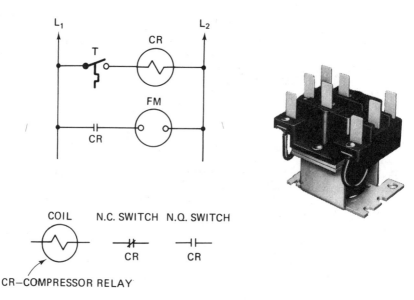

Figure 13-3 Relay coils and switches.

(g) Always show switches in their normal (de-energized) position.

(h) Thermostats with switching subbases, primary controls for oil burners, and other more complicated controls can be shown by terminals only in the main diagram. Subdiagrams are used when necessary to show the internal control circuits.

(i) It is common practice to start the diagram showing line-voltage circuits first and low-voltage (control) circuits second (Figure 13-4).

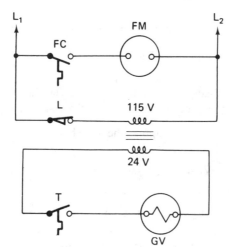

Figure 13-4 Line-voltage and low-voltage circuits schematic diagram.

Schematic Wiring Diagrams   Chap. 13

Rules for Drawing: Horizontal Style

Assuming that either a completely wired unit or a connection wiring diagram is available, the following is a step-by-step procedure for drawing a schematic:

Referring to the connecting wiring	Drawing the schematic diagram
1. Locate the source of power. Trace it back to the disconnect switch.	1. Draw two horizontal lines* representing L_1 and L_2, with sufficient space between them for the diagram. Draw in the disconnect switch.
2. Trace each circuit on the diagram, starting with L_1 and returning to L_2.	2. Draw each circuit on the diagram using a vertical line to connect L_1 through the switches, through the load to L_2.
3. Determine the names of each switch and load.	3. Make a legend by listing the names of the electrical components, together with the letters representing each. The letters are used on the diagram to identify the parts.

* Vertical lines could also be used to represent L_1 and L_2, in which case horizontal lines would then be used to represent the individual circuits.

A connection diagram usually shows the relative position of the various controls on the unit. A schematic diagram makes it possible to indicate the sequence of operation of the electrical devices. A verbal description of the electrical system may also reveal some useful facts about the operation of the unit. Thus, the connection diagram, the schematic diagram, and the verbal description are all useful in understanding how the unit operates electrically. To show how these three are related, a connection diagram and a schematic diagram will be constructed from the description of each circuit.

Power supply. Description: The power supply is 120-V, 60-Hz, single-phase (Figure 13.5). A fused disconnect is placed in the hot line to the furnace to disconnect the power when the furnace is not being used. The power supply consists of a hot wire and neutral wire. The circuit has a 20-A fuse.

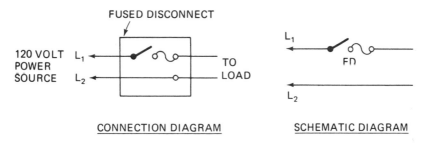

Figure 13-5 Power supply to furnace.

Circuits. *Description:* A fan motor operating on 120-V is placed in circuit 1 of Figure 13-6. It is controlled by a fan control. This fan control is located in the plenum or in the furnace cabinet by the heat exchanger. It is adjustable but to conserve energy is usually set to turn the fan on at 110°F (43°C) and off at 90°F (32°C). This permits the furnace to heat up before the fan turns on to deliver heated air to the building.

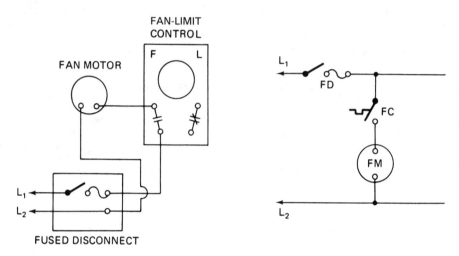

Figure 13-6 Fan circuit.

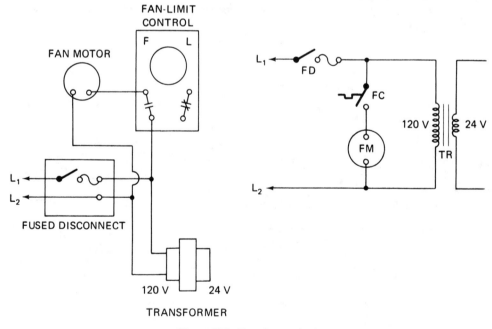

Figure 13-7 Transformer circuit.

Note that the fan control is part of a combination fan and limit control. Both use the same bimetal heat element. The limit control settings are higher than the fan control settings.

Description: The primary of a transformer is placed in a separate 120-V circuit, Circuit 2 (Figure 13-7). The transformer will be used to supply 24-V (secondary) power to the control circuits.

Description: This is a 24-V gas valve circuit (Figure 13-8). Circuit 3 includes the thermostat, gas valve, and limit control. When the thermostat calls for heat, the gas valve opens. The limit control will shut off the flow of gas should the air temperature leaving the furnace exceed 200°F (93°C).

Description: A manual switch, located in the subbase of the thermostat, is connected

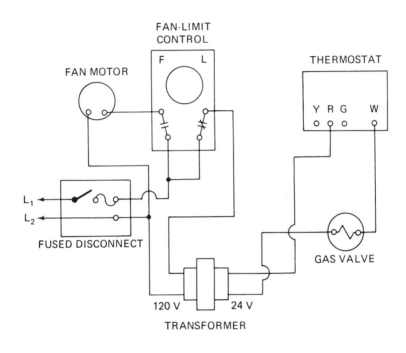

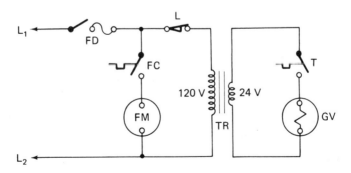

Figure 13-8 Gas valve circuit.

to an indoor fan relay, Circuit 4, so that the fan can be manually turned on for ventilation even though the gas is off (Figure 13-9). The relay switch is in the 120-V circuit in parallel with the fan control and the solenoid coil of the relay is in the 24-V circuit in series with the fan switch (FS).

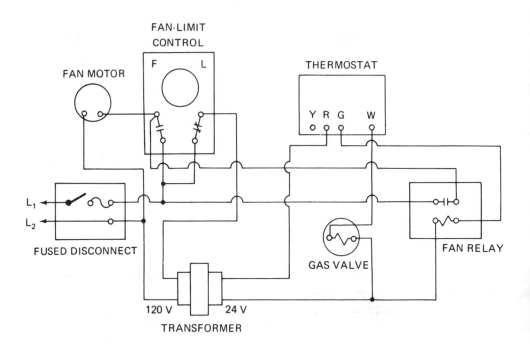

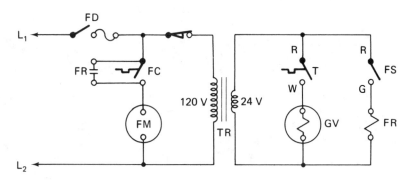

Figure 13-9 Manual fan circuit.

REVIEW PROBLEM 1

Draw a schematic wiring diagram from the connection diagram shown in Figure 13-10.

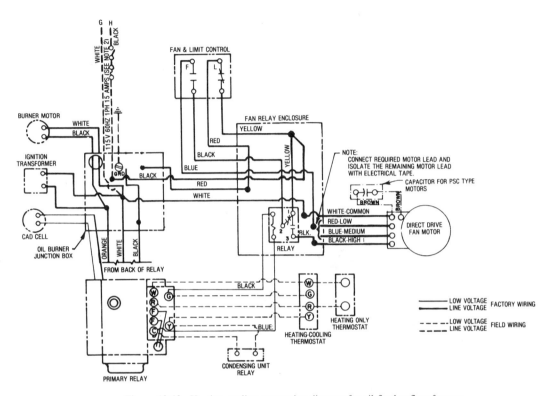

Figure 13-10 Heating-cooling connection diagram for oil-fired upflow furnace.

REVIEW PROBLEM 2

Draw a connection diagram from the schematic diagram shown in Figure 13-11.

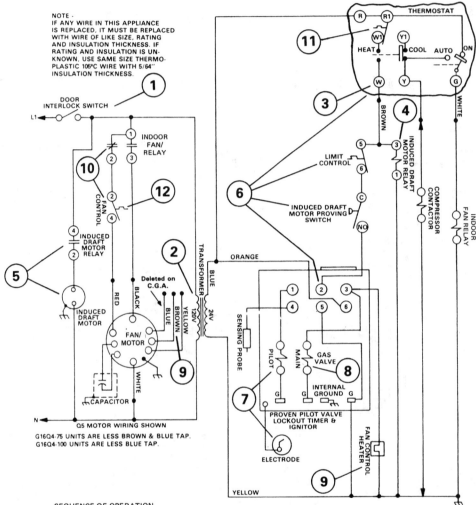

NOTE -
IF ANY WIRE IN THIS APPLIANCE
IS REPLACED, IT MUST BE REPLACED
WITH WIRE OF LIKE SIZE, RATING
AND INSULATION THICKNESS. IF
RATING AND INSULATION IS UN-
KNOWN, USE SAME SIZE THERMO-
PLASTIC 105°C WIRE WITH 5/64"
INSULATION THICKNESS.

G16Q4-75 UNITS ARE LESS BROWN & BLUE TAP.
G16Q4-100 UNITS ARE LESS BLUE TAP.

Q5 MOTOR WIRING SHOWN

SEQUENCE OF OPERATION

1. LINE POTENTIAL FEEDS THROUGH DOOR INTER-LOCK. ACCESS PANEL MUST BE IN PLACE TO ENERGIZE UNIT.

2. TRANSFORMER PROVIDES 24 VOLTS TO POWER CONTROL CIRCUIT.

3. ON A HEATING DEMAND, THERMOSTAT BULB MAKES PROVIDING 24 V AT "W" LEG.

4. INDUCED DRAFT MOTOR RELAY IS ENERGIZED FROM "W" LEG.

5. INDUCED DRAFT MOTOR RELAY N.O. CONTACTS CLOSE AND ENERGIZE THE INDUCED DRAFT MOTOR.

6. WHEN THE INDUCED DRAFT MOTOR COMES UP TO SPEED, THE INDUCED DRAFT MOTOR PROVING SWITCH CLOSES COMPLETING THE CIRCUIT FROM "W" LEG OF THERMOSTAT THROUGH LIMIT CONTROL TO IGNITION CONTROL TERMINAL 2.

7. PILOT GAS VALVE AND PILOT IGNITION SPARK ARE ENERGIZED.

8. AFTER PILOT FLAME HAS BEEN PROVEN BY IGNITION CONTROL, MAIN GAS VALVE IS ENERGIZED AND SPARK IS DE-ENERGIZED. (MAIN GAS VALVE WILL OPEN ONLY ON PROOF OF PILOT FLAME.)

9. AS THE MAIN GAS VALVE IS ENERGIZED, THE FAN CONTROL HEATER IS ACTIVATED.

10. IN APPROXIMATELY 30-80 SECONDS N.O. FAN CONTROL CONTACTS CLOSE ENERGIZING BLOWER MOTOR FROM N.C. BLOWER MOTOR RELAY CONTACTS TO THE HEATING SPEED TAP.

11. AS HEATING DEMAND IS SATISFIED, THERMO-STAT HEAT BULB BREAKS DE-ENERGIZING IGNITION CONTROL, GAS VALVE, AND FAN CONTROL HEATER.

12. BLOWER MOTOR CONTINUES RUNNING UNTIL FURNACE TEMPERATURE DROPS BELOW FAN CONTROL SET POINT.

Figure 13-11 Gas-fired upflow furnace schematic diagram.

CHAPTER 13 STUDY QUESTIONS

The answers to the study questions are found in the sections of this chapter under chapter topic indicated.

STUDY QUESTIONS	*CHAPTER TOPICS*
1. What is the purpose of a schematic wiring diagram?	*Understanding a schematic*
2. What is the purpose of the legend?	*Understanding a schematic*
3. How are the power lines drawn? How is a second-voltage power supply shown using a transformer?	*Rules for drawing*
4. If the power lines are vertical, what does each horizontal line represent?	*Rules for drawing*
5. What essential electrical devices must be shown in each circuit?	*Rules for drawing*
6. With two vertical lines representing the power supply, which line is usually shown "hot"?	*Rules for drawing*
7. With L_1 hot and L_2 neutral, where should the fused disconnect be placed?	*Rules for drawing*
8. In showing a relay, how is a switch of the relay shown to be connected (mechanically) to the relay coil?	*Rules for drawing*
9. How is the position of two switches shown, both capable of turning on the same load?	*Rules for drawing*
10. How is the position of two switches shown if both must be on to have the load operate?	*Rules for drawing*
11. How is it shown if one switch operates two loads?	*Rules for drawing*

14 Using Electrical Test Instruments

OBJECTIVES

After studying this chapter, the student will be able to:

- Use common electrical test instruments for service or troubleshooting

ELECTRICAL TEST INSTRUMENTS

To test the performance of a heating unit, or to troubleshoot service problems, requires the use of instruments. Since a heating unit has many electrical components, a heating technician should

- Know the unit electrically
- Be able to read and use schematic wiring diagrams
- Be able to use electrical test instruments

The reading and construction of schematic wiring diagrams was discussed in Chapter 13. The use of schematic diagrams is discussed in this chapter.

COMPONENT FUNCTIONS

To know the unit electrically means to understand exactly how each component functions. Figure 14-1 shows a simple electrical heating wiring arrangement for a forced air gas system. Two views are shown:

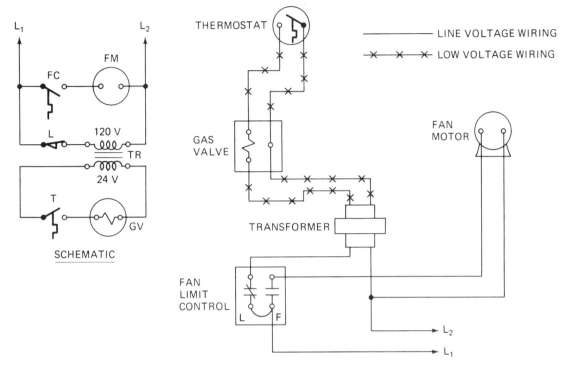

Figure 14-1 Electrical wiring for a 24-V forced warm air gas-fired furnace.

1. The schematic diagram

2. The connection diagram

Three load devices are shown:

1. Fan motor

2. Transformer

3. Gas valve

The fan motor turns the fan when it is supplied with power, in this case 120-V, single-phase, 60-Hz current.

The transformer, which has a primary voltage of 120 V and a secondary voltage of 24 V, is energized whenever power is supplied.

A solenoid type gas valve opens when it is energized and operates on 24-V power.

There is at least one automatic switch in each circuit. The fan has one, the transformer has one, and the gas valve has two. The following is a description of the types of switches used:

Component Functions

- The fan control turns on the fan when the bonnet temperature rises to the *cut-in* setting. It turns off the fan when the bonnet temperature drops to the *cut-out* setting.

- The limit control is a safety device that turns off the power to the transformer when the bonnet temperature rises to the cut-out setting. It turns on the power to the transformer automatically when the bonnet temperature drops to the cut-in setting.

- A combination gas valve has a built-in pilotstat. The pilotstat is a safety device operated by a thermocouple (not shown). When the pilot is burning properly, the N.O. contacts are closed, permitting the gas valve to open in response to the thermostat.

- The thermostat is a low-voltage (24-V) switch operated by a bimetal sensing element. When the room temperature drops, and the thermostat reaches its cut-in setting, the contacts close, and the gas valve opens (provided that the pilot flame is proven). When the room temperature rises to the cut-out setting of the thermostat, the contactor opens and the gas valve closes.

INSTRUMENT FUNCTIONS

A number of instruments are required in testing. These include

- A voltmeter to measure electrical potential

- An ammeter to measure rate of electrical current flow

- An ohmmeter to measure electrical resistance

- A wattmeter to measure electrical power

- A temperature tester to measure temperatures

Some meters measure a combination of characteristics. For example, a clamp-on ammeter that has provisions to measure amperes, volts, and ohms is available. A VOM multimeter that can measure volts, ohms, and milliamperes is available.

The following scales are typical. However, before purchasing an instrument it is important to verify that its features match specific service needs. For example, do its scales allow the measured values to be clearly read?

1. **DC Millivolt Scales:** 0 to 50, 0 to 500, 0 to 1500. These scales are used to read voltages on thermocouples and thermopiles. A millivolt is a thousandth ($\frac{1}{1000}$) volt.

2. **AC Voltage Scales:** 0 to 30, 0 to 500. These scales are used to read low-voltage control circuits and line-voltage circuits.

3. **AC Amperage Scales:** 0 to 15, 0 to 75. These scales are used for measuring amperage drawn by various low-voltage and line-voltage loads.

4. **Ohm Scales:** 0 to 400, 0 to 3000. These scales are used for resistance readings on all types of circuits and for continuity checks on all systems.

5. **Wattage Scales:** 0 to 300, 0 to 600, 0 to 1500, 0 to 3000. These scales are used to measure power input to a circuit or system.

6. **Temperature Scale:** 0 to 1200°F. This scale is used to check return air temperatures, discharge air temperatures and stack temperatures.

USING METERS

When using meters, the following points should be considered:

1. Always use the highest scale first; then work down until midscale readings are obtained. This prevents damage to the meter.

2. Always check the calibration of a meter before using it. For example, on an ohmmeter the two test leads are shorted together and the zero adjust knob turned until the needle reads zero resistance.

3. When using a clamp-on type ammeter, the sensitivity of the instrument can be increased by wrapping the conductor wire around the jaws. The sensitivity will be multiplied by the number of turns taken. For example; 10 loops of single-strand insulated thermostat wire can be wrapped around the jaws of an ammeter, as shown in Figure 14-2. If the meter is set to read on the 1 to 5-A scale, a reading of 2.5 A would be divided by 10 to arrive at the true reading 0.25 A.

$$\frac{\text{AMMETER READING}}{10 \text{ LOOPS}} = \text{ACTUAL AMPS}$$

$$\frac{2.5}{10} = 0.25 \text{ AMPS}$$

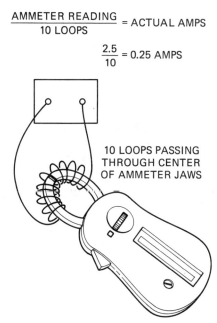

10 LOOPS PASSING THROUGH CENTER OF AMMETER JAWS

Figure 14-2 Method used to accurately read low amperage values with a clamp-on ammeter.

4. When using a clamp-on type of ammeter, be sure the clamp is around only one wire. If it encloses two wires, the current may be flowing in opposite directions, which could cause a zero reading even though current is actually flowing.

5. Always have a supply of the required meter fuses on hand. Certain special fuses may be difficult to obtain on short notice.

6. When measuring dc millivolts being delivered by a thermocouple in a circuit, an adapter is required to provide access to the internal connection (Figure 14-3). This adapter provides a visual indication of proper thermocouple operation. See Figure 14-4 for application.

7. The millivoltmeter is used when checking the output of pilot generators and thermocouples. See Figure 14-5.

8. The test meter shown in Figure 14-6 is used when testing burner equipment. It checks the flame signal current on systems using rectifying flame rod, photocell, infrared, or ultraviolet flame detectors.

Figure 14-3   Thermocouple tester. (Courtesy, Honeywell Inc.)

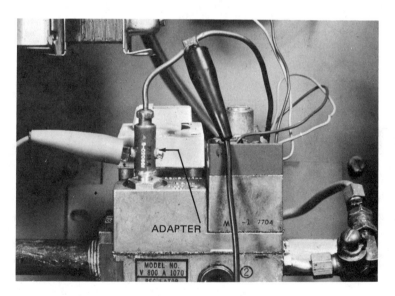

Figure 14-4   Adapter being used for thermocouple measurements.

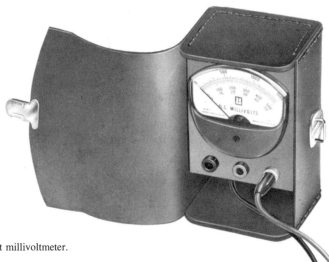

Figure 14-5 Direct current millivoltmeter.
(Courtesy, Honeywell Inc.)

RANGES: 0–50, 0–500, 0–1500

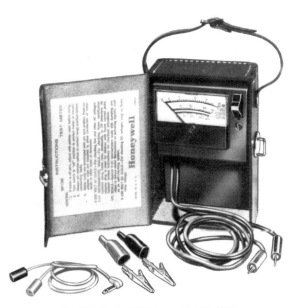

RANGES: 0–300 Vac — 20,000 OHMS
0–150 Vac — 40,000 OHMS

Figure 14-6 Combination ac/dc voltmeter
and dc microammeter. (Courtesy,
Honeywell Inc.)

Three types of readings that can be taken with an ohmmeter are shown in Figure 14-7.

1. No resistance ("short"), left illustration. Closed switch is given full-scale deflection, indicating 0 Ω.

2. Measurable resistance, middle illustration. Measurable resistance is providing less deflection or a specific ohm reading on the meter.

3. Infinite resistance ("open"), right illustration. There is no complete path for the ohmmeter current to flow through, so there is no deflection of the meter needle. The resistance is so high that it cannot be measured. The meter shows infinity (∞) representing an open circuit.

Note: It is important to remember when using an ohmmeter that it has its own source of power and must never be used to test a circuit that is "hot" (connected to power). All power must be off or the ohmmeter can be seriously damaged.

One good example of the use of an ohmmeter is in testing fuses (Figure 14-8). The

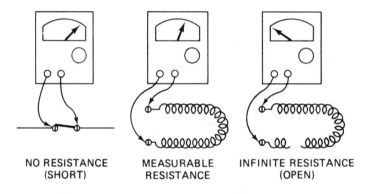

NO RESISTANCE   MEASURABLE   INFINITE RESISTANCE
(SHORT)   RESISTANCE   (OPEN)

Figure 14-7 Three types of readings taken with an ohmmeter.

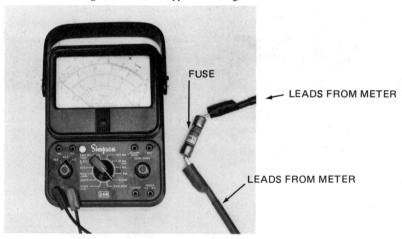

Figure 14-8 Ohm scale of multimeter being used for testing fuses. (Courtesy, Simpson Electric Company.)

fuse is removed from the power circuit and the ohmmeter is used to make a continuity check. If continuity (0 Ωs) is obtained when the meter leads are touching the two ends of the fuse, the fuse is good.

SELECTING THE PROPER INSTRUMENT

The most helpful procedure for deciding which instrument to use in troubleshooting is to check as follows:

1. If any part of the unit operates, the voltmeter or ammeter are normally used.

2. If no portion of the unit operates, a short circuit could be the problem and the ohmmeter is probably the best instrument to use.

When attempting to measure the resistance of any component, the possibility of obtaining an incorrect reading always exists when a part is wired into the system. In a parallel circuit when testing with an ohmmeter, it is necessary to disconnect one side of the component being tested to avoid the possibility of an incorrect reading of the resistance (Figure 14-9).

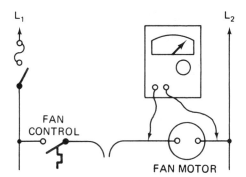

Figure 14-9. Disconnecting one side of parallel circuit when testing resistance with ohmmeter.

A wattmeter measures both amperage and volts simultaneously. This is necessary in an ac circuit because watts take into consideration the power factor. The *power factor* indicates the percent of the volts times the amperes that a consumer actually pays for. Since the peak of the volts and amperes does not usually occur at the same time, wattage is normally less than the product of the volts times the amperes.

Power Calculations

It may be necessary to calculate the power, measured in watts, consumed by a furnace or air conditioning unit. This can be accomplished by taking both voltage and amperage readings at the equipment and then inserting these values into the following formula. The power factor can be obtained from the electric company.

$$P = E \times I \times \text{PF}$$

where: P = power, watts

E = EMF, volts

I = current, amperes

PF = power factor

Substitute the sample values E = 120 V, I = 12 A, and PF = 0.90 into the formula:

$$P = 120 \text{ V} \times 12 \text{ A} \times 0.90 \text{ power factor} = 1296 \text{ W}$$

or approximately 1.3 kilowatts (kw), where k = 1000.

Figure 14-11 Digital snap-around volt-ammeter, audible and visual continuity. (Courtesy, A. W. Sperry, Inc.)
RANGES: 0-200/500 V ac
0-200/300 A ac

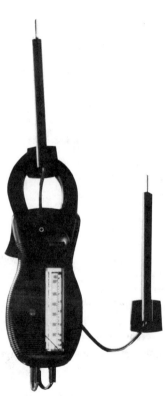

RANGES: 0-150/300/600 V ac
0-6/15/40/100/300 A ac
25-OHM MIDSCALE

Figure 14-10 Rotary scale clamp-on volt-ammeter-ohmmeter. (Courtesy, Amprobe Instrument.)

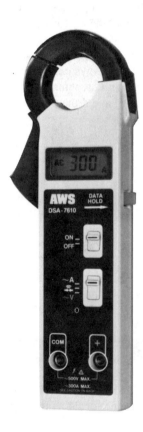

Figure 14-12 Clamp-on volt-ohm-ammeter, measures millisecond power surges. (Courtesy, TIF Instruments, Inc.)

RANGES: 0.1-1000 V ac
0.1-1000 A ac
0.1-800 Ω

Clamp-On Volt-Ammeter-Ohmmeters

The clamp-on style of volt-ammeter-ohmmeter is popular with service personnel. The instrument is easy to use and the variable scales are easy to read. See Figures 14-10, 14-11, and 14-12 for specifications. Figure 14-13 shows their application when troubleshooting motors.

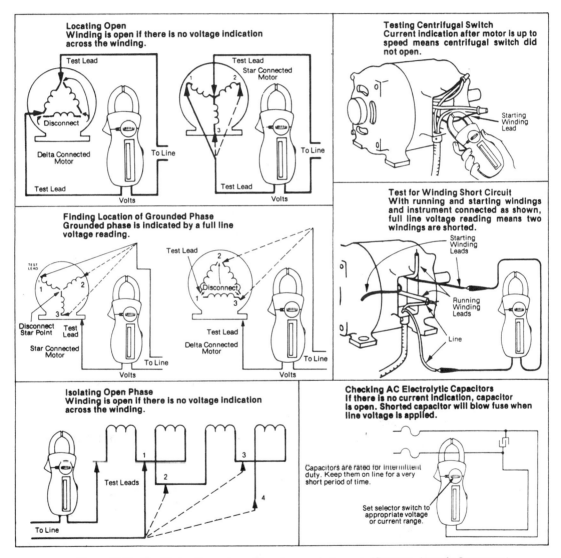

Figure 14-13 Troubleshooting motors with a clamp-on instrument. (Courtesy, Amprobe Instrument.)

Selecting the Proper Instrument

Voltprobe Tester

Figure 14-14 shows an instrument that is designed for measuring voltage only. Some checks that can be made with a voltprobe tester are shown in Figure 14-15.

Figure 14-14 Voltprobe voltage tester checks ten ac/dc voltage levels. (Courtesy, Amprobe Instrument.)

RANGES: 115/220/277/440/550 V ac
115/220/400/600/750 V dc

FINDING GROUNDED
SIDE OF LINE

CHECK FUSES

DETERMINE GROUNDED
SIDE OF MOTOR

Figure 14-15 Application of voltprobe tester. (Courtesy, Amprobe Instrument.)

Digital Multimeters

The digital type of meter is popular because it is considered to be accurate within ±0.05%. Some of the features of the digital meter are: auto setting of zero for each change of range; auto change of polarity as the signal changes polarity; noise rejection; removal of an ac line-frequency signal riding on a dc voltage; very high input resistance of 10 mΩ and higher, making it suitable for virtually any solid-state circuitry. Figures 14-16, 14-17, and 14-18 are examples of digital-type multimeters.

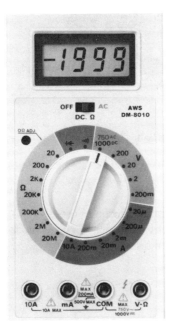

Figure 14-16 3½ digital rotary switch multimeter; electronic protection; 500-V ac/dc, audible continuity buzzer. (Courtesy, A.W. Sperry, Inc.)

RANGES: 0–200 μ/2/20/200/1000 V dc,
0–200 μ/2/20/200/750 V ac,
0–20 μ/200 μ, 2 m, 20 m, 200 m, 10 A ac/dc
0–20/200/2K, 20K, 200K, 2M/20 MΩ

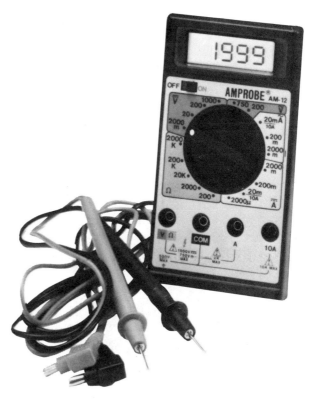

Figure 14-17 3½ rotary switch mutimeter, 20 ranges, ac/dc voltage, amps, resistance, low-battery indication, fused to 600 V ac/dc. (Courtesy, Amprobe Instrument.)

Selecting the Proper Instrument

RANGES, dc VOLTS 0–1000 V
SENSITIVITY 20,000 Ω PER VOLT
RANGES ac VOLTS 0–1000 V
SENSITIVITY 5,000 Ω PER VOLT
RANGE dc MILLIVOLTS 0–250 V
SENSITIVITY 20,000 Ω PER VOLT
RANGE dc MICROAMPERES 0–50 μA
VOLTAGE DROP 250 mV

| R X 1 | R X 100 | R X 10,000 |
| 0–2000 Ω | 0–200,000 Ω | 0–20 MΩ |

Figure 14-18 Digital multimeter. (Courtesy, Simpson Electric Company.)

Volt-Amp Recorder

When a permanent record of volts or amps is required, a portable recorder can be used. This is helpful for detecting and interpreting intermittent electrical problems. The recorder shown in Figure 14-19 can record up to three variables on the same paper chart.

Figure 14-19 Portable recorder for volts or amps; speeds troubleshooting; used with clamp-on volt-ammeter-ohmmeter. (Courtesy, Amprobe Instrument.)

Using Electrical Test Instruments   Chap. 14

TROUBLESHOOTING A UNIT ELECTRICALLY

Testing Part of a Unit

To troubleshoot a unit electrically assume, for example, that service is required on a gas-fired forced air unit, with wiring shown in Figure 14-1. The complaint is that the unit does not heat properly. The fan will not run. The gas burner cycles as a result of the limit control cycling on and off.

The first step is to review the schematic wiring diagram and eliminate from consideration any circuits that appear to be operating properly. In this case, the transformer and the gas valve circuits are eliminated. Now the testing can be confined to the fan motor circuit.

Since part of the unit does run, a voltmeter should be used for testing. By the process of elimination the source of the trouble is found.

First, measure the voltage across the ends of the circuit where the connection is made to L_1 and L_2 (Figure 14-20). The voltmeter reads 120 V, which is satisfactory.

Second, with one meter lead on L_2, place the other meter lead between the fan control and the motor (Figure 14-21). The meter reads 120 V. The bonnet temperature is 150°F. The fan control is set to turn the fan on at 120°F. Therefore, the fan control should be made and this checks out as satisfactory.

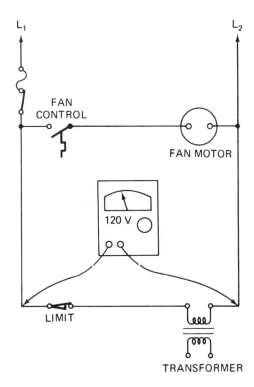

Figure 14-20 Measuring line voltage.

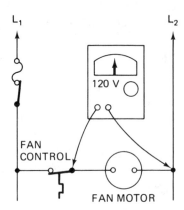

METER LEADS ON L₂ AND LOAD SIDE OF FAN
CONTROL SWITCH TO CHECK POWER AVAILABLE
FOR LOAD (MOTOR).

Figure 14-21 Placement of meter leads.

If the fan motor still does not run after the proper power has been supplied, it is an indication that the fan motor is defective and must be replaced.

The process of elimination can be used on any circuit where troubleshooting is required, regardless of the number of switches. Where power is being supplied to the load and the load does not operate, the load device is defective and needs to be replaced.

Testing a Complete Unit

In troubleshooting a complete unit, there are numerous electrical tests that can be made with the instruments. By the process of elimination, it is important to rule out as many of the circuits as possible that are not causing trouble.

The methods of testing various heating systems are indicated in the following diagrams:

1. Thermopile, self-generating, gas heating control system (Figure 14-22)

2. 24-V gas heating control system (Figure 14-23)

3. Line-voltage gas heating control system (Figure 14-24)

4. Oil burner control system (Figure 14-25)

5. Electric heating system (Figure 14-26)

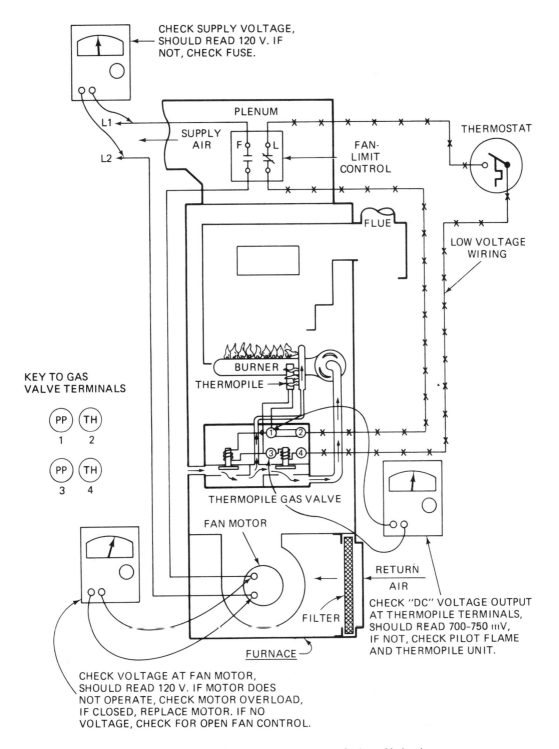

CHECK SUPPLY VOLTAGE, SHOULD READ 120 V. IF NOT, CHECK FUSE.

PLENUM

L1

SUPPLY AIR

F   L

L2

FAN-LIMIT CONTROL

THERMOSTAT

FLUE

LOW VOLTAGE WIRING

KEY TO GAS VALVE TERMINALS

PP TH
1   2

PP TH
3   4

BURNER

THERMOPILE

THERMOPILE GAS VALVE

FAN MOTOR

RETURN AIR

FILTER

FURNACE

CHECK "DC" VOLTAGE OUTPUT AT THERMOPILE TERMINALS, SHOULD READ 700-750 mV, IF NOT, CHECK PILOT FLAME AND THERMOPILE UNIT.

CHECK VOLTAGE AT FAN MOTOR, SHOULD READ 120 V. IF MOTOR DOES NOT OPERATE, CHECK MOTOR OVERLOAD, IF CLOSED, REPLACE MOTOR. IF NO VOLTAGE, CHECK FOR OPEN FAN CONTROL.

Figure 14-22 Thermopile system, gas-fired, troubleshooting.

Troubleshooting a Unit Electrically

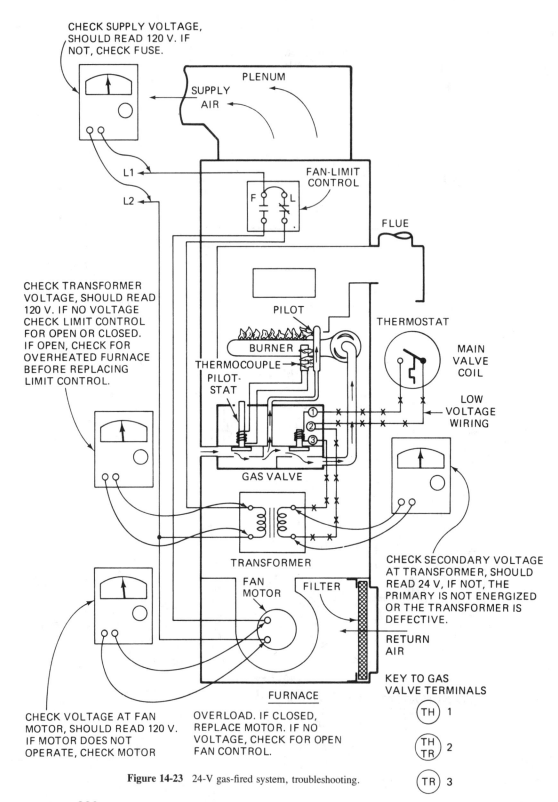

CHECK SUPPLY VOLTAGE, SHOULD READ 120 V. IF NOT, CHECK FUSE.

PLENUM

SUPPLY AIR

L1

L2

FAN-LIMIT CONTROL

F   L

FLUE

CHECK TRANSFORMER VOLTAGE, SHOULD READ 120 V. IF NO VOLTAGE CHECK LIMIT CONTROL FOR OPEN OR CLOSED. IF OPEN, CHECK FOR OVERHEATED FURNACE BEFORE REPLACING LIMIT CONTROL.

PILOT

BURNER

THERMOCOUPLE

PILOT-STAT

①
②
③

GAS VALVE

THERMOSTAT

MAIN VALVE COIL

LOW VOLTAGE WIRING

TRANSFORMER

CHECK SECONDARY VOLTAGE AT TRANSFORMER, SHOULD READ 24 V, IF NOT, THE PRIMARY IS NOT ENERGIZED OR THE TRANSFORMER IS DEFECTIVE.

FAN MOTOR

FILTER

RETURN AIR

KEY TO GAS VALVE TERMINALS

CHECK VOLTAGE AT FAN MOTOR, SHOULD READ 120 V. IF MOTOR DOES NOT OPERATE, CHECK MOTOR

OVERLOAD. IF CLOSED, REPLACE MOTOR. IF NO VOLTAGE, CHECK FOR OPEN FAN CONTROL.

FURNACE

TH 1

TH
TR 2

TR 3

Figure 14-23 24-V gas-fired system, troubleshooting.

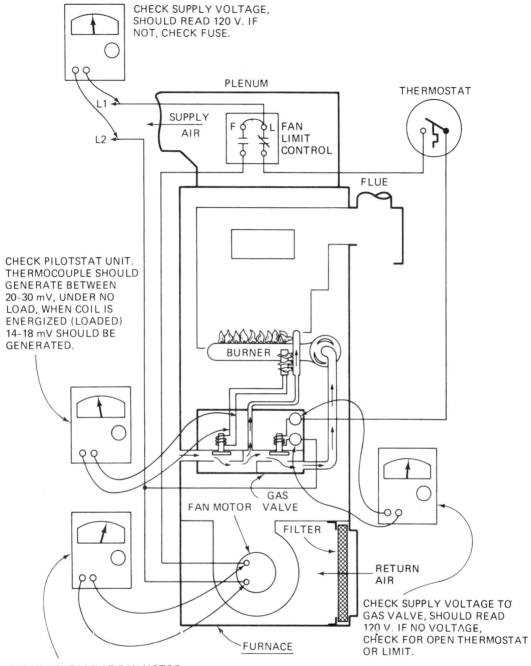

CHECK SUPPLY VOLTAGE, SHOULD READ 120 V. IF NOT, CHECK FUSE.

PLENUM

THERMOSTAT

L1

SUPPLY AIR

F L FAN LIMIT CONTROL

L2

FLUE

CHECK PILOTSTAT UNIT. THERMOCOUPLE SHOULD GENERATE BETWEEN 20–30 mV, UNDER NO LOAD, WHEN COIL IS ENERGIZED (LOADED) 14–18 mV SHOULD BE GENERATED.

BURNER

GAS VALVE

FAN MOTOR

FILTER

RETURN AIR

CHECK SUPPLY VOLTAGE TO GAS VALVE, SHOULD READ 120 V. IF NO VOLTAGE, CHECK FOR OPEN THERMOSTAT OR LIMIT.

FURNACE

CHECK VOLTAGE AT FAN MOTOR, SHOULD READ 120 V. IF MOTOR DOES NOT OPERATE, CHECK MOTOR OVERLOAD. IF CLOSED, REPLACE MOTOR. IF NO VOLTAGE, CHECK FOR OPEN FAN CONTROL.

Figure 14-24 120-V gas-fired system, troubleshooting.

283

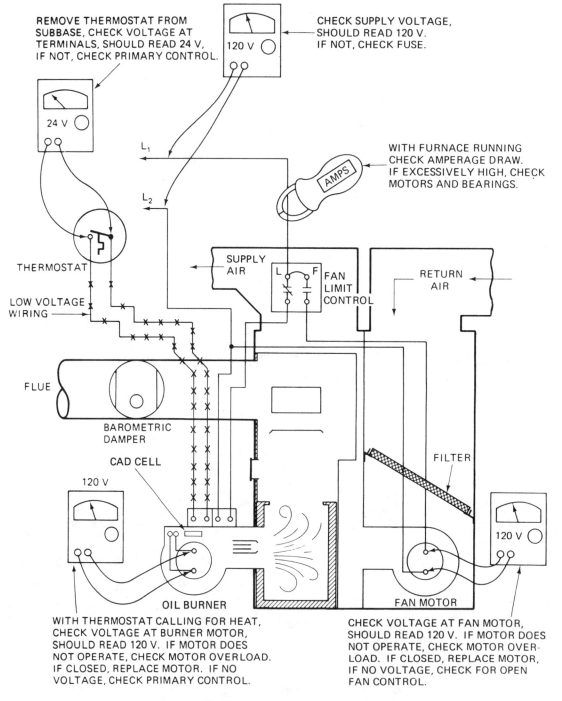

REMOVE THERMOSTAT FROM SUBBASE, CHECK VOLTAGE AT TERMINALS, SHOULD READ 24 V, IF NOT, CHECK PRIMARY CONTROL.

24 V

CHECK SUPPLY VOLTAGE, SHOULD READ 120 V. IF NOT, CHECK FUSE.

120 V

L_1

L_2

WITH FURNACE RUNNING CHECK AMPERAGE DRAW. IF EXCESSIVELY HIGH, CHECK MOTORS AND BEARINGS.

AMPS

THERMOSTAT

LOW VOLTAGE WIRING

SUPPLY AIR

L   F
FAN LIMIT CONTROL

RETURN AIR

FLUE

BAROMETRIC DAMPER

CAD CELL

120 V

FILTER

120 V

OIL BURNER

FAN MOTOR

WITH THERMOSTAT CALLING FOR HEAT, CHECK VOLTAGE AT BURNER MOTOR, SHOULD READ 120 V. IF MOTOR DOES NOT OPERATE, CHECK MOTOR OVERLOAD. IF CLOSED, REPLACE MOTOR. IF NO VOLTAGE, CHECK PRIMARY CONTROL.

CHECK VOLTAGE AT FAN MOTOR, SHOULD READ 120 V. IF MOTOR DOES NOT OPERATE, CHECK MOTOR OVER-LOAD. IF CLOSED, REPLACE MOTOR, IF NO VOLTAGE, CHECK FOR OPEN FAN CONTROL.

Figure 14-25 Oil burner troubleshooting, cad-cell primary safety control.

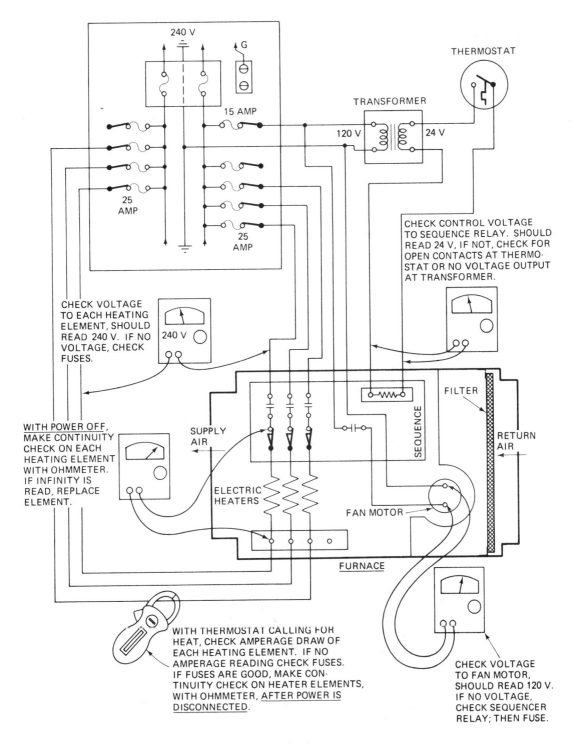

Figure 14-26 Electric heating system, troubleshooting.

Troubleshooting a Unit Electrically

RANGES:
dc VOLTS: 200 mV, 2, 20, 200, 1000 V
ac VOLTS: 200, 750 V
RESISTANCE: 200, 2K, 20K, 200K, 2M, 20 MΩ
dc AMPS: 200 μA, 2 mA, 20 mA, 200 mA, 2 A, 10 A

Figure 14-27 Flame-control tester combining digital multimeter and flame safety kit; includes flame simulator and flame current plug. (Courtesy, Thermal Engineering Co.)

EFFICIENCY AND AIR-BALANCING INSTRUMENTS

Flame-Control Tester

Figure 14-27 shows a flame-control tester, which includes a digital multimeter and a flame safety kit, designed to test all major brands of electronic ignition controls.

Figure 14-28 Combustion analyzer measures oxygen and stack temperature; large digital display programmed for six common fuels. (Courtesy, United Technologies, Bacharach.)

Combustion Analyzer

To determine the combustion efficiency of fuels an analyzer is required. A popular, hand-held model is shown in Figure 14-28. This tester quickly measures oxygen and flue-gas temperatures, then computes efficiency up to 99.9%.

Combustible Gas Detector

The accurate detection of combustible gases is extremely important and can be accomplished with a solid state electronic detector. Figure 14-29 shows a hand-held model capable of detecting leaks as small as 50-1000 parts per million (ppm), with an audible signal. Hydrocarbons, carbon monoxide and refrigerants are among the gases that can be detected.

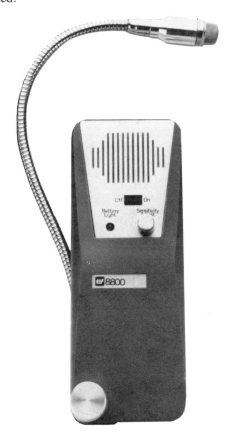

Figure 14-29 Solid-state electronic combustible gas detector; audible "Geiger counter" signal, adjustable sensitivity, continuous duty. (Courtesy, TIF Instruments, Inc.)

Temperature Testers

Temperature readings are often required when performing service work: Two types of temperature testers are shown in Figures 14-30 and 14-31. Both models use remote probes, which can be used to read air or liquid temperatures. Each also reads in either Fahrenheit or Celsius.

RANGES: −20 TO +1350°F
         −30 TO +750°C

Figure 14-30 Temperature tester, thermocouple-type. (Courtesy, Robinair Division, Sealed Power Corporation.)

LCD READOUT, DISPLAYS THREE
DIFFERENT TEMPERATURES
RANGE: −40 TO +1500°F

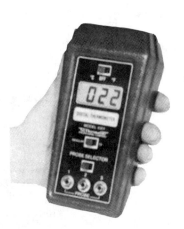

Figure 14-31 Hand-held digital thermometer. (Courtesy, Thermal Engineering Co.)

Air Meters

There are many types of testers used to read and measure air velocity, pressure and volume. Readings possible can include supply or return: grille velocity, duct air velocity, and pressure drops across cooling coils or air filters. It is also possible to measure furnace drafts and exhaust hood face velocities. See Figures 14-32, 14-33, and 14-34.

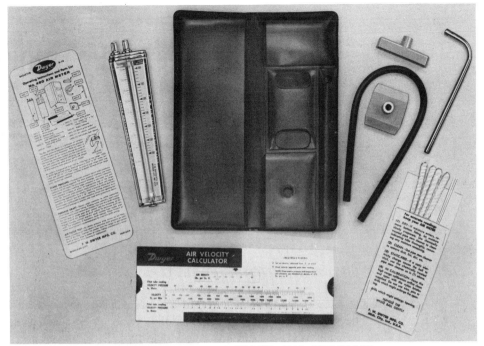

AIR VELOCITY: 260–1200 FT/MIN, 1000–4000 FT/MIN
STATIC PRESSURE: 0.005–0.09 IN., 0.05–1.0 IN. W.C.

Figure 14-32 Air meter kit; direct reading includes meter, probes, air velocity calculator. (Courtesy, Dwyer Instruments, Inc.)

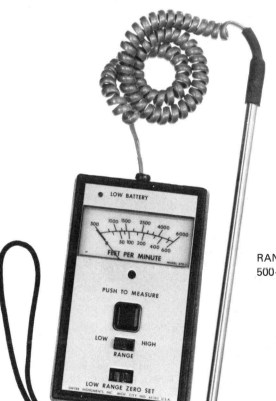

RANGES: 0–600 FT/MIN, 500–6000 FT/MIN.

Figure 14-33 Hand-held thermal anemometer, battery-powered with low-battery indicator. (Courtesy, Dwyer Instruments, Inc.)

MEASUREMENT AREA: 50 TO 500 IN.^{2}
VELOCITY: 170 TO 3000 FT/MIN; VOLUME 70–3000 FT^3/MIN

Figure 14-34 Volume-aire air balancer, reads cubic feet per minute and feet per minute directly. (Courtesy, TIF Instruments, Inc.)

HEAT PUMP SERVICE INSTRUMENTS AND TESTERS

In the servicing of heat pumps, many specialized instruments and equipment items are required. Included in this group are gauge manifolds, vacuum pumps and gauges, refrigerant charging equipment, and refrigerant leak detectors. These are shown in Figures 14-35 through 14-42.

When capacitor-related problems occur, an analyzer similar to the one shown in Figure 14-43 is a great help.

Figure 14-35 Heat pump manifold set: has third gauge for direct pressure check of the switching assembly, one compound gauge, and two high-pressure gauges. (Courtesy, Robinair Division, Sealed Power Corporation.)

Figure 14-36 Four-way, heavy-duty gauge manifold set; optical sight glass allows visual contact with refrigerant as it flows through gauges. (Courtesy, TIF Instruments, Inc.)

Figure 14-37 Vacuum pump, two-stage, rotary vane, direct-drive, high vacuum (20 microns), gas ballast, 115 V 60 Hz. (Courtesy, Robinair Division, Sealed Power Corporation.)

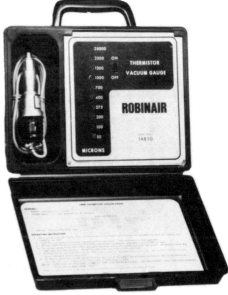

Figure 14-38 Thermistor vacuum gauge, solid-state circuitry, indicates vacuum levels from 25,000 to 50 microns, battery-operated, operating temperature 0°F to +120°F, storage temperature 0°F to +158°F. (Courtesy, Robinair Division, Sealed Power Corporation.)

Heat Pump Service Instruments and Testers

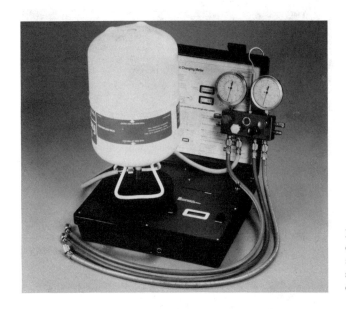

Figure 14-39 Electronic refrigerant charging meter, dispenses refrigerant into system in fractions of an ounce, from standard 30-lb cylinder; easy-to-read LCD display. (Courtesy, TIF Instruments, Inc.)

Figure 14-40 Charging cylinder compensates for volume fluctuations caused by temperature variations. Provides accuracy in recharging. Built-in heating element reduces charging time. Handles R-12, R-22, R-502. (Courtesy, Robinair Division, Sealed Power Corporation.)

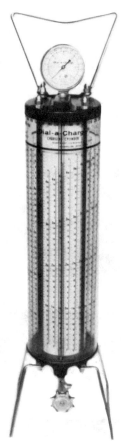

Figure 14-41 Refrigerant leak detector; portable, lightweight, battery-powered, sensor probe extends to 5 ft, detects leaks to ¹/₁₀ oz per year, ear phone. Operating temperature range: +30°F to +120°F. Optional 110-V ac adapter available. (Courtesy, Imperial Eastman.)

Figure 14-42 Refrigerant leak detector. Low-cost substitute for electronic leak detector. Leak is indicated by color of flame. Standard propane cylinder, replacement reactor plate. (Courtesy, Robinair Division, Sealed Power Corporation.)

Figure 14-43 Capacitor analyzer, four ranges of measurement, solid-state circuitry, fused to protect user and instrument, reads AC or DC voltages. (Courtesy, Control Power Systems, Inc.)

CHAPTER 14 STUDY QUESTIONS

The answers to the study questions are found in the sections of this chapter under the chapter topic indicated.

STUDY QUESTIONS	*CHAPTER TOPICS*
1. Explain the functions of the voltmeter, ammeter, ohmmeter, and wattmeter.	*Instrument functions*
2. In purchasing a meter, which scales are important on each of the commonly used meters?	*Selecting the proper instrument*
3. Name three important points in using electrical test instruments.	*Selecting the proper instrument*
4. Describe the types of readings that can be taken with an ohmmeter.	*Using meters*

5. Which meter has its own source of power?

Using meters

6. Which meter is good for testing fuses?

Using meters

7. Which meter requires calibration each time it is used?

Instrument functions

8. How many wires should be placed in the jaws of a clamp-on ammeter?

Selecting the proper instrument

9. When measuring dc millivolts delivered by a thermocouple, which special device is required?

Selecting the proper instrument

10. To eliminate the possibility of error, what precaution should be exercised in measuring a resistance in a parallel circuit?

Selecting the proper instrument

11. What is the formula for calculating watts in a power circuit?

Power calculations

12. If a voltmeter reads zero when placed across a switch when the power is on, what is the condition of the switch?

Selecting the proper instrument

13. In troubleshooting a defective unit, which circuits can be eliminated from the testing procedure?

Testing a complete unit

14. If no part of the unit operates, which instrument should be used for testing?

Selecting the proper instrument

15 External Furnace Wiring

OBJECTIVES

After studying this chapter, the student will be able to:

- Evaluate the external electrical wiring of a forced warm air furnace and troubleshoot where necessary

FIELD WIRING

External furnace wiring usually includes the wiring connections to the power supply and the thermostat (Figures 15-1 and 15-2). These connections are also described as *field wiring*, to distinguish them from the wiring done at the factory by the manufacturer. Field wiring is completed by the installation crew or the electrician on the job.

Where the furnace equipment includes accessories such as a humidifier, electronic air cleaner, or cooling, additional field wiring is required.

Since the performance of the furnace is dependent upon proper field wiring, special attention must be given to this particular part of the installation. Most manufacturers supply detailed instructions for connecting the thermostat and accessories to the furnace. Most field-wiring problems occur because of improper or inadequate connections to the building's power supply.

If cooling is not one of the accessories, most gas and oil furnaces can operate on a 15-A, 120-V single-phase ac branch circuit. Where electric heating or cooling equipment is installed, 240-V single-phase ac power is required. The amperes of service needed depends upon the size of the electric furnace or cooling unit.

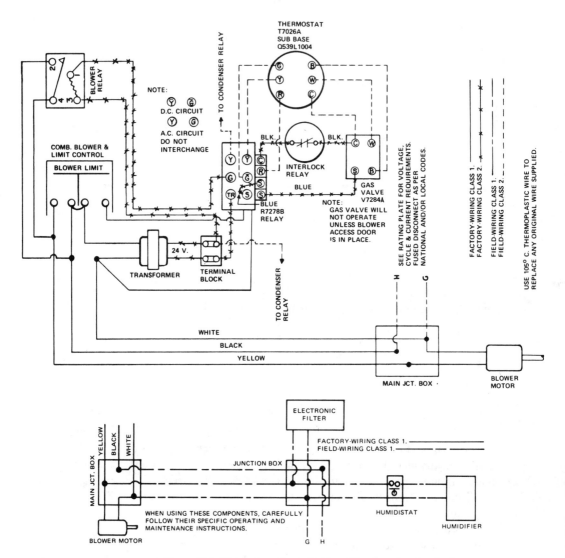

Figure 15-1 External gas furnace wiring. (Courtesy, Luxaire, Inc.)

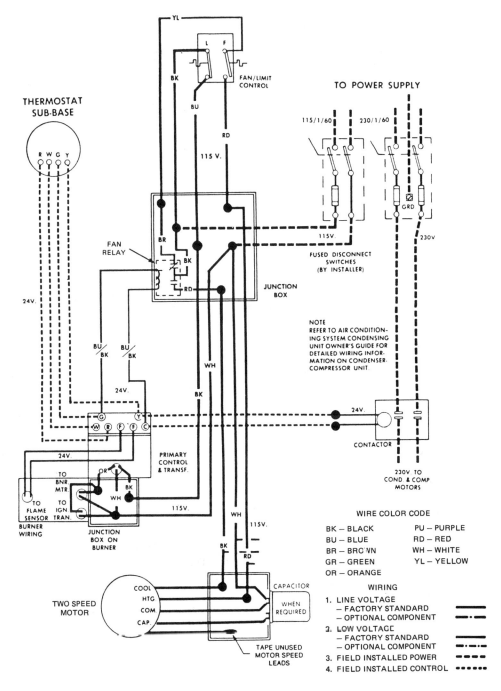

Figure 15-2 External wiring for oil furnace for heating and air-conditioning.

ANALYZING POWER SUPPLY

A building's electrical system must be analyzed to determine whether or not the existing power supply is adequate. If it is found to be inadequate, additional service needs to be installed. A building's electrical system includes the entire wiring of the building starting from the service entrance. The system can be studied from three standpoints:

1. Main power supply

2. Branch circuits

3. Materials and equipment

All wiring must be installed in accordance with the National Electrical Code and any local codes or regulations that apply.

Main Power Supply

The usual source of the main power supply to a building is an entrance cable, consisting of three wires. On newer services one of these wires is black (hot), one is red (hot), and the third is white (neutral). The size of these entrance wires determines the maximum size of the service panel that can be installed.

The entrance cable.   The wires in an entrance cable connect the incoming power lines with the building wiring. The cable is connected through the meter socket to the main service panel, as shown in Figure 15-3. Note that the neutral wire at the main panel is connected to a water pipe or other type of approved ground.

When it is necessary to increase the size or capacity of the service, an additional fuse panel or subpanel can be added to the main service panel. However, this is possible only when the entrance wiring is large enough to permit the extra load.

Building's ampere service.   A building's ampere service is the size or capacity of the power supply available from the main panel for electrical service within the building. The service is usually 60, 100, 150, or 200 A. If a home has an electric range, electric dryer, and central air-conditioning, 150-A service is needed. For homes having electric heating, 200-A service is required. The minimum service for a modern home is 100 A. Many older homes have only 60-A service. The service must always be large enough to supply the needs of the connected loads.

All residential services require a three-wire electric power supply. The size of the wire for various ampere services is as follows:

	Copper Wire	Aluminum & Copper Clad
•	60-A number 6	number 6
•	100-A number 4	number 2
•	150-A number 1	number 0
•	200-A number 2/0	number 3/0

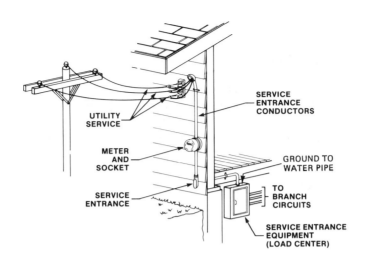

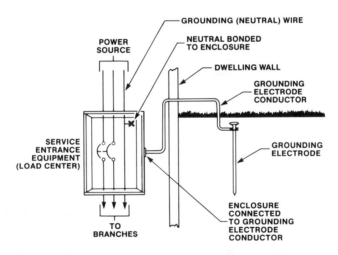

Figure 15-3 Typical service entrance arrangements, including one with neutral ground. (Courtesy, I-T-E Electrical Products.)

Branch Circuits

Branch circuits are the divisions of main power supply that are fused and connected to the loads in a building.

The main power supply is connected to the fuse or circuit breaker box, as shown in

Analyzing Power Supply

Figure 15-4. The two hot lines are fused. The voltage across the two hot lines is usually 208 or 240 V. The neutral line is grounded at the main service panel. The voltage from either of the hot lines to the neutral line is 120 V.

Types of branch circuits.   Branch circuits can be either 208/240 V (Figure 15-5) or 120 V (Figure 15-6). Branch circuits for 208/240 V have fuses in both hot lines. Branch circuits of 120 V have one fuse in the hot line and none in the neutral.

The main fuse box or circuit breaker can have both 208/240-V and 120-V branch circuits. The maximum fuse size on a 120-V branch is 20 A. A 20-A 120-V branch requires No. 12 wire minimum. A 15-A 120-V branch requires No. 14 wire minimum, or as required by local codes.

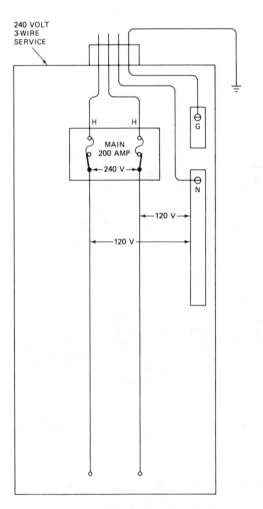

Figure 15-4   Electrical load center. (Courtesy, Bryant Electric.)

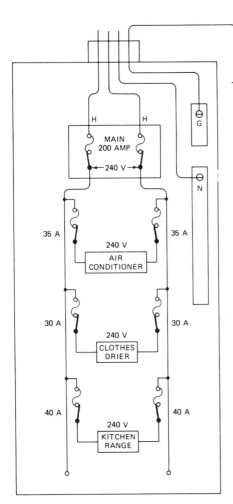

Figure 15-5 Electrical load center providing 240-V service. (Courtesy, Bryant Electric.)

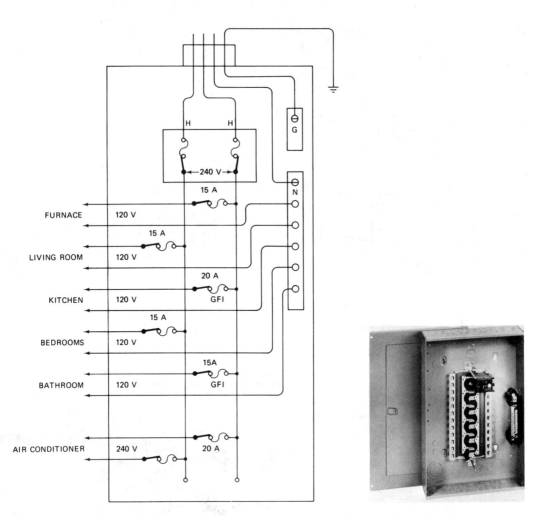

Figure 15-6 General-purpose electrical load center. (Courtesy, Bryant Electric.)

Grounding. The electrical terms grounding, grounded, and ground may be confusing. *Grounding* is the process of connecting to the earth a wire or other conductor from a motor frame or metal enclosure to a water pipe, buried plate, or other conducting material. Grounding is done chiefly for safety, and all mechanical equipment should be *grounded*. Modern three-pronged plugs and receptacles for 120-V circuits have a grounding wire (Figure 15-7).

A *ground* is the common return circuit in electric equipment whose potential is zero. A ground permits the current to get through or around the insulation to normally exposed metal parts that are hot, or "live."

A proper ground protects a user from electrical shock should a short circuit occur.

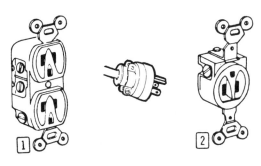

Figure 15-7 120-V three-pronged plug and receptacles. (Courtesy, Sears, Roebuck and Company.)

Low voltage. All load devices are designed to operate at a specified voltage, marked on the equipment. The voltage may be 120, 208, or 240 V. Most electrical equipment will tolerate a variation of voltage from 10% above to 10% below rated (specified) voltage. Thus, a motor rated at 120 V will operate with voltages between 108 and 132 V.

Low or high voltage is usually considered to be any voltage that is not within the tolerated range. Thus, if a 120-V motor is supplied with 100-V power, the voltage would be too low and the motor would probably fail to operate properly.

Low voltage is a much more common problem than high voltage for the reason that all current-carrying wire offers a resistance to flow, which results in a voltage drop. For example, a 50-ft length of No. 14 wire would have a 3½-V drop when carrying 15 A. However, this is not excessive since the resultant voltage is within the 10% allowable limit.

If a circuit is overloaded, the current rises above the rated current-carrying capacity of the wire and the voltage drop can easily exceed the 10% limit established for the load. The low-voltage condition that results from overloaded circuits can cause motors to fail or burn out.

All power supplies should be checked during peak load conditions to determine if proper voltage is being supplied. This should be done at the service entrance, at the furnace disconnect, and at load devices. If there is a problem at the service entrance, the power company should be contacted.

If there is a problem of overloaded circuits in the building, the owner should be notified and an electrician's services secured. If there is a problem in the furnace wiring, a service technician should look for defective wiring and/or check for proper sizes of wires and transformers.

Materials and Equipment

All electrical power devices are important when analyzing a building's electrical system. In addition, certain special equipment is required to complete the external electrical wiring system to the furnace. This equipment includes:

- Main panel
- Fused disconnect

- Power takeoff
- Cable
- Adapter for wire service conversion

Main panel. The existing main electrical panel may be suitable or it may need replacing, depending on power requirements for the equipment being installed. On new installations, the building plans should include adequate main panel service.

There are two types of panels: those with fuses (old style; Figure 15-8), and those with circuit breakers for the individual circuits (Figure 15-9). The circuit breaker type of panel has the advantage of being able to simply reset the breaker rather than having to replace the fuses, making it more convenient to service when an overload occurs. Both types of panels are available with delayed-action tripping to permit loads to draw extra current when starting without shutting down the power supply.

Figure 15-8 Fused service panel. (Courtesy, Sears, Roebuck and Company.)

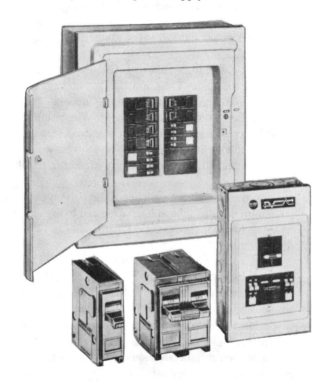

Figure 15-9 Circuit breaker service panel. (Courtesy, Sears, Roebuck and Company.)

Secondary load center. The secondary load center is connected below the service side of the main service breaker. This type has no main circuit breaker and is normally used downstream from the entrance panel. In Figure 15-10 the separate branch circuit breakers are wired in the same manner and serve the same purpose as the branch breakers in the main load center.

Fused disconnect. A fused disconnect is used to disconnect and protect a 120-V ac circuit and is located within a few feet from the unit it serves. It is sometimes called a "service switch" because it permits a convenient means for disconnecting the power to the furnace.

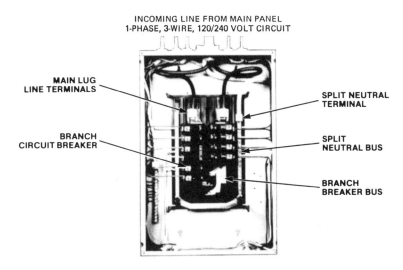

INCOMING LINE FROM MAIN PANEL
1-PHASE, 3-WIRE, 120/240 VOLT CIRCUIT

MAIN LUG
LINE TERMINALS

BRANCH
CIRCUIT BREAKER

SPLIT NEUTRAL
TERMINAL

SPLIT
NEUTRAL BUS

BRANCH
BREAKER BUS

Figure 15-10   Secondary electrical panel. (Courtesy, I-T-E Electrical Products.)

Cable.   Cable is a protective shield that encloses electrical wires. In most areas, all line-voltage wiring must be enclosed in approved-type cable with wire connections made in an approved junction box.

There are four types of cable (Figure 15-11):

1.   Indoor-type plastic-sheathed

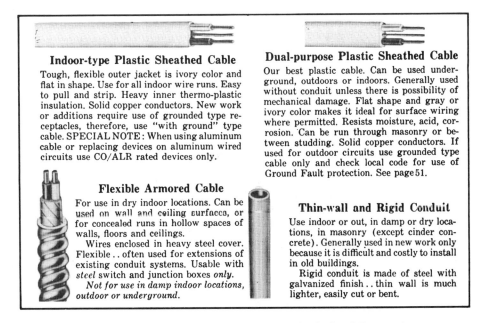

Indoor-type Plastic Sheathed Cable

Tough, flexible outer jacket is ivory color and flat in shape. Use for all indoor wire runs. Easy to pull and strip. Heavy inner thermo-plastic insulation. Solid copper conductors. New work or additions require use of grounded type receptacles, therefore, use "with ground" type cable. SPECIAL NOTE: When using aluminum cable or replacing devices on aluminum wired circuits use CO/ALR rated devices only.

Dual-purpose Plastic Sheathed Cable

Our best plastic cable. Can be used underground, outdoors or indoors. Generally used without conduit unless there is possibility of mechanical damage. Flat shape and gray or ivory color makes it ideal for surface wiring where permitted. Resists moisture, acid, corrosion. Can be run through masonry or between studding. Solid copper conductors. If used for outdoor circuits use grounded type cable only and check local code for use of Ground Fault protection. See page 51.

Flexible Armored Cable

For use in dry indoor locations. Can be used on wall and ceiling surfaces, or for concealed runs in hollow spaces of walls, floors and ceilings.

Wires enclosed in heavy steel cover. Flexible .. often used for extensions of existing conduit systems. Usable with *steel* switch and junction boxes *only.*

Not for use in damp indoor locations, outdoor or underground.

Thin-wall and Rigid Conduit

Use indoor or out, in damp or dry locations, in masonry (except cinder concrete). Generally used in new work only because it is difficult and costly to install in old buildings.

Rigid conduit is made of steel with galvanized finish .. thin wall is much lighter, easily cut or bent.

Figure 15-11   Types of cable. (Courtesy, Sears, Roebuck and Company.)

Analyzing Power Supply

2.　Dual-purpose plastic-sheathed

3.　Flexible armored

4.　Thin-wall and rigid conduit

The dual-purpose type of cable can be used outdoors or indoors without conduit. The method of connecting cable to junction boxes is shown in Figure 15-12 (nonmetallic cable) and Figure 15-13 (thin-wall conduit). Grounding is not required when using conduit.

Adapter.　An adapter converts two-wire service to three-wire, 120-V service. After proper grounding, existing systems which include only two wires may be converted to three-wire systems by use of an adapter arrangement, shown in Figure 15-14.

Ground fault interrupters.　Fuses and circuit breakers protect circuits and wire against overloads and short circuits but not against current leakage. Small amounts of leakage can occur without blowing a fuse or tripping a breaker. Under certain conditions the leakage can be hazardous.

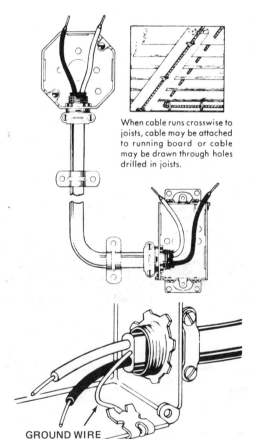

When cable runs crosswise to joists, cable may be attached to running board or cable may be drawn through holes drilled in joists.

GROUND WIRE

Figure 15-12　Nonmetallic cable connectors. (Courtesy, Sears, Roebuck and Company.)

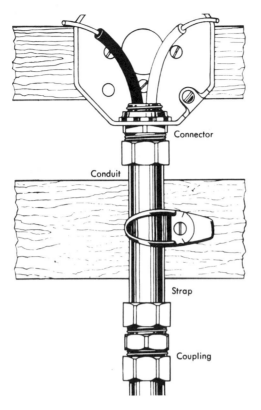

Figure 15-13 Thinwell (metallic) cable connectors. (Courtesy, Sears, Roebuck and Company.)

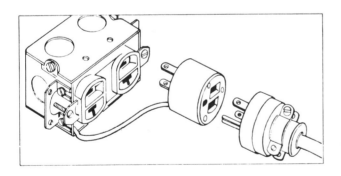

Figure 15-14 Adapter for conversion of two-wire to three-wire system. (Courtesy, Sears, Roebuck and Company.)

A relatively new product adapted for residential use is called the *ground fault circuit interrupter* (GFCI), see Figure 15-15. The GFCI is designed to detect and interrupt the power supply quickly enough to prevent a serious problem. After the problem is corrected the GFCI can be reset and power at that point will be restored.

The National Electrical Code recommends the use of GFCIs on all outdoor circuits. Local codes are especially strong on their use in conjunction with swimming pools that have any electrical connections.

Analyzing Power Supply

1. GROUND FAULT CIRCUIT INTERRUPTER FOR BATHROOMS AND OTHER AREAS, WHERE REQUIRED BY CODE.

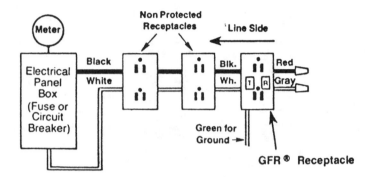

2. TYPICAL WIRING DIAGRAM FOR ADDITION OF GFR RECEPTACLE.

3. GFR FOR OUTDOOR USE, WEATHERPROOF, 20 AMP, DUPLEX RECEPTACLE.

4. BREAKER TYPE GFR, ONLY FITS SPECIFIC PANEL.

Figure 15-15 Ground fault circuit interrupters. (Courtesy, Bryant Electric.)

CHAPTER 15 STUDY QUESTIONS

The answers to the study questions are found in the sections of this chapter under the chapter topic indicated.

STUDY QUESTIONS	CHAPTER TOPIC
1. What field wiring is usually low voltage?	*Field wiring*

2. What is the usual color coding for the three entrance wires?   *Main power supply*

3. What is the service amperage for most gas furnaces?   *Field wiring*

4. What service amperage is required for residential electric heating?   *Building's amperage service*

5. How many fuses are required for a 240-V branch circuit?   *Types of branch circuits*

6. What is the range of voltage that can be used on a 120-V motor?   *Low voltage*

7. Name one circuit that requires a ground fault interrupter.   *Ground fault interrupters*

8. When should the power supply be checked for low-voltage conditions?   *Low voltage*

9. What is the connection to the main panel called when an additional fuse panel is added?   *The entrance cable*

10. What action should be taken if the voltage is too low coming to the residence?   *Low voltage*

11. How should an adapter be grounded?   *Adapter*

16 Controls Common to All Forced-Air Furnaces

OBJECTIVES

After studying this chapter, the student will be able to:

- Identify the common types of electrical control devices used on forced warm air furnaces

- Evaluate the performance of common types of controls in the system

FUNCTIONS OF CONTROLS

The function of automatic controls is to operate a system or unit in response to some variable condition. Automatic controls are used to turn the various electrical components (load devices) on and off. These devices operate in response to a controller that senses the room temperature or humidity, thereby activating the equipment to maintain the desired conditions.

Load devices that make up a heating unit are

- Fuel-burning device or heater

- Fan

- Humidifier

- Electrostatic air cleaner

- Cooling equipment

Each one of these load devices has some type of switch or switches that automatically or manually causes the device to operate. The automatic switches respond to variable conditions from a *sensor*. A sensor is a device that reacts to a change in conditions and is then capable of transmitting a response to one or more switching devices. For example, a thermostat senses the need for heat and switches on the heating unit. When the thermostat senses that enough heat has been supplied, it switches off the heating unit.

COMPONENTS OF CONTROL SYSTEMS

Five elements comprise the control system for a forced warm air heating unit:

1. Power supply
2. Controllers
3. Limit controls
4. Primary controls
5. Accessory controls

Power supply. The power supply furnishes the necessary current, at the proper voltage, to operate the various control devices. The fused disconnect and the transformer are parts of the power supply.

Controllers. Controllers sense the condition being regulated and perform the necessary switching action on the proper load device. The controller group includes such devices as the thermostat, the humidistat, and the fan control.

Limit controls. Limit controls shut off the firing device or heater when the maximum safe operating temperature is reached.

Primary controls. The gas valve, the flame detector relay for an oil burner, and the sequencer for electric furnaces are types of primary controls. A primary control usually includes some type of safety device. For example, on an oil furnace primary control, the burner will be shut off if a flame is not produced or goes out.

Accessory controls. Used to add special features to the control system. One of these is the fan relay, which permits the fan switch on a 24-V thermostat to operate a 120-V fan.

THERMOSTATS

Thermostats control the source of heat to closely maintain the selected temperature in the space being conditioned. A heating system should provide even (consistent) temperatures for the comfort of a building's occupants. It is said that people can sense a change of approximately 1½°F in temperature. A well-regulated system will provide less than 1°F variation.

A sensing element is usually bimetallic. Thus, the element is composed of two different metals; one is usually copper and the other Invar, bonded together. When heated, copper has a more rapid expansion rate than Invar. When the bimetal is heated, it changes shape. In a heating thermostat, this movement is mechanically connected to a switch that closes on a drop in temperature and opens on a rise in temperature (Figure 16-1).

Bimetallic elements are constructed in various shapes (Figure 16-2). A spiral-wound bimetallic element (Figure 16-3), is compact in construction. For this reason, it is the element used in many thermostats.

Switching action should take place rapidly to prevent arcing, which causes damage to the switch contacts. A magnet is used to provide rapid action. However, the most common type of switching action in use is the mercury tube arrangement (Figure 16-4). The electrical contacts of the switch are inside the tube together with a globule of mercury. The electrical contacts are located at one end of the tube. When the tube is tipped in one direction, the mercury makes an electrical connection between the contacts and the switch is closed. When the tube is tipped in the opposite direction, the mercury goes to the other end of the tube and the switch is opened.

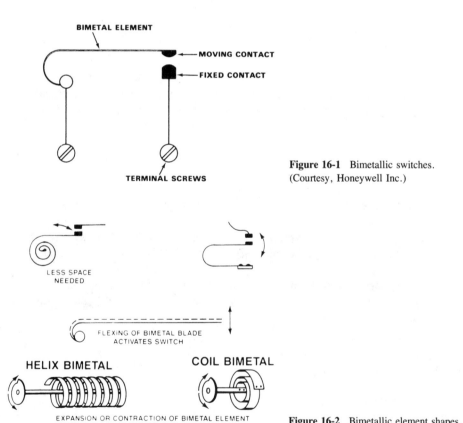

Figure 16-1 Bimetallic switches. (Courtesy, Honeywell Inc.)

Figure 16-2 Bimetallic element shapes. (Courtesy, Honeywell Inc.)

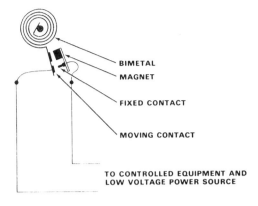

Figure 16-3 Spiral wound bimetallic element. (Courtesy, Honeywell Inc.)

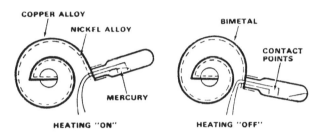

Figure 16-4 Mercury tube switching action. (Courtesy, Honeywell Inc.)

Electronic Temperature Sensing

Thermistors use various materials whose resistance lowers when the temperature rises and rises when their temperature lowers. Electronic sensing devices have no moving parts; as the temperature changes their resistance changes. An electronic device (thermostat) converts these changes in resistance into a control signal that turns burners, compressors, on and off. In Figure 16-5, different styles of thermistors and their symbol are shown.

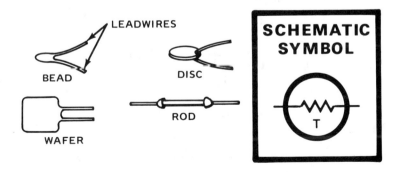

Figure 16-5 Typical thermistors and their schematic symbol. (Courtesy, Honeywell, Inc.)

Thermostats

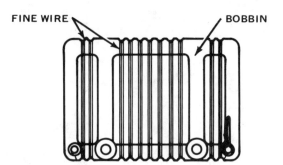

FINE WIRE   BOBBIN

Figure 16-6 A resistance bulb. (Courtesy, Honeywell Inc.)

Figure 16-6 shows another type of electronic temperature sensing device called a resistance bulb, which is a coil of fine wire wound around a bobbin.* The resistance of the wire increases as the temperature rises and decreases as the temperature falls, opposite that of a thermistor.

Types of Current

Most residential thermostats are of the low-voltage type (24 V). Low-voltage wires are easier to install between the thermostat and the heating unit. The construction of a low-voltage thermostat provides greater sensitivity to changing temperature conditions than does a line-voltage (120-V) thermostat. The materials can be of lighter construction and easier to move, with less chance for arcing.

Some self-generating systems (Figure 16-7) use a millivolt (usually 750-mV) power supply to operate the thermostat circuit. These thermostats are very similar in construction to low-voltage thermostats.

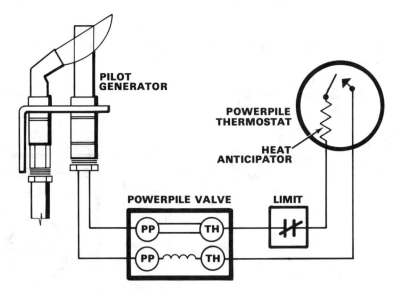

Figure 16-7 Powerpile self-powered system. (Courtesy, Honeywell Inc.)

* A bobbin is a small round device, or cylinder.

Purpose

Some thermostats are designed for heating only or for cooling only. Other thermostats are designed for a combination of both heating and cooling, (Figure 16-8). With the mercury tube design, a set of contacts is located at one end of the tube for heating and the other end for cooling. The cooling contacts make on a rise in temperature and break on a drop in temperature. The tube with both sets of contacts is attached to a single bimetallic element.

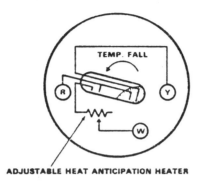

ADJUSTABLE HEAT ANTICIPATION HEATER

Figure 16-8 Diagram of the contacts in the mercury bulb. (Courtesy, Honeywell Inc.)

Anticipators

There is a lag (time delay) between the call for heat by the thermostat and the amount of time it takes for heat to reach a specific area. The differential of the thermostat plus the heat lag of the system could cause a wide variation in room temperature.

There is always a differential (difference) between the temperature at which the thermostat makes and the temperature at which it breaks (opens). For example, the thermostat may call for heat when the temperature falls to 70°F and shut the furnace off when the temperature rises to 72°F.

To provide closer control of room temperature, a heat *anticipator* is built into the thermostat (Figure 16-9). A heat anticipator consists of a resistance heater placed in series with the thermostat contacts. On a call for heat, current is supplied to the heater. This action heats the bimetallic element, causing it to respond somewhat ahead of the actual rise in room temperature. By supplying part of the heat with the anticipator, a lesser amount of room heat is required to meet the room thermostat setting. Thus, the furnace shuts off before the actual room temperature reaches the cutout point on the thermostat. Although the furnace continues to supply heat for a short period after the unit shuts off, the actual room temperature does not exceed the setting of the thermostat because the anticipator assists in producing even heating and prevents wide temperature variations.

The heat anticipator is adjustable and should be set at the amperage indicated on the primary control. Small variations from the required setting can be made by the service technician to improve performance on individual jobs.

Decreasing the setting of the anticipator increases the resistance of the anticipator, thus shortening the period that the furnace remains on (shortens the heating cycle). For even heating, the furnace should cycle 8 to 10 times per hour.

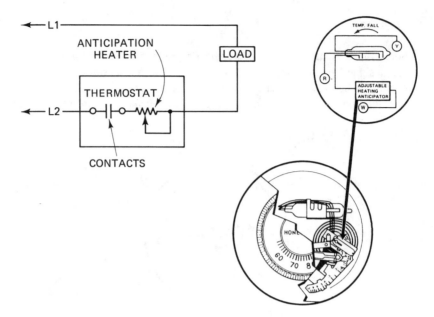

Figure 16-9 Series heat anticipator. (Courtesy, Honeywell Inc.)

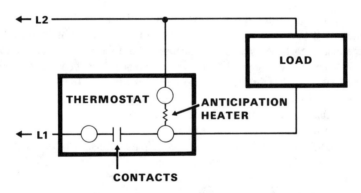

Figure 16-10 Parallel cooling anticipator. (Courtesy, Honeywell Inc.)

Anticipators are also supplied for thermostats that control cooling. A cooling anticipator (Figure 16-10) is placed in parallel with the thermostat contacts. Thus, heat is supplied to the bimetal on the off cycle (when cooling is off) and serves to decrease the length of the shutdown period.

Subbases

Most thermostats have some type of subbase, which serves as a mounting plate (Figure 16-11). A subbase provides a means for leveling and fastening a thermostat to the wall, and contains electrical connections and manual switches. Manual switches offer a home-

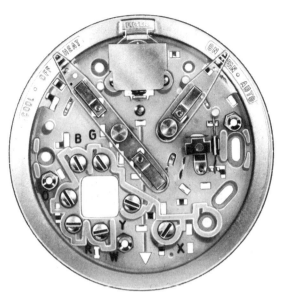

Figure 16-11 Thermostat subbase.
(Courtesy, Honeywell Inc.)

owner the choice of "heat-off-cool" and fan "auto-on." Switches on a subbase increase the number of functions that can be performed by a thermostat.

Although a thermostat has only a sensing element and one or two automatic switches, with the addition of subbase manual switches it offers a choice of many switching actions. The possible switching actions for the subbase shown in Figure 16-11 are described next.

Position 1.　One manual switch in heat position, the other in fan auto position. Heat source operates on a call for heat. Fan is operated by the fan controller.

Position 2.　One manual switch in heat position, the other in fan on position. Heat source operates on a call for heat. Fan runs continuously.

Position 3.　One manual switch in cool position, the other in fan auto position. Cooling equipment and fan operate on a call for cooling.

Position 4.　One manual switch in cool position, the other in fan on position. Cooling equipment operates on a call for cooling. Fan runs continuously.

As shown in Figure 16-12, the following switching actions can be clearly observed.

Position 1.　R and W make to call for heat.

Position 2.　R and W make to call for heat. R and G make from the manual switch to operate the fan continuously.

Position 3.　R and Y make to call for cooling. At the same time, R and G make to operate the fan.

Position 4.　R and Y make to call for cooling. R and G make from the manual switch to operate the fan continuously.

Wiring diagrams often show only the terminals of the thermostat and none of the internal circuiting.

Thermostats

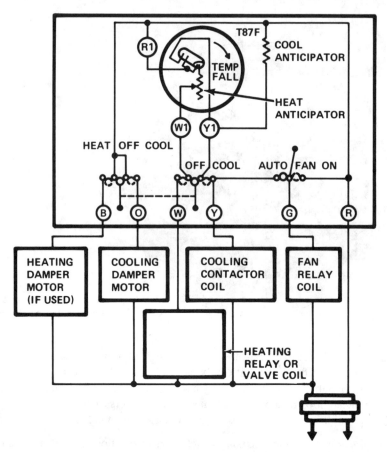

Figure 16-12 Diagram of the switching action that takes place in the thermostat subbase shown in Figure 16-11. (Courtesy, Honeywell Inc.)

Application and Installation

The following are some recommended procedures in the application and installation of thermostats.

- Select the thermostat that best meets the customers' needs.
- Select the thermostat designed for the specific type of application: heat only, heat-cool, heat pump, and so on.
- Select the location.
- Mount the thermostat approximately 5 ft above the floor.
- Select the anticipator setting that matches the equipment.
- Select proper location for outdoor sensor, if used.
- Seal up any openings in the wall under the mounting plate to eliminate infiltration.

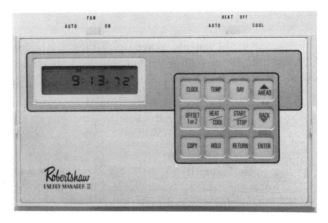

Figure 16-13 Seven-day programmable thermostat with digital display of temperature and time settings. (Courtesy, Robertshaw Controls Company.)

Programmable

The programmable thermostat is a solid-state microcomputer control with 7-day programming. This thermostat is designed with a full range of temperature setback-setup-offset capability. A battery is used to maintain the program and time during periods of power interruption. In Figure 16-13, there is a built-in cooling time delay to protect the compressor from damage due to short cycling.

The capability of setback-setup maximizes energy savings during unoccupied periods and during the night hours. The thermostat and control module shown in Figure 16-14 contains optional features that perform several functions:

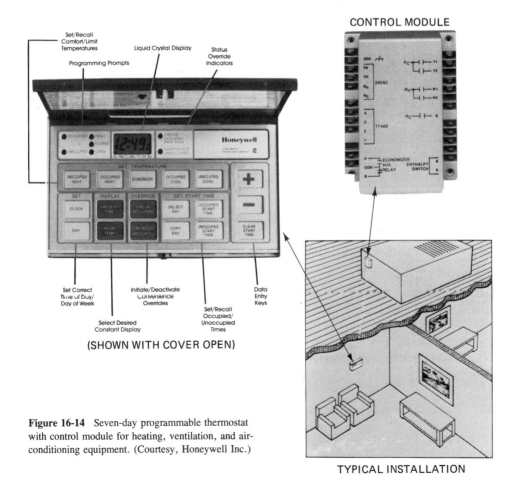

Figure 16-14 Seven-day programmable thermostat with control module for heating, ventilation, and air-conditioning equipment. (Courtesy, Honeywell Inc.)

1. **Controls Start-Up Times:** Automatically varies the daily start-up time depending on building load. If outdoor air is suitable temperature-wise, the building can be precooled.

2. **Controls Damper and Fan Operation:** Closing outdoor air dampers and allowing fan operation only on a call for heating or cooling during unoccupied periods.

In Figure 16-15, the energy savings for many cities are shown using four conditions of night setback. **Note:** Savings may vary some due to differences in equipment, insulation, and personal lifestyle.

% OF HEATING/COOLING ENERGY YOU COULD SAVE (BASED ON THE AVERAGE HOME)

	A	B	C	D		A	B	C	D		A	B	C	D
Albuquerque, NM	12%	24%	10%	16%	Detroit, MI	11%	21%	13%	22%	Omaha, NB	11%	20%	12%	19%
Atlanta, GA	15%	27%	12%	19%	Dodge City, KS	12%	23%	9%	15%	Philadelphia, PA	11%	24%	13%	20%
Atlantic City, NJ	12%	23%	13%	20%	Greensboro, NC	14%	25%	12%	19%	Phoenix, AZ	16%	30%	7%	11%
Billings, MT	10%	20%	9%	16%	Houston, TX	16%	30%	9%	14%	Pitsburgh, PA	11%	22%	13%	20%
Birmingham, AL	15%	28%	12%	17%	Indianapolis, IN	11%	22%	12%	19%	Portland, ME	10%	19%	15%	21%
Boise, ID	11%	22%	8%	15%	Jackson, MS	16%	30%	11%	17%	Portland, OR	13%	24%	11%	20%
Boston, MA	11%	22%	13%	20%	Jacksonville, FL	17%	30%	11%	17%	Providence, RI	11%	21%	16%	24%
Buffalo, NY	10%	20%	14%	22%	Kansas City, MO	12%	23%	10%	16%	Roanoke, VA	12%	24%	12%	19%
Burlington, VT	9%	18%	14%	22%	Las Vegas, NV	15%	27%	7%	11%	Salt Lake City, UT	11%	21%	10%	16%
Charleston, SC	16%	29%	13%	19%	Little Rock, AR	15%	27%	10%	16%	San Diego, CA	16%	30%	25%	33%
Cheyenne, WY	10%	19%	12%	17%	Los Angeles, CA	15%	30%	20%	27%	San Francisco, CA	14%	26%	14%	19%
Chicago, IL	11%	21%	13%	20%	Louisville, KY	13%	24%	11%	18%	Seattle, WA	12%	24%	16%	23%
Cincinnati, OH	12%	24%	12%	19%	Madison, WI	10%	19%	13%	19%	Sioux Falls, SD	10%	19%	11%	18%
Cleveland, OH	10%	21%	13%	21%	Memphis, TN	15%	26%	11%	17%	Spokane, WA	11%	20%	10%	18%
Colorado Springs, CO	11%	22%	11%	16%	Miami, FL	18%	30%	11%	17%	Springfield, MA	11%	20%	13%	20%
Columbus, OH	11%	22%	12%	19%	Milwaukee, WI	10%	19%	13%	19%	St. Louis, MO	12%	23%	11%	18%
Corpus Christi, TX	17%	30%	10%	15%	Minneapolis, MN	9%	18%	12%	20%	Syracuse, NY	11%	20%	13%	21%
Dallas, TX	15%	28%	9%	14%	New Orleans, LA	16%	30%	11%	17%	Washington, DC	13%	25%	13%	20%
Denver, CO	11%	22%	10%	17%	New York, NY	12%	23%	13%	20%	Wilmington, DE	12%	23%	13%	20%
Des Moines, IA	11%	20%	12%	19%	Oklahoma City, OK	14%	26%	11%	16%	©Copyright Honeywell, Inc.				

A	10°*	B	10°*	C	5°	D	5°

SINGLE	DOUBLE	SINGLE	DOUBLE
HEATING	HEATING	COOLING	COOLING
SETBACK	SETBACK	SETUP	SETUP
(70° to 60°	(70° to 60°	(75° to 80°	(75° to 80°
8 hours/day)	8 hours	11 hours/day)	9 hours/day,
	twice/day)		7 hours/night)

*Savings for a 5° heating setback are at least ½ of savings for a 10° setback.

Figure 16-15 Energy savings based on use of programmable thermostats. (Courtesy, Honeywell Inc.)

A *humidistat* (Figure 16-16) is a sensing control that measures the amount of humidity in the air and provides switching action for the humidifier. The sensing element is either human hair or nylon ribbon. These materials expand when moist and contract when dry. This movement is used to operate the switching mechanism.

The sensing element for the humidistat can be located either in the return air duct or in the space being conditioned (Figure 16-17). The humidistat is wired in such a way that humidity is added only when the fan is operating.

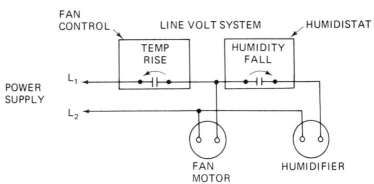

Figure 16-16 Humidistat. (Courtesy, Honeywell Inc.)

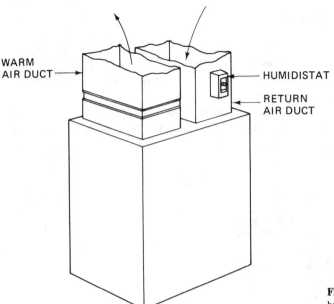

WARM
AIR DUCT

HUMIDISTAT

RETURN
AIR DUCT

Figure 16-17 Duct installation of humidistat.

FAN AND LIMIT CONTROLS

Fan (blower) and limit controls have separate functions in the heating system. However, they are discussed together since both can use the same sensing element and are, therefore, often combined into a single control.

The insertion element (sensor) can be made in a number of forms (Figure 16-18). Some are bimetallic and some are hydraulic. The hydraulic element is filled with liquid which expands when heated, moving a diaphragm connected to a switch.

The sensing element for these controls is inserted in the warm air plenum of the furnace. It must be located in the moving air stream, where it can quickly sense the warm air temperature rise.

Sensing elements are made in different lengths to fit various applications. When replacing equipment, the original insertion length should always be duplicated.

BIMETALIC
BLADE ELEMENT

BIMETALIC
FLAT SPIRAL ELEMENT

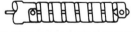

BIMETALIC HELIX ELEMENT

LOOPED TUBE ELEMENT

Figure 16-18 Types of insertion elements (sensors). (Courtesy, Honeywell Inc.)

Controls Common to All Forced-Air Furnaces   Chap. 16

Fan Controls

A fan control (Figure 16-19) senses the air temperature in the furnace plenum and, to prevent discomfort, turns on the fan when the air is sufficiently heated. There are two general types of fan controls:

- Temperature-sensing
- Timed fan start

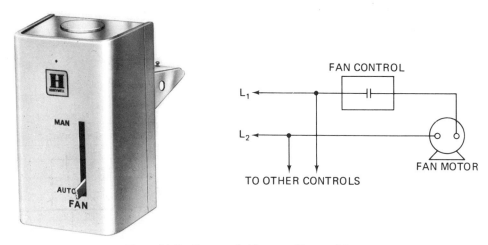

Figure 16-19 Fan control. (Courtesy, Honeywell Inc.)

Temperature-sensing. These controls depend on the gravity heating action of the furnace to move air across the sensing element. When the air temperature reaches the fan on temperature (usually about 110°F), the fan starts. When the thermostat is no longer calling for heat, the fan continues to run to move the remaining heat out of the furnace. The fan stops at the fan off temperature setting of the fan control (usually about 90°F). Most fan controls are adjustable so that changes in fan operation can be made to fit individual requirements. The fan control circuit is usually line voltage (120 V). The fan control switch is placed in series with the power to the fan motor. Some fan controls have a fixed differential. The fan on temperature can be set but the differential (fan on minus fan off temperature) is set at the factory. The fixed differential is normally 20 to 25°F.

Timed fan start. This control (Figure 16-20) is used in a downflow or horizontal furnace where gravity air movement over the heat exchanger cannot be depended upon to warm the sensing element. This control has a low-voltage (24-V) resistance heater, which is energized when the thermostat calls for heat. The fan starts approximately 60 s after the heat is turned on. Usually, the fan is turned off by a conventional temperature-sensing fan control. It is important that the manufacturer's instructions be followed for setting the heat anticipator in the thermostat.

Fan and Limit Controls

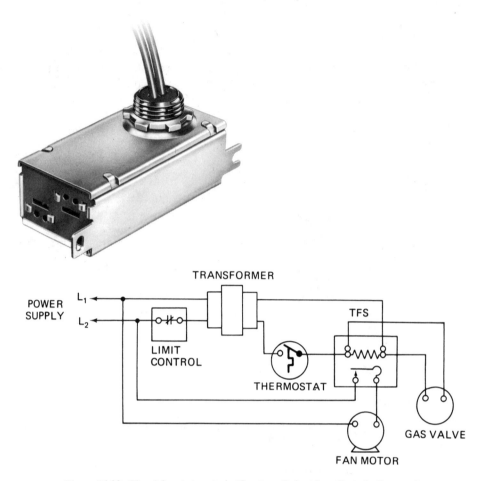

Figure 16-20 Timed fan start control. (Courtesy, Robertshaw Controls Company)

Limit Controls

The *limit control* is a safety device that shuts off the source of heat when the maximum safe operating temperature is reached (Figure 16-21). Like the fan control, it senses furnace plenum temperature or air temperature at the outlet. Warm air furnace limit controls are usually set to cut out at 200°F and automatically cut in at 175°F.

On a gas furnace the line-voltage limit control is placed in series with the transformer. On an oil furnace the line-voltage limit control is placed in series with the primary control. On an electric furnace, the limit controls are placed in series with the heating elements.

On a horizontal or downflow furnace, a secondary limit control is required (Figure 16-22). This control is located above the heating element and is usually set to cut out the source of heat when the sensing temperature reaches 145°F.

Where two limit controls are used, they are usually wired in series with each other. Thus, either limit control can turn off the source of heat.

Some secondary limit controls have a manual reset (not automatic). Some have an arrangement for switching on the fan when the limit contacts are opened.

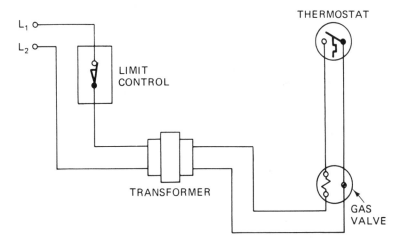

Figure 16-21 Limit control.

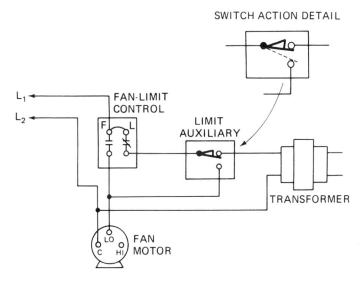

Figure 16-22 Secondary limit control.

Combinations

Since the fan and limit controls both use the same type of sensing element, they are often combined into one control (Figure 16-23).

This is helpful when both the fan and limit controls are of line-voltage type, since this simplifies the wiring. However, the fan and limit controls each have separate switches and separate terminals. The fan control can be wired for line voltage and the limit control for low voltage, if desired.

Fan and Limit Controls

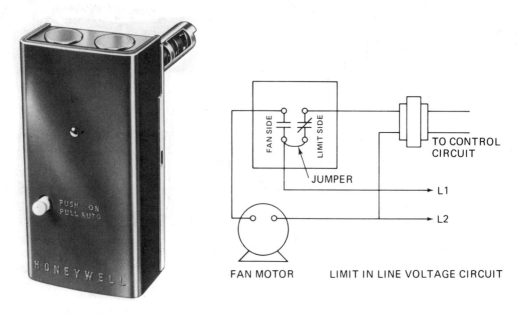

FAN SIDE

LIMIT SIDE

JUMPER

TO CONTROL CIRCUIT

L1

L2

FAN MOTOR   LIMIT IN LINE VOLTAGE CIRCUIT

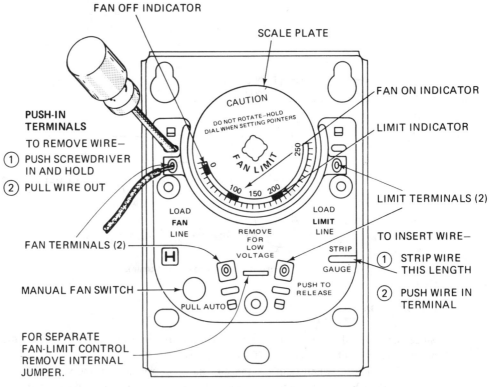

FAN OFF INDICATOR

SCALE PLATE

FAN ON INDICATOR

LIMIT INDICATOR

**PUSH-IN
TERMINALS**

TO REMOVE WIRE—

① PUSH SCREWDRIVER IN AND HOLD

② PULL WIRE OUT

CAUTION

DO NOT ROTATE—HOLD DIAL WHEN SETTING POINTERS

FAN LIMIT

0   100 150 200 250

LOAD
FAN
LINE

LOAD
LIMIT
LINE

LIMIT TERMINALS (2)

TO INSERT WIRE—

① STRIP WIRE THIS LENGTH

② PUSH WIRE IN TERMINAL

FAN TERMINALS (2)

REMOVE
FOR
LOW
VOLTAGE

STRIP

GAUGE

MANUAL FAN SWITCH

H

PUSH TO
RELEASE

PULL AUTO

FOR SEPARATE
FAN-LIMIT CONTROL
REMOVE INTERNAL
JUMPER.

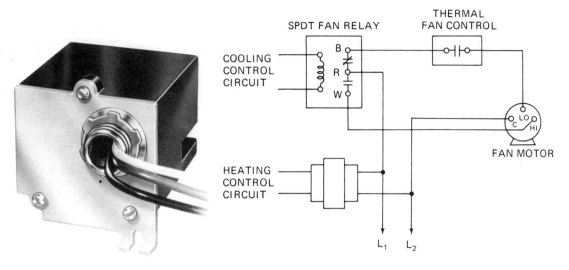

Figure 16-24 Two-speed fan control. (Courtesy, Honeywell Inc.)

Two-Speed Fan Controls

Two fan speeds can be obtained by adding a fan relay to a standard control system (Figure 16-24). The fan is usually operated at low speed on heating and high speed for ventilation or air-conditioning. The relay has a low-voltage coil in series with the G terminal on the thermostat. When the thermostat calls for cooling, the switch in the relay opens and an N.O. switch closes. This switches the fan from low to high speed.

CHAPTER 16 STUDY QUESTIONS

STUDY QUESTIONS	CHAPTER TOPICS
1. Describe the function of an automatic control system.	*Functions of controls*
2. Give a series of examples of load devices.	*Functions of controls*
3. Which basic element of the control system includes the sensor?	*Functions of controls*
4. Name and describe the five elements of a control system.	*Functions of controls*
5. What is the smallest temperature difference that most people can sense?	*Thermostats*
6. Describe the various types of sensing elements.	*Thermostats*
7. What metals are used in constructing bimetal sensors?	*Thermostats*

8. What is the rating of the low-voltage circuit used on thermostat circuits?

Thermostats

9. What is the largest number of switches usually found in a single mercury tube element?

Thermostats

10. What voltage is used in a self-generating system?

Types of current

11. How is the differential of a thermostat determined?

Anticipators

12. How many times an hour should a furnace cycle?

Anticipators

13. Why are the terminals on a thermostat identified by color code?

Thermostats

14. Describe an electronic temperature timing device.

Electronic temperature sensing

15. What are the additional features in a programmable thermostat?

Programmable

16. What type of sensing element does a humidistat have?

Humidistats

17. Why are fan and limit controls both placed on the same electrical device?

Fan and limit controls

18. Where is a timed fan-start switch used?

Timed fan start

19. How does a two-speed fan control operate?

Two-speed fan control

20. Where is the heat anticipator located and how is it adjusted?

Anticipators

17 Gas Furnace Controls

OBJECTIVES

After studying this chapter, the student will be able to:

- Identify the various electrical controls and circuits on a gas-fired furnace

- Determine the sequence of operation of the controls

- Service and troubleshoot the gas heating unit control system

USE OF GAS FURNACE CONTROLS

Broadly speaking, gas furnace controls are the electrical and mechanical equipment that manually or automatically operates the unit.

The controls used depend upon

1. Type of fuel or energy

2. Type of furnace

3. Optional accessories

The controls differ for gas, oil, or electric heat sources. They differ somewhat for the upflow and downflow units. They also become more complex as accessories such as humidifiers, electrostatic filters, and cooling are added.

Control circuits for a gas warm air heating unit are

1. Power supply circuit

2. Fan circuits

3. Pilot circuit

4. Fuel-burning or heater circuit

5. Accessory circuits

Both line-voltage and low-voltage circuits are required for some components. For example, a relay used to start a fan motor may have a low-voltage coil but the switch that starts the fan motor operates on line voltage.

Schematic diagrams are used in the study of circuits. Following is the key to the legends used on schematics described in this chapter.

CAP	Capacitor
CC	Compressor contactor
EAC	Electrostatic air cleaner
EP	Electric pilot
FC	Fan control
FM	Fan motor
FD	Fused disconnect
FR	Fan relay
G	Terminal
GV	Gas valve
H	Humidistat
HS	Humidification system
HU	Humidifier
L	Limit
LA	Limit auxiliary
$L_1 L_2$	Power supply
N	Neutral
NC	Normally closed
NO	Normally open

PPC	Pilot power control
SPDT	Single-pole double-throw
SPST	Single-pole single-throw
TFS	Timed fan start
THR	Thermocouple
TR	Transformer
W	Heating terminal
Y	Cooling terminal

Power Supply

The power supply circuit (Figure 17-1) usually consists of a 15-A source of 120-V ac power, a fused disconnect (FD) in the hot line, and a transformer (TR) to supply 24-V ac power to the low-voltage controls.

A single source of power is adequate unless a cooling accessory is added, in which case a separate source of 208/240-V ac power is required. Power for cooling requires DPDT disconnect with fuses in each "hot" line. Possibly an additional low-voltage transformer would be required, if the one used for heating does not have sufficient capacity.

Fan

The line-voltage circuit for a single-speed fan consists of a fan control (FC) in series with the fan motor (FM) connected across the power supply (Figure 17-2).

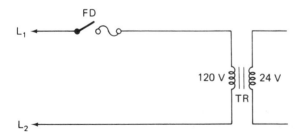

Figure 17-1 Power supply circuit with fused disconnection (FD) and transformer (TR).

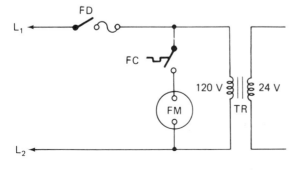

Figure 17-2 Fan circuit with fan control (FC) and fan motor (FM).

Many heating units have multiple-speed fans. The low speed is used for heating, while the high speed is used for cooling or ventilation.

The operation of the fan with a two-speed motor requires two circuits (Figure 17-3). There is a line voltage circuit to power the fan motor, and a low-voltage circuit to operate the switching circuit.

Under normal operation on heating, the fan motor (FM) is controlled by the fan control (FC). When operating the fan on high speed, the fan switch on the subbase of the thermostat can be moved to the "on" position. This action closes contact between R and G in the thermostat. Current flows through the coil of the cooling fan relay (FR), opening the NC switch and closing the NO switch operating the fan motor on high speed.

On a downflow or horizontal unit, the fan motor can be operated by a timed fan relay (TFS) (Figure 17-4). On these units, with the fan not running and the sensing element of the fan control located in the air outlet, the standard fan control cannot be used to start the fan.

On a call for heating, R and W make in the thermostat. The heater of the timed fan start (TFS) is energized. After about 45 s, the fan motor is operated by the TFS switch.

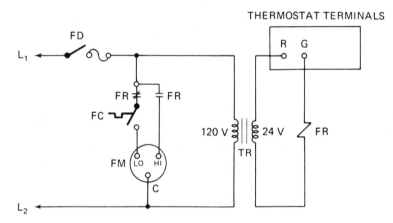

Figure 17-3 Two-speed fan motor with cooling fan relay (FR).

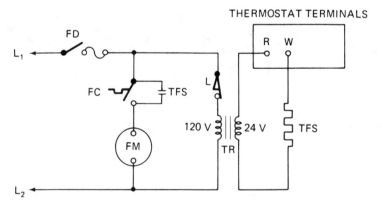

Figure 17-4 Fan control for downflow furnace using timed fan starts (TFS).

Gas Furnace Controls   Chap. 17

When the thermostat is satisfied and R and W break, the fan motor continues to operate until the leaving air temperature reaches the cut-out temperature setting of the fan control (FC).

Pilot

The gas safety circuit is powered by a thermocouple (Figure 17-5). When a satisfactory pilot is established the thermocouple generates approximately 30 MV to energize the safety control portion of the combination gas valve. Thus, the gas cannot enter the burner until a satisfactory pilot is established.

Most wiring diagrams omit the pilot circuit, since it is common to all combination gas systems and need not be repeated in each diagram.

Gas Valve

The gas valve circuit is in a low-voltage circuit (Figure 17-6). When the thermostat calls for heat, R and W make, energizing the gas valve because the limit control is normally closed.

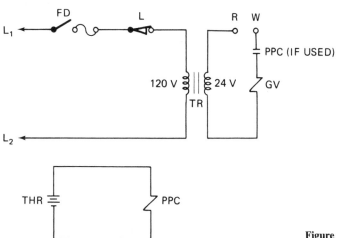

PILOT CIRCUIT WITH 30 MV THERMOCOUPLE (THR)
AND PILOT POWER UNIT (PPC)

Figure 17-5 Pilot circuit with 30-mV thermocouple (THR) and pilot power control (PPC).

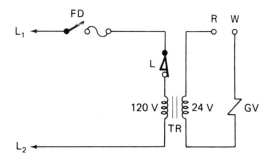

Figure 17-6 Gas valve (GV) circuit with limit control (L).

Circuits

Should excessive temperatures occur (usually 200°F in the plenum), the limit control opens the circuit to deenergize and close the gas valve. The limit control automatically restarts the burner when its cut-in temperature (usually 175°F) is reached.

On a downflow or horizontal furnace, a limit auxiliary (LA) control is used (Figure 17-7). The LA control is located in a position to sense gravity heat from the heating elements. If the fan fails to start, the LA control will sense excess heat (usually set to cut out at 145°F).

Limit controls are usually line voltage and placed in series with the transformer (Figure 17-8). Some line-voltage limit controls have a separate set of contacts that make when the limit breaks turning on the fan if, for any reason, it is not running.

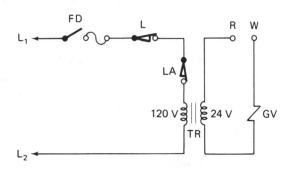

Figure 17-7 Gas valve (GV) circuit for downflow or horizontal furnace with limit control (L) and secondary limit (LA) in series with transformer.

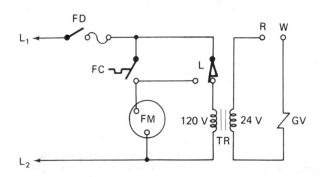

Figure 17-8 Single-pole double-throw (SPDT) limit control with set of contacts to operate fan on limit action.

Accessories

Figure 17-9 shows the schematic of accessory circuits. The humidistat (H) and humidifier (HU) are wired in series and connected to power only when the fan is running. The electrostatic air filter also operates only when the fan is running. These accessories are supplied with line-voltage power.

The cooling contactor (CC) is in series with the Y connection on the thermostat. When R and Y make, the cooling contactor coil is energized, operating the cooling unit.

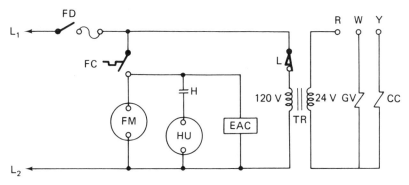

Figure 17-9 Accessory circuits.

TYPICAL WIRING DIAGRAMS

The foregoing schematic wiring diagrams illustrate the control circuits found on many heating furnaces. A schematic aids a service technician in understanding how the control system operates. However, many manufacturers supply only connection wiring diagrams for their equipment. Therefore, it may be necessary for a technician to construct a schematic in order to separate the circuits for testing and for diagnosing service problems.

Unfortunately, few standards exist that require manufacturers to conform in making connection wiring diagrams. However, if service technicians know the most common controls and their functions, with practice, they can interpret almost any diagram. In some instances when a diagram is not available, a technician can also prepare one to suit the equipment found on the job.

The following is a review of some typical connection diagrams supplied by various manufacturers for their equipment.

Upflow

The controls in an upflow gas furnace (Figure 17-10) include

- Thermostat
- Gas valve
- Combination fan and limit control
- Multispeed fan motor with run capacitor
- Transformer
- Fan relay

IF ANY OF THE ORIGINAL WIRE AS SUPPLIED WITH THE FURNACE
MUST BE REPLACED, IT MUST BE REPLACED WITH WIRING MATERIAL
HAVING A TEMPERATURE RATING OF AT LEAST 105°C.

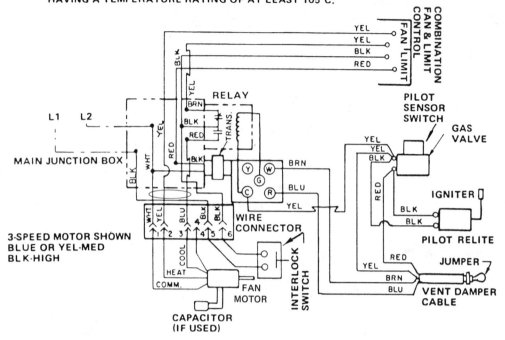

FACTORY WIRING ——————————

FIELD WIRING CLASS 1 —— · —— - —— - —— - - ——

Figure 17-10 Connection wiring diagram for upflow gas furnace. (Courtesy, Borg Warner Central Environmental Systems, Inc.)

Figure 17-11 Schematic diagram for upflow gas furnace in Figure 17-10. (Courtesy, Borg Warner Central Environmental Systems, Inc.)

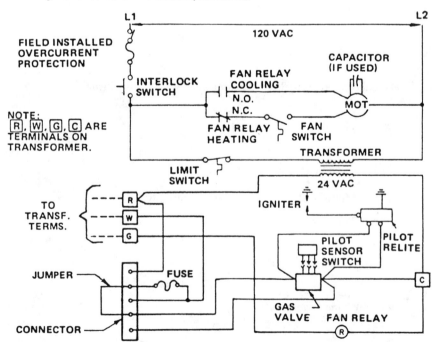

This system has been prepared for the addition of air conditioning so cooling can be added with very little modification of the control system. A schematic diagram for this unit can be constructed as shown in Figure 17-11.

Downflow

The controls in a downflow gas furnace (Figure 17-12) include

- Thermostat
- Gas valve
- Combination fan and limit control

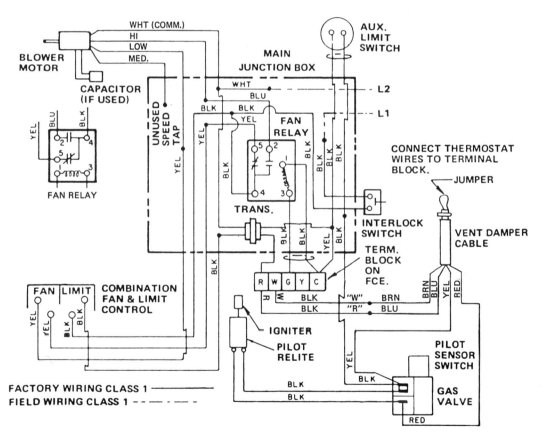

Figure 17-12 Connection wiring diagram for downflow gas furnace. (Courtesy, Borg Warner Central Environmental Systems, Inc.)

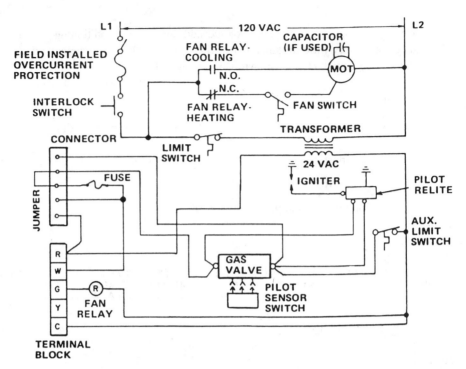

Figure 17-13 Schematic diagram for downflow gas furnace shown in Figure 17-12. (Courtesy, Borg Warner Central Environmental Systems, Inc.)

Controls in a Downflow Gas Furnace (continued)

- Auxiliary limit

- Fan motor with run capacitor

- Transformer

Note that Figures 17-12 and 17-13 do not show a timed fan start, which is common to many downflow (counterflow) units. On certain units, the fan control is located in such a position that it senses gravity heat from the heating elements, thus eliminating the need for a timed fan start.

Horizontal

A connection drawing for a horizontal gas furnace with cooling accessory (Figure 17-14) includes:

- Thermostat

- Gas valve

- Combination fan and limit control

- Auxiliary limit

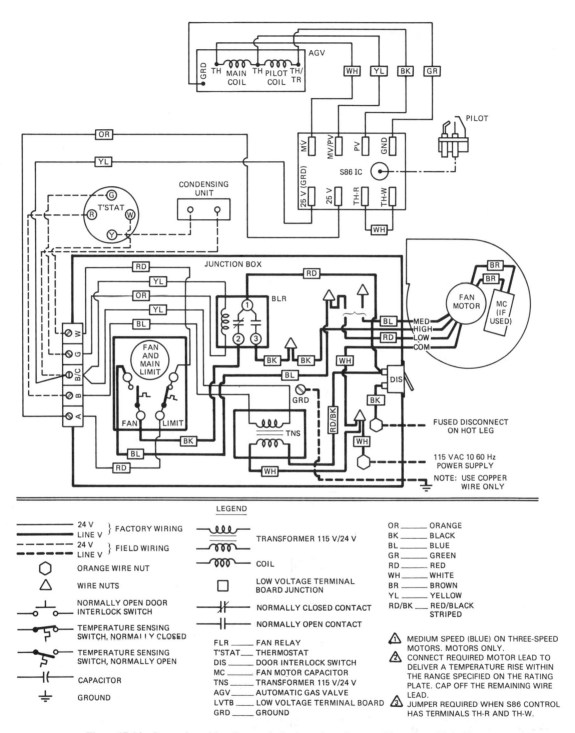

Figure 17-14 Connection wiring diagram for horizontal gas furnace with cooling added. (Courtesy, Borg Warner Central Environmental Systems, Inc.)

Typical Wiring Diagrams

- Fan motor

- Transformer

A schematic diagram for this unit can be constructed as shown in Figure 17-15.

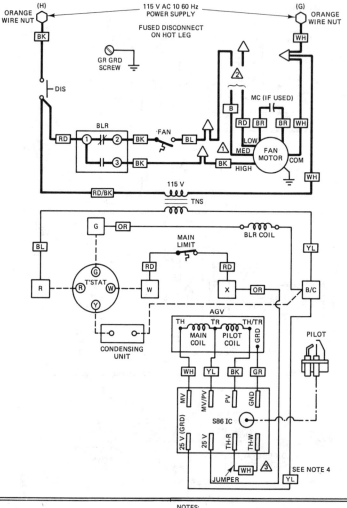

Figure 17-15 Schematic wiring diagram for horizontal gas furnace with cooling added. (Courtesy, Borg Warner Central Environmental Systems, Inc.)

⚠1 MEDIUM SPEED (BLUE) ON THREE-SPEED MOTORS. MOTORS ONLY.

⚠2 CONNECT REQUIRED MOTOR LEAD TO DELIVER A TEMPERATURE RISE WITHIN THE RANGE SPECIFIED ON THE RATING PLATE. CAP OFF THE REMAINING WIRE LEAD.

⚠3 JUMPER REQUIRED WHEN S86 CONTROL HAS TERMINALS TH-R AND TH-W.

━━━━━ FACTORY HIGH-VOLTAGE WIRING

───── FACTORY LOW-VOLTAGE WIRING

━ ━ ━ FIELD HIGH-VOLTAGE WIRING

NOTES:

(1) JUMPER FROM R TO G_H – REMOVED WHEN SPECIAL THERMOSTAT SUBBASE IS USED.

(2) ⊘ – SCREW TERMINALS FOR FIELD WIRING CONNECTIONS.

(3) ▭ – $\frac{1}{4}$-IN. QUICK CONNECT TERMINALS.

(4) ●∦● – HEATING FAN RELAY CONTACT IS
2A   NORMALLY CLOSED UNTIL 115 V AC IS APPLIED TO FURNACE.

(5) TO CHANGE MOTOR SPEED, MOVE BLK OR RED WIRE TO DESIRED SPEED SETTING.

(6) IF ANY OF THE ORIGINAL WIRE AS SUPPLIED WITH THE APPLIANCE MUST BE REPLACED, IT MUST BE REPLACED WITH AWM(105°C) WIRE OR ITS EQUIVALENT.

(7) MOTOR IS THERMALLY OVERLOAD PROTECTED.

(8) FACTORY SPEED SELECTION IS FOR AVERAGE CONDITIONS, SEE INSTALLATION INSTRUCTIONS FOR OPTIMUM SPEED SELECTION. MOTOR MAY BE 3 OR 4 SPEED.

(9) SYMBOLS ARE AN ELECTRICAL REPRESENTATION ONLY.

One special feature of this control system is that the purchaser has the option of installing electronic air cleaner controls and equipment. The connection diagram, Figure 17-16, shows the proper locations to connect the wiring for the electronic air cleaner.

Figure 17-16 Wiring diagram for upflow gas furnace with printed circuit control center. (Courtesy, Bryant Air Conditioning/Heating.)

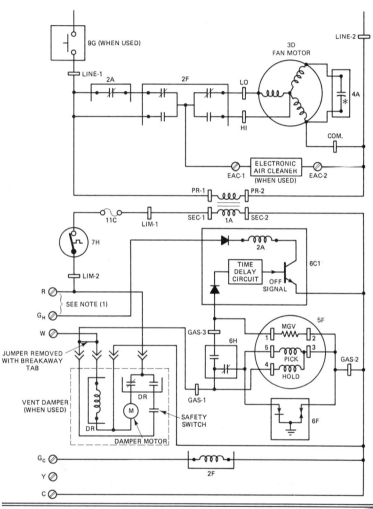

1A – TRANSFORMER 115/24
2A – RELAY - HEAT (SPST-NC)
2F – RELAY - COOL (DPDT)
3D – FAN MOTOR
4A – RUN CAPACITOR
5F – GAS VALVE
6C1 – PRINTED CIRCUIT BOARD
6F – PILOT IGNITER
6H – SAFETY PILOT (FLAME SENSING)
7H – LIMIT SWITCH (SPST-NC)
9G – FAN DOOR SWITCH (SPST-N.O.)
11C – FUSIBLE LINK
11E – GROUND LUG

━━━━━ FACTORY HIGH-VOLTAGE WIRING
───── FACTORY LOW-VOLTAGE WIRING
━ ━ ━ ━ FIELD HIGH-VOLTAGE WIRING

NOTES:
(1) JUMPER FROM R TO G_H – REMOVED WHEN SPECIAL THERMOSTAT SUBBASE IS USED.
(2) ⊘ – SCREW TERMINALS FOR FIELD WIRING CONNECTIONS.
(3) ▭ – $\frac{1}{4}$-IN. QUICK CONNECT TERMINALS.
(4) |•╫•| – HEATING FAN RELAY CONTACT IS
    2A   NORMALLY CLOSED UNTIL 115-V AC IS APPLIED TO FURNACE.
(5) TO CHANGE MOTOR SPEED, MOVE BLK OR RED WIRE TO DESIRED SPEED SETTING.
(6) IF ANY OF THE ORIGINAL WIRE AS SUPPLIED WITH THE APPLIANCE MUST BE REPLACED, IT MUST BE REPLACED WITH AWM(105°C) WIRE OR ITS EQUIVALENT.
(7) MOTOR IS THERMALLY OVERLOAD PROTECTED.
(8) FACTORY SPEED SELECTION IS FOR AVERAGE CONDITIONS, SEE INSTALLATION INSTRUCTIONS FOR OPTIMUM SPEED SELECTION. MOTOR MAY BE 3 OR 4 SPEED.
(9) SYMBOLS ARE AN ELECTRICAL REPRESENTATION ONLY.

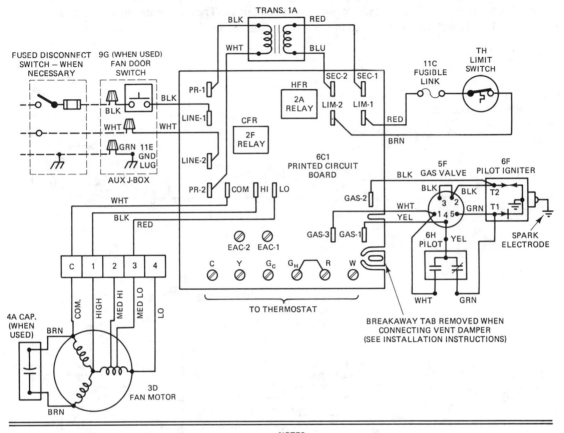

1A — TRANSFORMER 115/24
2A — RELAY - HEAT (SPST-NC)
2F — RELAY - COOL (DPDT)
3D — FAN MOTOR
4A — RUN CAPACITOR
5F — GAS VALVE
6C1 — PRINTED CIRCUIT BOARD
6F — PILOT IGNITER
6H — SAFETY PILOT (FLAME SENSING)
7H — LIMIT SWITCH (SPST-NC)
9G — FAN DOOR SWITCH (SPST-N.O.)
11C — FUSIBLE LINK
11E — GROUND LUG

━━━━━ FACTORY HIGH-VOLTAGE WIRING
───── FACTORY LOW-VOLTAGE WIRING
▬ ▬ ▬ ▬ FIELD HIGH-VOLTAGE WIRING

NOTES:
(1) JUMPER FROM R TO G_H – REMOVED WHEN SPECIAL THERMOSTAT SUBBASE IS USED.
(2) ⊘ – SCREW TERMINALS FOR FIELD WIRING CONNECTIONS.
(3) ▭ – $\frac{1}{4}$-IN. QUICK CONNECT TERMINALS.
(4) ●|┤┝●| – HEATING FAN RELAY CONTACT IS
    2A   NORMALLY CLOSED UNTIL 115 V AC IS APPLIED TO FURNACE.
(5) TO CHANGE MOTOR SPEED, MOVE BLK OR RED WIRE TO DESIRED SPEED SETTING.
(6) IF ANY OF THE ORIGINAL WIRE AS SUPPLIED WITH THE APPLIANCE MUST BE REPLACED, IT MUST BE REPLACED WITH AWM(105°C) WIRE OR ITS EQUIVALENT.
(7) MOTOR IS THERMALLY OVERLOAD PROTECTED.
(8) FACTORY SPEED SELECTION IS FOR AVERAGE CONDITIONS, SEE INSTALLATION INSTRUCTIONS FOR OPTIMUM SPEED SELECTION. MOTOR MAY BE 3 OR 4 SPEED.
(9) SYMBOLS ARE AN ELECTRICAL REPRESENTATION ONLY.

Figure 17-17 Connection diagram for upflow gas furnace with printed circuit control center. (Courtesy, Bryant Air Conditioning/Heating.)

The connection diagram shown in Figure 17-17 displays the wiring connections to the printed circuit board. Note the vent damper breakaway tab provided for installation of a vent damper. The printed circuit board is designed for ease of service in the field.

TESTING AND SERVICE

When performing service on a furnace, every effort is made to pinpoint the problem to a specific part or circuit. This avoids extra work in checking over the complete control system to find the problem. For example, if all parts of a furnace operate properly except the fan, the fan circuit can be tested separately to locate the malfunction.

In electrical troubleshooting, it is good practice to "start from power", that is, to start testing where power comes into the unit and continue testing in the problem area until power is either no longer being supplied, or with power available, the load does not operate. When reaching either point, the difficulty is located. For example, referring to Figure 17-11, if the complaint is that the fan will not run on high speed, the step-by-step troubleshooting procedure would be as follows:

1. Check power supply at load side of fused disconnect.

2. Jumper thermostat terminals R and G to determine if the relay will "pull in."

3. If the relay operates satisfactorily, check power supply at high-speed terminals of fan

4. If power is available at fan, and it still will not run, motor is defective

Use of Test Meters

Figure 17-18 shows five locations where a test meter can be used on a 24-V gas heating control system. These meters check out the following circuits:

- Power
- Fan
- Pilot
- Gas valve
- Transformer

No accessories are shown. However, if these circuits exist on equipment being serviced, meter readings can be taken at these parts in addition to the ones shown.

Component Testing and Troubleshooting

In troubleshooting, each component (or circuit) has the potential for certain problems that the service technician can check for or test. Some of these potential problems are as follows:

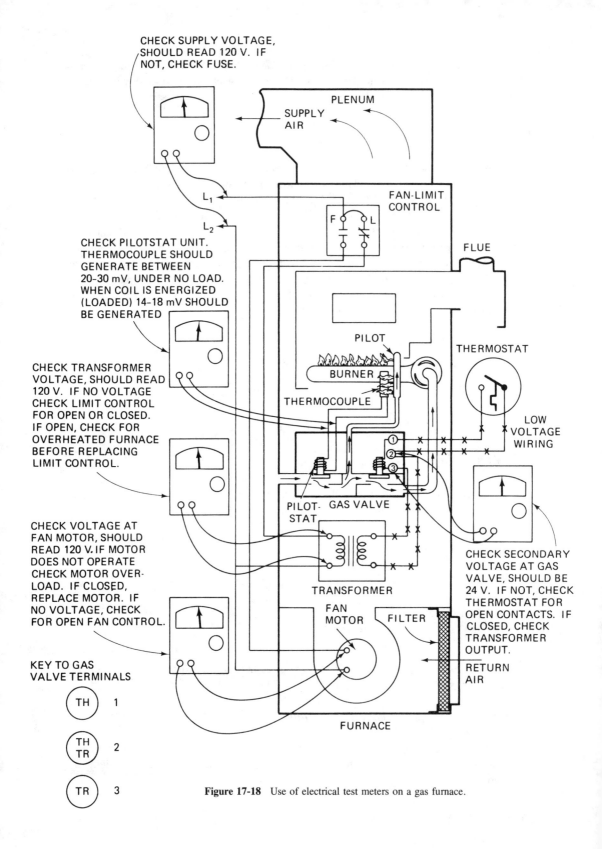

CHECK SUPPLY VOLTAGE, SHOULD READ 120 V. IF NOT, CHECK FUSE.

PLENUM

SUPPLY AIR

FAN-LIMIT CONTROL

L_1

L_2

F L

FLUE

CHECK PILOTSTAT UNIT. THERMOCOUPLE SHOULD GENERATE BETWEEN 20-30 mV, UNDER NO LOAD. WHEN COIL IS ENERGIZED (LOADED) 14-18 mV SHOULD BE GENERATED

PILOT

THERMOSTAT

BURNER

CHECK TRANSFORMER VOLTAGE, SHOULD READ 120 V. IF NO VOLTAGE CHECK LIMIT CONTROL FOR OPEN OR CLOSED. IF OPEN, CHECK FOR OVERHEATED FURNACE BEFORE REPLACING LIMIT CONTROL.

THERMOCOUPLE

LOW VOLTAGE WIRING

PILOT- GAS VALVE STAT

CHECK VOLTAGE AT FAN MOTOR, SHOULD READ 120 V. IF MOTOR DOES NOT OPERATE CHECK MOTOR OVERLOAD. IF CLOSED, REPLACE MOTOR. IF NO VOLTAGE, CHECK FOR OPEN FAN CONTROL.

TRANSFORMER

CHECK SECONDARY VOLTAGE AT GAS VALVE, SHOULD BE 24 V. IF NOT, CHECK THERMOSTAT FOR OPEN CONTACTS. IF CLOSED, CHECK TRANSFORMER OUTPUT.

FAN MOTOR

FILTER

RETURN AIR

KEY TO GAS VALVE TERMINALS

FURNACE

TH 1

TH TR 2

TR 3

Figure 17-18 Use of electrical test meters on a gas furnace.

1. *Power supply*
   (a) Switch open
   (b) Blown fuse or tripped breaker
   (c) Low voltages

2. *Thermostat*
   (a) Subbase switch turned off
   (b) Set too low
   (c) Loose connection
   (d) Improper anticipator setting

3. *Pilot*
   (a) Plugged orifice on pilot
   (b) Pilot blowing out due to draft
   (c) Too little or too much gas being supplied to pilot

4. *Thermocouple*
   (a) Loose connection
   (b) Too close or too far from flame
   (c) Defective thermocouple

5. *Transformer*
   (a) Low primary voltage
   (b) Defective transformer
   (c) Blown fuse in 24-V circuit

6. *Limit control*
   (a) Switch open
   (b) Loose connection
   (c) Defective control

7. *Gas valve*
   (a) Defective pilot safety power unit
   (b) Defective main gas valve

8. *Fan control*
   (a) Switch open
   (b) Improper setting
   (c) Defective control

Thermocouple Circuit

Millivoltmeter probes can be connected in the thermocouple circuit, as shown in Figure 17-19, using the special adapter. If the meter reading is less than 17 mV, there is insufficient power to operate the pilot safety power unit. This must be corrected by either improving the flame impingement on the thermocouple or by replacing the thermocouple.

Figure 17-19 Testing a thermocouple circuit.

Figure 17-20 Jumper across a control switch.

Adjusting the Anticipator Circuit on a Thermostat

Normally, the anticipator is set at the amperage shown on the gas valve. However, if this information is not available, the current flow in the gas valve circuit can be measured.

Testing a Control Switch

Fan-limit and other switches can be tested by placing a jumper across the switch contacts, as shown in Figure 17-20.

Gas Furnace Controls   Chap. 17

BURNER IGNITION

There are three types of gas burner ignition systems:

1. Pilot ignition system (intermittent)
2. Direct-spark ignition system
3. Silicon carbide ignition system

Pilot Ignition

The pilot ignition system (intermittent) is designed for low-voltage application on all types of residential gas-fired heating equipment.

Principle of operation. The thermostat powers the control to open the pilot burner gas valve and provide the ignition spark simultaneously. As soon as the pilot flame is established, the spark ceases and the main burner gas valve is energized. Should the flame not be established within a predetermined period, the system provides safety shutdown. (Sparking stops and pilot gas flow is interrupted.)

Electronic flame-sensing circuitry in the ignitor detects the presence or absence of the pilot burner flame. If the flame is not established during the trial-for-ignition period, the system closes the pilot gas valve and locks out. If the burner flame is extinguished during the duty cycle, the main gas valve will close and the ignitor will retry ignition before going into lockout.

Proper location of the electrode assembly is important for optimum system performance. It is recommended that there be approximately a $\frac{1}{8}$-in. gap between the electrodes and the pilot, as shown in Figure 17-21. This figure also shows the typical retrofit wiring for a pilot ignition system.

Figure 17-21 Typical retrofit wiring of an electronic ignition control. (Courtesy, Robertshaw Controls Company.)

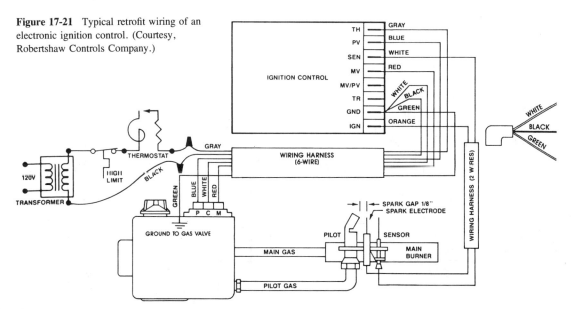

In Figure 17-22 the ignition system is used in a heat-cool application. This type of installation can be used with a two-stage gas valve.

Direct Spark Ignition

Direct spark ignition (DSI) does away with the pilot altogether and lights the main burner with an electric spark. Operation of the burner depends on continuous detection of the main burner flame by an electronic flame-sensing system.

Unlike the intermittent pilot ignition, DSI is required to light a significantly larger gas flow. Safety demands that ignition and flame detection occur in a few seconds.

Principle of operation. If the main burner lights, a circuit is completed from the flame sensor through the flame to the burner head and ground. This current flow proves the presence of the main burner flame and resets the lockout timer and at the same time interrupts the spark ignition circuit. The gas valve remains open as long as there is a call for heat and as long as the module continues to detect the presence of the main flame. Should the current flow be interrupted (flame-out), trial for ignition begins again.

If the safety lockout timing period ends before the main burner lights or before the flame sensor establishes enough current, the control module will go into safety lockout. When the module goes into safety lockout, power to the pulse generator is interrupted, the gas control circuit is interrupted, and the alarm circuit relay (if the module is so equipped) is energized. The module will stay locked out until it is reset by turning the thermostat down below room temperature for 30 s. Applying a DSI system is a complex engineering task best accomplished by the equipment manufacturer. So field-retrofitting the DSI controls is not a practical procedure. There are, however, times when components of DSI systems need replacing. Parts are available for this kind of job.

Ignition control units are installed with vent dampers. When a vent damper is in the system, the thermostat wire is connected to one side of the *end switch* circuit. The end

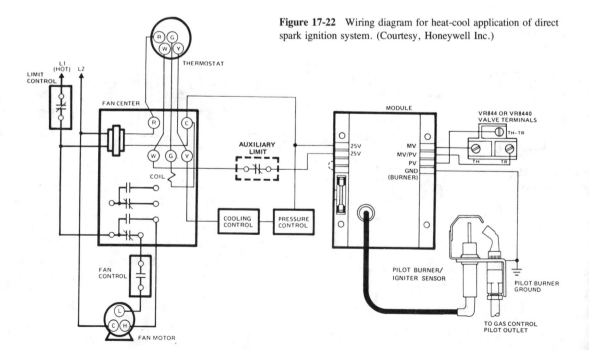

Figure 17-22 Wiring diagram for heat-cool application of direct spark ignition system. (Courtesy, Honeywell Inc.)

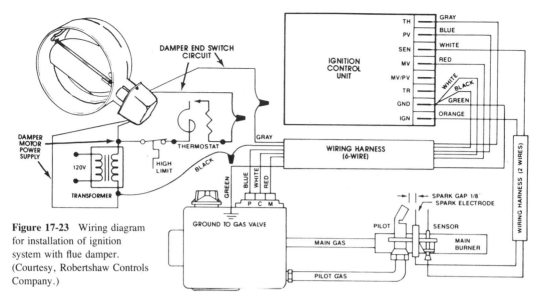

Figure 17-23 Wiring diagram for installation of ignition system with flue damper. (Courtesy, Robertshaw Controls Company.)

switch is closed only when the damper is fully open. Figure 17-23 shows the wiring connection for the damper end switch. **Warning:** Vent damper must be in the full open position before the ignition system is energized. Failure to verify this may cause a serious health hazard to occupants.

In some furnace wiring, one terminal of the secondary side of the transformer may be grounded, and this could damage the transformer. Therefore, it is important to determine which gas valve wire is grounded before making the connection to the wiring harness. This procedure is shown in Figure 17-24.

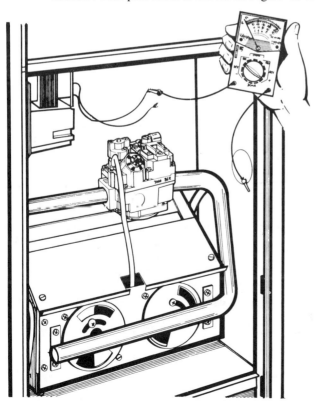

Figure 17-24 Procedure for checking ground side of transformer. (Courtesy, Robertshaw Controls Company.)

Ignition and flame-sensing hardware for direct spark ignition systems is available in different configurations. One of these is shown in Figure 17-25.

In Figure 17-26 the diagram shows a combined system in which the igniter and the sensor are one unit.

Silicon Carbide Ignition System

Principle of operation.   The system utilizes a silicon carbide element that performs a dual function of ignition and flame detection. The igniter is an electrically heated resistance element that thermally ignites the gas. The flame detector circuit utilizes flame rectification for monitoring the gas flame.

The igniter serves two functions. Upon a call for heat, the element is powered from the 120-V ac line and allowed to heat for 45 s (typical). Then the main valve is powered,

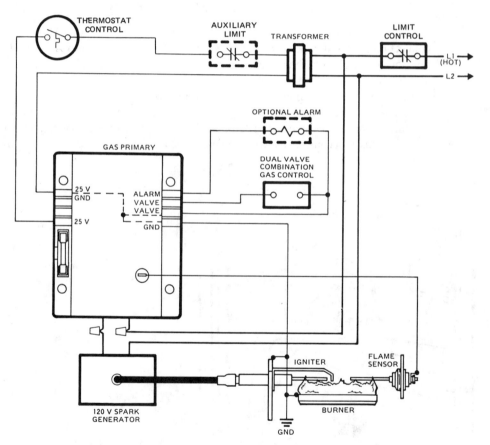

Figure 17-25 Connection wiring diagram of system with separate igniter and sensor. (Courtesy, Honeywell Inc.)

Gas Furnace Controls   Chap. 17

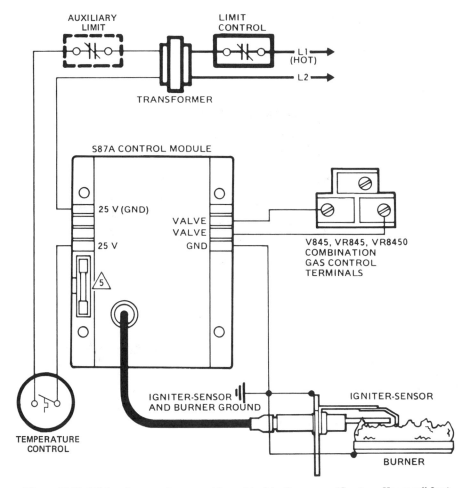

Figure 17-26 Wiring diagram of system with combined igniter-sensor. (Courtesy, Honeywell Inc.)

permitting gas to flow to the burner for the trial-for-ignition period, which is typically 7 s long, although other timings are available. At the end of this period, the igniter is switched from its heating function to that of a flame probe which checks for the presence of flame. If flame is present, the system will monitor it and hold the main valve open. If flame is not established within the trial-for-ignition period, the system will lock out, closing the main valve and shutting off power to the igniter. If a loss of flame occurs during the heating cycle, the system will recycle through the ignition sequence.

Silicon carbide ignition.   Proper location of the silicon carbide igniter is important for optimum system performance. It is recommended that the igniter be mounted temporarily using clamps or other suitable means so that the system can be tested before permanent mounting is accomplished. The igniter should be located so that its tip extends

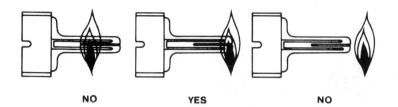

NO   **YES**   **NO**

Figure 17-27 Proper location of silicon carbide igniter element in relation to flame. (Courtesy, Fenwal Incorporated.)

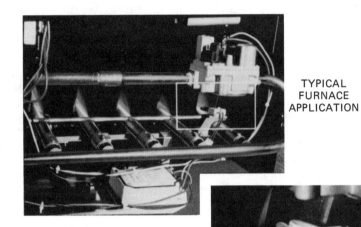

TYPICAL
FURNACE
APPLICATION

SILICONE CARBIDE
HIGH MASS IGNITION
SOURCE

Figure 17-28 Silicon carbide igniter located directly over burner outlet. (Courtesy, White-Rodgers Division of Emerson Electric Company.)

Figure 17-29 Connection wiring diagram for silicon carbide ignition system. (Courtesy, Fenwal Incorporated.)

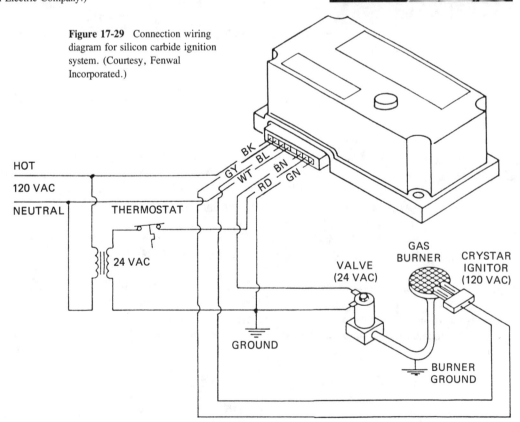

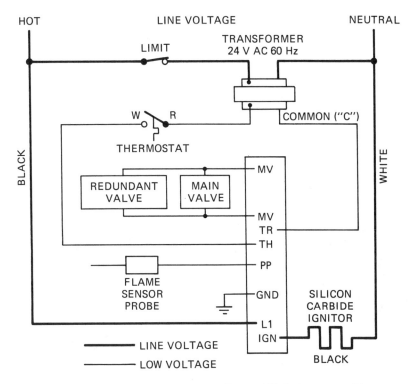

Figure 17-30 Schematic wiring diagram for silicon carbide igniter system. (Courtesy, White-Rodgers Division of Emerson Electric Company.)

$\frac{3}{4}$ in. through the center of the flame and about $\frac{1}{2}$ in. above the base of the flame, as shown in Figure 17-27 and 17-28.

Wiring diagrams for the silicon carbide systems are shown in Figures 17-29 and 17-30.

AUTOMATIC VENT DAMPER

An automatic vent damper system prevents heated air from wastefully going up the open vent when the furnace is not operating. Such a system consists of a damper assembly, a damper operator, and a wiring harness. The damper operator electrically interlocks with the spark ignition control in the spark ignition system. Different types and styles of damper operators are shown in Figures 17-31, 17-32, and 17-33.

Figure 17-31 Automatic vent damper requiring a redundant gas valve. (Courtesy, Honeywell Inc.)

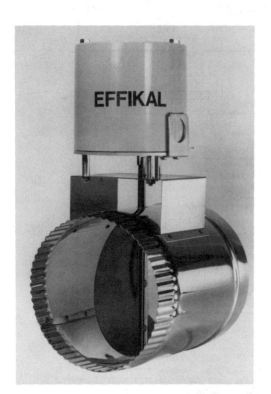

Figure 17-32 Automatic vent damper requiring a redundant gas valve. (Courtesy, Michigan Furnace Company.)

DAMPER BLADE

BLADE POSITION INDICATOR

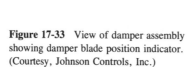

Figure 17-33 View of damper assembly showing damper blade position indicator. (Courtesy, Johnson Controls, Inc.)

MOTOR

PLUG

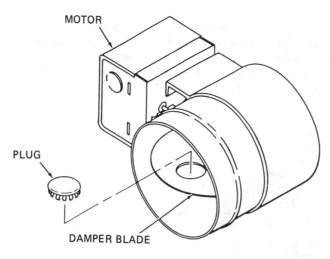

DAMPER BLADE

Figure 17-34 Application of vent damper to system using a standing pilot. (Courtesy, Honeywell Inc.)

Regardless of the burner ignition system used, the vent damper is always used with a dual-valve combination gas control or two main valves in the gas line to the burner manifold.

The dual (redundant) valves are required by safety codes. When a vent damper is installed on a gas furnace with a standing pilot, provision must be made for venting the products of combustion to the outside. To do this, the plug in the damper blade is removed as shown in Figure 17-34.

Wiring

All wiring or wiring harnesses must conform to local codes and ordinances. It is important to check the damper position after it is wired to be sure that the damper is fully open before the main burner is ignited. Figure 17-35 is a connection diagram and Figure 17-36 is a pictorial diagram. Both illustrate the wiring of vent dampers. Note that the

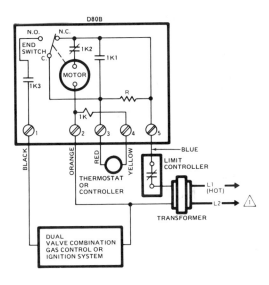

⚠ POWER SUPPLY. PROVIDE DISCONNECT MEANS AND OVERLOAD PROTECTION AS REQUIRED.

Figure 17-35 Connection wiring diagram for vent damper (Courtesy, Honeywell Inc.)

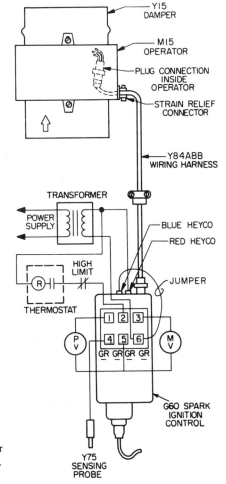

Figure 17-36 Pictorial wiring diagram for vent damper. (Courtesy, Johnson Controls, Inc.)

Automatic Vent Damper

wiring diagram in Figure 17-36 is designed for specific G60 controls used only with vent damper applications.

Installation

The vent damper must be located in the vent so that it serves only the appliance for which it is intended (Figure 17-37). If the vent damper is improperly installed, a hazardous condition—such as an explosion or carbon monoxide poisoning—could result. The damper must be mounted in an accessible location at least 6 in. from any combustible material or the heat exchanger. Make sure as well that the position indicator is easily visible when the damper installation is complete.

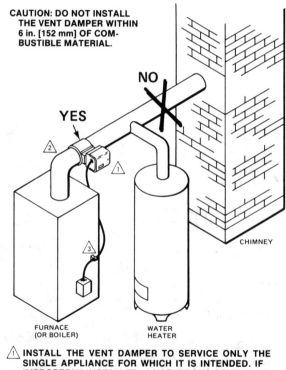

CAUTION: DO NOT INSTALL THE VENT DAMPER WITHIN 6 in. [152 mm] OF COMBUSTIBLE MATERIAL.

NO

YES

CHIMNEY

FURNACE (OR BOILER)

WATER HEATER

⚠1 INSTALL THE VENT DAMPER TO SERVICE ONLY THE SINGLE APPLIANCE FOR WHICH IT IS INTENDED. IF IMPROPERLY INSTALLED, A HAZARDOUS CONDITION, SUCH AS AN EXPLOSION OR CARBON MONOXIDE POISONING, COULD RESULT.

⚠2 DO NOT INSTALL THE VENT DAMPER ON VENT PIPE CURVE.

⚠3 DO NOT RUN WIRES NEAR HIGH TEMPERATURE SURFACES. USE STAND-OFF BRACKETS IF NECESSARY.

Figure 17-37 Proper installation of a vent damper (Courtesy, Honeywell Inc.)

CHAPTER 17 STUDY QUESTIONS

The answers to the study questions are found in the sections of this chapter under the chapter topics indicated.

STUDY QUESTIONS	CHAPTER TOPICS
1. Name the various circuits in a gas furnace control system.	*Circuits*
2. What power supply should be used on a standard gas furnace?	*Power supply*
3. How many circuits are required to operate a two-speed fan?	*Fan*
4. What are the components of a gas valve circuit?	*Gas valve*
5. What two thermostat terminals must close to provide a call for heating?	*Gas valve*
6. What is the cut-in temperature on a limit control with a 200°F cut-out point?	*Gas valve*
7. What is the usual cut-out temperature of a secondary limit control?	*Gas valve*
8. What are the two terminals that close on the thermostat to call for cooling?	*Accessories*
9. What circuit activates a timed fan start?	*Gas valve*
10. What accessory when added requires a secondary power supply?	*Power supply*
11. What type of furnace uses an auxiliary limit (LA) control?	*Gas valve*
12. In testing a fan relay, what voltage should be applied to the fan relay coil?	*Typical wiring diagrams*
13. Describe the three types of gas burner ignition systems.	*Burner ignition*
14. Describe the operation of an automatic vent damper.	*Automatic vent damper*
15. Where is the automatic vent damper placed and how is it wired into the control system?	*Automatic vent damper*

18 Oil Furnace Controls

OBJECTIVES

After studying this chapter, the student will be able to:

- Identify the various controls and circuits on an oil-fired furnace

- Determine the sequence of operation of the controls

- Service and troubleshoot the oil heating unit control system

USE OF OIL FURNACE CONTROLS

Many of the oil furnace controls are similar to those of gas furnaces. The main difference is in the control of the fuel-burning equipment. The major components controlled are:

- Oil burner (including ignition)

- Fan

- Accessories

As with gas furnaces, certain variations must be incorporated in the oil furnace control system to comply with various furnace models. A downflow furnace, for example, needs an auxiliary limit control and a timed fan start control, which are not required on an upflow furnace.

CIRCUITS

The control circuits for an oil-burning furnace consist of

- Power circuit
- Fan circuit
- Ignition circuit
- Oil burner circuit
- Accessory circuits

Primary Control

Several of the control circuits are combined in a single primary control to simplify control construction and field wiring. The primary control is a type of central control assembly that supplies power for the ignition, and oil burner circuits.

The primary control actuates the oil burner and provides a safety device which stops the operation of the burner if the flame fails to ignite or is extinguished for any reason. This safety device prevents any sizable quantity of unburned oil from flowing into the furnace, thus reducing the possibility of an explosion.

Two types of oil primary control sensors are commonly used:

1. Bimetallic sensor
2. Cad cell sensor

Bimetallic sensor. The bimetallic sensor type of oil primary control is often called a *stack relay* because it is normally placed in the flue pipe between the heat exchanger and the barometric damper. It includes a relay which permits the low-voltage (24-V) thermostat to operate the line-voltage (120-V) oil burner. The internal wiring for a bimetallic sensor type of primary control is shown in Figure 18-1.

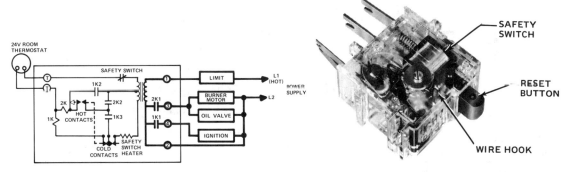

Figure 18-1 Internal wiring for a bimetallic sensor-type oil primary control with safety switch. (Courtesy, Honeywell Inc.)

The entry of the power supply (120-V ac) is shown at the top of the diagram. Line-voltage power is connected to the oil burner and to the transformer located in the primary control. The balance of the control operates on low voltage.

Figure 18-2 shows the installation of the bimetallic sensor (pyrotherm detector) in the furnace flue. Figure 18-3 shows the mechanical action that takes place when the bimetal expands as it senses heat from the flame. The normal position of the switches in this control are: cold contacts NC, hot contacts NO. When the bimetal is heated, the cold contacts break and the hot contacts make.

Referring to Figure 18-1, when the thermostat calls for heat, the cold contacts are made and the safety switch heater is energized. If the flame fails to light and the cold contacts continue closed, the safety switch heater will "warp out" (open) the safety switch. The heaters and switch constitute a type of heat relay. With current flowing through this circuit, about 90 s is required to trip (open) the safety switch. If the burner produces flame and heats the bimetallic element the switching occurs, opening the cold contacts and closing the hot contacts. This action causes the current to bypass the safety switch heater and the burner continues to run.

A stack relay type of primary control is shown in Figure 18-4. Line-voltage power is connected across terminals 1 and 2, and the oil burner motor is connected across 1 and 3. Constant ignition is also connected across terminals 1 and 3. Intermittent ignition is connected across terminals 1 and 4. The thermostat is connected to terminals T and T (W and B).

Two types of ignition are used in the field: constant and intermittent. With constant ignition the electrodes spark continuously. Intermittent ignition operates only when the burner is started. With constant ignition, both the oil burner motor and the ignition transformer are wired across terminals 1 and 3. Bimetallic-type stack relays are found on many furnaces now in the field. However, the new units are usually equipped with a cad-cell type of primary control.

For the service technician's protection, it is important that the hot line of the power supply be brought to the number 1 terminal. In accordance with good practice, the switching action of this control should be in the hot line.

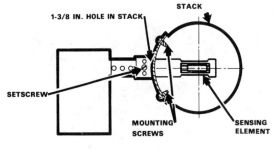

LOCATE DETECTOR

—DIRECTLY IN HOT STACK GASES.
—AHEAD AT ANY DRAFT REGULATOR.
—IN THE OUTSIDE CURVE OF AN ELBOW
   IF ELBOW LOCATION IS NECESSARY.

Figure 18-2 Pyrotherm flame detector. (Courtesy, Honeywell Inc.)

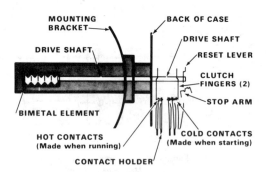

Figure 18-3 Pyrotherm flame detector operation. (Courtesy, Honeywell Inc.)

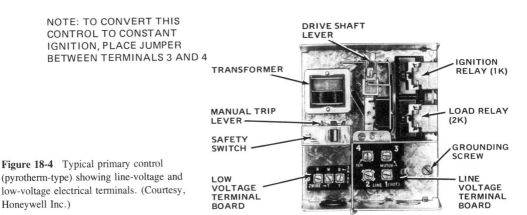

NOTE: TO CONVERT THIS CONTROL TO CONSTANT IGNITION, PLACE JUMPER BETWEEN TERMINALS 3 AND 4

DRIVE SHAFT LEVER

TRANSFORMER

IGNITION RELAY (1K)

MANUAL TRIP LEVER

LOAD RELAY (2K)

SAFETY SWITCH

GROUNDING SCREW

LOW VOLTAGE TERMINAL BOARD

LINE VOLTAGE TERMINAL BOARD

Figure 18-4 Typical primary control (pyrotherm-type) showing line-voltage and low-voltage electrical terminals. (Courtesy, Honeywell Inc.)

If the thermostat is calling for heat, 120-V ac power must be available at terminals 1 and 3, on a constant ignition system. However, if intermittent ignition is used, 120-V ac power must also be available at terminals 1 and 4. The thermostat terminals can be jumpered to simulate the thermostat calling for heat.

The control should be tested without supplying heat to the bimetallic element. When this is done, the safety switch should shut off the power to the burner in about 90 s. If heat is supplied to the bimetallic element, the burner should continue to run.

Sometimes these controls get "out of step." That is, the cold contacts do not remake when the bimetal cools down. This should be corrected by following the restepping procedure shown in Figure 18-5.

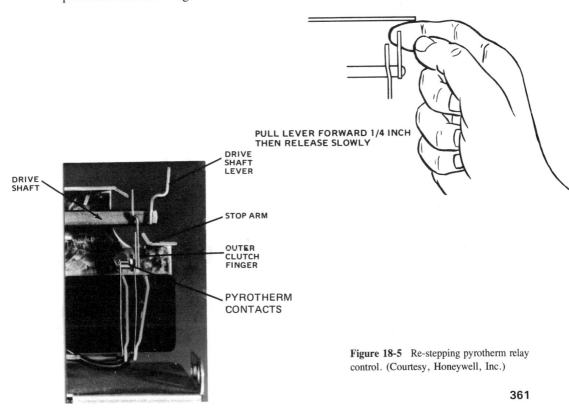

PULL LEVER FORWARD 1/4 INCH THEN RELEASE SLOWLY

DRIVE SHAFT LEVER

STOP ARM

OUTER CLUTCH FINGER

PYROTHERM CONTACTS

DRIVE SHAFT

Figure 18-5 Re-stepping pyrotherm relay control. (Courtesy, Honeywell, Inc.)

361

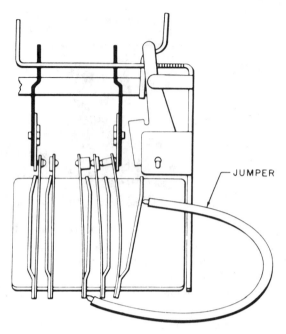

JUMPER

Figure 18-6 Use of jumper to test cold contacts on pyrotherm relay control. (Courtesy, Honeywell Inc.)

To test the contact terminals, jumper across the cold contacts, as shown in Figure 18-6. If the bimetal is cold and contacts cannot be restepped, replace the primary control.

Stack relays have some built-in limitations. They are slow acting due to the thermal lag of the bimetal. Wiring must be completed in the field, so performance cannot be fully checked by the manufacturer. The bimetal element is exposed to the products of combustion and requires more maintenance than the cad-cell-type detector. Stack relays are no longer used in new installations. However, they are used for the replacement of defective units. All new residential oil heating systems utilize cad-cell primary controls.

Cad-cell sensor. A cad cell is shown in Figure 18-7 and its location is shown in 18-8. The cad-cell primary control has one feature that is not present in the bimetallic sensor. If the cad cell senses stray light (light not from the flame) before the thermostat

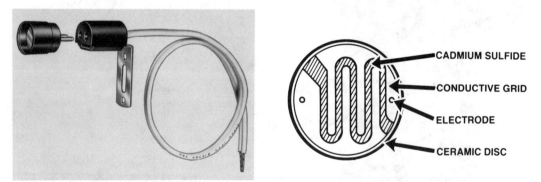

CADMIUM SULFIDE

CONDUCTIVE GRID

ELECTRODE

CERAMIC DISC

Figure 18-7 Cad-cell assembly and details of face. (Courtesy, Honeywell, Inc.)

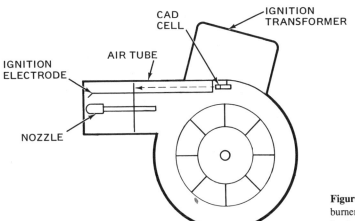

Figure 18-8 Cad-cell location in oil burner assembly. (Courtesy, Honeywell Inc.)

calls for heat, the burner cannot be started by the thermostat. This is a protective arrangement. Therefore, when testing the operation of the cad-cell primary, block off all light that might reach the cad cell. (see Figure 18-9.)

The cad cell itself can be tested with a suitable ohmmeter. The ohmmeter must be capable of reading up to 100,000 Ω. In the absence of light, the cad cell should have a resistance of about 100,000 Ω. In the presence of light, its resistance should not exceed 1500 Ω.

To test the primary control, start the burner and within 30 s jump the cad-cell terminals with a 1000–1500-Ω resistor. If the burner continues to run, the cad-cell primary is operating correctly. In actual operation, a poor or inadequate oil burner flame can be

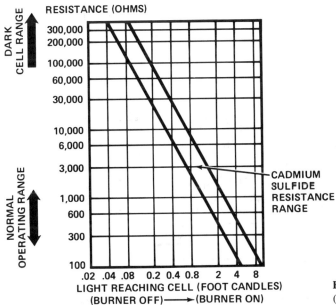

Figure 18-9 Cad cell responding to light. (Courtesy, Honeywell Inc.)

Circuits

a problem. The safety arrangement on a cad-cell primary control usually stops the burner in about 30 s if the cad cell does not sense an adequate flame.

Electrical. The ability of the cad cell to change electrical resistance when exposed to different intensities of light makes possible the operation of a safety control circuit.

Figure 18-10 shows the internal wiring connections for the primary cad-cell types of primary control as well as the internal circuiting. The power (120-V ac) connection to the burner and primary control transformer are shown on the left side of the diagram. The balance of the control is low voltage (24-V ac). The thermostat and the cad cell are shown connected to the left side of the primary control.

When the thermostat calls for heat, the oil burner starts and the safety switch heater is energized. If the flame fails to ignite, the heater warps out the safety switch in about 30 s, turning off the burner. If the flame is produced, it is sensed by the cad cell. This causes the safety switch heater to be bypassed and the burner stays on.

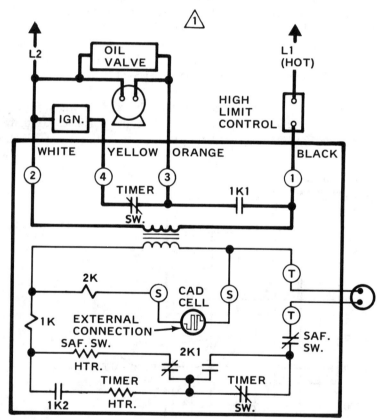

⚠ PROVIDE OVERLOAD PROTECTION AND DISCONNECT MEANS AS REQUIRED.

Figure 18-10 Wiring for cad-cell-type oil primary control (Courtesy, Honeywell Inc.)

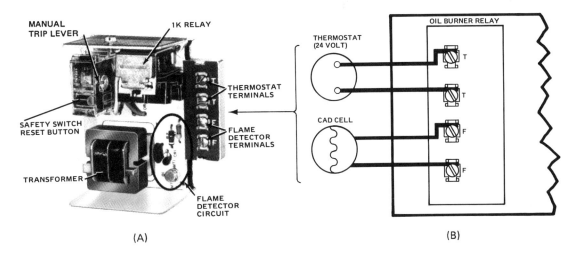

Figure 18-11 Cad-cell primary control showing thermostat and flame detector terminals. (Courtesy, Honeywell Inc.)

The cad-cell primary control power supply (120-V ac) is wired to the black (hot) and white (neutral) connections. The oil burner motor is wired to the white and orange connections. The thermostat is connected to terminals T and T. The cad cell is connected to terminals S and S (or F and F), as shown in Figure 18-11.

Options Available. There are two important options available on the cad-cell primary control:

1. Constant or intermittent ignition

2. Variations in motor control arrangement

On constant ignition both the oil burner motor and the ignition transformer are wired across the white and orange connections. On intermittent ignition, the motor is wired across white and orange, and the ignition transformer is wired across white and yellow.

Solid State. Solid-state technology is based on manipulating semiconductors to perform different functions in an electronic circuit.

The solid-state circuit, which replaces the sensitive relay in cad-cell primaries, consists of two resistors, one capacitor, and two solid-state switches. One of these is a bilateral switch, and the other is a triac, as shown in Figure 18-12.

The triac acts as a NO switch. It will conduct current between terminals A and B after a triggering current is applied to the gate terminal. It will continue to conduct after the triggering current is removed until current between A and B drops to zero. At this time, it becomes nonconducting, and another triggering signal is required before it will conduct again.

The bilateral switch is frequently used to trigger a Triac. When only terminals 1 and 2 are used, it acts as a resistor until a certain voltage, called the "breakover voltage," is reached. This voltage is very small, on the order of 8 V. When the breakover voltage

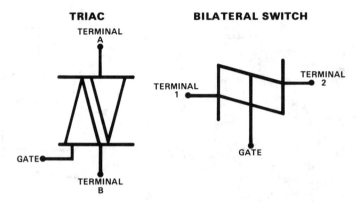

TRIAC   **BILATERAL SWITCH**

Figure 18-12   Solid-state switches. (Courtesy, Honeywell Inc.)

is passed, the resistance of the switch collapses and current flows. When the bilateral switch is used as a 3-terminal device, current is applied to the gate terminal to change the breakover voltage.

In Figure 18-13 which shows a solid-state flame-sensing circuit, the resistors and the capacitor in the cad-cell primary are not, strictly speaking, solid-state devices, but they are used extensively in solid-state circuits. A resistor simply opposes the flow of current. A capacitor, in a dc circuit, blocks the flow of current. In an ac circuit, the capacitor stores current on one half-cycle and releases it on the reverse half-cycle. Resistor R1 in Figure 18-13 determines the voltage drop across the F-F terminals, and resistor R2 protects the solid-state components from abnormally high voltages. The capacitor provides an extra burst of current each half-cycle to ensure that the Triac is triggered when necessary. The solid-state flame-sensing circuit is less affected by ambient light hitting the cad cell than is a comparable sensitive relay.

Sequence of Operation.   The schematic of an intermittent ignition model of a cad-cell primary control is shown in Figure 18-14. When the line switch is closed, the internal transformer is powered, whether or not the thermostat is calling for heat. A line-voltage thermostat can be used with this control if terminals T-T on the primary are jumpered. In this case, the primary and cad cell will not be powered until the thermostat calls for heat.

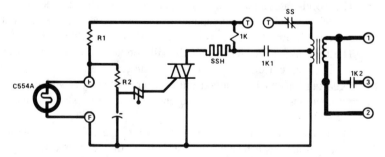

Figure 18-13   Solid-state flame-sensing circuit. (Courtesy, Honeywell Inc.)

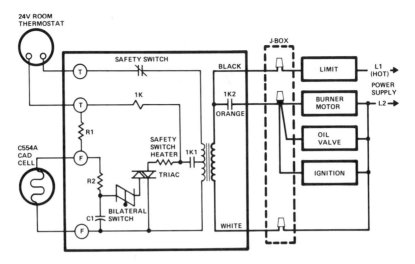

Figure 18-14 Wiring diagram for cad-cell primary. (Courtesy, Honeywell Inc.)

The solid-state flame-sensing circuit is designed so that the Triac will conduct current only when cad-cell resistance is high, indicating no flame. If cad-cell resistance is high, the voltage across the bilateral switch exceeds the breakover voltage, causing it to conduct and trigger the Triac. The capacitor provides a current pulse each half-cycle to make sure the breakover voltage is exceeded.

On flame failure, cad-cell resistance increases until the Triac is energized. The safety switch heats until the bimetal warps enough to break the circuit and stop the burner. The primary control must be reset before the burner can be restarted.

If there is a power failure during a call for heat, the burner shuts down safely and automatically. The system automatically returns to normal operation when power is restored.

Cad-cell versus thermal detection. Regardless of the type of detector and primary control used to supervise the burner, there are basic similarities in the general operation of the primary control. In all systems, a call for heat energizes the burner and starts the safety switch heater. If flame is established, the flame detector (thermal or optical) acts to bypass the safety switch heater and allows the burner to run.

The steps taken by the cad cell to bypass the safety switch heater and allow the burner to run are comparable to the steps taken by the stack detector. The cad cell's sighting of the flame and lowering its resistance is matched by the thermal detector's bimetal element "feeling" the change in stack gas temperature and moving the drive shaft outward. The pull-in of the sensitive relay or electronic network is matched by the opening of the stack relay contacts.

The actions of both detectors when flame is proved have the same result: the breaking of the safety switch heater circuit.

Compare the parts of a thermal flame detector to the cad cell detector. The electronic

Circuits   **367**

THERMAL DETECTION

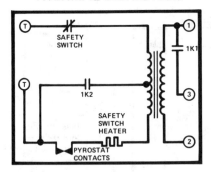

1. 1K PULLS IN, ENERGIZES BURNER.
2. SS HEATS THROUGH PYROSTAT CONTACTS.
3. FLAME ESTABLISHED, PYROSTAT CONTACTS OPEN.
4. SS HEATER IS BYPASSED.

CAD CELL DETECTION

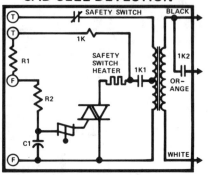

1. 1K PULLS IN, ENERGIZES BURNER.
2. SS HEATS THROUGH TRIAC.
3. FLAME ESTABLISHED, TRIAC STOPS CONDUCTING.
4. SS HEATER IS BYPASSED.

Figure 18-15   Basic primary control function. (Courtesy, Honeywell Inc.)

network replaces the Pyrostat contacts, and the light sensitive cell replaces the heat sensitive bimetal element, as shown in Figure 18-15.

The cad cell has certain advantages over the thermal detector. Its response time is faster than the bimetal's. On exposure to light its resistance drops almost immediately, while the bimetal reacts slowly to a relatively slow change in stack temperature. Because of this faster response the cell is better suited to modern installations. The cad cell is also well suited to the "package" concept since it and its associated primary control can be completely installed and wired by the burner manufacturer.

Power Circuit

Following is the key to the schematic diagrams used in the study of the power circuit and the other circuits described in this chapter.

BK	Black-wire color	FC	Fan control
BL	Blue-wire color	FM	Fan motor
G	Green-wire color	FR	Fan relay
OR	Orange-wire color	L	Limit
R	Red-wire color	LA	Limit auxiliary
W	White-wire color	L_1 L_2	Line 1, line 2 of power supply
Y	Yellow-wire color	S	Cad-cell terminal
C	24-V common conn.	T	Thermostat terminal
CC	Compressor relay	TFS	Timed fan start

Referring to the power circuit shown in Figure 18-16, 120-V ac power is supplied to the primary control. A fused disconnect is placed in the hot side of the line. A limit control is wired in series with the hot side of the power supply (L_1) and the black connection on the primary control. The transformer is a part of the primary control.

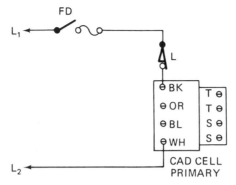

Figure 18-16 Power circuit.

Fan Circuit

The simplest type of fan circuit consists of a fan control in series with a single-speed fan motor, as shown in Figure 18-17.

Using a multiple-speed fan motor the switch on the subbase of the thermostat changes the fan speed, as shown in Figure 18-18.

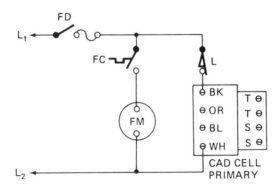

Figure 18-17 Fan circuit with single-speed fan motor.

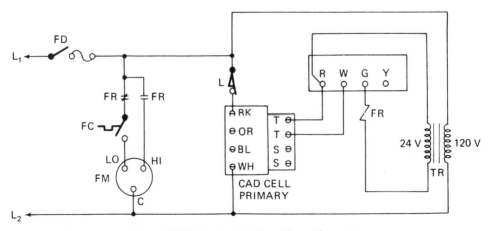

Figure 18-18 Fan circuit with multispeed fan motor.

Circuits

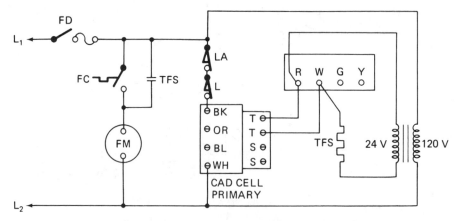

Figure 18-19 Fan circuit for downflow and horizontal furnaces.

On downflow and horizontal furnaces, a timed fan start (TFS) is used to start the fan and the fan control (FC) stops it, as shown in Figure 18-19. An auxiliary limit control is used in addition to the regular limit control and is wired in series with the primary control.

Ignition and Oil Burner Circuits

Ignition and oil burner circuits are shown in Figure 18-20. The ignition transformer is wired in parallel with the oil burner motor on a constant ignition system. The burner is wired to the orange and white connections on the primary control.

Accessory Circuits

Accessories for oil furnaces can be added in a manner similar to those shown in Chapter 17 for gas furnaces. A separate transformer is usually required for control circuit power when cooling is added. See Figures 18-18 and 18-19.

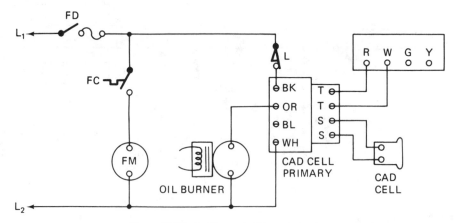

Figure 18-20 Ignition and oil burner circuits.

TYPICAL WIRING DIAGRAMS

Upflow

Figure 18-21 shows a typical connection diagram for an upflow oil furnace. Note that on this unit most of the wiring connections are brought to a common junction box. Since

Figure 18-21 Heat-cool connection wiring diagram for upflow oil furnace. (Courtesy, Comfortmaker, Snyder General Corporation.)

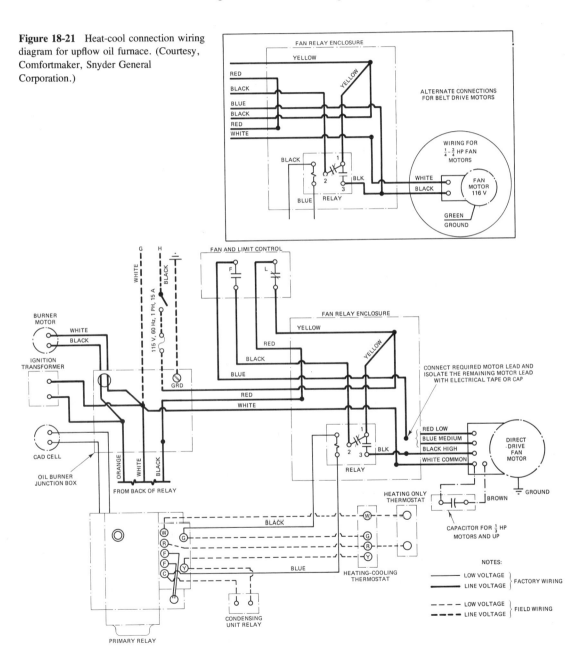

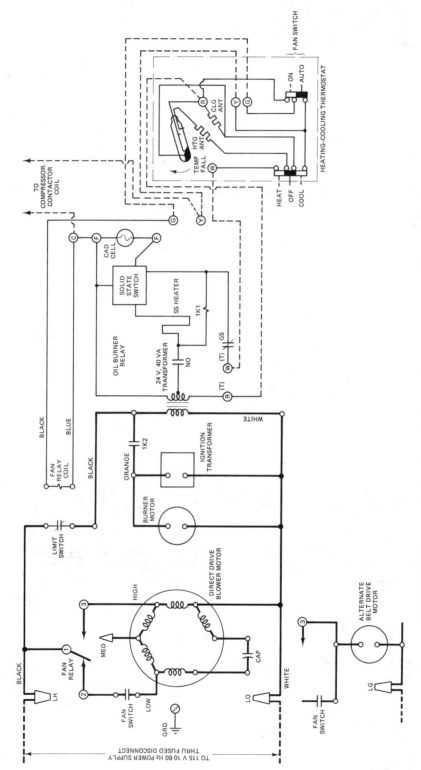

Figure 18-22 Heat-cool schematic wiring diagram for upflow oil furnace. (Courtesy, Comfort-maker, Snyder General Corporation.)

both the fan and limit controls are of line-voltage type, a jumper can be used between common terminals. The schematic wiring diagram for the upflow unit is shown in Figure 18-22.

Oil Furnace with MultiSpeed Fan Motor

Figure 18-23 shows a connection diagram for an oil furnace with multispeed fan motor. All wiring connections are made either in the primary control junction box or in a separate junction box that includes the indoor fan relay. The schematic wiring diagram for the oil furnace with multispeed fan motor is shown in Figure 18-24.

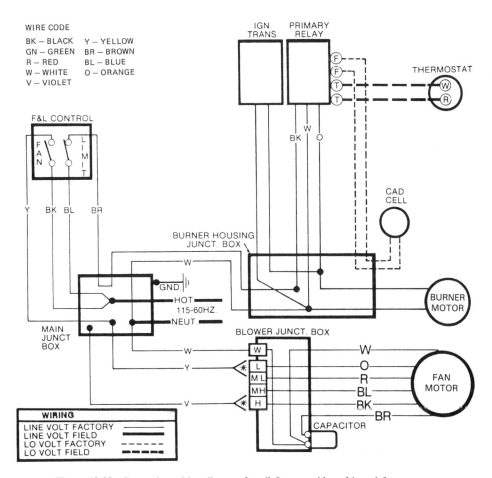

Figure 18-23 Connection wiring diagram for oil furnace with multispeed fan motor. (Courtesy, Heil-Quaker.)

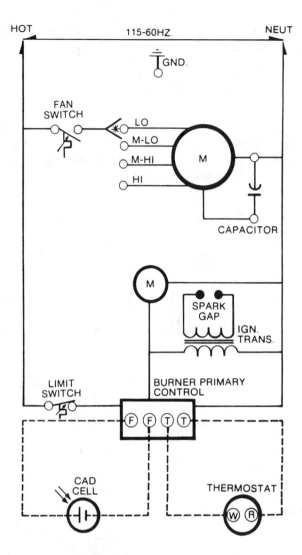

Figure 18-24 Schematic wiring diagram for oil furnace with multispeed fan motor. (Courtesy, Heil-Quaker.)

OPERATION OF VENT DAMPER

The damper operator opens and closes the vent damper upon demand of the room thermostat. The damper must be fully open before the oil burner control is energized through the vent damper relay. A typical wiring installation and damper location is shown in Figure 18-25.

The automatic vent damper system in Figure 18-26 is to be used only with oil burner primary controls, which sense the presence of combustion by light from the oil flame. The connection diagram in Figure 18-27 shows the internal wiring to the oil burner and thermostat.

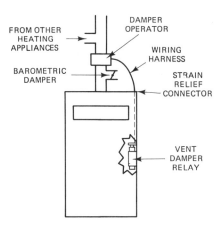

Figure 18-25 Typical damper location and wiring. (Courtesy, Johnson Control, Inc.)

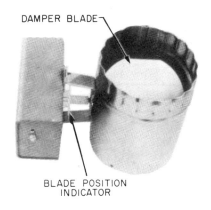

Figure 18-26 View of damper assembly showing damper blade position indicator. (Courtesy, Johnson Controls, Inc.)

Figure 18-27 Connection wiring diagram for a vent damper installation. (Courtesy, Johnson Controls, Inc.)

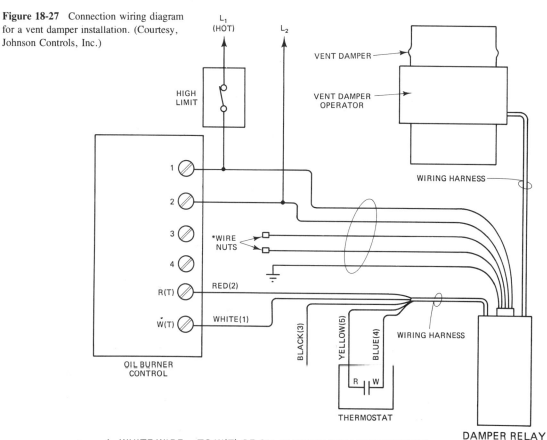

1. WHITE WIRE – TO W(T) OF OIL BURNER PRIMARY CONTROL
2. RED WIRE – TO R(T) OF OIL BURNER PRIMARY CONTROL
3. BLACK WIRE – TO C OF OIL BURNER PRIMARY CONTROL
4. BLUE WIRE – INSERT WIRE FROM W OF THERMOSTAT
5. YELLOW WIRE – INSERT WIRE FROM R OF THERMOSTAT

In troubleshooting an oil-fired furnace, attention should be given to the electrical and fluid flows through the furnace, for the following reasons:

- Electrical power is required to operate the control system, ignite the fuel, and energize the loads.

- Fuel oil is required for combustion.

- Air is required for combustion and to convey heat from the furnace to the spaces being heated.

Electricity, oil, and air each have a circuit or path of movement through the furnace. Each must be supplied in the proper place, in the proper quantity, and at the proper time.

Troubleshooting the fuel oil and air supply have been covered in other chapters. Therefore, the concern here is chiefly electrical power and control.

Use of Test Meters

Figure 18-28 shows the use of various test meters in measuring current in the electrical system of the furnace. The technique in electrical troubleshooting is to "start from power" and follow the availability of power through the control system to the load. If the power supply is stopped for any reason along the proper path, the reason for the stoppage should be determined, and corrected. If power in the proper quantity is supplied to the load and it does not operate, the load device is at fault.

Seven locations where meter readings are taken along the path of the electrical current are shown in Figure 18-28. Locations to be checked are

1. Voltage supply to the unit

2. Voltage across the limit control, to determine if this control switch is properly closed

3. Voltage across the thermostat, to be certain that it is calling for heat

4. Voltage at the oil burner motor and ignition transformer, to be certain that 120-V ac is being supplied

5. Voltage across the fan control, to determine that it is calling for fan operation

6. Voltage at the fan motor, to be certain that 120-V ac is being supplied

7. Amperage to the fan motor, to measure the running amperes. This should agree with the data on the motor nameplate

In meter readings 2, 3, and 5, a voltmeter is used to test a switch. If the switch is open, a voltage shows on the meter. If the switch is closed, the voltmeter reads zero.

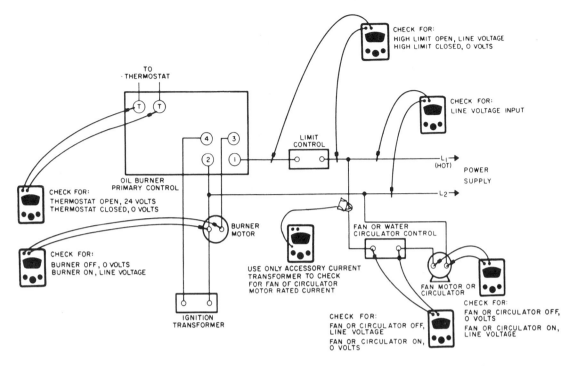

NOTE: WHEN CHECKING TO DETERMINE IF ANY SWITCH IS OPEN OR CLOSED: CHECK VOLTAGE ACROSS SWITCH WITH POWER ON; ZERO VOLTAGE INDICATES SWITCH IS CLOSED; IF ANY VOLTAGE IS INDICATED, SWITCH IS OPEN.

Figure 18-28 The use of various electrical meters in troubleshooting oil burner systems. (Courtesy, Honeywell Inc.)

Testing Components

The most complex element in an oil-fired furnace control system is the primary control. Therefore, it is this element that has the greatest potential need for service. Specific testing procedures are necessary to determine if the primary control is functioning properly.

Other Servicing Techniques

Most oil-burning furnaces have a manual test overload on the oil burner motor and a reset-type safety switch on the primary control. After an overload, these devices must be manually reset. The tripping of an overload switch is an indicator of a problem that must be found and corrected. Resetting the overload switches may start the equipment but unless the problem is resolved, nuisance tripout will continue to recur.

Regardless of the complaint, much time can often be saved at first by checking the following routine conditions:

- Does the tank contain fuel?

Troubleshooting and Service

- Is power being delivered to the building?

- Are all hand-operated switches closed?

- Are all hand valves in the oil supply line open?

- Are all limit controls in their normal (closed) position?

- Is the thermostat calling for heat?

- Are all overload switches closed?

Low voltage can cause such problems as low oil pump speed, motor burnouts from overload, and burners that fail to operate because relays do not pull in.

The power supply voltage should be checked while the greatest power usage is occurring. Low voltage should never be overlooked as a source of service problems. Where the service to the building is at fault, the local power company should be contacted. If the problem is within the building, the services of an electrician may be required to solve the problem.

CHAPTER 18 STUDY QUESTIONS

The answers to the study questions are found in the sections of this chapter under the chapter topics indicated.

STUDY QUESTIONS	CHAPTER TOPICS
1. What are the various circuits in an oil burner control system?	*Circuits*
2. What are the two types of primary controls?	*Primary controls*
3. On the stack type relay, are the cold contacts normally open or closed when starting?	*Bimetallic sensor*
4. What is the light sensitive material on a cad cell?	*Cad-cell sensor*
5. What is the resistance of a cad cell in the absence of light?	*Cad-cell sensor*
6. To which terminals of the primary control is the cad cell connected?	*Cad-cell sensor*
7. How many low-voltage terminals are on the cad-cell primary control?	*Cad-cell sensor*
8. On the cad-cell primary control, which terminal is used for the hot side of the power supply?	*Cad-cell sensor*
9. On the bimetal stack relay, which terminals are used for the power supply?	*Bimetallic sensor*
10. In testing a switch with a voltmeter, a reading of zero indicates what position of the switch?	*Use of test meters*
11. On a stack relay, if the flame fails, how long before the burner will go on safety?	*Bimetallic sensor*

12. What is the resistance of the cad cell when it senses light?

Cad-cell sensor

13. Describe the solid-state cad-cell circuit.

Solid-state sensor

14. What are the components of a vent damper circuit and how are they wired?

Operation of vent dampers

15. Which control requires the most service on an oil burner control system?

Testing components

19 Electric Heating

OBJECTIVES

After studying this chapter, the student will be able to:

- Identify the various types of controls and circuits used on an electric furnace
- Determine the sequence of operation of the controls
- Service and troubleshoot the electric furnace control system

CONVERSION OF ELECTRICITY TO HEAT

An electric heating furnace converts energy in the form of electricity to heat. The conversion takes place in resistance heaters.

Electric furnaces differ from gas or oil furnaces in that no heat exchanger is required. Return air from the space being heated passes directly over the resistance heaters and into the supply air plenum.

The amount of heat supplied depends upon the number and size of the resistance heaters used. The conversion of electricity to heat (the heat equivalent for 1 W of electrical power) takes place in accordance with the following formula:

$$1 \text{ W} = 3.415 \text{ Btu}$$

Figure 19-1 shows an electric forced warm air furnace (upflow model). Return air is brought into the blower compartment through the filters, then passed over the heating elements and sent out into the distribution system.

An electric furnace requires no flue. All of the heat produced is used in heating the building. Input is equal to output. Thus, it operates at 100% efficiency.

Major components, excluding the controls, are:

- Heating elements

- Blower and motor assembly

- Furnace enclosure

- Accessories, such as filters, humidifier, and cooling (optional)

TYPICAL ELECTRIC FURNACE FEATURES

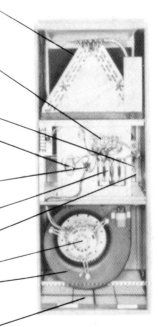

BUILT-IN COOLING COIL COMPARTMENT — Slide-in type for easier conversion to summer cooling. Accommodates 1½, 2, 2½, and 3 ton air conditioner cooling coils. See note on reverse side on heat pump installation.

CONTROLS — On demand from the wall thermostat, the heating elements are energized by electrical contactors. The 15 thru 30 KW versions have the blower motor interlocked with each stage for safety. Easily two staged.

LIMIT SWITCH — Thermal snap disc in each heating element shuts off power automatically if system air temperature becomes excessive.

BUILT-IN TRANSFORMER — Provides power supply for heating and optional cooling controls.

BLOWER RELAY — Provides automatic blower speed change-over to meet heating and cooling air delivery requirements.

BRANCH CIRCUIT FUSING — Factory installed in models rated over 48 amps.

HEATING ELEMENTS — Nickel-chrome wire with individual fusible links for long life. Entire assembly slides out for easy maintenance.

MOTOR — Multi-speed for both heating and cooling.

BLOWER — Heated air is quietly circulated by large volume centrifugal blower that is matched to the electrical heating system for efficiency. Slides out for easy maintenance.

FILTERS — Twin permanent type slide out from front for easy cleaning on all models except Models EFC5 and EFC10.

Figure 19-1 Electric forced warm air furnace, upflow model. (Courtesy, Bard Manufacturing Company.)

Following is the key to the schematic diagrams used in this chapter.

AC	Auxiliary contacts	L	Limit control
C	24-V common connection	$L_1 L_2$	Line 1, line 2 of power supply
FC	Fan control	OT	Outdoor thermostat
FD	Fused disconnect	R	Red wire, thermostat connection
FL	Fuse link	SQ	Sequencer
FM	Fan motor	TFS	Timed fan start
FU	Fuse	TR	Transformer
HR	Heat relay	W	White wire, thermostat connection

Heating Elements

The heating elements are made of Nichrome, a metal consisting chiefly of nickel and chromium. Heating elements are rated in kilowatts of electrical power consumed (1 kW = 1000 W).

A typical heating element assembly is shown in Figure 19-2. The Nichrome wire is

Figure 19-2 Typical heating element.

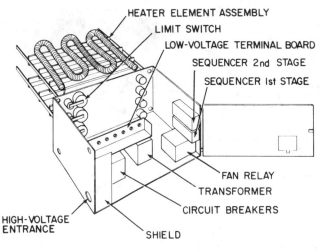

HEATER ELEMENT ASSEMBLY
LIMIT SWITCH
LOW-VOLTAGE TERMINAL BOARD
SEQUENCER 2nd STAGE
SEQUENCER lst STAGE
FAN RELAY
TRANSFORMER
CIRCUIT BREAKERS
SHIELD
HIGH-VOLTAGE ENTRANCE

Figure 19-3 Heater element assembly with circuit breakers. (Courtesy, Bryant Air Conditioning.)

Electric Heating   Chap. 19

supported by insulating material placed in such a way as to provide a minimum amount of air resistance and a maximum amount of contact between the air and the resistance heaters.

Each element assembly contains a thermal fuse and a safety limit switch (Figure 19-3). The safety limit switch is shown in schematic form in Figure 19-4. The limit switch is usually set to open at 160°F and close when the temperature drops to 125°F. The thermal fuse, a backup for the safety limit switch, is set to open at a temperature slightly higher than the limit switch.

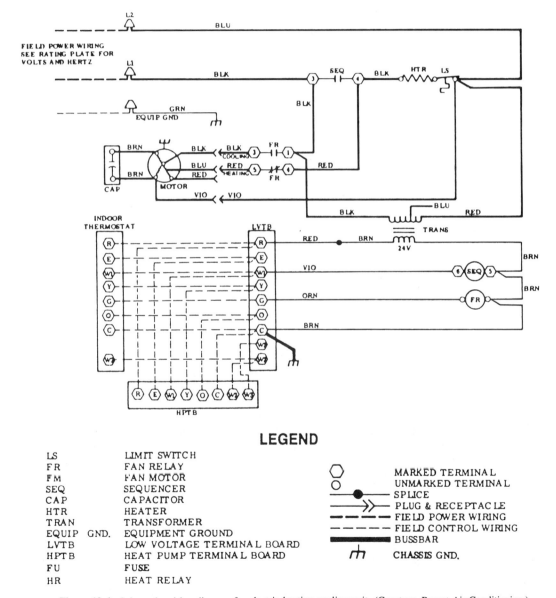

LEGEND

LS	LIMIT SWITCH	⬡	MARKED TERMINAL
FR	FAN RELAY	○	UNMARKED TERMINAL
FM	FAN MOTOR	●	SPLICE
SEQ	SEQUENCER	→»	PLUG & RECEPTACLE
CAP	CAPACITOR		
HTR	HEATER	▬ ▬ ▬	FIELD POWER WIRING
TRAN	TRANSFORMER	─ ─ ─ ─	FIELD CONTROL WIRING
EQUIP GND.	EQUIPMENT GROUND	▬▬▬	BUSSBAR
LVTB	LOW VOLTAGE TERMINAL BOARD		
HPTB	HEAT PUMP TERMINAL BOARD	⎍	CHASSIS GND.
FU	FUSE		
HR	HEAT RELAY		

Figure 19-4 Schematic wiring diagram for electric heating-cooling unit. (Courtesy, Bryant Air Conditioning.)

Electric Furnace Components

In addition to the safety controls in the element assembly, each assembly is fused where it connects to the power supply. Thus, triple safety protection is provided.

Electric furnaces have various individual numbers and sizes of heating element assemblies, depending on the total capacity of the equipment. Elements are placed on the line (power supply) in stages so as not to overload the electrical system on startup. In most units, the minimum size of an element energized or de-energized at one time is 5 kW (17,075 Btuh). Figure 19-4 shows how the heater sequencer operates each stage.

Fan and Motor Assembly

The fan and motor assembly is similar to that used on a gas or oil furnace. Fans may be either direct-drive or belt-driven. There is a trend toward the use of multispeed direct-drive fans, since they facilitate adjustment of the air flow by changing the blower speed. This is usually necessary when cooling is added, since larger air quantities and, consequently, higher speeds are required.

Enclosures

The exterior of the casing is similar to that of a gas or oil furnace but without the flue pipe connection. The interior is designed to permit the air to flow over the heating elements. The section supporting the heating elements is usually insulated from the exterior casing by an air space.

Accessories

Filters, humidifiers, and cooling are added to an electric heating furnace in a manner similar to gas and oil furnaces. Electric heating, therefore, can provide all of the related climate control features provided by other types of fuel.

POWER SUPPLY

The power supply for an electric furnace is 208/240-V, single-phase, 60-Hz. This power is supplied by three wires: two are hot and one is neutral. Fused disconnects are placed in the hot lines leading to the furnace. The National Electric Code limits the amount of service in a single circuit to 48 A. Therefore, if the running current exceeds this amount, additional circuits and fused disconnects must be provided.

The fuses for 48-A service must not exceed 60 A. This is a National Electric Code requirement, specifying that fuses should not exceed 125% of full-load amperes (48 × 1.25 = 60).

All wiring must be enclosed in conduit with proper connectors. Since 280/240 V is considerably more dangerous than lower voltages, every possible protection must be provided. The National Electric Code also requires that the furnace be grounded. The ground wire in the power supply is provided for this purpose.

Since the control system for an electric furnace includes more electrical parts than are in a gas or oil furnace, the wiring is more involved. It is extremely important to use a schematic diagram to assist in troubleshooting. If a schematic is not available from the manufacturer, one should be drawn by the service technician.

The control system consists of the following electrical circuits:

- Power circuit

- Fan circuit

- Heating element circuits

- Control circuits operated from the thermostat

Power Circuit

The power supply consists of one or more 208/240-V ac sources, directed through fused disconnects to the load circuits, including the 208/240-V/24-V transformer. The load lines are both hot, as shown in Figure 19-5.

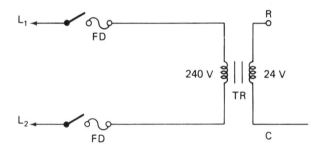

Figure 19-5   Power circuit showing hot load lines.

Fan Circuit

The fan circuits on an electric furnace are similar to those used with gas or oil except for the following changes:

1.   The fan motor is usually 208/240-V ac.

2.   A timed fan start is used to start the fan. This is usually a part of the sequencer (an electrical device for staging the loads).

3.   The fan starts from the timed fan start but is stopped by the regular thermal fan control.

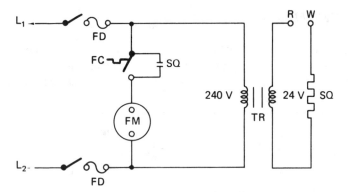

Figure 19-6 Type of fan circuit.

Details of the fan circuit arrangement are shown in Figure 19-6. When the thermostat calls for heating, R and W in the thermostat are made, energizing the low-voltage heater in the sequencer. After approximately 45 s, the fan operates. Just as soon as the temperature leaving the furnace rises to the fan control cut-in temperature, this control makes. However, it has no effect on the fan since it is already running.

Approximately 45 s after the thermostat is satisfied, the timed fan start switch opens. However, it has no effect on the fan since the fan control is made. When the leaving air temperature drops to the cut-out setting of the fan control, the fan stops.

Heating Element Circuits

The heating element assemblies are connected in parallel to the power supply. These assemblies are turned on by the sequencer or heat relays so that the load is gradually placed on the line. Each heating element has a sequencer switch wired in series with the element to start its operation. Figure 19-7 shows the fan and the heating elements operated by a sequencer.

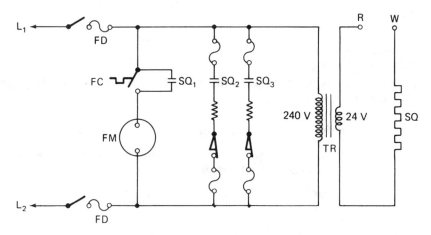

Figure 19-7 Fan and heating elements operated by a sequencer.

Electric Heating   Chap. 19

Control Circuits

When the thermostat calls for heating, R and W make, energizing the low-voltage heater (SQ) in the sequencer. In approximately 45 s, the switch to the fan (SQ$_1$) and the first heating element (SQ$_2$) are made simultaneously. Approximately 30 s later, the switch to the second heater element (SQ$_3$) is made. If additional heating elements are used, there is a comparable 30-s delay before each succeeding element is operated.

A two-stage thermostat is used on some systems. This thermostat has two mercury-bulb switches, one for each stage. The first stage is set to make at a temperature a few degrees higher than the second stage. The first stage controls the fan and some of the heating elements. The second stage controls the balance of the heating elements.

Referring to Figure 19-8, when the first stage of the thermostat calls for heat, R and W$_1$ make, energizing the heater SQ in the sequencer. This action switches on the first element and the fan, then the second element will be energized in 30 s. If the room temperature continues to drop to the setting of the second stage of the thermostat, R and W$_2$ are made, energizing the heat relay heater (HR). In approximately 45 s the switch to the third heating element (HR$_1$) will be made, operating the final stage of heating.

The second-stage thermostat can also be an outdoor thermostat rather than a part of the first-stage thermostat assembly. The low-voltage control circuit for this type of installation is shown in Figure 19-9.

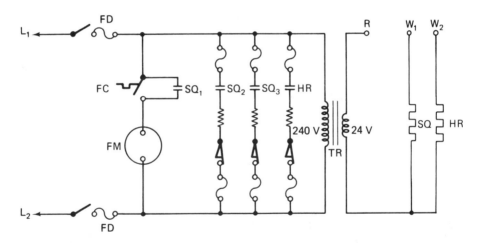

Figure 19-8 Thermostat assembly in two-stage heating.

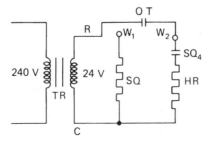

Figure 19-9 Use of outdoor thermostat.

Control System

387

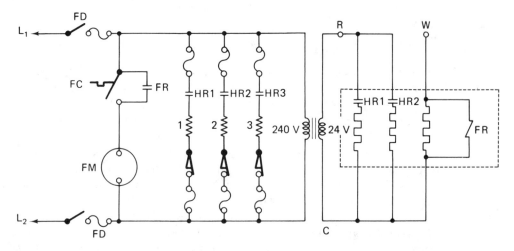

Figure 19-10 Use of heat relays (single-stage thermostat).

The first-stage (standard) thermostat operates the first-stage heating in the usual manner. A switch on the sequencer (SQ_4), an auxiliary switch, is also made in stage 1 to permit the second stage to operate. When the outside temperature reaches the setting of the outdoor thermostat (OT), the second-stage heating is operated in a manner similar to that shown in Figure 19-8.

Separate heat relays for each load can be used as an alternative to the use of the sequencer for staging the loads on an electric heating furnace. These relays function in a manner similar to the sequencer, as shown in Figure 19-10.

When R and W make, the heater on heat relay 1 (HR_1) is energized along with the fan relay (FR). In this arrangement the fan starts immediately and in about 30 s heat relay 1 switch (HR_1) closes, operating the first heater element. At the same time, the other HR_1 switch in the 24-V circuit closes, energizing the heater on heat relay 2. In approximately 30 s, the two switches (HR_2) in heat relay 2 close. One operates heating element 2 and the other energizes the heater in heat relay 3. In approximately 30 s the switch (HR_3) closes, operating heating element 3. Thus, the fan and all heating elements are placed on the line in sequence, as shown in Figure 19-11.

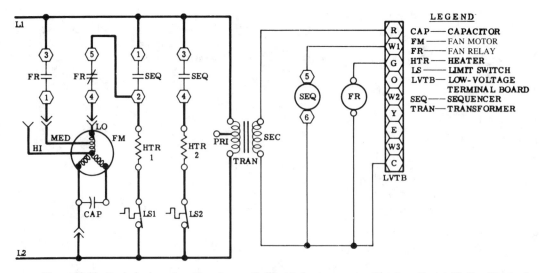

Figure 19-11 Typical schematic wiring diagram for electric heat sequencer. (Courtesy, Bryant Air Conditioning.)

A typical example of the use of sequencer to stage the loads on an electric furnace is shown in Figures 19-11 and 19-12.

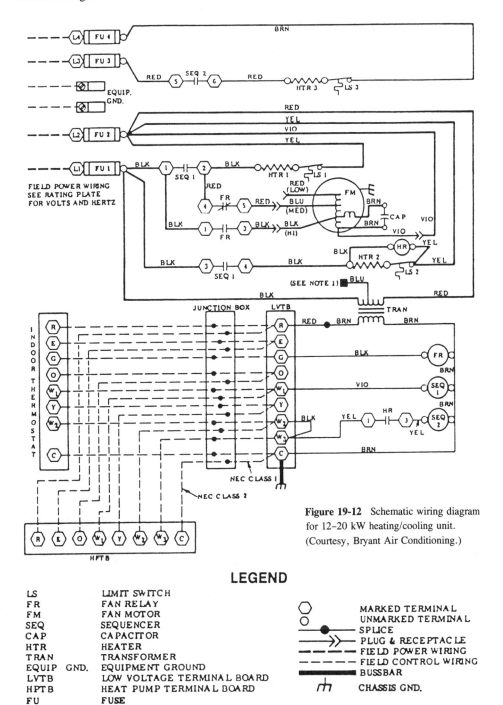

Figure 19-12 Schematic wiring diagram for 12–20 kW heating/cooling unit. (Courtesy, Bryant Air Conditioning.)

LEGEND

LS	LIMIT SWITCH	
FR	FAN RELAY	
FM	FAN MOTOR	
SEQ	SEQUENCER	
CAP	CAPACITOR	
HTR	HEATER	
TRAN	TRANSFORMER	
EQUIP GND.	EQUIPMENT GROUND	
LVTB	LOW VOLTAGE TERMINAL BOARD	
HPTB	HEAT PUMP TERMINAL BOARD	
FU	FUSE	
HR	HEAT RELAY	

MARKED TERMINAL
UNMARKED TERMINAL
SPLICE
PLUG & RECEPTACLE
FIELD POWER WIRING
FIELD CONTROL WIRING
BUSSBAR
CHASSIS GND.

389

The furnace shown in Figure 19-11 has two heating elements. This unit uses a single-stage thermostat. When R and W are made in the thermostat, the fan immediately starts on low speed. At the same time, the heater in the sequencer is energized and the heater elements are operated in stages at approximately 30-s intervals. The fan can be turned on manually to high speed at any time by making 1 and 3 in the fan circuit as shown in Figure 19-12.

The set of normally open contacts of energized sequencer SEQ (between 1 and 2) closes and completes the circuit through the set of N.C. contacts of indoor fan relay FR (between 5 and 4) to the low-speed tap of indoor fan motor FM. The fan motor starts instantly. The circuit to heater elements HTR 1 is also completed and these elements are energized.

After a short built-in time delay that prevents both heater elements from energizing simultaneously, the set of N.O. contacts of energized sequencer SEQ (between 3 and 4) closes and completes the circuit to heater elements HTR 2 and these elements are energized.

The fan motor and the energized heater elements remain on until the room temperature rises to a point above the heating control setting of the room thermostat. At this point, the electrical connection between thermostat terminal R to terminal W (or W1) opens. This open circuit de-energizes sequencer coil SEQ. The electric heating cycle is now off until there is another demand for heating by the room thermostat.

SERVICE AND TROUBLESHOOTING

The methods for checking at the thermostat and the fan motor of an electric furnace are similar to those used for gas and oil furnaces. The external wiring of an electric furnace has a fused disconnect (or disconnects) similar to a gas furnace but uses a higher voltage and more power. The method of checking the external wiring is similar to that used for gas and oil furnaces, with additional allowances for the larger power supply.

In troubleshooting, it is good practice to use the nature of the complaint as a key to the area in which service is required. For example, if the complaint of a homeowner is that the fan will not run, troubleshooting should be confined to this area until the problem is found and corrected.

If the complaint is more general, such as no heat, then a thorough and systematic check of the electrical system must be made. This requires an electrical check, starting where power is available and tracing through the electrical system to determine where it is no longer available. Switches must be checked to be sure that they are in their proper positions. Loads must be checked to be certain that they operate when supplied with the proper power.

A schematic wiring diagram is extremely helpful in determining the sequence in which power travels through the unit and for checking the correct operation of switches and loads.

Insufficient heat

1. **System or Building Incomplete:**   Your new furnace will not produce proper comfort until all construction has been completed and all insulation is in place.

2. **Building Not Properly Winterized:**   If a drafty conditions exists, we suggest installation of storm doors and windows, as needed. If walls or ceiling are excessively cold, proper insulation (if practicable to install) will do much to reduce fuel bills and improve comfort.

3. **Furnace Overloaded:**   This can happen when a dwelling is enlarged (by adding on rooms or opening up previously unused attic space). Have a heating engineer check the required heat load against the furnace capacity. He or she will make proper and economical recommendations for solving this problem

4. **Power Supply Turned Off:**   Close switch.

5. **Low Power Supply Voltage:**   Contact power company.

6. **Main Fuse Blown:**   Contact a service technician or the power company if they have a service department.

7. **Incorrect Thermostat Anticipator Setting:**   Correct setting

8. **Fan Operating at Too High a Speed Resulting in a Low Temperature Rise:**   reconnect fan motor to next lower speed

9. **Unit Cycling on Limit Controls Because of Inadequate Air Circulation:**
   (a)   Dirty air filter—clean or replace filter
   (b)   Fan wheel blades dirty—clean blades
   (c)   Duct dampers closed—open dampers
   (d)   Registers closed or restricted—open registers
   (e)   Fan motor nonoperational—contact a serviceperson.

Other causes of insufficient heat could be open heater element or elements, blown element fuses, blown fan motor and transformer fuses, blown thermal link fuses, shorted contactor control, shorted wiring, shorted transformer, loose terminal connections, and so on. Any of these malfunctions require the services of a technician or electrician.

Rooms too hot or some too cold

1. **Thermostat Located Incorrectly:**   Read section in this manual on locating thermostat—and relocate it as necessary.

2. **System Out of Balance:**   Readjust dampers.

3. **Registers Blocked:** Check carefully to make sure that rugs or furniture are not covering or blocking discharge or return air registers.

4. **Air Passages Blocked:** Check to see that return air passages are not blocked. Remove obstructions such as fallen insulation.

Fan/motor noisy

Check fan assembly for loose bolts; then lubricate motor bearings.

Checking Power

It is essential that proper power be supplied to the equipment and to load devices in the furnace. Manufacturers' data on the nameplate indicates the proper voltage. Most equipment can be operated within a range of 10% above or below the rated voltage. If power is not available within these limits, the equipment will not operate properly.

Checking Switches

(a) **Voltmeter:** This test can be used only when power is on and the voltmeter leads are placed across the two terminals of the switch. When the switch is closed, the voltmeter reads 0. When the switch is open, the voltmeter reads the voltage in the circuit.

(b) **Ohmmeter:** *This test is used only when the power is off.* The leads of the ohmmeter are placed across the two terminals of the switch. The switch must be disconnected from the circuit. A 0 reading indicates that the switch is closed. An ∞ (infinity) reading indicates the switch is open.

(c) **Jumper:** This test is used with power on. If a jumper across the two terminals of the switch operates the load, the switch is open.

Checking Loads

(a) **Voltmeter:** Test with power on. Determine if proper voltage is available at the load. With proper voltage the load should operate.

(b) **Ammeter:** This test is performed with power on.

The ammeter test is used to check the current used by the total furnace or any one of its load components (Figure 19-13). The meter readings are compared with the data on the nameplate. This test offers an excellent means of checking the current through the sequencer to be certain that the elements are being staged on at the proper time. The jaws of the clamp-on ammeter are placed around one of the main power supply lines.

Figure 19-13 Ammeter used to read current draw of electric furnace.

CHAPTER 19 STUDY QUESTIONS

The answers to the study questions are found in the sections of this chapter under the chapter topic indicated.

STUDY QUESTIONS	*CHAPTER TOPIC*
1. What is the principal difference between the electric heating furnace and other types?	*Conversion of electricity to heat*
2. What is the heat equivalent of 1 W?	*Conversion of electricity to heat*
3. What is the efficiency of an electric furnace?	*Electric furnace components*
4. What is the cut-out temperature on an electric furnace limit control?	*Heating elements*
5. What is the maximum-sized heating element?	*Heating elements*
6. What voltage is supplied to an electric furnace?	*Power supply*
7. What are the voltages on a control circuit transformer on an electric furnace?	*Power circuit*
8. Are the heating elements connected in series or parallel?	*Heating element circuits*
9. What is the purpose of the sequencer?	*Heating element circuits*
10. The outdoor thermostat is used in place of what type of room thermostat?	*Heating element circuits*
11. What instrument is used to check the flow of current through the heating elements?	*Checking loads*
12. What are the causes of insufficient heat?	*Service hints*
13. What causes rooms to be too hot?	*Service hints*
14. Should the fan always operate when the heating elements are on?	*Fan circuit*

20 Heating System Maintenance and Customer Relations

OBJECTIVES

After studying this chapter, the student will be able to:

- Determine the maintenance requirements for a heating system
- Instruct the owner on proper care and operation of the system

IMPORTANCE OF PROPER MAINTENANCE

Any mechanical equipment requires proper maintenance to continue its original efficiency. Heating systems are no exception. With proper care, a heating system will provide good performance for many years. In addition to producing periodic maintenance, the contractor can often upgrade the system when new technology is available.

The maintenance items that should receive attention include the following:

1. Testing and adjusting the fuel burning unit
2. Cleaning the air passages of the system
3. Servicing the fan-motor assembly
4. Rebalancing the system
5. Adjusting the thermostat anticipator and fan control
6. Testing the power and safety controls

7. Cleaning the heat exchangers

8. Changing air filters

9. Servicing accessories

10. Upgrading the equipment wherever possible

TESTING AND ADJUSTING

Information on combustion is covered in Chapter 6. The use of various types of combustion test instruments is supplied in Chapters 8, 9, and 14. It is important to adjust the fuel-burning unit to produce the highest efficiency that can be continuously maintained. The firing rate of the fuel and the supply of combustion air are the principal adjustments.

The firing rate of the fuel should be set to match the input requirements of the furnace indicated on the nameplate. For example, on a gas furnace if the input rating is 100,000 Btuh and the heating value of the gas is 1000 Btu/ft^3, the rate at which gas should be supplied is 100 ft^3/hr. This can be tested by turning the thermostat up and timing the gas flow through the meter. If the input is incorrect, an adjustment can be made at the gas pressure regulator or to the size of the burner orifices. On an oil burner, the size of the nozzle and the oil pressure will determine the firing rate.

Gas Furnace

Observe the flame. It should be a soft blue color without yellow tips. Adjust primary air if necessary. If the flame will not clean up when adjusted, remove the burners and clean them both inside and outside.

Measure the gas pressure (Figure 20-1). It should be 3.5 in. W.C. for natural gas and 10.0 in. W.C. for liquid petroleum gas. Measurements are made at the manifold pressure tap with main burners operating and with other gas-burning appliances in operation.

Figure 20-1 Measuring manifold gas pressure.

Check the thermocouple. The thermocouple, under no load, should generate 18–30 mV dc. When under load, it should generate at least 7 mV dc.

Oil Furnace

Clean the burner (Figure 20-2) and run a complete combustion test. Replace the oil burner nozzle if necessary. Adjust the air volume for maximum efficiency. Replace the oil line filter. Clean the bimetallic element on the stack relay (if used).

Observe the flame after the burner is restarted. The flame should be yellow in color and centered in the combustion chamber.

At this point a final adjustment should be made using proper test instruments. Unless otherwise specified in appliance manufacturer's instructions, the unit should be set as follows: After allowing 10 min for warm-up, air should be set so the smoke number is no greater than 1; less than number 1 smoke is desired. (**Note:** Occasionally a new heating unit requires more time than this to burn cleanly due to the oil film on heater surfaces.) Carbon dioxide measured in the stack (ahead of draft control) should be at least 8% for oil rates 1.0 gal/h or less and 9% for oil rates over 1.0 gal/h. The unit should be started and stopped several times to assure good operation.

Check the oil pressure (Figure 20-3). It should be 100 psig during operation and 85 psig immediately after shutdown. Motor life will be increased by proper oiling. Use a few drops of nondetergent oil at both motor oil holes twice each year. The line filter cartridge should be replaced every year to avoid contamination of the fuel unit and atomizing nozzle. Finally, the area around the heating unit should be kept clean and free of any combustible materials, especially papers and oil rags.

Figure 20-2 Typical oil burner assembly. (Courtesy, R. W. Beckett Company.)

Figure 20-3 Checking the oil pressure. (Courtesy, Sundstrand Hydraulics.)

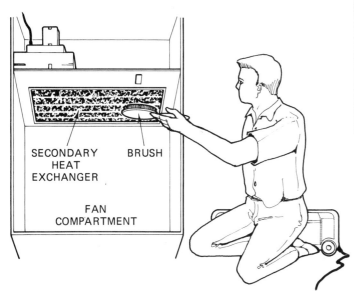

SECONDARY HEAT EXCHANGER

BRUSH

FAN COMPARTMENT

Figure 20-4 Cleaning secondary heat exchanger.

Electric Furnace

Set the thermostat to call for heat. Check by reading the incoming power amperage to be certain that all heater elements are operating.

On the three- and four-element furnaces that are equipped with a fused disconnect block, both legs of the heating elements are provided with cartridge fuses internal to the furnace. Two elements and the blower are grouped together on a 60-A fuse. On three-element furnaces, a single element is fused at 30-A.

Cleaning Air Passages

If construction work has taken place in the area or if the occupant is negligent in keeping the filters clean, there may be a layer of airborne dust on the outside surface of the heat exchangers. This surface needs to be kept clean.

Particularly on high-efficiency furnaces, the external surface of the secondary heat exchanger will collect debris. Stiff bristle brushes can be used to dislodge foreign material, and a commercial vacuum cleaner can be used to remove dirt and lint.

On high-efficiency furnaces it may be necessary to remove the blower to reach the secondary heat exchanger for cleaning, as shown in Figure 20-4. Brush strokes must be in the direction of the finned surface to avoid damage to the fins.

Inspect and clean the blades of the fan wheel using a brush and vacuum. Care should be taken not to dislodge balance weights (clips) that may be on the fan wheel.

Testing and Adjusting

The fan-motor assembly requires periodic attention. The unit may be belt-driven, as shown in Figure 7-12, or direct-driven, as shown in Figure 7-13. Most direct-drive units have multiple-speed arrangements.

Some motors and bearings require lubrication, and some do not. Oil or grease should be applied in accordance with the manufacturer's instructions.

Clean out the blades of the fan wheel. Motors that require oil should be oiled twice a year. If there is more than ⅛-in. end play on the shaft, move the thrust collar closer to the bearing.

Furnace fans are designed to rotate in one direction; therefore, it is important to determine proper rotation at the time of installation or when changing the fan motor (Figure 20-5). If it becomes necessary to reverse the rotation, follow the instructions on the motor terminal block for reversing the lead wires. The directions are usually found under the cover where the lead wires enter the motor.

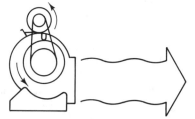

Figure 20-5 Determining fan rotation.

It is important to determine if the proper amount of air is being supplied by the fan-motor assembly. The easiest way to determine the volume of air handled by the furnace is to measure the temperature rise through the furnace. The temperature rise plus the output rating of the furnace provides the information necessary for calculating the cubic feet per minute handled by the fan:

$$\text{ft}^3/\text{min} = \frac{\text{output Btuh}}{\text{temperature rise} \times 1.08}$$

If the air volume handled by the fan does not comply with the manufacturer's requirement, the fan speed must be adjusted.

Belt-Driven Fans

If the unit is belt-driven, the speed of the fan can be changed by adjusting the variable pitch motor pulley, as shown in Figure 20-6. To adjust fan speed, loosen the set screw in the outer flange outward to decrease fan speed or inward to increase speed. The outer flange must be rotated by half-turns to avoid damage to the threads, but the flange should not be rotated outward so that the belt is riding on the hub rather than on the flanges of the pulley. After each adjustment of the motor pulley, lock the outer flange in place by

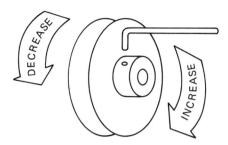

Figure 20-6 Adjustment of variable speed pulley.

tightening the set screw on the flat of the pulley hub. Line up the fan and motor pulleys by using a straightedge across two outer edges of the fan pulley, and adjust the pulley on the motor shaft so that the belt is parallel with the straightedge. Tighten the set screw securely on the flat of the motor shaft.

Most fan motors rotate at 1725 rev/min. The following table shows how the revolutions per minute can be increased or decreased by changing either the diameter of the motor pulley or the fan pulley.

EQUIPMENT SPEED rev/min
For Motors turning 1725 rev/min

Diameter of Motor Pulley	Diameter of pulley on equipment (inches)					
	5	6	7	8	9	10
1.25	431	359	308	270	240	216
1.50	518	431	370	323	288	259
1.75	604	503	431	377	335	302
2.00	690	575	493	431	383	345
2.25	776	646	554	485	431	388
2.50	862	719	616	539	479	431
2.75	949	791	678	593	527	474
3.00	1035	862	739	647	575	518
3.25	1121	934	801	701	623	561
3.50	1208	1006	862	755	671	604
3.75	1294	1078	924	809	719	647
4.00	1380	1150	986	862	767	690

$$\text{rev/min of equipment} = \frac{\text{rev/min of motor} \times \text{diameter of motor pulley}}{\text{diameter of equipment pully}}$$

For example, if the motor pulley is 2.00 in diameter and the fan pulley is 6 in., the fan would turn at 575 rev/min. If the motor pulley is increased in diameter to 3.00 in., the revolution per minute would increase to 862. It should be noted that an increase in fan revolutions per minute increases the amperage draw on the motor.

Some procedures relating to belt installation, alignment, and adjustments of belt-drive fans are shown in Figure 20-7.

Servicing Fan-Motor Assembly

WIPE OFF PULLEYS AND BELT with a clean rag to get rid of all oil and dirt. Dirt and grease are tough abrasives that cause the belt to wear out faster, throwing it out of balance and shortening its life.

INSTALL V-BELT in pulley grooves by loosening the belt take-up or the adjusting screw on the motor. Do not "roll" or "snap" the belt on the pulleys; this causes much more strain than the pulleys should have. Be sure the belt doesn't "bottom" in the pulley grooves.

ALIGN BOTH PULLEYS AND SHAFTS by moving the motor on its motor mount. You can do this "by eye," but you're a lot safer if you hold a straight edge flush against the blower pulley, then move the motor until the belt is absolutely parallel to the straight edge.

HERE'S A SHORT-CUT WAY TO CHECK PULLEY ALIGNMENT: Sight down the top of the belt from slightly above it. If the belt is straight where it leaves the pulley and does not bend, you can bet that the alignment is reasonably good.

CHECK BELT TENSION before proceeding further. Remember that a V-belt "rides" the inside of the pulley faces. Since the sides of the belt wedge in the pulleys, the V-belt does not have to be tight. It should be as loose as possible without slipping in the pulley grooves.

USE THIS RULE-OF-THUMB FOR ADJUSTING BELT TENSION: Using the belt take-up or motor adjusting screw, tighten the belt until the slack side can be depressed about ¾" for each foot of span between the pulleys. WARNING: EXCESSIVE BELT TENSION IS THE MOST FREQUENT CAUSE OF BEARING WEAR AND RESULTING NOISE.

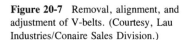

Figure 20-7 Removal, alignment, and adjustment of V-belts. (Courtesy, Lau Industries/Conaire Sales Division.)

Direct-Drive Fans

Direct-drive fans (see Figure 20-8a) are more popular than the belt-driven type because they require less maintenance. Furnaces that are equipped for air-conditioning are supplied with a multispeed motor. Multispeed motors have several connections in the motor windings, which allow the selection of different speeds. Most electric motors have a wiring diagram attached to the motor casing or to the underside of the plate that covers the motor terminals. The motor connections shown in Figure 20-8b are for a three-speed capacitor-start motor.

When cooling is added to an existing furnace, the evaporator coil adds an additional pressure drop in the distribution system. In most cases, cooling also requires more air than heating. If the furnace does not already have a multispeed motor for the fan, it is advisable to install one. For heating, the fan speed is usually slower than that used for cooling. A combination fan relay and transformer (Figure 20-9) can be installed. This

(A) DIRECT-DRIVE FAN

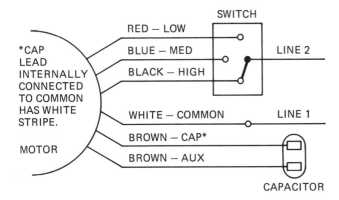

SWITCH

RED — LOW

BLUE — MED

BLACK — HIGH

LINE 2

*CAP LEAD INTERNALLY CONNECTED TO COMMON HAS WHITE STRIPE.

WHITE — COMMON   LINE 1

MOTOR

BROWN — CAP*

BROWN — AUX

CAPACITOR

(B) CONNECTIONS ON THREE-SPEED, CAPACITOR-START MOTOR.

Figure 20-8 Direct drive, multispeed fan, with capacitor start motor. (a) (Courtesy, Conaire Division, Philips Industries, Inc.) (b) (Courtesy, Universal Electric.)

Figure 20-9 Combination fan relay and transformer.

Servicing Fan-Motor Assembly

control provides a means of automatically changing the speed of the fan motor from heating to cooling.

The use of the fan relay and transformer as applied to single-speed fans is shown in Figure 20-10a, and that for two-speed fans is shown in Figure 20-10b.

Some helpful instructions on the maintenance of belt-driven and direct-drive fans are given in Figure 20-11.

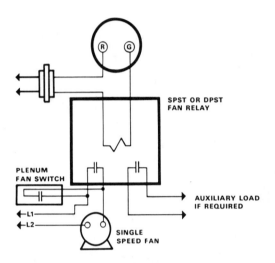

In the system shown, a call for cooling makes R-G in the thermostat and completes the circuit through the fan relay coil. The relay pulls in to energize the system fan. The plenum fan switch, for controlling the fan in the heating mode, is wired in parallel with the normally open fan relay contacts.

(A) SINGLE SPEED FAN

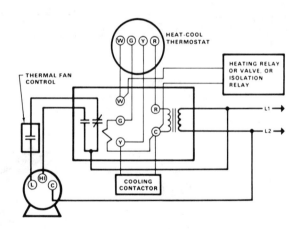

Low speed fan operation in heating mode is maintained through a normally closed contact in the fan relay. When the fan relay coil is energized on a call for cooling by the thermostat, this contact opens. This cuts off power to the low speed fan, and the normally open contacts close to energize the high speed windings of the fan motor.

Figure 20-10 Application of fan relay and transformer. (Courtesy, Honeywell Inc.)

(B) TWO SPEED FAN

	BELT DRIVE	DIRECT DRIVE
PULLEYS . . . BE SURE THEY ARE TIGHT ON THEIR SHAFTS AND ARE IN LINE	✓	
BELT . . . IF WORN, REPLACE IT AFTER DETERMINING AND CORRECTING THE CAUSE OF WEAR (BELT TOO LOOSE, BELT TOO TIGHT, PULLEYS NOT IN LINE, SHAFTS NOT PARALLEL, DIRT AND GREASE ON BELT AND PULLEYS, AND SO ON).	✓	
ELECTRICAL CONNECTIONS . . . BE SURE LEAD CABLE IS RESILIENTLY ANCHORED AND CANNOT RATTLE OR TRANSMIT VIBRATIONS.	✓	✓
FAN OUTLET . . . SEE THAT THE OUTLET IS CENTERED IN THE BLOWER OPENING OF THE UNIT AND SEALED AGAINST AIR LEAKAGE.	✓	✓
NOISE . . . MAKE SURE THERE IS NO METAL-TO-METAL CONTACT.	✓	✓
FAN BEARINGS . . . WORN BEARINGS MEAN TROUBLE. REPLACE BEARINGS AND SHAFT IF NECESSARY.	✓	
WHEEL . . . SEE THAT THE WHEEL IS CENTERED IN THE BLOWER HOUSING, AND THAT THE THRUST COLLARS ARE TIGHT ON THE SHAFT.	✓	✓
LUBRICATION . . . OIL THE MOTOR AND FAN BEARINGS, IF NEEDED.	✓	
FILTERS . . . FILTERS SHOULD BE REPLACED AT THE BEGINNING OF EACH SEASON, AND SHOULD BE CHANGED DURING THE SEASON, UNLESS A PERMANENT TYPE IS FOUND.	✓	✓

Figure 20-11 Handy checklist for belt-driven and direct-drive fans. (Courtesy, Lau Industries, Conaire Sales Division.)

REBALANCING THE SYSTEM

After a forced warm air system has been in use for a period of time, some rooms may be heating better than others. Therefore, rebalancing the system is in order.

Air balancing is performed by adjusting the branch-duct dampers to produce uniform temperatures throughout the building (Figure 20-12). The procedure is as follows:

1. Place a thermometer in each room, at table height.

2. Open all supply and return air duct dampers.

3. Open all grilles and register dampers.

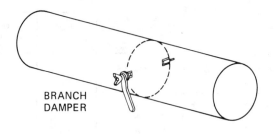

BRANCH
DAMPER

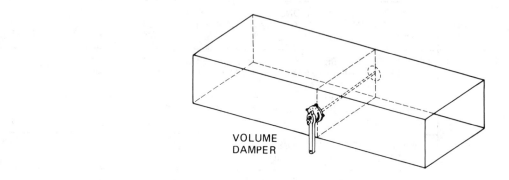

VOLUME
DAMPER

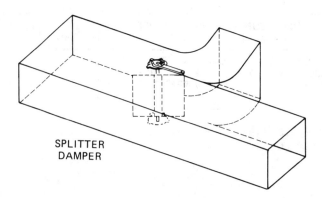

SPLITTER
DAMPER

Figure 20-12 Damper adjustment.

4. Set the thermostat to call for heat.

5. Adjust the dampers while furnace is running to produce uniform temperatures in all the rooms.

The balancing should be done during weather cold enough to permit continuous operation of the heating equipment for a substantial period of time. Continuous fan operation with the furnace cycling at the rate of 8 to 10 times per hour provides good conditions for balancing.

ADJUSTING THE THERMOSTAT ANTICIPATOR AND FAN CONTROL

The thermostat anticipator is adjusted to control the length of the operating cycle. Raising the amperage setting of the anticipator lengthens the cycle. Lowering the amperage setting of the anticipator shortens the cycle.

Most anticipators are marked with a series of current (amperage) settings. A moveable arm can be positioned at the required amperage. The normal setting is indicated on the gas valve. Changes, however, are often necessary to improve the operating characteristics of a specific installation.

A typical heating thermostat anticipator is shown in Figure 20-13. The thermostat should be secure and level and all wiring connections should be tight. Any dust or lint that may have collected on the moving parts should be carefully removed.

Where continuous fan action is not used, the fan control on an upflow furnace starts the fan when the bonnet temperature reaches its cut-in point (Figure 20-14). If the fan is delivering air that is too cool for comfort, the cut-in point of the fan control can be raised. It is advantageous to have the longest possible fan-on time and still not blow cold air. The differential of the fan control (cut-in temperature minus cut-out temperature) should be great enough to prevent short cycling of the fan.

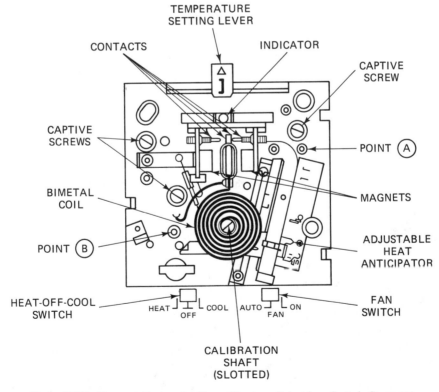

Figure 20-13 Thermostat base and subbase. (Courtesy, Robertshaw Controls Company.)

Adjusting the Thermostat Anticipator and Fan Control

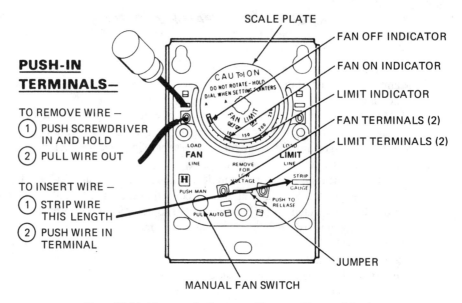

PUSH-IN TERMINALS—

TO REMOVE WIRE —

① PUSH SCREWDRIVER IN AND HOLD

② PULL WIRE OUT

TO INSERT WIRE —

① STRIP WIRE THIS LENGTH

② PUSH WIRE IN TERMINAL

SCALE PLATE

FAN OFF INDICATOR

FAN ON INDICATOR

LIMIT INDICATOR

FAN TERMINALS (2)

LIMIT TERMINALS (2)

JUMPER

MANUAL FAN SWITCH

Figure 20-14 Fan control adjustment. (Courtesy, Honeywell Inc.)

TESTING THE POWER AND SAFETY CONTROLS

It is important to use a separately fused branch electrical circuit containing a properly sized fuse or circuit breaker for the furnace. A means for disconnecting the furnace must be located within sight of it and readily accessible to it.

Check the supply voltage to be certain that the proper power is being delivered to the furnace. To check the supply voltage to determine that it is adequate, the following procedure is recommended:

1. On a gas-fired, forced-air furnace, remove the transformer; then check the power supply leads in the junction box (Figure 20-15).

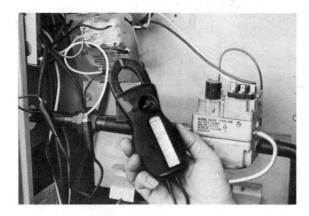

Figure 20-15 Checking the power supply on a gas-fired furnace.

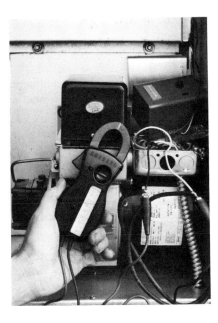

Figure 20-16 Checking the power supply on an oil-fired furnace.

2. On an oil-fired, forced-air furnace, remove the cad-cell control from the top of the oil burner assembly; then check the power supply leads in the junction box (Figure 20-16).

Check to be sure that all wiring connections are tight and that wiring insulation is in good condition. With a thermometer, check the cut-out point of the limit control by shutting down the fan. Bonnet temperature must not exceed 200°F.

SAFETY CHECK OF THE LIMIT CONTROL

The limit control shuts off the combustion control system and energizes the circulating-air fan motor if the furnace overheats.

The recommended method of checking the limit control is to gradually block off the return air after the furnace has been operating for a period of at least 5 min. As soon as the limit has proven safe, the return-air opening should be unblocked to permit normal air circulation. By using this method to check the limit control, it can be established that the limit is functioning properly and will provide a fail-safe if there is a motor failure. (The downflow or horizontal furnaces have a manual reset limit switch located on the fan housing.)

On high-efficiency furnaces, there are many sensing switches and safeguard controls that must be checked to be certain that the equipment will run properly.

SAFETY CHECK OF FLOW-SENSING SWITCH

1. Turn off 115-V power to furnace.

2. Remove the control door and disconnect the inducer motor lead wires from the inducer printed-circuit board.

3. Turn on 115-V power to furnace.

4. Close the thermostat switch as if making a normal furnace start. The pilot should light and then cycle off and on. If the main burners do not light, the flow-sensing switch is functioning properly.

5. Turn off 115-V power to furnace.

6. Reconnect the inducer motor wires, replace the control door, and turn on 115-V power.

SAFETY CHECK OF DRAFT SAFEGUARD SWITCH

The purpose of this control is to permit the safe shutdown of the furnace during certain blocked flue conditions.

1. Disconnect power to the furnace and remove the vent pipe from furnace outlet collar. Be sure to allow time for the vent pipe to cool down before removing.

2. Set the room thermostat above room temperature and restore power to furnace.

3. After normal startup, allow furnace to operate for 2 min; then block (100%) flue outlet. Furnace should cycle off within 2 min.

4. Reconnect vent pipe to furnace outlet collar.

5. Wait 5 min and then reset draft safeguard switch.

CLEANING THE HEAT EXCHANGER

The only time that it is necessary to disassemble the furnace and clean the interior surface of the heat exchanger is when the fuel-burning device is out of adjustment and sooting

Figure 20-17 Cleaning heat exchanger.

occurs in the flue passages. On some conventional furnaces it is possible to use a brush to dislodge the soot (Figure 20-17) and a vacuum to remove it.

On high-efficiency furnaces, two heat exchangers may require cleaning. A typical location of these heat exchangers is shown in Figure 20-18.

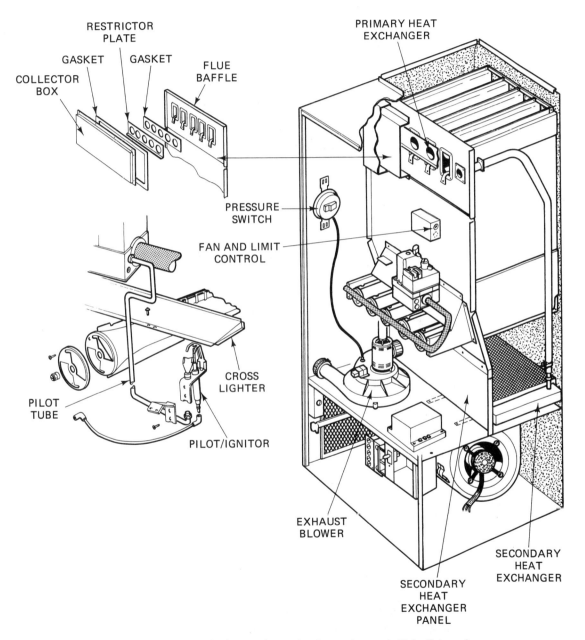

Figure 20-18 Location of primary and secondary heat exchangers in high-efficiency furnace.

Cleaning the Heat Exchanger

Figure 20-19 Replacing air filters. (Courtesy, American Air Filter Company.)

CHANGING AIR FILTERS

Clean or replace air filters as often as necessary to permit proper air flow. Replacement filters should be similar in material, thickness, and size, to those removed (Figure 20-19).

The air filters must be clean when testing any system for air volume. A dirty filter creates an unnecessary restriction, thereby reducing air volume.

SERVICING ACCESSORIES

Clean and service accessories in accordance with manufacturer's instructions. Humidifiers may require cleaning more than once a year depending on water conditions.

The condenser surface on condensing units used for cooling must be kept clean. Condenser fans usually require lubrication.

UPGRADING THE FURNACE

The owner should be advised of any advanced technology that will improve efficiency or comfort. These items include programmable thermostats, flue dampers, electronic ignition, and so forth.

CUSTOMER RELATIONS

Good practice in customer relations has many benefits. Continuing good relationships with customers increase their awareness of the responsibility they have toward properly maintaining the equipment. Satisfied customers usually mean repeat business and new customers. Here are some of the important areas in this relationship:

1. Instructions about equipment care

2. Service company communication

3. Warranty

4. Service record

A service technician should produce a positive relationship with the customer since he or she may be the only company representative the customer ever meets. Appearance and attitude reflect the service technician's role in fostering customer relations. Neatness also counts in regard to tools. Technicians should be outfitted with proper tools required for the job and have thorough training, not only in the use of tools required for specific equipment but also in customer relationships.

Instructions for Equipment Care

Discuss with the owner the features of the installation, how the system operates, and the proper care of the system. Post information similar to the ''Maintenance and Care'' forms shown in Figures 20-20 and 20-21.

Service Company Communications

The name and telephone number of the service company should be displayed in a prominent location near the installation. A service log should be attached to the furnace and kept up to date by any technician servicing the unit.

Warranty

The manufacturer's limited warranty (Figure 20-22) and the contractor's warranty should be supplied to the owner. Although the manufacturer does not include labor in replacing a defective part during the first year, usually the contractor's warranty does. Manufacturers often offer an extended warranty on parts such as heat exchangers (Figure 20-23).

Service Record

It is important to leave the owner with a record of a service call. This is part of the communication system between the owner and the customer. This record shows what has been done and when the work was performed. It is also helpful to the contractor for informing his or her employees about the history of an installation when additional work is required. A sample combustion service record for an oil-fired installation is shown in Figure 20-24.

MAINTENANCE AND CARE FOR THE OWNER OF A GAS-FIRED FURNACE

Warning:

1. TURN OFF ELECTRICAL POWER SUPPLY TO YOUR FURNACE BEFORE REMOVING ACCESS DOORS TO SERVICE OR PERFORM MAINTENANCE.

2. When removing access doors or performing maintenance functions inside your furnace, be aware of sharp sheet metal parts and screws. BE EXTREMELY CAREFUL WHEN HANDLING PARTS OR REACHING INTO THE UNIT.

AIR FILTER

The air filter should be checked at least every 6 to 8 weeks and changed or cleaned whenever it becomes dirty.

The size of the air filter varies, depending on the furnace model and size. When replacing your furnace filter, always use the same size and type of filter that was originally supplied.

Warning: NEVER OPERATE YOUR FURNACE WITHOUT A FILTER IN PLACE.

Failure to heed this warning may result in damage to the furnace blower motor. An accumulation of dust and lint on internal parts of your furnace can cause a loss of efficiency and, in some cases, fire.

When inspecting, cleaning, or replacing the air filter in your furnace, refer to the appropriate following procedures that apply to your particular furnace.

1. Turn OFF the electrical supply to the furnace. Remove the control and fan access doors, respectively.

2. Gently remove the filter and carefully turn the dirty side up (if dirty) to avoid dislodging dirt from the filter.

3. If the filter is dirty, wash it in a sink or bathtub or outside with a garden hose. Always use cold water, and use a mild liquid detergent if necessary. Then, allow the filter to air dry.

4. Reinstall the clean filter with the crosshatch binding side facing the furnace fan. Be sure that the filter retainer is under the flange on the furnace casing.

5. Replace the fan and control access doors, and restore electrical power to your furnace.

COMBUSTION AREA AND VENT SYSTEM

The combustion area and vent system should be visually inspected before each heating season. An accumulation of dirt, soot, or rust can result in loss of efficiency and improper performance. Accumulations on the main burners can result in the burners firing out of normal time sequence. This delayed ignition is characterized by an especially loud sound that can be quite alarming.

Caution: If your furnace makes an especially loud noise when the main burners are ignited by the pilot, shut down your furnace and call your service person.

1. Turn OFF the electrical supply to your furnace and remove the access doors.

2. Carefully inspect the gas burner and pilot areas for dirt, rust, or scale. Then, inspect the flue connection area and flue pipe for rust.

Caution: If dirt, rust, soot, or scale accumulations are found, call your service person.

Figure 20-20 Typical gas-fired furnace maintenance and care instructions.

MAINTENANCE AND CARE FOR THE OWNER OF
AN OIL-FIRED FURNACE

SAFETY INFORMATION

Warning: These instructions are intended to aid you in the safe operation and proper maintenance of your oil furnace. Read these instructions thoroughly before attempting to operate the furnace. The purpose of WARNINGS and CAUTIONS in these instructions is to call attention to the possible danger of personal injury or equipment damage; they deserve careful attention and understanding. If you do not understand any part of these instructions, contact a qualified licensed service person for clarification.

1. Do not attempt to light the burner manually with a match or other flame.
2. Do not attempt to start the burner with oil or oil vapors in the combustion chamber.
3. Do not operate the furnace without all fan doors and compartment covers securely in place.
4. Do not attach any kind of device to the flue or vent.
5. Always shut off electrical power to the furnace before attempting any maintenance.

HOW YOUR SYSTEM OPERATES

As the flame from the oil burner warms the heat exchanger, the fan switch will start the fan operation. Warm air should now gently circulate from the supply diffusers throughout the dwelling and return to the furnace through return air grille(s).

When the temperature of the circulating air reaches the temperature setting of the thermostat, the oil burner will stop operation, the heat exchanger will cool, and the fan operation will soon be interrupted.

OPERATING INSTRUCTIONS

Burner operation

1. Set the room thermostat above room temperature.
2. Turn the electric switch on. The burner should start automatically.
3. After burner starts, reset the room thermostat for desired temperature.

If Burner Does Not Start

1. Check the fuse in the burner circuit.
2. Make sure the room thermostat is set above the room temperature.

Warning: An explosion or flash fire can occur if the combustion chamber is not free of oil when using the primary control reset button. Make sure the combustion chamber is free of oil before using the reset button.

3. Wait 5 minutes in order to allow the control to cool so that it will recycle. Reset the primary control.
4. If the burner still does not start, call your service person.

Note: CAD CELL MAY BE EXPOSED TO DIRECT ARTIFICIAL LIGHT OR SUNLIGHT, WHICH MAY ENTER THROUGH THE BURNER AIR-CONTROL BAND.

ANNUAL MAINTENANCE

1. Before the heating season, lubricate the burner motor using SAE No. 20 motor oil.

Caution: Do not oil more than necessary. Follow the instructions attached to the fan housing.

2. Have the burner, heating unit, and all controls checked by your service contractor to assure proper operation during the heating season.

TO CHANGE OIL FILTER

1. Turn electric switch off.
2. Close the oil-line valve at tank.
3. Carefully remove the lower section of the filter assembly containing the oil filter cartridge.
4. Drain excess oil from the oil line into a container; then dispose of the oil and the old cartridge.
5. Place a new filter cartridge in the filter assembly and screw it back into place.
6. Loosen the "bleed" screw on top of oil cartridge assembly, allowing air to be purged. Tighten the bleed screw.
7. Open valve in oil line at tank.

THINGS YOU MAY DO

1. **Warning:** Disconnect the main power to the unit before attempting any maintenance.
2. Keep the air filters clean.

Caution: DO NOT OPERATE YOUR SYSTEM FOR EXTENDED PERIODS WITHOUT FILTERS. ANY RECIRCULATED DUST PARTICLES WILL BE HEATED AND CHARRED BY CONTACT WITH THE FURNACE HEAT EXCHANGER. THIS RESIDUE WILL SOIL CEILINGS, WALLS, DRAPES, CARPETS, AND OTHER HOUSEHOLD ARTICLES.

LUBRICATION INSTRUCTIONS

Highboy Units

In order to oil the motor and fan, it is necessary to slide the fan out of the furnace. Remove the fan panel on the front of the furnace and slide the fan section out.

Counterflow Units

In order to oil the motor and fan, it is necessary to remove the upper inner panel of the fan compartment. Follow the instructions on the label.

Lowboy and Horizontal Units

In order to oil the motor and fan, it is necessary to remove only the fan compartment door. The fan is positioned within the compartment to make the fan bearings accessible for oiling.

Proper belt tension is important and may be checked by depressing the belt at a point halfway between the pulleys approximately 1 in. Belt tension may be adjusted by turning the adjustment screw attached to motor base to raise or lower motor.

Figure 20-21 Typical oil-fired furnace maintenance and care instructions.

DELUXE INDOOR GAS-FIRED FURNACE
LIMITED WARRANTY

ONE-YEAR WARRANTY — This BDP COMPANY product is warranted to be free from defects in material and workmanship under normal use and maintenance for a period of one year from the date of installation whether or not actual use begins on that date. A new or remanufactured part, at BDP COMPANY'S sole option, to replace any defective part will be provided without charge for the part itself, PROVIDED the defective part is returned to our distributor through a qualified servicing dealer. The replacement part assumes the unused portion of the warranty. This warranty applies only to the product in its original installation location and is voided if the product is reinstalled elsewhere.

THIS WARRANTY DOES NOT INCLUDE LABOR OR OTHER COSTS incurred for diagnosing, repairing, removing, installing, shipping, servicing or handling of either defective parts or replacement parts. Such costs may be covered by a separate warranty provided by the installer.

EXTENDED 19-YEAR WARRANTY ON HEAT EXCHANGER ONLY — During the second through twentieth years after the start of the 1-YEAR WARRANTY, BDP COMPANY further warrants the heat exchanger against defects in material or workmanship under normal use and maintenance. BDP COMPANY will, at BDP COMPANY'S sole option, either provide a new or remanufactured heat exchanger under the same conditions as stated in the 1-YEAR WARRANTY, OR allow a credit in the amount of the then current retail selling price of an equivalent heat exchanger toward the purchase of a new BRYANT, DAY & NIGHT or PAYNE gas furnace, PROVIDED the defective heat exchanger is returned to our distributor through a qualified servicing dealer.

THIS WARRANTY DOES NOT INCLUDE LABOR or other costs incurred for repairing, removing, installing, shipping, servicing or handling of either defective parts or complete furnace or replacement parts or complete furnace. Such costs are the responsibility of the owner.

LIMITATION OF WARRANTIES — ALL IMPLIED WARRANTIES INCLUDING IMPLIED WARRANTIES OF MERCHANTABILITY, ARE HEREBY LIMITED IN DURATION TO THE PERIOD FOR WHICH EACH LIMITED WARRANTY IS GIVEN. THE EXPRESSED WARRANTIES MADE IN THIS WARRANTY ARE EXCLUSIVE AND MAY NOT BE ALTERED, ENLARGED OR CHANGED BY ANY DISTRIBUTOR, DEALER OR OTHER PERSON WHATSOEVER.

ALL WORK UNDER THE TERMS OF THIS WARRANTY SHALL BE PERFORMED DURING NORMAL WORKING HOURS. ALL REPLACEMENT PARTS, WHETHER NEW OR REMANUFACTURED, ASSUME AS THEIR WARRANTY PERIOD ONLY THE REMAINING TIME PERIOD OF THIS WARRANTY.

BDP COMPANY WILL NOT BE RESPONSIBLE FOR:

1. Normal maintenance as outlined in the owner's instructions.
2. Damage or repairs required as a consequence of faulty installation or application by others.
3. Failure to start due to voltage conditions, blown fuses, open circuit breakers, or other damages due to the inadequacy or interruption of electrical service.
4. Damage or repairs needed as a consequence of any application, abuse, improper servicing, unauthorized alteration, or improper operation.
5. Damage as a result of floods, winds, fires, lightning, accidents, corrosive atmosphere, or other conditions beyond the control of BDP COMPANY.
6. Parts not supplied or designated by BDP COMPANY.
7. BDP COMPANY products installed outside the continental United States of America, Alaska, Hawaii, and Canada.
8. Electricity or fuel costs or increases in electricity or fuel costs from any reason whatsoever including additional or unusual use of supplemental electric heat.
9. ANY SPECIAL, INDIRECT, CONSEQUENTIAL, PROPERTY, OR COMMERCIAL DAMAGE OF ANY NATURE WHATSOEVER.

Some states do not allow the exclusion or limitation of incidental or consequential damages and some states do not allow limitations on how long an implied warranty lasts, so the above limitations may not apply to you.

This warranty gives you specific legal rights, and you may also have other rights which vary from state to state.

FOR SERVICE OR REPAIR, FOLLOW THESE STEPS IN ORDER:

FIRST: Contact the installer. You may find his name on the product or in your Owner's Packet. If his name is not known, call your builder if yours is a new residence.

SECOND: Contact the nearest distributor. (See telephone pages.)

THIRD: Contact:

BDP COMPANY	or	BDP COMPANY
Consumer Relations Department		Consumer Relations Department
7310 West Morris Street		855 Anaheim-Puente Road
Indianapolis, Indiana 46231		City of Industry, California 91749
Phone: (317) 243-0851		Phone: (213) 964-1211

Model No. _____   Unit Serial No. _____

Date of Installation _____   Installed by _____

Name of Owner _____   Address of Installation _____

Figure 20-22 Sample of limited warranty. (Courtesy, BDP Company.)

Heating Equipment Warranty

Heating equipment manufactured by Duomatic Olsen Inc. is warranted to the original owner against defects in workmanship and material for 1 year from the date of original installation. Blower, motor controls and other electrical or mechanical components which are not manufactured by Duomatic Olsen Inc. are not warranted by Duomatic Olsen Inc. but are warranted by their respective manufacturer.

In addition to the above warranty, the heat exchanger and electric heat elements are warranted by Duomatic Olsen Inc. against failure under normal use due to defects in workmanship or material as set out in the following table:

PRODUCT	MODEL NUMBER PREFIX	DURATION OF WARRANTY	COST TO OWNER OF REPLACEMENT PART EXPRESSED AS A PERCENTAGE OF THE RETAIL PRICE PREVAILING AT THE TIME OF REPLACEMENT
Gas Residential Furnaces with sectional steel Heat Exchangers	HBS, WBS	20 years	First 10 years after date of original installation — None 11–12th year — 50% 13–14th year — 60% 15–16th year — 70% 17–18th year — 80% 19–20th year — 90%
Gas Unit Heaters with aluminized sectional Heat Exchangers	KUS	5 years	None
Oil Furnaces with drum type Heat Exchangers	HTL, WTL, BCL	20 years	First 10 years after date of original installation — None 11–12th year — 50% 13–14th year — 60% 15–16th year — 70% 17–18th year — 80% 19–20th year — 90%
Oil Furnaces with drum type Heat Exchangers	DOS	10 years	None
Solid Fuel and Multi Fuel Furnace Heat Exchangers	CWO-B, CWO-C BBC, CWF	10 years	None
Solid Fuel Boiler (Vessel Only)	WBA	10 years	None

The obligation of Duomatic Olsen Inc. under the above warranties is limited to repairing or replacing with new or reconditioned parts at the discretion of Duomatic Olsen Inc. or its authorized agent any part which Duomatic Olsen Inc. or its authorized agent finds defective without charge to the original owner other than the charge specified in the above table F.O.B. factory.

Save as stated herein, the above warranties do not include any freight, mileage, labor, taxes or other expenses incurred by the original owner if any part warranted by Duomatic Olsen Inc. requires replacement.

This warranty applies only when this heating equipment:

1. Is sold and installed within the boundaries of United States of America.
2. Is installed in accordance with our instructions, by certified installers where applicable, and with good practice and accepted standards.
3. Has been fired with proper type of fuel, has been maintained in accordance with our instructions and good operating practice.
4. Has not been fired at an input in excess of its rated or designed input capacity.
5. Has not been operated without adequate air circulation over the heating element or without proper limit to warm air temperature; has not been damaged through malice, ignorance, accident or faulty installation.
6. Is installed where standard or normal atmosphere prevails and the unit is not subject to excessive humidity, dust conditions, or chemical atmosphere of any type or kind which may cause accelerated metal corrosion.
7. In relation to Item No. 6 Duomatic Olsen Inc. will not assume laboratory costs where test return positive.

If any of the above conditions exist or have affected this product, the warranty is null and void. This warranty is the sole guarantee extended by Duomatic Olsen Inc. and is given in lieu of all other representations, warranties or covenants, expressed or implied, statutory or otherwise, whether as to merchantability, fitness of purpose or otherwise. This warranty is for the sole benefit of the original owner and may not be transferred.

RETAIN FOR REFERENCE:

MODEL NO.: .... DATE OF INSTALLATION: ....

SERIAL NO.: .... INSTALLER: ....

DUOMATIC OLSEN INC., TILBURY, ONTARIO, CANADA

Figure 20-23 Sample warranty. (Courtesy, Duomatic Olsen Inc.)

COMBUSTION SERVICE RECORD

HIGH PRESSURE GUN-TYPE BURNERS

For Use with BACHARACH Combustion Testing Instruments

Owner _John Doe_
Street _426 Maple Drive_
City _Centerville_   Phone _CE-5481-J_
If not home get key _428 Maple Drive_
Occupant _Same_
Street _____
City _____   Phone _____
Work Authorized ☑ by Owner ☐ by Occupant

John Doe
<small>signature of person authorizing work</small>

Order No. _4244_   Date _____
Taken by _Smith_

Condition Reported

☐ No Fire   ☑ Insufficient Heat
☑ Excessive Oil Consumption   ☐ Odor
☐ Burner Ignites, then Goes Out   ☐ Noise
☐ Burner puffs . . . ☐ On Start; ☐ On Stop
OTHER _____

When Service Wanted
DATE _____ TIME _Before Noon_
☐ PHONE FOR APPOINTMENT _____

Job Assigned to:
NAME _Ryan_   DATE _____

Job Completed:
DATE _____ TIME _10 AM_
BY _Tom Ryan_
<small>Signature of Service Man</small>

I—Preparing for Combustion Test

1. Open main burner switch.
2. Inspect and clean out accumulated oil in combustion chamber.
3. Advance thermostat. (5-10° F.)
4. Close remote control burner switch.
5. Make ¼" diameter hole in flue pipe and overfire

(for BACHARACH test instruments).
6. Insert TEMPOINT thermometer (200-1000° F. range). through ¼" diameter hole in flue pipe.
7. Open inspection port or door.
8. Adjust flame mirror.
9. Close main burner switch. (Starting burner.)

II—Combustion Test Procedure and Inspection Data

STEP	Observe—and mark with √		1	2	3	4
1	FLAME IGNITION	Instant	✓	✓		
		Delayed				
		Doesn't Ignite				
2	FLAME COLOR	Orange		✓		
	If flame shows two colors check both	Yellow	✓	✓		
		White				
		Sparks				
3	FLAME SHAPE	Uniform	✓			
		Lop-sided				
4	FLAME IMPINGEMENT	At bottom				
		At sides				
		At rear				
5	ODOR	None	✓			
	Near burner, observation door, draft regulator	Slight				
		Heavy				
6	NOISE	Rattle				
	Mark (x) when Excessive	Hum				
	Mark (√) if Moderate	Pulsation				
		Start				
		Running				
		After fire				
7	SOOT DEPOSIT	Flue				
	Mark (x) if Heavy;	Comb. Chamber				
	(√) if Light;					
	(o) if None	Furnace/Boiler				

STEP	Observe—and write in data		1	2	3	4
8	(Close observation door) OVERFIRE DRAFT in inches Water		.030	.020		
9	TEMPOINT READING FLUE GAS TEMP. °F. When constant temperature is reached		710	610		

STEP	Observe—and write in data		1	2	3	4
10	BASEMENT AIR TEMP. °F.		60	60		
11	NET STACK TEMP. °F. Subtract basement temp. (step 10) from flue gas temp. (step 9)		650	550		
12	FLUE DRAFT in inches water. (use same hole used for stack temp. test)		.035	.025		
13	FYRITE READING % CO₂ (use same hole used for stack temp. test)		5½	9½		
14	TRUE-SPOT SMOKE READING (use same hole used for stack temp. test)		½	1		
15	FIRE EFFICIENCY FINDER % COMBUSTION EFFICIENCY		60¼	76½		
16	(Open Main Burner Switch) FLAME CUT-OFF (Seconds) Estimate time required in seconds for flame to disappear after burner stops		2	2		
17	(Close Main Burner Switch) OIL PRESSURE (psi) Measured with oil gauge installed on pump					
18	FEED LINE SUCTION (inches) Measured with vacuum gauge installed in feed line					
19	(Open Main Burner Switch Remove Nozzle Assembly) NOZZLE (service if necessary, then reinstall)	Size—Gph				
		Type—S/H				
		Spray Angle				
20	COMBUSTION CHAMBER SIZE	Depth "				
		Length "				
		Width "				
		Area sq. in.				

III—Adjustments and Repairs

Make adjustments, install replacements, and tune-up as required. Indicate, in spaces provided below, work done before repeating the tests listed under "II".

Write in "A" for "Adjust"; "C" for "Clean", "R" for "Replace". Mark "√" for other work, and describe it on the back of this sheet, if necessary.

WORK PERFORMED	BEFORE TEST NO.			
	2	3	4	
BURNER AIR SHUTTER	A			
SEAL AIR LEAKS	✓			
BURNER AIR BLOWER	C			
TURBULATOR				
AIR CONE				
BAROMETRIC DAMPER	A			
BURNER IGNITION— SAFETY CONTROL				
LIMIT CONTROL				
ELECTRODES				
ELECTRODE CABLE				
TRANSFORMER				
AIR FILTERS	R			
NOZZLE				
NOZZLE STRAINER				
PUMP STRAINER				
PUMP				
OIL FILTER	R			
OIL PRESSURE				
PUMP CUT OFF				
COMBUSTION CHAMBER				
BURNER POSITION				
BELT-COUPLING				
OIL LINE				
CHIMNEY REPAIRS				
FURNACE/BOILER CLEANED				

IV—Final Inspection

(a) Repeat the combustion check-ups listed under "II", and enter data in proper spaces.

(b) Check each of the following for proper setting, operation, or condition.

☑ MAIN BURNER SWITCH   ☑ THERMOSTAT
☑ BLOWER CONTROL   ☑ LIMIT CONTROL
☑ PUMP CONTROL   ☑ LUBRICATION
☐ LOW WATER CUT OFF   ☑ OIL LEAKS
☑ CIRCULATING-AIR FAN   ☑ AIR FILTERS
CONDITION OF FUEL OIL _good_
FLAME FAILURE CUT OFF TIME _120_ SEC.
IGNITION CUT OFF TIME _15_ SEC.

Figure 20-24 Sample combustion service record for oil-fired heating units. (Courtesy, Bacharach Instrument Company.)

CHAPTER 20 STUDY QUESTIONS

The answers to the study questions are found in the sections of this chapter under the chapter topic indicated.

STUDY QUESTIONS	CHAPTER TOPIC
1. Name ten items that are included under furnace maintenance.	*Importance of proper maintenance.*
2. Which parts of the furnace require adjustment?	*Importance of proper maintenance*
3. How should the firing rate of the furnace be determined?	*Testing and adjusting*
4. How is the air quantity determined?	*Servicing fan-motor assembly*
5. What is the relation of the amount of air required for cooling to the amount required for heating?	*Direct-drive fans*
6. In balancing the air flow, where are the thermometers located?	*Rebalancing the system*
7. How often should the furnace cycle per hour?	*Adjusting the thermostat anticipator and fan control*
8. How often should the fan motor be lubricated?	*Servicing fan-motor assembly*
9. What is the proper color for a gas flame?	*Gas furnace*
10. How frequently should oil burners be serviced?	*Oil furnace*
11. What is the maximum time that heat exchangers are under warranty?	*Warranty*
12. What are the important areas of concern in customer relations?	*Customer relations*

21 Energy Conservation

OBJECTIVES

After studying this chapter, the student will be able to:

- Recommend the construction factors to reduce the building exposure losses

- Determine the value of retrofit measures to reduce the use of energy required for heating

- State the types of auxiliary equipment or modifications that are available for energy conservation

ENERGY CONSERVATION MEASURES

The diagram in Figure 21-1 shows the extent to which space heating contributes to the nation's use of energy. Nearly 18% of the total energy consumed is required for heating . Further, by adding domestic hot water and air-conditioning, the proportions of energy used rises to about 25% of the total amount. Although heating is an essential element of our existence, only recently has a great deal of attention been directed to conserving this valuable natural resource.

In other areas of the text a number of ways to conserve energy are shown, including the use of high-efficiency furnaces and heat pumps, the improved use of controls, and so on. This chapter is devoted primarily to describing how the building envelope can be improved to save energy. Included also are other conservation measures for specific applications. This information is divided into the following three areas:

418

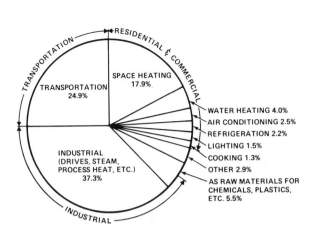

Figure 21-1 U.S. energy needs.
(Courtesy, Honeywell Inc.)

1. Reducing exposure losses

2. Reducing outside air infiltration

3. Using other retrofit measures

Although heating installation and service people are not directly concerned with the construction of the building, they are frequently called upon to offer recommendations for reducing the size of the heating load and for improving comfort levels. A good understanding of the construction factors and other modifications to improve performance can be a valuable asset.

Reducing Exposure Losses

Figure 21-2 shows the exposure losses for a typical, well-built house. The construction shown includes fiberboard sheathing, insulated doors, dual-glazed windows, R-19 ceiling insulation, and R-11 wall insulation. Variations in the size and shape of the house and its window area will alter the heat loss distribution. Typical losses are as follows.

Exposure	Percent of Total Heat Loss
Frame walls	17
Ceiling	5
Basement walls	20
Basement floor	1
Windows	16
Doors	3
Air leakage	38

Some reduction in the heat loss can be accomplished by adopting the options shown in Figure 21-3.

Energy Conservation Measures

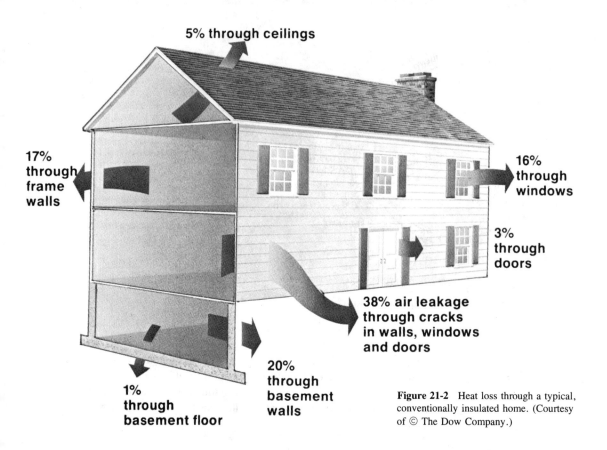

5% through ceilings

17% through frame walls

16% through windows

3% through doors

38% air leakage through cracks in walls, windows and doors

1% through basement floor

20% through basement walls

Figure 21-2 Heat loss through a typical, conventionally insulated home. (Courtesy of © The Dow Company.)

OPTION:	APPROXIMATE SAVINGS ON HOME HEAT LOSS:
CEILING: RAISE INSULATION FROM R-19 TO R-30	2%
WALL (4″ STUD): RAISE INSULATION FROM R-11 TO R-13	1%
WALL (6″ STUD): RAISE INSULATION FROM R-11 TO R-19	5%
WINDOWS: CHANGE FROM DUAL GLAZING TO TRIPLE GLAZING	5%
SHEATHING: SWITCH FROM CONVENTIONAL FIBERBOARD TO 1 IN. OF R-5.41 SHEATHING AND INSTALL FROM ROOFLINE TO SILL PLATE	14%
SHEATHING: SWITCH FROM CONVENTIONAL FIBERBOARD TO 1 IN. OF R-5.41 SHEATHING AND INSTALL FROM ROOFLINE TO FROSTLINE	24%

Figure 21-3 Thermal improvement options.

Insulation. The insulating values of various types of materials are commonly given in terms of R-factors, where R represents the resistance of the material or materials to thermal loss—that is, the R-value is the ability of the insulation to slow the transfer of heat. Higher R-values represent more insulating ability.

The following table shows the insulating values of certain substances, given in terms of 1 in. of thickness.

Material	Density (lb/ft³)	Thermal resistance (R) (in./thickness)
Glass fiber	9.5–11.0	4.00
Vermiculite, expanded	7.0–8.2	2.08
Mineral wool, resin binder	15.0	3.45
Expanded polystyrene, extruded	2.2	5.00

Figure 21-4 shows the amount of either *batts* or *loose fill* material required to achieve various insulating values. For example, 6 in. of glass mineral fiber batts are needed to produce R-19 thermal resistance. Using loose fill, 8¾ in. are required to produce the

BATTS OR BLANKETS

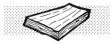

INSULATION VALUE	GLASS MINERAL FIBER INCHES	ROCK MINERAL FIBER INCHES
R-11	3½	3
R-13	3⅝	3½
R-19	ⓖ 6	5½
R-22	6½	6
R-26	8¼	7
R-30	9½	8½
R-38	12	11

LOOSE FILL (POURED OR BLOWN)

INSULATION VALUE	**GLASS MINERAL FIBER INCHES	BAGS/1000 SQ. FT.	**ROCK MINERAL FIBER INCHES	BAGS/1000 SQ. FT.	***CELLULOSIC FIBER INCHES
R-11	5	11	3¾	23	3
R-13	6	13½	4¾	28	3½
R-19	ⓐ 8¾	20	6½	38	5⅛
R-22	10	22	7½	45	6
R-26	12	27	9½	56	7
R-30	13¾	30	10¼	62	8⅛
R-38	17½	40	12¾	77	10¼

**Blown mineral fiber insulation has both a depth and density relationship. R-values depend upon both number of inches and bags per 1,000 square feet of insulation.

***According to the National Cellulose Insulation Manufacturers Association, blown cellulose insulation shall have an R-value that is greater than or equal to 3.70 per inch of thickness with a density not to exceed 3 pounds per cubic foot.

Figure 21-4 R-values related to insulation thickness. (Courtesy, U.S. Department of Energy.)

INCHES	PERCENT REDUCTION IN HT. TRANSFER	PERCENT GAIN FROM PREVIOUS FIGURE	TOTAL GAINS POSSIBLE BEYOND 4 IN. OF INSULATION
0			
1	65.5%	65.5%	
2	79.2%	13.7%	
4	88.3%	9.1%	
6	92.0%	3.7%	5.5% FROM 4 TO 8 IN.
8	93.8%	1.8%	6.7% FROM 4 TO 10 IN.
10	95.0%	1.2%	7.5% FROM 4 TO 12 IN.
12	95.8%	0.8%	

Figure 21-5 Energy loss reduction equated to inches of ceiling insulation.

same R-number. The number of bags of loose fill required per 1000 ft^2, to provide the various thicknesses is also shown.

Referring to ceiling insulation shown in Figure 21-5, the optimum thickness of insulation is approximately 4 in. Doubling this thickness to 8 in., increases the insulating value by only 5.5%, and tripling the amount of insulation increases it by only 7.5%.

A comparison of the various types of insulation with reference to such qualities as ease of application, fire resistance, and vapor barrier requirements is given in Figure 21-6.

Attic ventilation. Related to the use of attic insulation is the need for adequate attic ventilation. In summer the attic temperature can be excessive unless the attic is well ventilated. Two means are available: (1) natural ventilation and (2) the use of an exhaust fan. The selection depends on the attic construction and the feasibility of providing the necessary openings.

The following two methods of providing *natural ventilation* can be used. In making a selection, the important element to consider is the amount of net vent area each would provide. As noted in Figure 21-7, the recommended net vent area is dependent on the method used.

Natural Ventilation Method	Recommended Net Vent Area
1. Continuous ridge vents plus soffit	1. 1.5 in.^{2}/ft^2 of ceiling area
2. Gable, roof, or turbine vents plus soffit	2. 3.0 in.^{2}/ft^2 of ceiling area

TYPE	COMMENTS	APPLICATION
BATTS/BLANKETS Preformed glass fiber or rock wool with or without vapor barrier backing	Fire resistant, moisture resistant, easy to handle for do-it-yourself installation, least expensive and most commonly available.	Unfinished attic floor, rafters, underside of floors, between studs
RIGID BOARD 1. Extruded polystyrene bead 2. Extruded polystyrene 3. Urethane 4. Glass fiber	All have high R-values for relatively small thickness. 1, 2, 3: Are not fire resistant, require installation by contractor with ½-in. gypsum board to insure fire safety. 3: Is its own vapor barrier; however, when in contact with liquid water, it should have a skin to prevent degrading. 1, 4: Require addition of vapor barrier. 2: Is its own barrier.	Basement walls, new construction frame walls, commonly used as an outer sheathing between siding and studs
LOOSE FILL (POURED IN) 1. Glass fiber 2. Rock wool 3. Treated cellulosic fiber	All easy to install, require vapor barrier bought and applied separately. Vapor barrier may be impossible to install in existing walls. 1, 2: Fire resistant, moisture resistant 3: Check label to make sure material meets federal specifications for fire and moisture resistance and R-value	Unfinished attic floor uninsulated existing walls
LOOSE FILL (BLOWN IN) 1. Glass fiber 2. Rock wool 3. Treated cellulosic fiber	All require vapor barrier bought separately, all require space to be filled completely. Vapor barrier may be impossible to install in existing walls. 1, 2: Fire resistant, moisture resistant. 3: Fills up spaces most consistently. When blown into closed spaces, has slightly higher R-value, check label for fire and moisture resistance and R-value.	Unfinished attic floor, finished attic floor, finished frame walls, underside of floors.

Figure 21-6 Insulation materials chart. (Courtesy, U.S. Department of Energy.)

Energy Conservation Measures

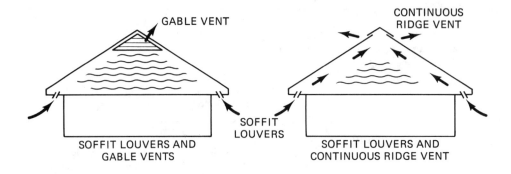

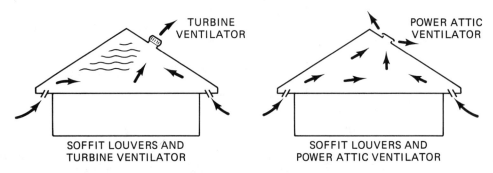

Figure 21-7 Types of attic ventilation. (Courtesy, U.S. Department of Energy.)

Powered ventilation consists of a thermostatically controlled vent placed near the peak of the roof in the center of the attic. If the house is large (over 2000 ft^2), or has a T- or L-shaped configuration, more than one is needed. The fan capacity of the ventilator should provide a minimum of 1.5 ft^3/min per square foot of ceiling area. Soffit vents, which provide intake air, should have a minimum of 80 in.^{2} of net free area for each 100 ft^3/min of ventilator capacity. The thermostat should be set to turn on at 100°F and off at 85°F.

Vapor barriers.   To protect the insulation against condensation, a vapor barrier is recommended. An excellent example of energy-efficient wall construction is shown in Figure 21-8. Note the position of the polyethylene vapor barrier and the use of sheathing with a high R-factor.

The U-factor.   Thus far the discussion of insulation had centered around the R-factor, the resistance of a material to the flow of heat. A more useful factor in determining heat load is the U-factor.

POLYETHYLENE
VAPOR BARRIER

2x4 FRAMING

HIGH-R
SHEATHING

GYPSUM
WALLBOARD

FIBERGLAS
UNFACED
BATT INSULATION

EXTERIOR
SIDING

Figure 21-8 An example of energy-efficient wall construction. (Courtesy, Owens/Corning Fiberglas Corporation.

The U-factor is the reciprocal of the R-factor; thus

$$U = \frac{1}{R}$$

The U-factor is an overall heat transfer coefficient. It represents the amount of heat in

Energy Conservation Measures

Btuh units that will flow through a given material or materials per square foot of surface area per degree of difference in temperature. For example, if the R-valve is R13, the U-factor is

$$U = \frac{1}{R} = \frac{1}{13} = 0.08 \text{ Btuh/ft}^2/°F$$

Applying this to an exposed wall, the R-factor is the sum total of the R-factors of the individual components in the wall. The following tabulation illustrates the determination of the R-factor for a wall made up of various components. Note that this wall has a total R-factor of 15.18. This amount represents the resistance of the wall to the flow of heat through it.

Material or Surface	R-Factor
Exterior surface resistance	0.17
Bevel-lapped siding, ½ × 8 in.	0.81
Fiberboard insulating sheathing, ¾ in.	2.10
Insulation, mineral wool batts, 3½ in.	11.00
⅜-in. gypsum lath and ⅜-in. plaster	0.42
Interior surface resistance	0.68
Total R-factor	15.18

In most northern climates it is good practice to provide construction of walls with an R-factor of 15.0 or greater and ceilings with a factor of 25.0 or greater. Windows should be constructed with double glass or single glass with a storm window.

To convert to a U-factor in the preceding example, where the R-factor for the exposed wall is 15.18, the heat-transfer coefficient is determined as follows:

$$U = \frac{1}{R} = \frac{1}{15.18} = 0.07 \text{ Btuh/ft}^2/°F$$

The U-factor is calculated in Btuh/ft^2 of surface per degree of difference in temperature. With this information, the effectiveness of adding insulation can be evaluated in terms of heat savings.

Energy-efficient windows. Windows with built-in thermal barrier reduce the heat loss through the glass and the framing, as shown in Figure 21-9. One window manufacturer's rating chart is shown in Figure 21-10. Note the inclusion of single-glazed, insulating glass, double-glazed, and triple-glazed units. The total unit U- and R-values are given for each, as is the percent relative humidity when condensation will appear on the innermost surface. The inside-glass surface temperature is also shown. All these factors are based on an outside temperature of 0°F, an inside temperature of 70°F, no inside air movement, and uniform heating conditions.

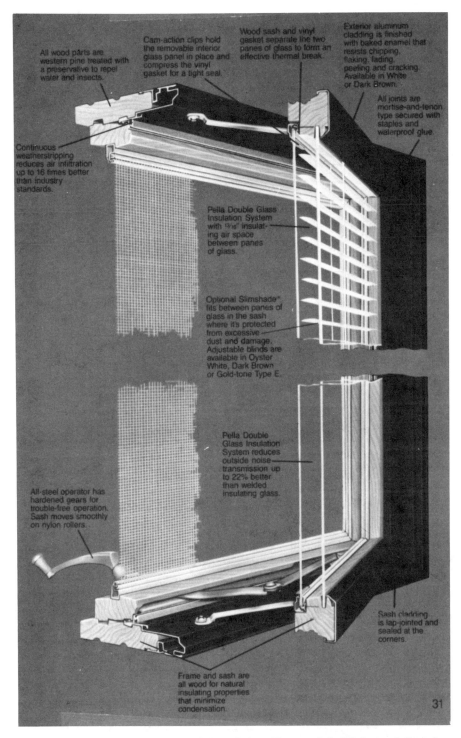

Figure 21-9 Double-glazed, energy-efficient window. (Courtesy, Pella Windows and Doors.)

Energy Conservation Measures

427

WINDOW MANUFACTURER'S RATING CHART

Anderson® Windows and Gliding Patio Doors	Average		Percent Relative Humidity When Condensation Appears On Innermost Glass Surface	Inside Glass Surface Temperature	Type of Glazing
	Unit "U" Value	Unit "R" Value			
SINGLE GLAZED					
Prefinished Basement/Utility	1.04	.96	12%	14°F	Single-Pane Glass
DOUBLE-PANE INSULATING GLASS					
Perma-Shield® Gliding Patio Door—White All Sizes Except PS 5	0.58	1.72	35%	41°F	Double-Pane Insulating Safety Glass
Perma-Shield® Picture Window CP35/AP53	0.55	1.82	36%	41°F	Double-Pane Insulating Glass
Perma-Shield® Casement/Awning, Perma-Shield® Gliding, Perma-Shield® Narroline Double-Hung, Primed Casement	0.52	1.92	37%	42°F	Double-Pane Insulating Glass
Perma-Shield® Gliding Patio Door—Terratone, All Sizes PS 5—White	0.47	2.13	43%	46°F	Double-Pane Insulating Safety Glass
Primed Casement Picture Windows	0.44	2.27	45%	47°F	Double-Pane Insulating Glass

DOUBLE-GLAZED					
Prefinished Basement/Utility	0.48	2.08	41%	45°F	Single-Pane Glass with Outside Storm Panel
TRIPLE-PANE INSULATING GLASS					
Perma-Shield® Gliding Patio Door, White and Terratone All Sizes	0.39	2.56	50%	51°F	
Perma-Shield® Narroline Picture Window, Perma-Shield® Casement and Awning Picture Windows, CP35, AP53	0.37	2.70	50%	51°F	Triple-Pane Insulating Glass
Perma-Shield® Casement and Awning Vent and Picture Window Units	0.35	2.86	52%	52°F	Triple-Pane Insulating Glass
TRIPLE-GLAZED					
Perma-Shield® Narroline Double-Hung, Perma-Shield® Gliding	0.33	3.03	53%	52°F	Double-Pane Insulating Glass with Combination
Perma-Shield® Casement, Perma-Shield® Awning, Primed Casement	0.32	3.12	55%	53°F	Double-Pane Insulating Glass with Outside Storm Panel
ROOF WINDOW					
Roof Window (at 45° angle)	0.33	3.03	53%	52°F	Double-Pane Tempered Insulating Glass

Figure 21-10 Insulating values for various types of windows. (Courtesy, Anderson Corporation.)

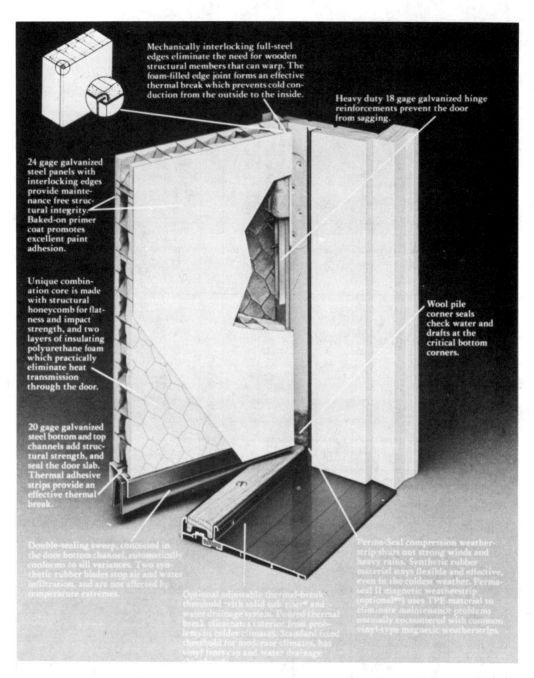

Mechanically interlocking full-steel edges eliminate the need for wooden structural members that can warp. The foam-filled edge joint forms an effective thermal break which prevents cold conduction from the outside to the inside.

Heavy duty 18 gage galvanized hinge reinforcements prevent the door from sagging.

24 gage galvanized steel panels with interlocking edges provide maintenance free structural integrity. Baked-on primer coat promotes excellent paint adhesion.

Unique combination core is made with structural honeycomb for flatness and impact strength, and two layers of insulating polyurethane foam which practically eliminate heat transmission through the door.

Wool pile corner seals check water and drafts at the critical bottom corners.

20 gage galvanized steel bottom and top channels add structural strength, and seal the door slab. Thermal adhesive strips provide an effective thermal break.

Double-sealing sweep, concealed in the door bottom channel, automatically conforms to sill variances. Two synthetic rubber blades stop air and water infiltration, and are not affected by temperature extremes.

Optional adjustable thermal-break threshold with solid oak riser* and water drainage system. Poured thermal break eliminates interior frost problems in colder climates. Standard fixed threshold for moderate climates, has vinyl frost cap and water drainage.

Perma-Seal compression weatherstrip shuts out strong winds and heavy rains. Synthetic rubber material stays flexible and effective, even in the coldest weather. Perma-seal II magnetic weatherstrip (optional*) uses TPE material to eliminate maintenance problems normally encountered with common vinyl-type magnetic weatherstrips.

Figure 21-11 An example of energy-efficient door construction. (Courtesy, Perma-Door by American Standard.)

Energy-efficient doors. Energy-efficient doors are available. These are doors that incorporate either polystyrene or polyurethane insulation and a thermal barrier to also reduce heat loss through the framing (Figure 21-11). One door manufacturer's rating chart gives the overall R-factor for various types of door construction (Figure 21-12). With the use of a full polyurethane core, the R-factor is 15.15, which is almost equal to the wall factor of 15.18 calculated for the exposed wall in the preceding example. With such a door a storm door is virtually unnecessary. In fact, a storm door might be counterproductive because of the tendency to leave the primary door open at times to avoid the inconvenience of opening and closing two doors.

	R factor
Solid core wood door	2.90*
Stile and rail wood door	2.79*
Hollow core wood door	2.18*
Steel door with polystyrene core	7.14
Steel door with ¾″ urethane "honeycomb" core	8.42
Storm door (aluminum)	1.84**
THERMA-TRU door (with a full polyurethane core door)	15.15

*R-factor reference according to ASHRAE (American Society of Heating, Refrigeration and Air Conditioning Engineers) figures.
**Based on engineering calculations.

Figure 21-12 R-factors for various types of exterior doors. (Courtesy, Pease Company, Ever-Strait Division.)

Weatherstripping. Weatherstripping and caulking around doors, windows, and other wall penetrations stop the entry of outside air into a building. Even if no noticeable drafts are present, air movement can be occurring. A typical 3-ft-wide door with a $\frac{1}{8}$-in. separation at the threshold may not produce a noticeable draft; however, $4\frac{1}{2}$ in.^{2} of open area exist. This is equivalent to a hole $1\frac{3}{16}$ in. in diameter (see Figure 21-13).

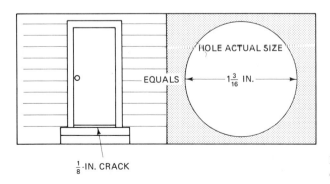

$\frac{1}{8}$-IN. CRACK

Figure 21-13 Door clearance of ⅛ in. is equivalent to area of 1³/₁₆-in. hole.

Reducing Air Leakage

There are many ways to tighten up a structure to reduce air infiltration. However, it is first essential to find out where the leakage is occurring. A number of contractors are offering "house doctor" service, which consists of a scientific means of finding the leakage areas and then implementing measures to close the openings. The original research for the house doctor concept was conducted by the Lawrence Berkeley Laboratory at the University of California.

There are two main sources of leakage: (1) through building materials and (2) at intersections where two building components meet. It is a simple matter to install a vapor barrier under plasterboard when a new house is constructed. On existing houses, it may be impractical. The use of a vapor barrier greatly reduces the air leakage through building materials.

Some examples of intersections are floors with walls, walls with ceilings, chimneys with floors and walls, and penetrations in the wall, floor, or ceiling to accommodate fixtures for plumbing, electric switches and outlets, or light switches. Air leakage can also occur through bypasses from the basement and the house interior to the attic. These bypasses are most often found in wall cavities and around chimneys, vents, and flue pipes. Wherever the leak is found, it must be eliminated. This is the function of the house doctor.

Diagnostic procedure

1. *Install a blower door*, constructed as shown in Figure 21-14. This panel fits into the door frame and includes a variable-speed blower that is used to depressurize (suck out) or pressurize (blow into) the house. A measurement of the

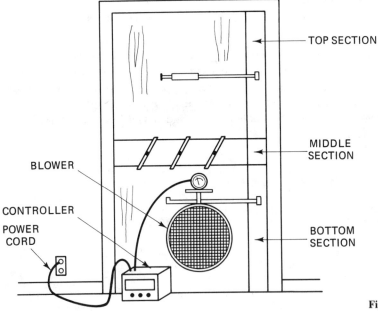

Figure 21-14 Blower door.

pressure in the house during this process is an indication of the tightness of the house.

2. *Use an infrared scanner* to locate the leaks. This is a heat-sensitive television-like camera, which shows the warm spots as bright spots. It is used on the outside of the house during pressurization in the winter. Warm air escaping is detected by the scanner.

3. *Use smokesticks* to locate the leaks. A smokestick is a lighted torch that emits dense smoke, which will follow the direction of air currents. These are commercially available and are used on the inside of the house when the house is pressurized. Smoke is carried through the cracks and holes by air being forced out of the house.

It is usually good practice to separate the main part of the house from the attic and basement in making pressurization and depressurization tests to assist in locating leakage areas.

Method of installing a blower door. The parts used for the blower door consist of the following, illustrated in the figures indicated:

Description	Figure
1. Bottom section: fan/motor assembly	21-14
2. Top section	21-14
3. Aluminum middle section	21-14
4. Controller unit with revolutions per minute	21-14
5. Inclined manometer	21-15 and 21-16
6. Plastic tube: 3 pieces	
7. Connecting power cords for controller and fan	21-14

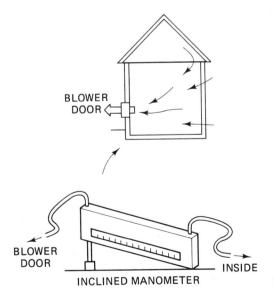

Figure 21-15 Depressurization.

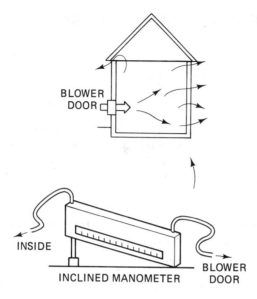

Figure 21-16 Pressurization.

The procedure for installing the blower door is as follows:

1. Move the bottom and top sections into place and tighten against door frame.

2. Install the middle section and tighten into place.

3. Connect the controller unit and plug in power cord.

4. Connect the manometer using the plastic tubes.

To measure pressurization, the upper end of the manometer should sense indoor pressure, and the lower end should sense outdoor pressure. To measure depressurization, reverse the connections (Figures 21-15 and 21-16).

Making pressure measurements. Before any measurements are made, design-ventilation openings in the building must be closed. These include exterior windows and doors, chimney dampers, attic doors, kitchen range hoods, bathroom vents, and so on. The heating system for the house should be turned off while the tests are made. During pressurization, the readings on the inclined manometer should reach 0.12 in. W.C. If they do not, large openings in the building envelope such as fireplaces have not been properly covered. The revolutions per minute of the fan should be recorded, so that a similar test can be made, to assess the improvement after retrofit measures have been performed.

Determining the leakage sites. Use the infrared scanner and the smokesticks to determine when leakage is occurring. Inspect the house to determine remedial measures to tighten the construction. Some retrofit measures that can be used include the following:

1. Seal holes around pipes and wire.

2. Seal cracks around beams in open beam ceilings.

3. Seal cracks around heating registers and exhaust fan cutouts.

4. Seal cracks around edges of fireplaces and mantelpieces.

5. Seal cracks inside and around built-in cabinets and bookshelves.

6. Seal holes in recessed fluorescent light fixtures.

7. Seal gaps beneath baseboards and moulding and behind electric baseboard heaters.

8. Install a fireplace seal-tight damper in the chimney flue.

9. Weatherstrip and caulk leaky windows and doors and seal cracks around the window and door frames.

Air-to-air heat exchangers. Cutting down infiltration and reducing air leakage can create nearly airtight homes. This can cause problems unless some form of ventilation is provided. Some of the problems caused by airtight houses are as follows:

1. **Condensation.** Humidity from people, cooking, washing, and plants cause windows to fog or paint to peel, and so on.

2. **Odors.** Odors from cooking, bathrooms, and smoking linger in the house.

3. **Contaminants.** Toxic substances such as formaldehyde from building materials, benzopyrene from smoking, nitrogen dioxide and carbon monoxide from gas stoves, and radon gas, which escapes from the soil, can all rise to high levels when houses are not properly ventilated (Figure 21-17).

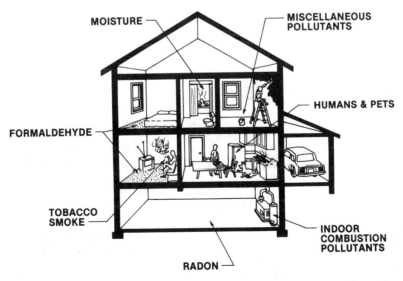

Figure 21-17 Sources of indoor pollution. (Courtesy, U.S. Department of Energy.)

Energy Conservation Measures

The air-to-air heat exchanger is a device for recovering heat from exhaust air and using it to heat air supplied from the outside for ventilation. The illustration in Figure 21-18 shows how this heat-recovery unit operates. In winter, fresh, dry cold air is forced through the multipath heat exchanger core and stale, warm indoor air is forced through in the opposite direction. The fresh air temperature rises 80% or more of the indoor-outdoor temperature difference. The rate of air flow can be regulated by the homeowner to meet individual needs. During the colder winter months, some moisture in the exhaust air can freeze when subjected to low outside temperatures. The unit includes automatic defrost to insure proper operation during severe winter conditions. A humidistat can be provided to switch the fan speed to control indoor humidity levels.

Figure 21-19 illustrates the application of an air-to-air heat exchange system in a typical home. The best mounting location is usually the basement adjacent to other mechanicals or in the laundry area. Select a location with the best relationship to the ductwork and as close as possible to the outside wall. As provision for a condensate drain will have to be made, a plumbing stack, fixture, or floor drain should be handy. The unit may be mounted between or below the floor joists, on wall brackets, or on the floor.

Costs can be substantially reduced when installing a central, ducted system in new construction or retrofitting an existing system if the proper planning takes place in advance. Exchanger manufacturers should be consulted in the design phase of the project to facilitate this planning process. Ductwork layout and design must be planned for, and many problems can be avoided if the system is well integrated into the house design (Figure 21-20).

Because the heat exchanger is a ventilation device, not a heating appliance, some designers use stud cavities in walls, joist cavities in floors, and dropped ceilings as a low-cost, ready-made ductwork for the heat exchange system, thus saving money on the purchase of additional ductwork. In some areas, codes may forbid some of these practices, and some manufacturers who employ this type of ducting advise special treatment of these spaces.

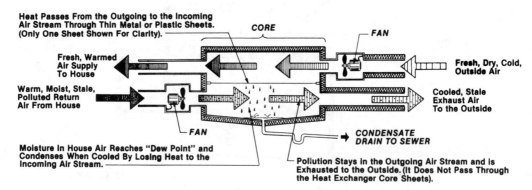

Figure 21-18 Operation of air-to-air heat exchanger. (Courtesy, U.S. Department of Energy.)

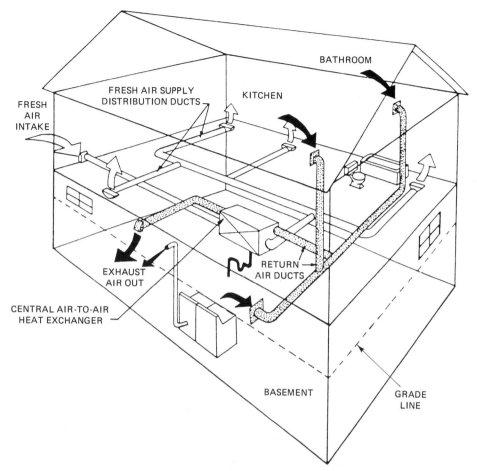

Figure 21-19 Application of an air-to-air heat exchanger in a typical home. (Courtesy, U.S. Department of Energy.)

Using Other Retrofit Measures

There is a continuing effort among manufacturers to offer new products to reduce energy consumption. Some of these products fit specific requirements while others have more general applications. In the following section various measures that have unique features are described. The list is not complete due to the dynamic nature of research and development being carried on in this field. The student should be constantly on the alert for new ideas and products which conserve energy.

The topics that are discussed in this section include the following:

1. Fireplace treatment

2. Use of heat pump hot water heaters

Energy Conservation Measures **437**

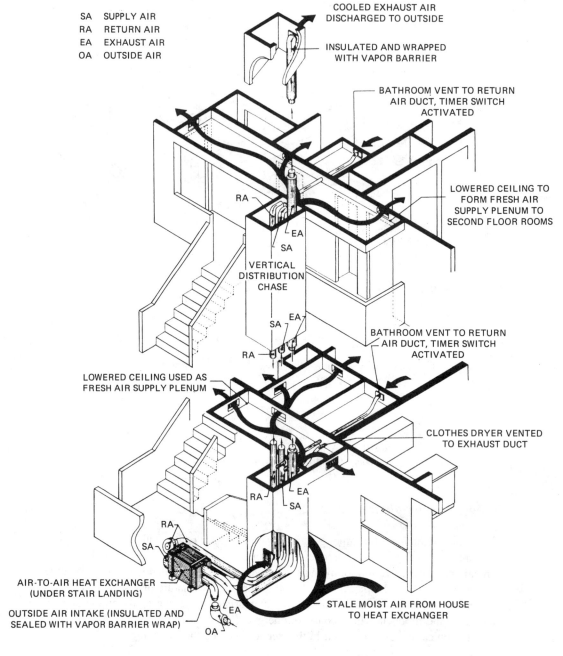

SA   SUPPLY AIR
RA   RETURN AIR
EA   EXHAUST AIR
OA   OUTSIDE AIR

COOLED EXHAUST AIR
DISCHARGED TO OUTSIDE

INSULATED AND WRAPPED
WITH VAPOR BARRIER

BATHROOM VENT TO RETURN
AIR DUCT, TIMER SWITCH
ACTIVATED

RA

LOWERED CEILING TO
FORM FRESH AIR
SUPPLY PLENUM TO
SECOND FLOOR ROOMS

EA
SA

VERTICAL
DISTRIBUTION
CHASE

SA   EA

RA

BATHROOM VENT TO RETURN
AIR DUCT, TIMER SWITCH
ACTIVATED

LOWERED CEILING USED AS
FRESH AIR SUPPLY PLENUM

CLOTHES DRYER VENTED
TO EXHAUST DUCT

RA   EA
SA

RA

SA

AIR-TO-AIR HEAT EXCHANGER
(UNDER STAIR LANDING)

OUTSIDE AIR INTAKE (INSULATED AND
SEALED WITH VAPOR BARRIER WRAP)

EA

OA

STALE MOIST AIR FROM HOUSE
TO HEAT EXCHANGER

Figure 21-20 An isometric view of an integrated, central, ducted air-to-air heat exchanger for a two-story house. (Courtesy, U.S. Department of Energy.)

3. Use of more efficient lighting

4. Alterations to the heating unit

5. Using programmed thermostats

6. Using solar heating

7. Improved maintenance

Fireplace treatment.   The open fireplace can be a source of considerable heat loss. To prevent this, it is recommended that wood-burning fireplaces be installed with separate outside air intake vents for combustion air. This provision replaces the normal drawing of already heated air from within the house. Glass doors on the unit also channel radiant heat into the room while preventing warm air from escaping up the chimney, as shown in Figure 21-21.

Using heat pumps for hot water.   Heat-recovery units that use rejected energy for heating hot water are now available on many residential cooling and heat pump units. These units are valuable for supplementing the conventional hot water heater.

Complete package heat pump–hot water heaters are also available. They operate the year around in the heating mode to supplement the standard gas or electric units (see Chapter 11 for information on heat pumps).

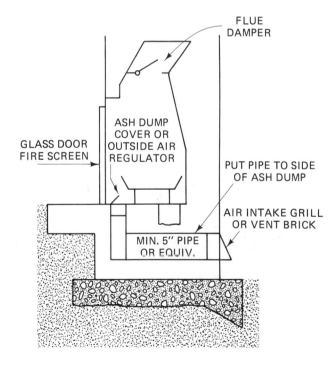

Figure 21-21 An example of an energy-efficient fireplace.

Using more efficient lighting. Energy-efficient fluorescent lighting is recommended whenever appropriate. Fluorescent lights produce from 55 to 92 lumens of light per watt, compared to 15 to 25 lumens per watt for incandescent light. A lumen is a measure of the flow of light.

Fluorescent lights have a longer life than incandescent bulbs. The average life of a fluorescent bulb is around 20,000 h as compared to less than 1000 h for incandescent bulbs.

Alterations to the heating unit. Alterations to the heating unit to improve efficiency have been included in earlier chapters of the text and should be consulted for complete information. Important measures to consider for retrofitting include

1. Replacing the unit with a high-efficiency furnace (see Chapter 10)

2. Sizing the furnace to fit the load (see Chapter 3)

3. Installing vent dampers and electronic ignition (see Chapters 8 and 17)

Using programmable thermostats. The use of an automatic temperature setback is one example of a system modification that can be made (Figure 21-22). A 5 to 20% savings in fuel can be realized by lowering the temperature in the space 5°F for 8 h each night. A savings of 9 to 16% can be realized by lowering the space temperature 10°F for 8 h at night. A table showing night setback savings for various parts of the country is shown in Figure 21-23.

Using solar heating. Solar heating is used by a homeowner principally for

1. Heating space

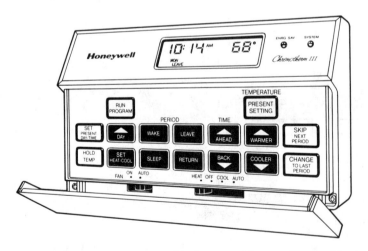

Figure 21-22 Seven-day programmable thermostat. (Courtesy, Honeywell Inc.)

	①	②	③	④		①	②	③	④
ALBUQUERQUE, NM	12%	24%	16%	16%	LOS ANGELES, CA	15%	30%	20%	27%
ATLANTA, GA	15%	27%	12%	19%	LOUISVILLE, KY	13%	24%	%	18%
ATLANTIC CITY, NJ	12%	23%	13%	20%	MADISON, WI	10%	19%	%	19%
BILLINGS, MT	10%	20%	9%	16%	MEMPHIS, TN	15%	26%	11%	17%
BIRMINGHAM, AL	15%	28%	12%	17%	MIAMI, FL	18%	30%	11%	17%
BOISE, ID	11%	22%	8%	15%	MILWAUKEE, WI	10%	19%	13%	19%
BOSTON, MA	11%	22%	13%	20%	MINNEAPOLIS, MN	9%	18%	12%	20%
BUFFALO, NY	10%	20%	14%	22%	NEW ORLEANS, LA	16%	30%	11%	17%
BURLINGTON, VT	9%	18%	14%	22%	NEW YORK, NY	12%	23%	13%	20%
CHARLESTON, SC	16%	29%	13%	19%	OKLAHOMA CITY, OK	14%	26%	11%	16%
CHEYENNE, WY	10%	19%	12%	17%	OMAHA, NE	11%	20%	12%	19%
CHICAGO, IL	11%	21%	13%	20%	PHILADELPHIA, PA	11%	24%	13%	20%
CINCINNATI, OH	12%	24%	12%	19%	PHOENIX, AZ	16%	30%	%	11%
CLEVELAND, OH	10%	21%	13%	21%	PITTSBURGH, PA	11%	22%	13%	20%
COLORADO SPRINGS, CO	11%	22%	11%	16%	PORTLAND, ME	10%	19%	15%	21%
COLUMBUS, OH	11%	22%	12%	19%	PORTLAND, OR	13%	24%	11%	20%
CORPUS CHRISTI, TX	17%	30%	10%	15%	PROVIDENCE, RI	11%	21%	16%	24%
DALLAS, TX	15%	28%	9%	14%	ROANOKE, VA	12%	24%	12%	19%
DENVER, CO	11%	22%	10%	17%	SALT LAKE CITY, UT	11%	21%	10%	16%
DES MOINES, IA	11%	20%	12%	19%	SAN DIEGO, CA	16%	30%	25%	33%
DETROIT, MI	11%	21%	13%	22%	SAN FRANCISCO, CA	14%	26%	14%	19%
DODGE CITY, KS	12%	23%	9%	15%	SEATTLE, WA	12%	24%	16%	23%
GREENSBORO, NC	14%	25%	12%	19%	SIOUX FALLS, SD	10%	19%	11%	18%
HOUSTON, TX	16%	30%	9%	14%	SPOKANE, WA	11%	20%	10%	18%
INDIANAPOLIS, IN	11%	22%	12%	19%	SPRINGFIELD, MA	11%	20%	13%	20%
JACKSON, MS	16%	30%	%	17%	ST. LOUIS, MO	12%	23%	11%	18%
JACKSONVILLE, FL	17%	30%	%	17%	SYRACUSE, NY	11%	20%	13%	21%
KANSAS CITY, MO	12%	23%	10%	16%	WASHINGTON, DC	13%	25%	13%	20%
LAS VEGAS, NV	15%	27%	%	11%	WILMINGTON, DE	12%	23%	10%	20%
LITTLE ROCK, AR	15%	27%	10%	16%	©Copyright Honeywell, Inc.				

① 10° * SINGLE HEATING SETBACK 70° TO 60° 8 HOURS/DAY

② 10° * DOUBLE HEATING SETBACK 70° TO 60° 8 HOURS/DAY, TWICE/DAY

③ 5° SINGLE COOLING SETUP 75° TO 80° 11 HOURS/DAY

④ 5° DOUBLE COOLING SETUP 75° TO 80° 9 HOURS/DAY, 7 HOURS/NIGHT

*SAVINGS FOR A 5° HEATING SETBACK ARE AT LEAST $\frac{1}{2}$ OF SAVINGS FOR A 10° SETBACK.

ACTUAL SAVINGS DEPEND ON YOUR HOME, GEOGRAPHIC LOCATION, NUMBER OF SETBACKS AND AMOUNT OF SETBACK DEGREES.

Figure 21-23 Percentage of heat/cooling energy savings with thermostat setback in average home. (Courtesy, Honeywell Inc.)

2. Heating domestic hot water

3. Heating swimming pool water

From an economic standpoint, domestic hot water solar heating has the greatest return for the average homeowner, since hot water is needed year around. This type of heating permits utilization of the summer solar radiation, which is greater than that available in winter for most parts of the country. Figure 21-24 shows a solar closed-system domestic water heating package. This particular package consists of a series of components, hooked up and ready to be connected to collectors and water tank. The collectors and tank are not part of the package, so they must be ordered separately. Any good closed system using collectors of ample capacity can be used.

Swimming pool water solar heating also utilizes the summer heat to advantage. A simple hookup is shown in Figure 21-25.

Improved maintenance.   Firing devices should be cleaned and serviced on a regular basis. Throwaway filters should be replaced when dirty. Motors should be oiled. Regular maintenance is important on any heating system; if maintenance is neglected, the efficiency and reliability of the system will decrease. Where efficiency can be easily

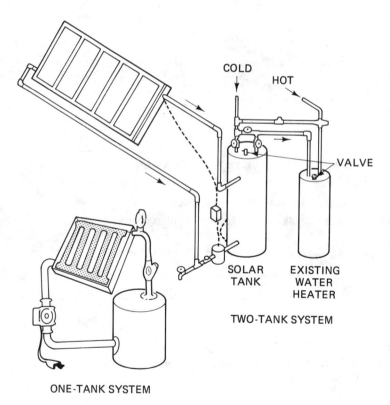

Figure 21-24   Solar domestic hot water system. (Courtesy, Detroit Edison.)

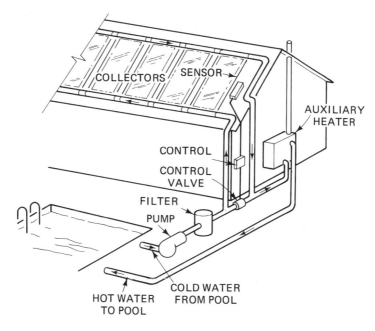

Figure 21-25 Solar swimming pool heating system. (Courtesy, Detroit Edison.)

measured, as on an oil-fired installation, this should be done at least once a year to assure good performance.

Distribution systems should be kept clean. Thermostats should be kept in calibration. Ductwork should be balanced to provide an even distribution of heat. The thermostat location should be changed or the thermostat replaced if it does not provide adequate temperature control. Proper maintenance is essentially good housekeeping practice, which results in improved performance.

Many new types of energy-saving devices are becoming available on the market because of the urgent need for saving fuel. Anyone involved in the heating business should carefully evaluate these innovations, since fuel should be saved by all practical means.

CHAPTER 21 STUDY QUESTIONS

The answers to the study questions are found in the sections of this chapter under the chapter topic indicated.

STUDY QUESTIONS | *CHAPTER TOPICS*

1. What percentage of the total energy consumed in the United States is used for heating? | *Energy conservation measures*

2. What does an R-factor represent in terms of insulating value? | *Insulation*

3.   What is the largest factor in the thermal resistance of a properly constructed wall?   *Insulation*

4.   What should the R-factor be for a ceiling, in keeping with good practice?   *Insulation*

5.   An R-factor of 13 is equivalent to what U-factor?   *Insulation*

6.   What percentage of the heat loss of an average house is due to air leakage?   *Reducing exposure losses*

7.   What is the density of expanded polystyrene in pounds per square foot?   *Insulation*

8.   What is the increase in insulating value in changing 4-in. of insulation to 12-in.?   *Insulation*

9.   What is the recommended net vent area for continuous ridge vents?   *Attic ventilation*

10.   What R-factor is practical for a polystyrene core door?   *Energy-efficient doors*

11.   Describe the blower door method of testing the air leakage of a residence.   *Reducing air leakage*

12.   How is an air-to-air heat exchanger used?   *Air-to-air heat exchangers*

13.   What is the best method of reducing heated-air losses from a fireplace?   *Fireplace treatment*

14.   What types of lighting are most energy-efficient for residences?   *Using more efficient lighting*

APPENDICES

RESIDENTIAL HEATING SYSTEM TROUBLE-ANALYSIS CHART

COMPLAINT	AREA OF TROUBLE	POSSIBLE CAUSES	CORRECTIVE ACTION
No heat	Power Supply	1. Tripped overload. 2. Open switch. 3. Bad transformer. 4. Bad connection. 5. Line voltage fluctuating or too low.	1. Determine cause – replace fuse or reset breaker. 2. Correct. 3. Replace. 4. Correct. 5. Inform power company.
	Thermostat	Refer to Thermostat Trouble Analysis Chart	
	Limit	1. System out on limit. 2. Manual reset limit tripped. 3. Dirty or pitted contacts. 4. Poor connection. 5. Defective.	1. Determine cause. 2. Reset, correct cause. 3. Clean or replace. 4. Correct. 5. Replace.
	Fuel delivery and pilot system (gas)	1a. Bad main or pilot gas valve. 1b. Bad thermocouple, thermopile, or power unit. 2. Fuel line blocked or low pressure.	1. Refer to the gas handbook for complete troubleshooting procedures for gas control systems. 2. Check manual valves, check for obstructions, check street supply, refer to equipment manufacturer's instructions.
	Fuel delivery	1. Failure in primary control. 2. No oil being delivered (primary control okay). 3. No ignition (primary control okay).	1. Refer to the oil handbook for complete troubleshooting, procedures for oil control systems. 2. Check for empty tank, blocked fuel line, bad oil valve or pump clogged nozzle; refer to equipment manufacturer's instructions. 3. Check connections, transformer, electrode spacing, insulators; refer to equipment manufacturer's instructions.
Not enough heat	Thermostat	Refer to Thermostat Trouble Analysis Chart	
	Limit	1. Set too low. 2. Improperly located.	1. Raise setting. 2. Relocate if necessary; consult equipment manufacturer.

(Courtesy, Honeywell Inc.)

RESIDENTIAL HEATING SYSTEM TROUBLE-ANALYSIS CHART
(*continued*)

COMPLAINT	AREA OF TROUBLE	POSSIBLE CAUSES	CORRECTIVE ACTION
Low Input	Low Input (gas or oil)	1. Undersized furnace or boiler. 2. Poor burner adjustment. 3. Sooted heat exchanger. 4. Poor draft. 5. Low boiler water. 6. Distribution system improperly balanced. 7. Failure of fan or circulator. 8. Low fan output 9. Restricted air flow.	1. Replace if condition extreme. 2. Refer to manufacturer's instructions. 3. Determine cause (poor draft, burner adjustment, etc.) and correct. 4. Clean system; check chimney size and design. 5. Add make up water. 6. Correct 7. Repair according to manufacturer's instructions. 8. Adjust pulley for higher speed. 9. Check filters; check obstructions in ducts or in front of registers.
	Low input (gas)	1. Improperly adjusted pressure regulator. 2. Improperly sized orifice—too small. 3. Malfunctioning regulator. 4. Clogged burner orifice. 5. Malfunctioning gas gas valve. 6. Dirt in valve restricting gas flow. 7. Manual valve partially closed. 8. Low supply pressure from gas main.	1. Adjust regulator to proper manifold pressure. 2. Replace with manufacturer's recommended size. 3. Replace regulator. 4. Clean or replace burner orifice. 5. Repair or replace. 6. Clean valve and seat. 7. Move to full open position. 8. Call gas company.
	Low input (oil)	1. Clogged oil filter or fuel line. 2. Clogged, faulty, or improperly sized nozzle. 3. Defective or improperly adjusted pump.	1. Replace filter and/or clean fuel line. 2. Clean or replace nozzle. 3. Replace or readjust pump pressure.
Too much heat, or overshoot	Thermostat	Refer to Thermostat Trouble Analysis Chart.	

(Courtesy, Honeywell Inc.)

THERMOSTAT TROUBLE-ANALYSIS CHART

CONDITION

T/S INDICATES ROOM THERMOSTAT.

T/S jumpered: System won't work	T/S jumpered: System works	Room temp overshoots T/S setting	Room temp doesn't reach T/S setting	T/S seems out of calibration	T/S cycles too often	T/S doesn't cycle often enough	Room temp swings excessively	POSSIBLE CAUSES
x								T/S not at fault; Check elsewhere
	x							T/S mounted on cold wall
	x							T/S wiring hole not plugged
	x							T/S exposed to cold drafts
	x				x		x	T/S not exposed to circulating air
	x	x	x					T/S not mounted level (mercury switch type)
	x	x	x					T/S not properly calibrated
			x					Heating plant too small or underfired
x								Limit control set abnormally low
	x							T/S exposed to direct rays of sun
	x							T/S affected by heat from fireplace
	x							T/S affected by lamp, TV or appliances
	x							T/S affected by stove or oven
	x							T/S is mounted on warm wall
	x							T/S mounted near register or radiator
	x				x		x	T/S heater set too high
				x				T/S heater set too low
	x				x			Heating plant too large or input excessive
	x				x		x	T/S does not have heater
x	x				x			T/S contacts are dirty
x								Low-voltage control circuit open
x								Low-voltage transformer burned out
x								Main valve operator is bad
x		x	x					Bad terminals, staking, splicing or soldering
	x							T/S damaged
		x	x					Clogged filter in forced warm air system

THERMOSTATS WITH ADJUSTABLE HEAT ANTICIPATOR SCALE ADJUSTMENT

Adjust heater to match current rating of primary control; this rating is usually stamped on the control nameplate. Move the indicator on the scale to correspond with this rating, and the heater will be properly adjusted for optimum comfort with most types of heating systems.

A slightly higher setting to obtain longer "burner-on" times (and thus fewer cycles per hour) may be desirable on some systems such as a one-pipe steam system. Example—If "burner-on" time is too short, proceed as follows:

If the nominal heater setting is 0.4, adjust to 0.45 setting and check system operation, adjust to 0.5 setting and recheck, etc., until the desired "burner-on" time is obtained. If the nominal heater setting is 0.2, adjust to 0.225 to achieve the desired burner-on time.

If the room temperature overshoots the thermostat setting excessively, decreasing the burner-on time may result in more constant temperature. To accomplish this, adjust the heater setting from the nominal 0.4 down to 0.35, or from the nominal 0.2 down to 0.18, and recheck operation of the system.

(Courtesy, Honeywell Inc.)

HEATING SERVICE GUIDE:
Forced-Air Furnace Checklist, Burners Gas-Fired

CONDITIONS	POSSIBLE CAUSES	POSSIBLE CURES
FLAME TOO LARGE	1. PRESSURE REG. SET TOO HIGH. 2. DEFECTIVE REGULATOR 3. BURNER ORIFICE TOO LARGE.	1. RESET, USING MANOMETER 2. REPLACE 3. REPLACE WITH CORRECT SIZE.
NOISY FLAME	1. TOO MUCH PRIMARY AIR. 2. NOISY PILOT 3. BURR IN ORIFICE	1. ADJUST AIR SHUTTERS 2. REDUCE PILOT GAS· 3. REMOVE BURR OR REPLACE ORIFICE
YELLOW TIP FLAME	1. TOO LITTLE PRIMARY AIR. 2. CLOGGED BURNER PORTS 3. MISALIGNED ORIFICES 4. CLOGGED DRAFT HOOD	1. ADJUST AIR SHUTTERS 2. CLEAN PORTS 3. REALIGN 4. CLEAN
FLOATING FLAME	1. BLOCKED VENTING 2. INSUFFICIENT PRIMARY AIR	1. CLEAN 2. INCREASE PRIMARY AIR SUPPLY

DELAYED IGNITION	1. IMPROPER PILOT LOCATION.
	2. PILOT FLAME TOO SMALL.
	
	3. BURNER PORTS CLOGGED
	   NEAR PILOT
	4. LOW PRESSURE
		1. REPOSITION PILOT.
		2. CHECK ORIFICE, CLEAN,
		   INCREASE PILOT GAS.
		3. CLEAN PORTS
		
		4. ADJUST PRESSURE REGULATOR.

FAILURE TO IGNITE	1. MAIN GAS OFF 2. BURNED OUT FUSE 3. LIMIT SWITCH DEFECTIVE 4. POOR ELECTRICAL CONNECTIONS. 5. DEFECT GAS VALVE. 6. DEFECTIVE THERMOSTAT.	1. OPEN MANUAL VALVE. 2. REPLACE 3. REPLACE 4. CHECK, CLEAN AND TIGHTEN. 5. REPLACE 6. REPLACE

BURNER WON'T TURNOFF	1. POOR THERMOSTAT LOCATION.
	2. DEFECTIVE THERMOSTAT.
	
	3. LIMIT SWITCH MALADJUSTED.
	4. SHORT CIRCUIT
	
	5. DEFECTIVE OR STICKING AUTOMATIC
	   VALVE
		1. RELOCATE
		2. CHECK CALIBRATION. CHECK
		   SWITCH AND CONTACTS.
		   REPLACE.
		3. REPLACE
		4. CHECK OPERATION AT
		   VALVE. LOOK FOR
		   SHORT AND CORRECT.
		5. CLEAN OR REPLACE.

RAPID BURNER CYCLING	1. CLOGGED FILTERS. 2. EXCESSIVE ANTICIPATION. 3. LIMIT SETTING TOO LOW. 4. POOR THERMOSTAT LOCATION.	1. CLEAN OR REPLACE. 2. ADJUST THERMOSTAT ANTICIPATOR FOR LONGER CYCLES. 3. READJUST OR REPLACE LIMIT. 4. RELOCATE.
RAPID FAN CYCLING	1. FAN SWITCH DIFF. TOO LOW. 2. BLOWER SPEED TOO HIGH.	1. READJUST OR REPLACE. 2. READJUST TO LOWER SPEED.
BLOWER WON'T STOP	1. MANUAL FAN "ON". 2. FAN SWITCH DEFECTIVE. 3. SHORTS	1. SWITCH TO AUTOMATIC. 2. REPLACE 3. CHECK WIRING AND CORRECT.

II   MOTOR AND BLOWER

CONDITION·	POSSIBLE CAUSES	POSSIBLE CURES
NOISY	1. FAN BLADES LOOSE. 2. BELT TENSION IMPROPER. 3. PULLEYS OUT OF ALIGNMENT. 4. BEARINGS DRY. 5. DEFECTIVE BELT. 6. BELT RUBBING.	1. REPLACE OR TIGHTEN. 2. READJUST (USUALLY 1 INCH SLACK) 3. REALIGN 4. LUBRICATE 5. REPLACE 6. REPOSITION

(Courtesy, Robertshaw Controls Company.)

Appendices

PILOT BURNER SERVICE-ANALYSIS CHART

CONDITION

Pilot cannot be lighted	Pilot out when reset knob released	Pilot outage during system use	Pilot burning but on safety shutdown	Pilot flame lazy, yellow	Pilot flame waving, blue	Pilot flame small, blue	Pilot flame noisy, lifting, blowing	Pilot flame hard, sharp	POSSIBLE CAUSES
x									Pilot gas supply is turned off
x									Pilot gas line not purged of air
x	x					x			Pilot burner orifice is clogged (replace)
x									Lighting knob not being held depressed
x									Reset button not being held depressed
x									Lighting knob not set at pilot position
x						x			Pilot gas flow adjustment is closed off
	x	x				x			Gas supply pressure is too low
	x	x							Pilot unshielded from excessive draft
	x								Lighting knob released too soon
	x								Reset button released too soon
	x	x	x						Thermocouple or thermopile is bad
	x	x	x						Pilotstat power unit is bad
	x	x	x						Power unit connection dirty, loose or wet
	x	x	x						Pilot flame is improper size
	x	x	x						Powerpile terminals shorted or loose
	x								Thermocouple cold junction too hot
	x			x					Pilot burner lint screen clogged
	x								Pilot unshielded from burner concussion
				x					Pilot burner primary air opening clogged
				x					Pilot burner orifice is too large
					x				Pilot unshielded from combustion products
						x		x	Pilot burner orifice too small
							x		Pilot gas pressure too high
								x	Typical of mfd., butane-air and propane-air
x	x					x			Pilot filter clogged
			x						Excessive ambient temperature
		x	x						Incorrect or marginal appliance venting
		x							Gas line too small or restricted

(Courtesy, Honeywell Inc.)

Q15 AND Q16 DIRECT-SPARK IGNITION
INSTALLATION TROUBLESHOOTING
WHEN SPARK IS PRESENT BUT PILOT WILL NOT LIGHT

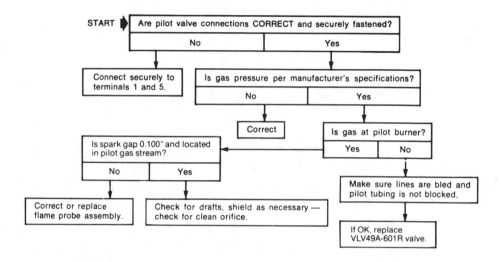

Q15 AND Q16 DIRECT-SPARK IGNITION
INSTALLATION TROUBLESHOOTING
WHEN PILOT LIGHTS BUT MAIN VALVE WILL NOT COME ON

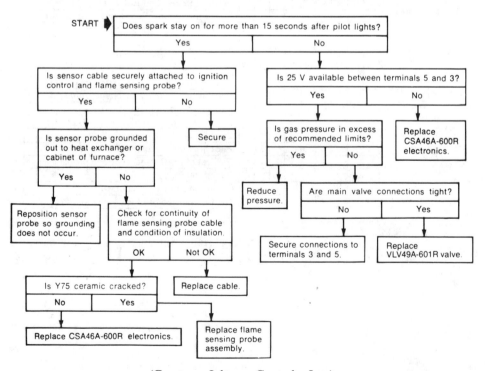

(Courtesy, Johnson Controls, Inc.)

S87 DIRECT-SPARK IGNITION SYSTEM TROUBLESHOOTING

Start the system by setting the temperature controller to call for heat. Observe the system response and establish the type of malfunction or deviation from normal operation using the appropriate table.

Use the table by following the instructions in the boxes. If the condition is true or okay (answer: yes), go down to the next box. If the condition is not true or not okay (answer: no), go to the box to the right. Continue checking and answering conditions in each box until a problem and/or repair is explained. After any maintenance or repair, the troubleshooting sequence should be repeated until normal system operation is obtained.

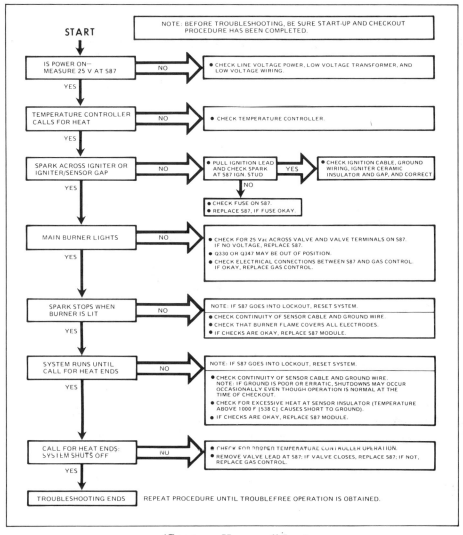

(Courtesy, Honeywell Inc.)

S89A DIRECT-SPARK IGNITION GAS PRIMARY TROUBLESHOOTING

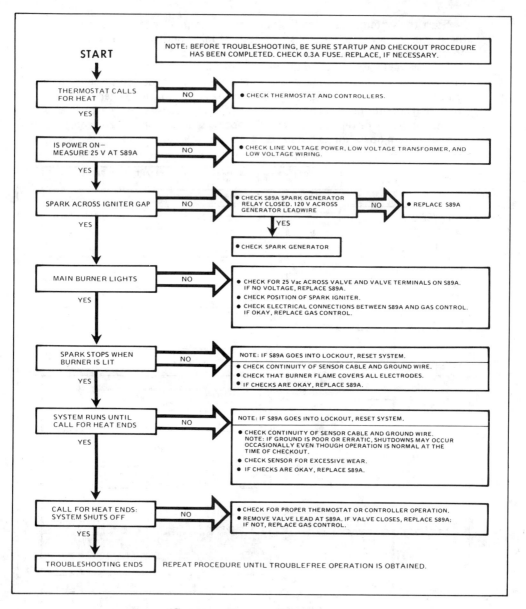

(Courtesy, Honeywell Inc.)

S825 DIRECT-SPARK IGNITION SYSTEM TROUBLESHOOTING

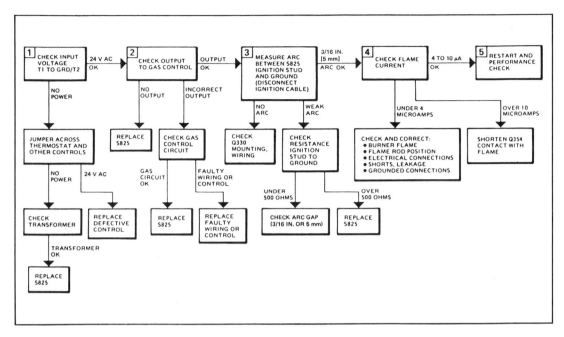

(Courtesy, Honeywell Inc.)

S825 QUICK REFERENCE TROUBLESHOOTING CHART
Direct-Spark Ignition System

PROBLEM		POSSIBLE CAUSE	CORRECTIVE ACTION
IGNITION SPARK	BURNER ACTION		
NONE	NO GAS FLOW	No power to S825.	1. Check transformer voltage. 2. Jumper thermostat or high limit. If system starts, replace defective control.
NORMAL	NO GAS FLOW	1. Gas controls wired incorrectly. 2. S825 output to gas control defective. 3. Gas control defective. 4. Separate transformer in S825D gas control circuit defective.	1. Check wiring. 2. Check S825 output. If no output, replace S825. (ON S825C, DO NOT SHORT TERMINALS VALVE 3 AND VALVE 5.) 3. Check resistance of gas control operator. Replace gas control if infinite resistance (open circuit). 4. Check for 24 Vac. If 0 V, check primary. If primary voltage OK, replace transformer.
NORMAL OR WEAK SPARK	SLOW (DELAYED) LIGHT OFF	Check Q330 Spark Igniter- 1. Incorrect spark gap. 2. Weak spark. 3. Dirty ceramic. 4. Incorrect Q330 location or position.	1. Bend tip of outer (ground) electrode. 2. Check resistance of stud terminal to ground. If over 500 ohms, replace S825. Keep ignition cable from touching any metal—use standoffs. 3. Clean ceramic with rag. 4. Relocate Q330.
SPARK KEEPS RECYCLING	EXCESSIVE RELAY CHATTER-ING ON S825D	One transformer is used both to power S825D and gas controls. 1. Transformer not properly sized (inadequate VA). 2. Transformer of poor quality. 3. Lifting flame.	1. Replace with transformer of adequate VA. 2. Replace with higher quality transformer. 3. Reduce gas input or primary air input to burner.

(Courtesy, Honeywell Inc.)

S825 QUICK REFERENCE TROUBLESHOOTING CHART (CONTINUED)
Direct-Spark Ignition System

PROBLEM		POSSIBLE CAUSE	CORRECTIVE ACTION
IGNITION SPARK	BURNER ACTION		
NORMAL	NORMAL START BUT SYSTEM LOCKS OUT IN LOCKOUT TIMING	Check W354 Flame Sensor— 1. Dirty ceramic. 2. Unstable flame on sensor element. 3. Incorrect Q354 location or position. 4. Incorrect gas input to burner. 5. Excessive draft. 6. Q354 flame rod grounded. 7. Q354 mounting bracket not properly grounded.	1. Clean ceramic with rag. 2. Check flame character-istics. If flame OK, install two Q354s in parallel on opposite sides of burner. Check flame current (4 to 10 milliamps and steady). 3. Relocate Q354. 4. See Checking Burner Input. 5. Install shield. 6. Check location—bend rod away from burner. 7. Check grounding.
NONE OR VERY WEAK SPARK	NORMAL START BUT SYSTEM LOCKS OUT IN LOCKOUT TIMING	1. Incorrect Q330 spark gap. 2. Weak spark. 3. Dirty ceramic. 4. Other short to ground. 5. Q330 mounting bracket not properly grounded. 6. No spark output from S825.	1. Bend tip of outer (grd) electrode to 3/16 in. [4.8 mm]. 2. Check resistance of stud terminal to ground. If over 500 ohms, replace S825. Keep ignition cable from touching metal—use standoffs. 3. Clean ceramic with rag. 4. Check wiring. 5. Check grounding. 6. Check resistance of stud terminal to ground. If over 500 ohms, replace S825.
NORMAL	GAS CONTROL WON'T OPEN	1. Separate transformer in S825D gas control circuit defective. 2. Gas controls wired incorrectly. 3. S825 output to gas control defective. 4. Gas control defective.	1. Check for 24 Vac. If 0 V, check primary. If primary voltage OK, replace transformer. 2. Check wiring. 3. Check S825 output. If no output, replace S825. (ON S825C, DO NOT SHORT TERMINALS VALVE 3 AND VALVE 5.) 4. Check resistance of gas control operator. Replace gas control if infinite resistance (open circuit).

(Courtesy, Honeywell Inc.)

S86 INTERMITTENT PILOT SYSTEM TROUBLESHOOTING

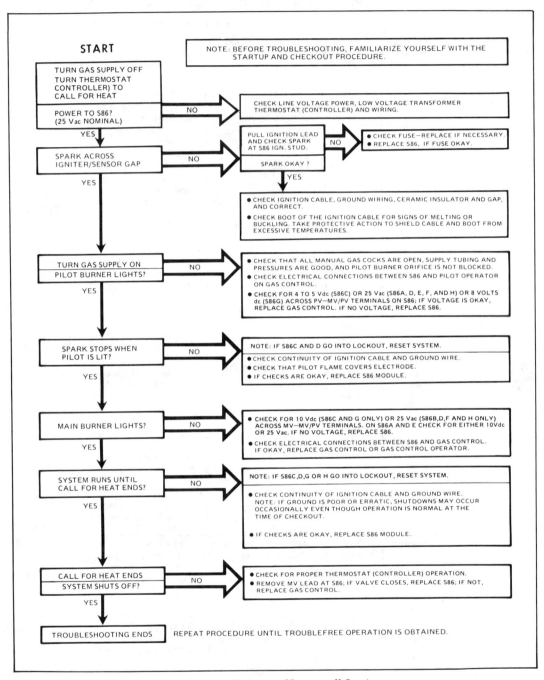

START

TURN GAS SUPPLY OFF
TURN THERMOSTAT
(CONTROLLER) TO
CALL FOR HEAT

NOTE: BEFORE TROUBLESHOOTING, FAMILIARIZE YOURSELF WITH THE
STARTUP AND CHECKOUT PROCEDURE.

POWER TO S86?
(25 Vac NOMINAL)   NO →   CHECK LINE VOLTAGE POWER, LOW VOLTAGE TRANSFORMER
                            THERMOSTAT (CONTROLLER) AND WIRING.

YES

SPARK ACROSS
IGNITER/SENSOR GAP   NO →   PULL IGNITION LEAD
                              AND CHECK SPARK
                              AT S86 IGN. STUD.   NO →   ● CHECK FUSE—REPLACE IF NECESSARY.
                                                            ● REPLACE S86, IF FUSE OKAY.
                              SPARK OKAY ?

YES   YES

● CHECK IGNITION CABLE, GROUND WIRING, CERAMIC INSULATOR AND GAP,
  AND CORRECT.
● CHECK BOOT OF THE IGNITION CABLE FOR SIGNS OF MELTING OR
  BUCKLING. TAKE PROTECTIVE ACTION TO SHIELD CABLE AND BOOT FROM
  EXCESSIVE TEMPERATURES.

TURN GAS SUPPLY ON
PILOT BURNER LIGHTS?   NO →   ● CHECK THAT ALL MANUAL GAS COCKS ARE OPEN, SUPPLY TUBING AND
                                 PRESSURES ARE GOOD, AND PILOT BURNER ORIFICE IS NOT BLOCKED.
                               ● CHECK ELECTRICAL CONNECTIONS BETWEEN S86 AND PILOT OPERATOR
YES   ON GAS CONTROL.
                               ● CHECK FOR 4 TO 5 Vdc (S86C) OR 25 Vac (S86A, D, E, F, AND H) OR 8 VOLTS
                                 dc (S86G) ACROSS PV—MV/PV TERMINALS ON S86; IF VOLTAGE IS OKAY,
                                 REPLACE GAS CONTROL. IF NO VOLTAGE, REPLACE S86.

SPARK STOPS WHEN
PILOT IS LIT?   NO →   NOTE: IF S86C AND D GO INTO LOCKOUT, RESET SYSTEM.
                        ● CHECK CONTINUITY OF IGNITION CABLE AND GROUND WIRE.
YES   ● CHECK THAT PILOT FLAME COVERS ELECTRODE.
                        ● IF CHECKS ARE OKAY, REPLACE S86 MODULE.

MAIN BURNER LIGHTS?   NO →   ● CHECK FOR 10 Vdc (S86C AND G ONLY) OR 25 Vac (S86B,D,F AND H ONLY)
                               ACROSS MV—MV/PV TERMINALS. ON S86A AND E CHECK FOR EITHER 10Vdc
                               OR 25 Vac. IF NO VOLTAGE, REPLACE S86.
YES   ● CHECK ELECTRICAL CONNECTIONS BETWEEN S86 AND GAS CONTROL.
                               IF OKAY, REPLACE GAS CONTROL OR GAS CONTROL OPERATOR.

SYSTEM RUNS UNTIL
CALL FOR HEAT ENDS?   NO →   NOTE: IF S86C,D,G OR H GO INTO LOCKOUT, RESET SYSTEM.

                              ● CHECK CONTINUITY OF IGNITION CABLE AND GROUND WIRE.
YES   NOTE: IF GROUND IS POOR OR ERRATIC, SHUTDOWNS MAY OCCUR
                                OCCASIONALLY EVEN THOUGH OPERATION IS NORMAL AT THE
                                TIME OF CHECKOUT.

                              ● IF CHECKS ARE OKAY, REPLACE S86 MODULE.

CALL FOR HEAT ENDS
SYSTEM SHUTS OFF?   NO →   ● CHECK FOR PROPER THERMOSTAT (CONTROLLER) OPERATION.
                            ● REMOVE MV LEAD AT S86; IF VALVE CLOSES, REPLACE S86; IF NOT,
YES   REPLACE GAS CONTROL.

TROUBLESHOOTING ENDS   REPEAT PROCEDURE UNTIL TROUBLEFREE OPERATION IS OBTAINED.

(Courtesy, Honeywell Inc.)

S89C HOT-SURFACE IGNITION-CONTROL TROUBLESHOOTING

Start the system by setting the thermostat (temperature controller) to call for heat. Observe the system response and establish the type of malfunction or deviation from normal operation by using the flow chart below.

Follow the instructions in the boxes. If the condition is true or okay (answer is yes), go down to the next box.

If the condition is not true or not okay (answer is no), go to the box at right. Continue checking and answering conditions in each box until a problem and/or repair is explained. After any maintenance or repair, the troubleshooting sequence should be repeated until normal system operation is obtained.

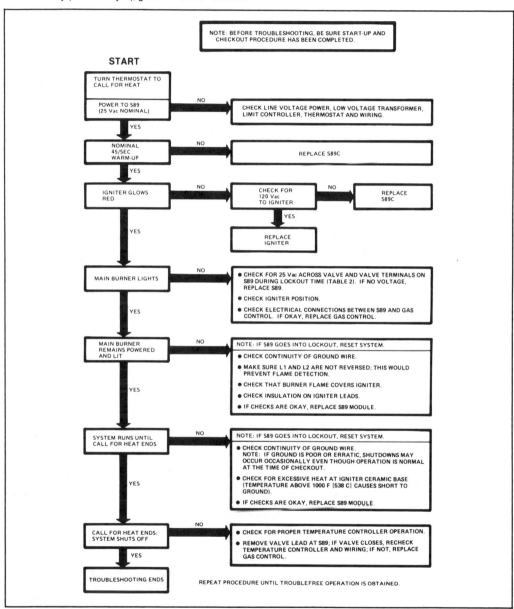

(Courtesy, Honeywell Inc.)

MAIN BURNER AND PILOT BURNER, ORIFICE SIZE CHART

Input (Btu/h) per spud	Natural gas: 1020 Btu — 0.65 SG 3 ½ in. WC manifold		Propane: 2500 Btu — 1.5 SG 11 in. WC manifold	
	Drill size	Decimal tolerance	Drill size	Decimal tolerance
12,000	51	0.064–0.067	60	0.038–0.040
15,000	48	0.073–0.076	58	0.040–0.042
20,000	43	0.086–0.089	55	0.050–0.052
25,000	41	0.093–0.096	53	0.056–0.059
27,500	39	0.097–0.100	53	0.060–0.063
40,000	32	0.113–0.116	49	0.070–0.073
50,000	30	0.124–0.128	46	0.078–0.081
60,000	27	0.140–0.144	43	0.086–0.089
70,000	22	0.153–0.157	42	0.090–0.093
80,000	20	0.156–0.161	40	0.095–0.098
90,000	17	0.168–0.173	38	0.098–0.101
100,000	13	0.180–0.185	35	0.107–0.110
105,000	11	0.186–0.191	34	0.108–0.111
110,000	10	0.188–0.193	33	0.109–0.113
125,000	5	0.200–0.205	1/8	0.121–0.125
135,000	3	0.208–0.213	30	0.124–0.128
140,000	7/32	0.214–0.219	30	0.124–0.128
150,000	1	0.223–0.228	29	0.132–0.136
160,000	A	0.229–0.234	28	0.136–0.140
175,000	C	0.237–0.242	27	0.140–0.144
190,000	E	0.245–0.250	25	0.145–0.149
200,000	F	0.252–0.257	23	0.150–0.154
210,000	H	0.261–0.266	21	0.154–0.159
220,000	I	0.267–0.272	20	0.156–0.161
240,000	K	0.276–0.281	18	0.164–0.169
260,000	M	0.290–0.295	16	0.172–0.177
280,000	5/16	0.307–0.312	13	0.180–0.185
300,000	O	0.311–0.316	11	0.186–0.191
310,000	P	0.318–0.323	9	0.191–0.196
320,000	21/64	0.323–0.328	7	0.196–0.201

(Courtesy, Luxaire, Inc.)

OIL FURNACE ROUTINE PERFORMANCE CHECKS
AND TROUBLESHOOTING

1. Check Shut-Off Valve and Line Filter. Replace or clean cartridge in line filter if dirty. Be sure to open shut-off valve.

2. Check Nozzle Assembly. Replace the nozzle according to manufacturer's recommendations when needed.

Important: Use proper designed tools for removal of nozzle from firing head.

3. Check Strainer. Clean strainer using clean fuel oil or kerosene. Install new cover gasket. Replace strainer if necessary.

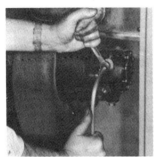

4. Check Connections. Tighten all connections and fittings in the intake line and unused intake port plugs.

5. Pressure Setting. Insert pressure gage in gage port. Normal pressure setting should be at 100 PSI. Check manufacturer's pressure setting recommendation on each installation being serviced.

6. Insert Vacuum gage in unused intake port. Check for abnormally high intake vacuum.

TROUBLESHOOTING

	cause	remedy
NO OIL FLOW AT NOZZLE	Oil level below intake line in supply tank	*Fill tank with oil.*
	Clogged strainer or filter	*Remove and clean strainer. Repack filter element.*
	Clogged nozzle	*Replace nozzle.*
	Air leak in intake line	*Tighten all fittings in intake line. Tighten unused intake port plug. Tighten in-line valve stem packing gland. Check filter cover and gasket.*
	Restricted intake line (High vacuum reading)	*Replace any kinked tubing and check any valves in intake line.*
	A two pipe system that becomes airbound	*Check and insert by-pass plug.*
	A single-pipe system that becomes airbound (Model J unit only)	*Loosen gage port plug or easy flow valve and drain oil until foam is gone in bleed hose.*
	Slipping or broken coupling	*Tighten or replace coupling.*
	Rotation of motor and fuel unit is not the same as indicated by arrow on pad at top of unit	*Install fuel unit with correct rotation.*
	Frozen pump shaft	*Return unit to approved service station or Sundstrand factory for repair. Check for water and dirt in tank.*

(Courtesy, Sundstrand Hydraulics, Inc.)

OIL FURNACE TROUBLESHOOTING (CONTINUED)

	cause	remedy
OIL LEAK	Loose plugs or fittings	*Dope with good quality thread sealer.*
	Leak at pressure adjusting end cap nut	*Fibre washer may have been left out after adjustment of valve spring. Replace the washer.*
	Blown seal (single pipe system)	*Check to see if by-pass plug has been left in unit. Replace fuel unit.*
	Blown seal (two pipe system)	*Check for kinked tubing or other obstructions in return line. Replace fuel unit.*
	Seal leaking	*Replace fuel unit.*
NOISY OPERATION	Bad coupling alignment	*Loosen fuel unit mounting screws slightly and shift fuel unit in different positions until noise is eliminated. Retighten mounting screws.*
	Air in inlet line	*Check all connections.*
	Tank hum on two-pipe system and inside tank	*Install return line hum eliminator.*
PULSATING PRESSURE	Partially clogged strainer or filter	*Remove and clean strainer. Replace filter element.*
	Air leak in intake line	*Tighten all fittings and valve packing in intake line.*
	Air leaking around cover	*Be sure strainer cover screws are tightened securely.*
LOW OIL PRESSURE	Defective gage	*Check gage against master gage, or other gage.*
	Nozzle capacity is greater than fuel unit capacity	*Replace fuel unit with unit of correct capacity.*

IMPROPER NOZZLE CUT-OFF

To determine the cause of improper cut-off, insert a pressure gage in the nozzle port of the fuel unit. After a minute of operation shut burner down. If the pressure drops and stabilizes above 0 P.S.I., the fuel unit is operating properly and air is the cause of improper cut-off. If, however, the pressure drops to 0 P.S.I., fuel unit should be replaced.

Filter leaks	*Check face of cover and gasket for damage.*
Strainer cover loose	*Tighten 8 screws on cover.*
Air pocket between cut-off valve and nozzle	*Run burner, stopping and starting unit, until smoke and after-fire disappears.*
Air leak in intake line	*Tighten intake fittings and packing nut on shut-off valve. Tighten unused intake port plug.*
Partially clogged nozzle strainer	*Clean strainer or change nozzle.*

(Courtesy, Sundstrand Hydraulics, Inc.)

OIL NOZZLE SELECTION

OIL BURNER NOZZLE INTERCHANGE CHART

STEINER 30°-90°	DELAVAN 30° — 90°
H/PH	A
S (.5 — 2.0) or Q	A or W
S/SS (2.25 +)	B
HAGO 30°-90°	**DELAVAN 30° — 90°**
SS	A
H	A or W
ES/P	B
MONARCH 30°-90°	**DELAVAN 30° — 90°**
R/NS/PL	A
AR	A or W
PLP	B

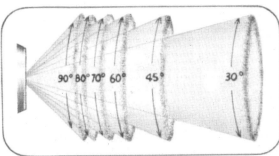

90° 80° 70° 60° 45° 30°

VARIETY OF SPRAY ANGLES

EFFECTS OF PRESSURE ON NOZZLE FLOW RATE

NOZZLE RATING AT 100 PSI	NOZZLE FLOW RATES IN GALLONS PER HOUR (Approx.)					
	80 PSI	120 PSI	140 PSI	160 PSI	200 PSI	300 PSI
.50	0.45	0.55	0.59	0.63	0.70	0.86
.65	0.58	0.71	0.77	0.82	0.92	1.12
.75	0.67	0.82	0.89	0.95	1.05	1.30
.85	0.76	0.93	1.00	1.08	1.20	1.47
.90	0.81	0.99	1.07	1.14	1.27	1.56
1.00	0.89	1.10	1.18	1.27	1.41	1.73
1.10	0.99	1.21	1.30	1.39	1.55	1.90
1.20	1.07	1.31	1.41	1.51	1.70	2.08
1.25	1.12	1.37	1.48	1.58	1.76	2.16
1.35	1.21	1.48	1.60	1.71	1.91	2.34
1.50	1.34	1.64	1.78	1.90	2.12	2.60
1.65	1.48	1.81	1.95	2.09	2.33	2.86
1.75	1.57	1.92	2.07	2.22	2.48	3.03
2.00	1.79	2.19	2.37	2.53	2.82	3.48
2.25	2.01	2.47	2.66	2.85	3.18	3.90
2.50	2.24	2.74	2.96	3.16	3.54	4.33
2.75	2.44	3.00	3.24	3.48	3.90	4.75
3.00	2.69	3.29	3.55	3.80	4.25	5.20
3.25	2.90	3.56	3.83	4.10	4.60	5.63
3.50	3.10	3.82	4.13	4.42	4.95	6.06
4.00	3.55	4.37	4.70	5.05	5.65	6.92
4.50	4.00	4.92	5.30	5.70	6.35	7.80
5.00	4.45	5.46	5.90	6.30	7.05	8.65
5.50	4.90	6.00	6.50	6.95	7.75	9.52
6.00	5.35	6.56	7.10	7.60	8.50	10.4
6.50	5.80	7.10	7.65	8.20	9.20	11.2
7.00	6.22	7.65	8.25	8.85	9.90	12.1
7.50	6.65	8.20	8.85	9.50	10.6	13.0
8.00	7.10	8.75	9.43	10.1	11.3	13.8
8.50	7.55	9.30	10.0	10.7	12.0	14.7
9.00	8.00	9.85	10.6	11.4	12.7	15.6
9.50	8.45	10.4	11.2	12.0	13.4	16.4
10.00	8.90	10.9	11.8	12.6	14.1	17.3
11.00	9.80	12.0	13.0	13.9	15.5	19.0
12.00	10.7	13.1	14.1	15.1	17.0	20.8
13.00	11.6	14.2	15.3	16.4	18.4	22.5
14.00	12.4	15.3	16.5	17.7	19.8	24.2
15.00	13.3	16.4	17.7	19.0	21.2	26.0
16.00	14.2	17.5	18.9	20.2	22.6	27.7
17.00	15.1	18.6	20.0	21.5	24.0	29.4
18.00	16.0	19.7	21.2	22.8	25.4	31.2
19.00	16.9	20.8	22.4	24.0	26.8	33.0
20.00	17.8	21.9	23.6	25.3	28.3	34.6
22.00	19.6	24.0	26.0	27.8	31.0	38.0
24.00	21.4	26.2	28.3	30.3	34.0	41.5
26.00	23.2	28.4	30.6	32.8	36.8	45.0
28.00	25.0	30.6	33.0	35.4	39.6	48.5
30.00	26.7	32.8	35.4	38.0	42.4	52.0
32.00	28.4	35.0	37.8	40.5	45.2	55.5
35.00	31.2	38.2	41.3	44.0	49.5	60.5
40.00	35.6	43.8	47.0	50.5	56.5	69.0
45.00	40.0	49.0	53.0	57.0	63.5	78.0
50.00	44.5	54.5	59.0	63.0	70.5	86.5

(Courtesy, Delavan Corporation.)

DETERMINING OIL-FLOW RATES AND COMBUSTION CHAMBER SIZE

PROPER FLOW RATES

Oil burner nozzles are available in a wide selection of flow rates, all but eliminating the need for specially calibrated nozzles. For example, between 1.00 GPH and 2.00 GPH inclusive, seven different flow rates are available. The following guidelines may be used for determining the proper flow rates:

The proper size nozzle for a given burner unit is sometimes stamped on the name plate of the unit.

If the unit rating is given in BTU per hour input, the nozzle size may be determined by . . .

$$GPH = \frac{BTU\ Input}{140,000}$$

If the unit rating is given in BTU output . .

$$GPH = \frac{BTU\ Output}{(Efficiency\ \%) \times 140,000}$$

On a steam job, if the total square feet of steam radiation, including piping, is known.

$$GPH = \frac{Total\ Ft^2\ of\ Steam \times 240}{(Efficiency\ \%) \times 140,000}$$

If the system is hot water operating at 180° and the total square feet of radiation, including piping, is known . . .

$$GPH = \frac{Total\ Ft^2\ of\ Hot\ Water \times 165}{(Efficiency\ \%) \times 140,000}$$

Generally, with hot water and warm air heat, the smallest flow rate that will adequately heat the house on the coldest day is the most economical in operation.

RECOMMENDED COMBUSTION CHAMBER DIMENSIONS

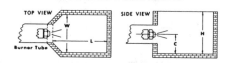

Nozzle Size or Rating (GPH)	Spray Angle	Square or Rectangular Combustion Chamber				Round Chamber (Diameter in inches)
		L Length (in.)	W Width (in.)	H Height (in.)	C Nozzle Height (in.)	
0.50 – 0.65	80°	8	8	11	4	9
0.75 – 0.85	60°	10	8	12	4	*
	80°	9	9	13	5	10
	45°	14	7	12	4	*
1.00 – 1.10	60°	11	9	13	5	*
	80°	10	10	14	6	11
	45°	15	8	11	5	*
1.25 – 1.35	60°	12	10	14	6	*
	80°	11	11	15	7	12
	45°	16	10	12	6	*
1.50 – 1.65	60°	13	11	14	7	*
	80°	12	12	15	7	13
	45°	18	11	14	6	*
1.75 – 2.00	60°	15	12	15	7	*
	80°	14	13	16	8	15
	45°	18	12	14	7	*
2.25 – 2.50	60°	17	13	15	8	*
	80°	15	14	16	8	16
	45°	20	13	15	7	*
3.00	60°	19	14	17	8	*
	80°	18	16	18	9	17

* Recommend oblong chamber for narrow sprays.

NOTES: These dimensions are for average conversion burners. Burners with special firing heads may require special chambers.

Higher backwall, flame baffle or corbelled backwall increase efficiency on many jobs.

Combustion chamber floor should be insulated on conversion jobs.

For larger nozzle sizes, use the same approximate proportions and 90 sq. in. of floor area per 1 gph.

For FlameCone installations, use approximately 65 sq. in. of floor area per 1 gph.

(Courtesy, Delavan Corporation.)

OIL BURNER SETUP AND TROUBLESHOOTING GUIDE

1. Check the pump oil pressure with a ¼″ NPT pressure gauge. Pressure should be a steady 100 PSI. Adjust, if necessary.
2. An oil filter must be installed on all furnace installations to insure reliable service and a clean oil supply. It should be located as close to the furnace as possible and have the following minimum capacities.
   A. One Pipe System—5 gal/hr
   B. Two Pipe System—20 gal/hr
3. Proper instrumentation must be used to set the correct smoke and draft readings.
   A. Allow the furnace to fire for at least five minutes.
   B. Use a smoke tester to adjust the air band setting to achieve a 0+ smoke.
   C. Use a draft gauge to adjust the barometric draft regulator to achieve a stack draft between −.025″ w.c. and −.035″ w.c. The pressure differential for the over the fire draft should be +.005″ w.c. to +.015″ w.c. (For firing rates from 1.5 GPH to 3.0 GPH, a pressure differential of up to +.02″ w.c. is acceptable.)
   D. If these readings and differential cannot be attained, a problem exists which must be solved before proceeding further.
4. Make sure that the furnace is level (or tilted up to 3° backwards) and is flat on the floor. If the furnace must be mounted on blocks then it must be supported along its entire length with a frame and additional blocking.
5. A one pipe system is recommended for gravity feed only. Up to an eight foot lift is allowable if the system is absolutely airtight.
   Rule of Thumb: Allow 1″ HG (mercury) of vacuum for each foot of vertical lift and 1″ HG (mercury) of vacuum for each 10′ of horizontal run.

For a two pipe system, follow the chart below.

Figures in body of table are total allowable feet of line length (Vertical + Horizontal) given feet of lift in column at left for pumps set 2 pipe.

FEET VERTICAL LIFT	1 Stage		2 Stage		WEBSTER 1 Stage "J" ONLY	
	⅜″ OD TUBING	½″ OD TUBING	⅜″ OD TUBING	½″ OD TUBING	⅜″ OD TUBING	½″ OD TUBING
0	50	100	75	100	100	100
1	46	100	71	100	93	100
2	42	100	68	100	85	100
3	39	100	64	100	78	100
4	35	100	60	100	70	100
5	31	95	56	100	63	100
6	27	83	53	100	55	100
7	24	72	49	100	48	100
8	20	60	45	100	40	100
9	16	49	41	100	33	99
10	12	38	38	100	25	76
11		27	34	100	18	53
12		15	30	91		31
13			26	80		
14			23	68		
15			19	57		
16				46		
17				34		
18				23		

This chart does not allow for any added restrictions such as line filter, elbows, sharp bends, check valves, etc.

Problem	Solution
Excessive oil dripping from nozzle after shutdown	Slight amount of oil normal. All air must be purged from oil line. —turn burner on, then open purge valve on pump. —close purge valve on pump before burner is shut down. Check all fittings (especially on suction side of pump) for tightness. —all connections should be flare type rather than compression type.
Oil running back down blast tube	Check above solutions for excessive oil dripping. Check tightness of nozzle. Check if nozzle is cross threaded. Check if furnace is level or up to a 3° tilt backwards.
Oil dripping into burner housing or between blast tube and burner housing	Check above solutions. Check if gasket is between mounting plate and housing. Check if screws holding mounting plate to housing are tight.
Misalignment of nozzle	Check locking nut on electrode assembly. Should be only hand tight plus 1/4 turn.
End cone distortion	Check alignment of electrode/oil pipe assembly. Check nozzle to face of end cone dimension. Should be 1″. If distortion is severe, check above and replace end cone. Check oil spray pattern—replace nozzle if necessary.
Delayed ignition	Check electrode to nozzle dimension. —0 to 1/16″ in front of nozzle. —1/2″ above nozzle ℄. —1/8″ between electrodes. Check oil spray pattern replace nozzle if necessary.

OIL BURNER TROUBLESHOOTING GUIDE

Most oil burner service calls fall into one of 4 basic categories:
1. No heat.
2. System overheats house.
3. System underheats house.
4. Miscellaneous complaints.

The following troubleshooting summary provides a guide to common possible causes of each of these complaints.

NO-HEAT COMPLAINTS

When troubleshooting a "no-heat" complaint, always check the following basic points first.
1. Make sure power is on at the main switch.
2. Make sure burner motor fuse isn't blown.
3. Check burner on-off switch. If switch is off, make sure combustion chamber is free of oil or oil vapor, then turn switch to ON position.
4. Check oil supply.
5. Make sure manual oil valves are open.
6. Make sure limit switches are closed.
7. Reset safety switch and set thermostat to call for heat.

After completing these checks, run through starting procedure. If system still does not operate properly, note point at which sequence fails.

Check the appropriate table to determine which parts of the system are most likely to be the cause of the trouble.

BURNER MOTOR DOESN'T START

CAN INDICATE	POSSIBLE CAUSE	CORRECTIVE ACTION
Trouble in primary	See cad-cell troubleshooting, or stack relay troubleshooting, as applicable.	
Trouble in thermostat	1. Broken wires, loose connections. 2. Dirty contacts. 3. Defective thermostat.	1. Replace broken wires, tighten connections. 2. Clean contacts. 3. Replace thermostat.
Faulty burner components	1. Broken wires, loose connections. 2. Motor start switch or thermal overload switch open. 3. Defective motor. 4. Defective pump.	See instructions supplied with heating equipment.

(Courtesy, Honeywell Inc.)

OIL BURNER TROUBLESHOOTING GUIDE (CONTINUED)

BURNER MOTOR STARTS–NO FLAME IS ESTABLISHED

CAN INDICATE	POSSIBLE CAUSE	CORRECTIVE ACTION
Trouble in primary	See cad-cell troubleshooting, or stack relay trouble-shooting, as applicable.	
Trouble in ignition system	1. Loose connection, broken wires between ignition transformer and primary.	1. Replace broken wires, tighten connections.
	2. Defective transformer.	2. Replace transformer.
	3. Ignition electrodes a. improperly positioned. b. spaced too far apart. c. loose. d. dirty.	3. Check manufacturer's instructions.
	4. Ceramic insulators dirty, shorted, damaged.	4. Replace electrode asssembly.
Faulty burner components	1. Dirty nozzle.	See instructions supplied with heating equipment.
	2. Nozzle loose, misaligned, worn.	
	3. Clogged oil pump strainer.	
	4. Clogged oil line.	
	5. Air leak in suction line.	
	6. Defective pressure regulator valve.	
	7. Defective pump.	
	8. Improper draft.	
	9. Water in oil.	
	10. Oil too heavy.	

BURNER MOTOR STARTS, FLAME GOES ON AND OFF AFTER STARTUP

CAN INDICATE	POSSIBLE CAUSE	CORRECTIVE ACTION
Trouble in primary	1. Dirty ignition or motor relay contacts.	1. Clean appropriate contacts.
	2. Burned out contacts.	2. Replace primary.
Trouble in limit control(s)	1. Dirty contacts.	1. Clean contacts.
	2. High and low limit settings too close or differential set too wide.	2. Readjust setting(s) and/or differential.
Trouble in thermostat	1. Broken wires, loose connections.	1. Replace broken wires, tighten connections.
	2. Differential set too close.	2. Reset differential.
	3. Anticipator defective.	3. Replace thermostat.
	4. Thermostat defective.	4. Replace thermostat.
Faulty burner components	1. Clogged or dirty oil lines.	See instructions supplied with heating equipment.
	2. Fluctuating water level (hydronic systems).	

(Courtesy, Honeywell Inc.)

OIL BURNER TROUBLESHOOTING GUIDE (CONTINUED)

SYSTEM OVERHEATS HOUSE

CAN INDICATE	POSSIBLE CAUSE	CORRECTIVE ACTION
Trouble at primary	1. Defective primary.	1. With burner running, disconnect one low voltage thermostat lead from primary control terminal. If relay doesn't drop out, replace primary.
Trouble at thermostat	1. Wiring shorted. 2. Thermostat out of calibration. 3. Defective or incorrect heat anticipator in the circuit. Anticipator improperly set. 4. Thermostat stuck in ON position. 5. Thermostat improperly located in the area under control, or draft on stat through wall.	1. Repair or replace wiring. 2. Recalibrate with accurate thermometer. 3. Replace or readjust anticipator. Replace thermostat if necessary. 4. Repair or replace thermostat. 5. Relocate thermostat. It must be out of drafts, away from radiating surfaces, ducts, steam pipes, and sunny locations.
Trouble in distribution system	1. Ductwork closed to area where thermostat is located. 2. Flow control valve (hot water) stuck in ON position. 3. Circulator does not stop running.	1. Open ductwork. 2. Repair or replace valve. 3. Check circulator circuits and/or replace circulator switching device.
Trouble at limit control	1. Limit not operating (or set too high). 2. Aquastat limit in wrong location or set too high.	1. Replace (or reset). 2. Relocate or reset as necessary.
Faulty burner components	1. Extremely oversized system. 2. Oil leaking into chamber. 3. System control valves stuck in ON position. 4. Hot water circulator does not stop running.	See instructions supplied by manufacturer of heating equipment.

(Courtesy, Honeywell Inc.)

SYSTEM UNDERHEATS HOUSE

CAN INDICATE	POSSIBLE CAUSE	CORRECTIVE ACTION
Trouble at thermostat	1. Open or loose wiring. 2. Contacts dirty. 3. Thermostat out of calibration. 4. Defective or incorrect heat anticipator in circuit. Anticipator improperly set. 5. Thermostat stuck in OFF position. 6. Thermostat improperly located. 7. Chronotherm clock thermostat 12 hours out-of-phase.	1. Repair or replace wiring. 2. Clean carefully. 3. Recalibrate thermostat with an accurate thermometer. 4. Replace or readjust anticipator. Replace thermostat if necessary. 5. Repair or replace thermostat. 6. Relocate to sense more accurately. 7. Advance setting 12 hours.
Trouble at the high or low limit controller	1. Controller set too low. 2. Slow to return to ON position. 3. Controller defective.	1. Raise set point. 2. Adjust differential. 3. Replace.
Trouble at blower (for forced air system)	1. Cutting out or recycling on overload. 2. Burned out blower motor. 3. Running too slow, or inadequate capacity. 4. Fan belt broken.	See instructions supplied with heating equipment.
System defects	1. Undersized furnace (possible if addition has been made to house) or boiler system. 2. Distribution system closed or inadequate. 3. Poor chimney draft. 4. Sooted heat exchanger. 5. Dirty warm air filters. 6. Dirty boiler water (steam system).	See instructions supplied with heating equipment.
Faulty burner system components	1. Fuel line clogged. 2. Impurities in oil, or strainer plugged. 3. Air in fuel line, or excess air in system. 4. Nozzle dirty, loose, or improperly sized. 5. Low oil pressure, or defective pump. 6. Motor does not come to proper speed. 7. Inoperative or inadequate circulator (hydronic system).	See instructions supplied with heating equipment.

(Courtesy, Honeywell Inc.)

EQUIPMENT REQUIRED FOR TROUBLESHOOTING OIL FURNACES

EQUIPMENT REQUIRED
1. Screwdriver
2. 0-150V ac Voltmeter
3. 1500 Ohm Resistor
4. Insulated Jumper Wires
5. Ohmmeter

CAUTION

Since checking must be done with live circuits, the troubleshooter must observe all the necessary precautions to avoid danger of electrical shock or equipment damage.

TROUBLESHOOTING PROCEDURES
Oil burner does not start when thermostat calls for heat

PRELIMINARY CHECKS:
1. Make sure limit switches are closed and that contacts are clean.
2. Check for line voltage power at primary. With thermostat calling for heat, voltage between burner terminals 1 and 2 (or black and white leadwires) on primary should be 120V.

PROCEED AS FOLLOWS AFTER
COMPLETING PRELIMINARY CHECKS:

PROCEDURE	CORRECTIVE ACTION	
	BURNER STARTS	BURNER DOESN'T START
1. Jumper thermostat terminals— Low volt stat—at primary; Line volt stat—at thermostat.	1. Trouble is in thermostat circuit. Check stat and wiring connections.	1. Trouble is in cad cell or primary. Go to step 2.
2. Disconnect 1 cad cell lead.	2. Cad cell is seeing external light or is defective, or cad cell connections are shorted. Go to step 3.	2. Disconnect line switch; check all wiring connections. Tighten any loose connections and retest. If burner still doesn't start, replace primary.
3. Stop burner and reconnect cad cell. Make sure F-F is not shorted, shield cad cell from external light, and jumper T-T terminals to start burner.	3. Eliminate external light source or permanently shield cad cell.	3. Replace cad cell.

(Courtesy, Honeywell Inc.)

TROUBLESHOOTING PROCEDURES (CONTINUED)
Oil burner starts, then locks out on safety

PROCEDURE	CORRECTIVE ACTION	
	BURNER LOCKS OUT	BURNER KEEPS RUNNING
1. Reset safety switch by pushing red safety switch button.	–	–
2. Disconnect cad cell leadwires at primary. If ohmmeter is available, connect cad cell leads to ohmmeter.	–	–
3. Jumper thermostat terminals to start burner— Low volt stat—at primary; Line volt stat—at thermostat.	–	–
4. After flame is established, but before safety switch locks out, jumper F-F terminals. Use 1500 ohm resistor or jumper wire if ohmmeter is not available.	4. Primary control is defective—replace. (If there is any doubt F-F terminals were jumpered within safety switch timing, wait 5 minutes, then repeat steps 1-4.)	4. Check cad cell using procedure A or B below.
A. PROCEDURE WHEN OHMMETER IS NOT USED		
5a. Open line switch, remove 1500 ohm resistor and reconnect cad cell leads to F-F terminals.	–	–
6a. Unplug cell and clean face with soft cloth. Check sighting for clear view of flame. Replace cell in socket.	–	–
7a. Close line switch, reset safety switch, and jumper T-T terminals to start burner.	7a. Replace cad cell, go to step 8a.	7a. Cad cell is OK.
8a. Reset safety switch and restart burner.	8a. Check detector view of flame, flame shape, and oil nozzle. If flame is normal and detector has good view of flame, check for open circuits in socket assembly wiring. Replace assembly if necessary. With delayed oil valve, check delay timing.	8a. Cad cell and socket assembly are OK.

(Courtesy, Honeywell Inc.)

TROUBLESHOOTING PROCEDURES (CONTINUED)
Oil burner starts, then locks out on safety

B. PROCEDURE WHEN OHMMETER IS USED

5b. Take ohmmeter reading with burner running and locate reading in table below. Read across to determine cause and corrective action.	–	–

OHMMETER READING	CAUSE	ACTION
0 ohms.	Short circuit.	Check for pinched cad cell leadwires.
Less than 1600 ohms but not 0.	Cad cell and application are operating correctly.	None.
Over 1600 ohms but not infinite.	Dirty or defective cell, improper sighting, or improper air adjustment.	1. Clean cell face and recheck. 2. Check flame sighting. 3. Replace cell and recheck. 4. Adjust air band to get good reading.
Infinite resistance.	Open circuit.	Check for improper wiring, loose cell in holder, or defective cell.

(Courtesy, Honeywell Inc.)

ELECTRIC FURNACE TROUBLESHOOTING GUIDE

Center of chart states basic trouble. Begin there.

Adjacent partial circles state specific troubles that could cause basic trouble. Determine which of these specific troubles exist before proceeding further.

Remaining partial circles state various contributing troubles to specific trouble. Determine contributing trouble or troubles before attempting correction.

Numbers in chart are for explanation and guidance. Where no numbers are shown, the statement is considered to be self-explanatory.

[Courtesy, SJC Corp (formerly Tappan Air Conditioning).]

ELECTRIC FURNACE TROUBLESHOOTING GUIDE (CONTINUED)

1. Check voltage at motor leads. Be sure to use common (white) and lead going to sequencer switch. Black, if high speed, blue, if medium speed and red, if low speed. Voltage should be 230 plus or minus 10%.

2. Remove wires from line voltage slave switch on number 1 sequencer. Check with continuity tester to determine that switch is closed and making contact. When attaching wires, make sure they are connected to top and bottom terminals. The center post is not used.

3. Check fuse on fuse block that feeds common leg (white) to blower motor.

4. Check to see that 24 volts is present at heater terminals on first sequencer.

5. Jumper R to W_1 on terminal board. If unit starts to operate after normal delay (not more than 50 seconds), trouble is in stat or stat wiring. Next, remove stat and jumper R and W terminals. If unit starts problem is in thermostat, not in wiring.

6. Check fuses on block feeding primary side of transformer.

7. If 230 or 208 volts is being supplied to primary side, check for 24 volts on the secondary. If 24 volts is not present on secondary, the transformer is defective.

8. Check line voltage to transformer for proper primary lead connections. Yellow lead for 230V; red lead for 208V.

9. If there is 24 volts to the heater and switch does not operate, the switch is defective.

10. Check model and size of furnace. Refer to the installation instructions to determine if thermostat is set for proper heat anticipation.

11. Check low voltage wiring at terminal block.

12. Check amp draw on each strip to determine if they are heating.

13. Check fuses feeding each leg of elements not heating.

14. With a voltmeter, ohmmeter or continuity light, check fusible link, limit switch and element. Be sure to shut off power and disconnect voltage leads if using ohmmeter or continuity light.

15. Place jumper across W_1 and W_2 terminals — first on terminal board, then on stat to determine if stat is operative. If this energizes the second stage, the stat is defective.

16. Place jumper across terminals of outdoor stat. If strip energizes, stat is defective.

17. If unit is operating on 208 volts instead of 240 volts, the heating capacity is 75% of rating.

18. Shut off power, remove cap and pull out internal overload. Check terminals 1 and 3 with a continuity tester.

19. Check capacitor. If capacitor is defective, shorted or burned out, motor will not run.

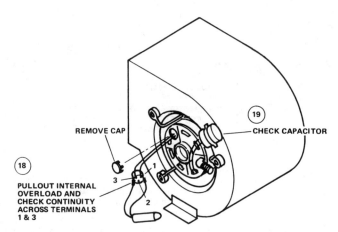

Internal Overload and Capacitor Check

[Courtesy, SJC Corp (formerly Tappan Air Conditioning).]

HEATING-COOLING THERMOSTAT TROUBLESHOOTING

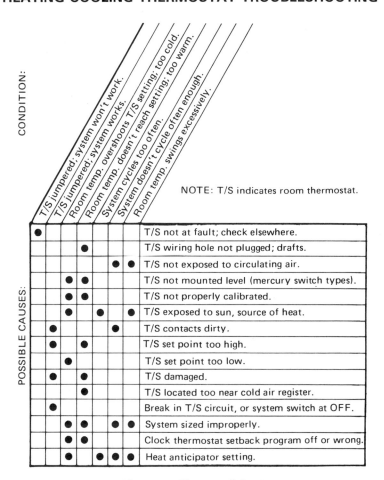

CONDITION:

- T/S jumpered: system won't work.
- T/S jumpered: system works.
- Room temp. overshoots T/S setting; too warm.
- Room temp. doesn't reach setting; too cold.
- System cycles too often.
- System doesn't cycle often enough.
- Room temp. swings excessively.

NOTE: T/S indicates room thermostat.

POSSIBLE CAUSES:

●							T/S not at fault; check elsewhere.
		●					T/S wiring hole not plugged; drafts.
				●	●		T/S not exposed to circulating air.
	●	●					T/S not mounted level (mercury switch types).
	●	●					T/S not properly calibrated.
	●		●		●		T/S exposed to sun, source of heat.
●			●				T/S contacts dirty.
●		●					T/S set point too high.
	●						T/S set point too low.
●		●					T/S damaged.
		●					T/S located too near cold air register.
●							Break in T/S circuit, or system switch at OFF.
	●	●		●	●		System sized improperly.
	●	●					Clock thermostat setback program off or wrong.
	●		●	●	●		Heat anticipator setting.

(Courtesy, Honeywell Inc.)

T8082 CHRONOTHERM THERMOSTAT TROUBLESHOOTING

CLOCK RUNS BUT—	CHECK	CORRECTING ACTION
A. Setup/setback temperature program 12 hours off.	Program dial in proper day or night phase.	Turn clock ahead 12 hours.
B. Dwelling does not warm up at programmed time.	Heating system may need more time to warm up dwelling.	Move red pin(s) one-half hour earlier on the program dial.
C. Temperature setup or setback occurs at the wrong times.	Program pins are at incorrect location.	Relocate pins to desired settings.
D. Dwelling temperatures not correct.	1. Thermostat set point lever positions. 2. Subbase switch positions. 3. Thermostat—move both levers to end of scale: a. right (red) for heat. b. left (blue) for cool.	1. Reset to desired temperatures. 2. Reset to desired positions. 3. Heat or cooling system should start. If not, call dealer service technician.
E. Stops.	1. Voltage across R and W wallplate terminals (if heating-only system). 2. Voltage across R and unmarked wallplate terminals (if cooling-only system). 3. Voltage across R and W subbase terminals (if heating-cooling system). 4. Battery (see "J" below).	1. Voltage must be 15–30 Vac. 2. Voltage must be 15–30 Vac. 3. Voltage must be 15–30 Vac. 4. Voltage 2.5–3.0 Vdc.
F. Stops after about 7 days.	1. Pilotstat system.	1. Relight pilot, or 2. Restart clock in fall, or 3. Add isolating relay. or 4. Convert primary valve to V800 type.
G. DSI or IP system goes into lockout.	Check IP and DSI system for T8082 compatibility	1. Install isolating relay.
H. Flue damper does not function properly.	—	1. Install isolating relay.
I. Stops after a period of time. 1. 2-wire cooling-only system. 2. Hydronic heating system with RA19, RA89, R4832, R845 or R847 relays. (Occurs only during 100% cooling or heating load.)	1. Cooling equipment. On systems with undersized cooling equipment the OFF cycle will be insufficient to provide adequate clock operation during prolonged cooling periods. 2. System voltage insufficient to change clock during prolonged periods of burner activity.	1. Move temperature control levers to upper end (90°) for 30 minutes to recharge battery for another week. 2. Move temperature control levers to the low end of scale (40°) for 30 minutes to recharge battery for another week.

CLOCK DOES NOT RUN—	CHECK	CORRECTING ACTION
J. No 24 V power to thermostat.	Fuse or circuit breaker to furnace, furnace switch, 24 V control circuit transformer, thermostat wire connections, thermostat-wallplate connections.	1. Restore power. See instructions to: 2. Charge battery. 3. Set clock. 4. Start clock. 5. Return to normal operation.
K. Batteries won't hold charge.	Clock will not run with 24 V power to wallplate. Check metal contact springs on back of thermostat.	1. Replace battery pack with Part No. 191127B. 2. Charge battery. 3. Start clock. 4. Return to normal operation. Straighten bent spring contacts.
L. Clock won't run with battery pack replacement and 24 V power to thermostat.	—	Replace thermostat.

(Courtesy, Honeywell Inc.)

FLUE GAS DAMPER—SERVICE-ANALYSIS CHART

Symptom	Check Procedure	Remedy
Damper will not open	1. Remove cover from damper operator. With power to furnace "on" and thermostat calling for heat, check voltage (24 V nominal) across terminals 1 and 4.	1a. If voltage is present, go to step 2. 1b. If no voltage is seen: (b1) the white lead is open or loose at its terminations. (b2) the problem is not in the damper.
	2. Remove white lead from terminal 4 and blue lead from terminal 1. Check continuity between terminals 1 and 4.	2a. If there is continuity with some resistance, go to step 3. 2b. If there is no continuity, replace the motor operator assembly.
	3. Is return spring broken?	3. Replace spring.
	4. Is damper housing or plate distorted?	4. Repair or replace housing assembly.
Damper will not close	1. Is 115-V power connected to furnace?	1. Damper will remain open if there is no power supply.
	2. Is thermostat calling for heat?	2. Thermostat must be "off" for damper to close.
	3. Is damper connected to printed circuit board in furnace electrical box?	3. Make sure the edge connector is positioned so that the terminals contact the printed circuit.
	4. Remove cover from damper operator. Check voltage (24 V nominal) across terminals 1 and 2.	4a. If voltage is present: (a1) but motor does not operate, replace the motor operator assembly. (a2) and the motor operates, the coupling or cotter pin retainer for the damper shaft is broken. Replace as necessary. (a3) and the motor stalls, the damper shaft is binding. Repair or replace the housing assembly. 4b. If no voltage is seen: (b1) there is an open circuit in the blue or red lead leading to terminals 1 and 2. (b2) the problem is not in the damper,
Damper closes and opens, but gas valve or ignition system does not operate.	1. Remove cover from damper operator. With power to furnace "on," thermostat calling for heat, and damper in open position, check voltage (24 V nominal) across terminals 1 and 3 on damper terminal board.	1a. If voltage is seen, problem is not in the damper. 1b. If no voltage is seen: (b1) the black lead in the edge connector is loose. (b2) replace the motor operator assembly.

(Courtesy, Honeywell Inc.)

PROCEDURE FOR INSTALLING ELECTRICALLY OPERATED
AUTOMATIC VENT DAMPER
Devices on existing appliances

This procedure is intended as a guide to aid in safely installing an automatic vent damper device on an existing appliance.

This procedure is based on the assumption that the history of the specific appliance has been one of safe and satisfactory operation.

This procedure is predicated on central furnace, boiler and water heater installations, and it should be recognized that generalized procedures cannot anticipate all situations. Accordingly, in some cases deviation from this procedure may be necessary to determine safe operation of the equipment.

The following steps are to be followed in making the modifications:

1. Perform a safety inspection of the existing appliance installation. See procedure (A) for a recommended procedure for such a safety inspection.

2. Shut off all gas and electricity to the appliance. To shut off gas use the shutoff valve in the supply line to the appliance.

3. Install the automatic vent damper device in strict accordance with the manufacturer's installation instructions. Make certain the device is not located in that portion of the venting system which serves any appliance other than the one for which the damper is installed.

4. Make certain wiring connections are tight and wires are positioned and secured so they will not be able to contact high temperature locations.

5. When an additional automatic valve has been incorporated or an existing gas control replaced, conduct a gas leakage test of the appliance piping and control system downstream of the shutoff valve in the supply line to the appliance.

6. Visually inspect the modified venting system for proper horizontal pitch.

7. Check that the damper and gas valve(s) are in the correct operating sequence.

   (a) The damper must be in the full open position <u>before</u> the gas valve(s) opens.

   (b) The damper must remain in the full open position while the gas valve(s) is open.

   (c) The gas valve(s) must be closed before the damper <u>begins</u> its return to the closed position.

   (d) The damper shall remain in the closed position during the off cycle of the appliance.

8. Determine the amperage draw of the gas control circuit and damper device.

   (a) Check appliance transformer for adequate capacity.

   (b) Check heat anticipator in comfort thermostat to determine it is properly adjusted.

9. Sequence the appliance through at least three normal operating cycles.

10. Insofar as is practical, close all building doors and windows and all doors between the space in which the appliance is located and other spaces of the building. Turn on clothes dryers. Turn on any exhaust fans, such as range hoods and bathroom exhausts, so they will operate at maximum speed. Do not operate a summer exhaust fan. Close fireplace dampers.

11. Place appliance in operation. <u>Follow the lighting instructions.</u> Adjust thermostat so appliance will operate continuously.

12. Test for spillage at the draft hood relief opening after 5 minutes of main burner operation. Use draft gage, flame of a match or candle, or smoke from a cigarette, cigar or pipe.

13. (a) Visually determine that main burner gas is burning properly: i.e., no floating, lifting or flashback. Adjust the primary air shutter(s) as required.

    (b) If the appliance is equipped with high and low flame controlling or flame modulation, check for proper main burner operation at low flame.

14. Determine that the pilot(s) is burning properly and that main burner ignition is satisfactory by interrupting and reestablishing the electrical supply to the appliance in any convenient manner. Test the pilot safety device to determine it is operating properly by extinguishing the pilot burner(s) when the main burner(s) is off and determining, after 3 minutes, that the main burner gas does not flow upon a call for heat.

15. <u>Applicable only to furnaces</u> — Check both the limit control and the fan control for proper operation. Limit control operation can be checked by blocking the circulating air inlet or temporarily disconnecting the electrical supply to the blower motor and determining that the limit control acts to shut off the main burner gas.

16. <u>Applicable only to boilers</u> —

    (a) Determine that the water pumps are in operating condition.

    (b) Test low water cutoffs, automatic feed controls, pressure and temperature limit controls and relief valves in accordance with the manufacturer's recommendations to determine they are in operating condition.

(Courtesy, Johnson Controls, Inc.)

Q15 AND Q16 SPARK IGNITION INSTALLATION TROUBLESHOOTING, NO SPARK

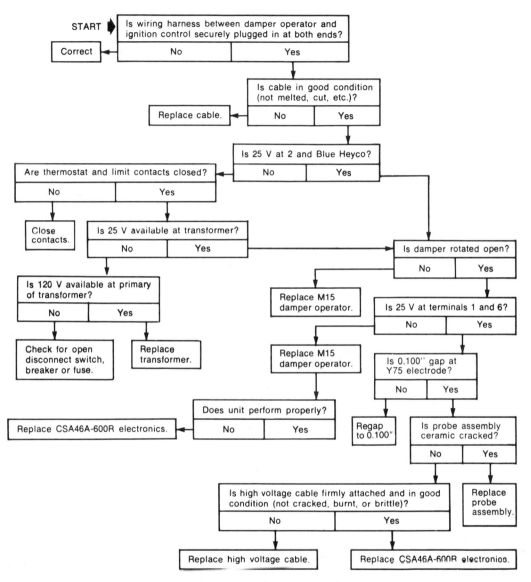

(Courtesy, Johnson Controls, Inc.)

FLUE GAS VENTING—REPLACEMENT INSTALLATIONS

I. The vent is a critical part of the heating system. It should *always* be examined prior to installation of the furnace.

II. When installing high-efficiency furnaces on a venting system that is "marginal," the following suggestions may help:

    A. Set furnace to full input rate. New furnaces are commonly set conservatively at factory.

B. Minimize restrictions in vent connector — use as few elbows as possible.

C. Insulate any long horizontal single-wall vent connector with 1/2-in. insulation or use double-wall pipe.

D. Follow recommendations in flow charts regarding application of 58SC, SS, DH induced-draft furnaces on existing chimney.

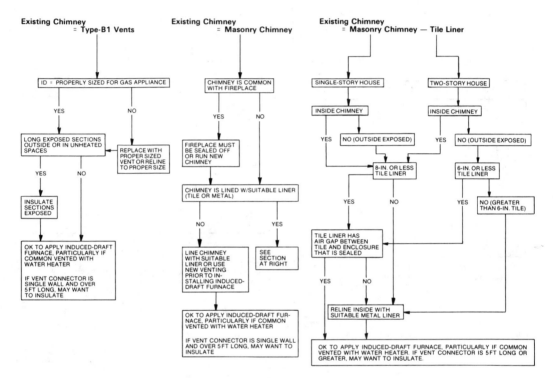

(Courtesy, Carrier Corporation.)

CAPACITY OF TYPE B DOUBLE-WALL VENTS
SERVING A SINGLE APPLIANCE

Height H	Lateral L	Vent Diameter—D						
		3''	4''	5''	6''	7''	8''	10''
		Maximum Appliance Input Rating in Thousands of Btu Per Hour						
6'	0	46	86	141	205	285	370	570
	2'	36	67	105	157	217	285	455
	6'	32	61	100	149	205	273	435
	12'	28	55	91	137	190	255	406
8'	0	50	94	155	235	320	415	660
	2'	40	75	120	180	247	322	515
	8'	35	66	109	165	227	303	490
	16'	28	58	96	148	206	281	458
10'	0	53	100	166	255	345	450	720
	2'	42	81	129	195	273	355	560
	10'	36	70	115	175	245	330	525
	20'	NR	60	100	154	217	300	486
15'	0	58	112	187	285	390	525	840
	2'	48	93	150	225	316	414	675
	15'	37	76	128	198	275	373	610
	30'	NR	60	107	169	243	328	553
20'	0	61	119	202	307	430	575	930
	2'	51	100	166	249	346	470	755
	10'	44	89	150	228	321	443	710
	20'	35	78	134	206	295	410	665
	30'	NR	68	120	186	273	380	626

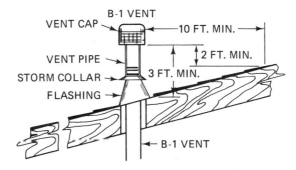

(Courtesy, BDP Company.)

HIGH-EFFICIENCY FURNACE
COMBUSTION AIR START-UP, ADJUSTMENT, AND SAFETY CHECK

A. Adjusting Tuning Valve

Before firing the furnace, the pressure drop through the heat exchanger must be adjusted for maximum efficiency. The pressure drop adjustment is accomplished with the tuning valve as follows:

NOTE: Be sure that the gas supply to the furnace is turned off.

1. Install field-supplied plastic tee between pressure tap on bottom of gas valve and pressure tube as shown in the figure below.
2. Install second field-supplied plastic tee between pressure switch and pressure tube from collector box as shown.
3. Connect slope gauge to tees as shown.
4. Close R-W circuit to start inducer motor.
5. Adjust tuning valve to obtain 0.83 ± 0.01 inches negative water column.
6. Remove handle from tuning valve and recheck pressure. Store in safe place.
7. Open R-W circuit.
8. Disconnect slope gauge.
9. Remove plastic tees and reconnect factory pressure tubes to gas valve and pressure switch.
10. Turn on gas supply to furnace.

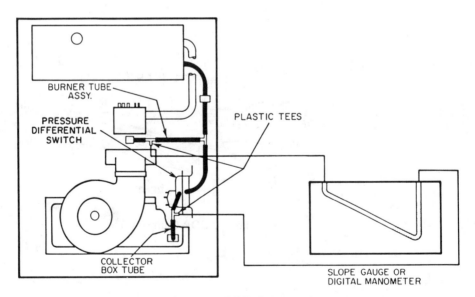

(Courtesy, BDP Company.)

PRINTED CIRCUIT FAN CONTROL CENTER

Each furnace features a fan control center. This will aid the installer and serviceman when installing and servicing the unit. A low-voltage terminal board is marked for easy connection of field wiring.

The main furnace control box features an adjustable blower-off timing device. The off timing delay can be varied over a range of 90 to 240 s by turning the off timing adjustment control in the direction indicated on the label attached to the side of the control box. After a change in adjustment, the time-delay circuit must be energized at least 4 min. This will saturate the solid-state circuit so that the off time delay will be the same as during normal furnace operation. The off timing adjustment is set at the factory for a delay of approximately 240 s.

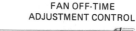

FAN OFF-TIME
ADJUSTMENT CONTROL

(Courtesy, BDP Company.)

MEASURING HEAT PUMP EFFICIENCY

The efficiency of heat pump equipment is usually measured using a number called Coefficient of Performance (COP).

To calculate a unit's COP, apply this formula:

$$COP = \frac{\text{Unit Capacity (Btuh)}}{\text{Unit Consumption (watts) x 3.413}}$$

Let's calculate the COP of a unit whose capacity is 36,000 Btuh and is consuming 3,880 watt at an outside temperature of 45 F. The calculation looks like this:

$$COP = \frac{36,000 \text{ Btu}}{3,880 \text{ watts x 3.413 Btu/watt}}$$

$$COP = \frac{36,000}{13,242} = 2.7$$

The COP of this unit is 2.7. That is, it is 2.7 times as efficient as electric resistance heating under the same conditions.

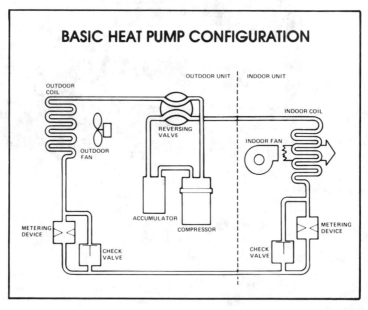

BASIC HEAT PUMP CONFIGURATION

(Courtesy, Honeywell Inc.)

ELECTRONIC AIR-CLEANER SERVICE

GENERAL DESCRIPTION

The F50 Electronic Air Cleaner replaced the F45 and F46 and was introduced in 1972 for use in central systems with capacities up to 2000 cfm. It uses the FC37A Electronic Cells.

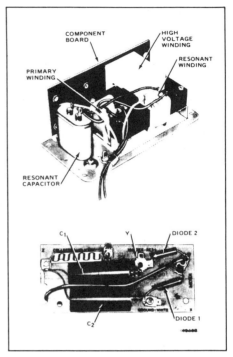

INTERNAL SCHEMATIC DIAGRAM

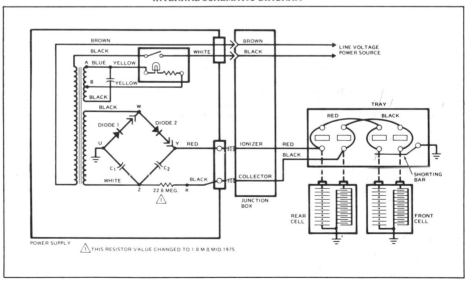

(Courtesy, Honeywell Inc.)

ELECTRONIC AIR-CLEANER SERVICE (CONTINUED)

CHECKOUT AND TROUBLESHOOTING

SERVICE AIDS

☐ High voltage test meter – ac and dc.
☐ Spare diode (137073A) with alligator clip.

PREPARATION

1. Check to see that the electronic cells are clean, dry, and properly installed in the air cleaner cabinet.

2. To energize the air cleaner, turn on the system fan and turn air cleaner switch ON.

NORMAL VOLTAGES

	WITH CELLS	WITHOUT CELLS
Ionizer	7,500–8,500V dc	8,500–9,600V dc
Collector	3,000V dc minimum	3,500–4,800V dc
Transformer Secondary	–	3,200–4,100V ac

ELECTRICAL TROUBLESHOOTING

Check out the electrical components of the F50 by observing the indicator light under various operating conditions. Follow the flow chart and refer to the instructions for checking components when indicated.

CHECK ELECTRONIC CELLS

When diagnostic checks indicate a possible problem in the electronic cells, inspect them carefully for any sign of mechanical damage. Check for short circuits from contacts to ground.

CHECK VOLTAGE DOUBLER CIRCUIT

1. Check voltage across each capacitor with opposite diode unplugged. If both capacitor and diode are good, the voltage will be over 3,500V dc.

2. Check diode by substitution and if the voltage still isn't right, replace the capacitor.

CHECK HIGH VOLTAGE TRANSFORMER

1. Disconnect black wire from the resonant capacitor.

2. Energize the air cleaner and measure *resonant winding* voltage.

    a. If this voltage is over 150V ac, the resonant capacitor is defective or the transformer secondary winding is open.

        (1) De-energize the power supply and check for continuity of the secondary winding.

    b. If this voltage is under 150V ac, the transformer is defective and must be replaced.

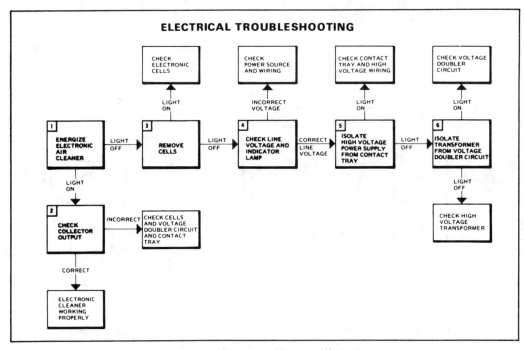

ELECTRICAL TROUBLESHOOTING

(Courtesy, Honeywell Inc.)

Airflow. It is important to install the air cleaner so that the airflow is evenly distributed across the face of the cell. Do this with:

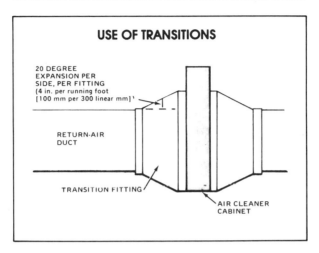

Offset. If the duct connection to the furnace allows inadequate clearance for the F50, shorten the lateral trunk or attach an offset to the elbow.

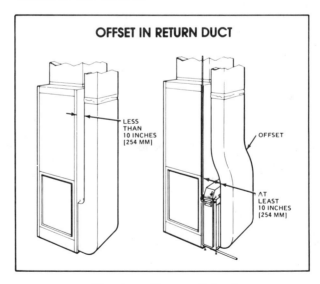

(Courtesy, Honeywell Inc.)

MEASUREMENT OF PRESSURE WITH A MANOMETER

Pressure is defined as a force per unit area — and the most accurate way to measure low air pressure is to balance a column of liquid of known weight against it and measure the height of the liquid column so balanced. The units of measure commonly used are inches of mercury (in. Hg.), using mercury as the fluid and inches of water (in. W.C.), using water or oil as the fluid.

Instruments employing this principle are called manometers. The simplest form is the basic and well-known U-tube manometer (Fig. 1). This device indicates the difference between two pressures (differential pressure), or between a single pressure and atmosphere (gage pressure), when one side is open to atmosphere.

If a U-tube is filled to the half way point with water and air pressure is exerted on one of the columns, the fluid will be displaced. Thus one leg of water column will rise and the other falls. The difference in height "h" which is the *sum* of the readings above and below the half way point, indicates the pressure in inches of water column.

The U-tube manometer is a primary standard because the difference in height between the two columns is always a true indication of the pressure regardless of variations in the internal diameter of the tubing.

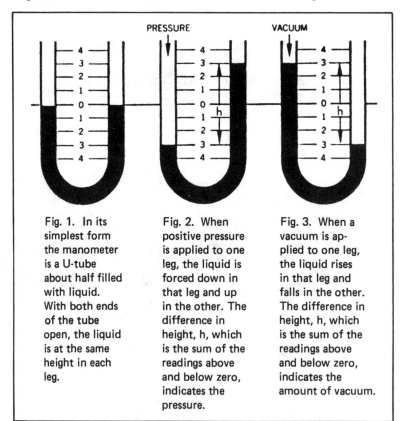

Fig. 1. In its simplest form the manometer is a U-tube about half filled with liquid. With both ends of the tube open, the liquid is at the same height in each leg.

Fig. 2. When positive pressure is applied to one leg, the liquid is forced down in that leg and up in the other. The difference in height, h, which is the sum of the readings above and below zero, indicates the pressure.

Fig. 3. When a vacuum is applied to one leg, the liquid rises in that leg and falls in the other. The difference in height, h, which is the sum of the readings above and below zero, indicates the amount of vacuum.

(Courtesy, Dwyer Instruments, Inc.)

Appendices

MEASUREMENT OF AIR VELOCITY WITH A MANOMETER

To measure air velocity, connect a Dwyer Durablock inclined manometer to a Pitot tube in the air stream as shown. This method requires only a static tap plus a simple tube in center of duct to pick up total pressure. The differential pressure reading on the manometer is velocity pressure, which may be converted to air velocity by calculation or reference to conversion charts.

Dwyer stainless steel Pitot tubes are made in numerous lengths and configurations to serve in the smallest to the largest duct sizes.

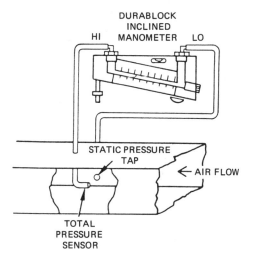

(Courtesy, Dwyer Instruments, Inc.)

CAPACITY TABLE FOR HEATING AND COOLING
Converting cubic feet per minute to Btuh
at various register and diffuser temperatures

	HEATING*			COOLING**		
REGISTER TEMPERATURE	120°	140°	160°	65°	60°	55°
TEMPERATURE RISE (OR DROP)	50°	70°	90°	15°	20°	25°
CFM						
50	2,700	3,780	4,860	1,050	1,400	1,755
75	4,050	5,670	7,290	1,580	2,110	2,630
100	5,400	7,560	9,720	2,110	2,810	3,510
125	6,750	9,450	12,150	2,630	3,510	4,390
150	8,100	11,340	14,580	3,160	4,210	5,265
175	9,450	13,230	17,010	3,685	4,915	6,140
200	10,800	15,120	19,440	4,210	5,620	7,020
250	13,500	18,900	24,300	5,265	7,020	8,775
300	16,200	22,680	29,160	6,320	8,425	10,530
350	18,900	26,460	34,020	7,370	9,830	12,285
400	21,600	30,240	38,880	8,425	11,230	14,040
450	24,300	34,020	43,740	9,480	12,640	15,795
500	27,000	37,800	48,600	10,530	14,040	17,550
600	32,400	45,360	58,320	12,640	16,850	21,060
700	37,800	52,920	68,040	14,740	19,660	24,570
800	43,200	60,480	77,760	16,850	22,460	28,080
900	48,600	68,040	87,480	18,950	25,270	31,590
1000	54,000	75,600	97,200	21,060	28,080	35,100
1200	64,800	90,720	116,640	25,270	33,700	42,120
1400	75,600	105,840	136,080	29,480	39,310	49,140
1600	86,400	120,960	155,520	33,700	44,930	56,160
1800	97,200	136,080	174,960	37,910	50,540	63,180
2000	108,000	151,200	194,400	42,120	56,160	70,200
2200	118,800	166,320	213,840	46,330	61,780	77,220
2400	129,600	181,440	233,280	50,540	67,390	84,240

*Based on 70° Return Air
**Based on 80° Return Air
  Total Cooling Btuh = Sensible + Latent. Latent = 30% of Total

(Courtesy, Hart & Cooling Manufacturing Company.)

GUIDE FOR SIZING FUSES

Dual-Element Time-Delay Fuse

● **Main Service**—Size fuse according to method in ●.

● **Feeder Circuit With No Motor Loads.** The fuse size must be at least 125% of the continuous load† plus 100% of the non continuous load. Do not size the fuse larger than the ampacity of the conductor*.

● **Feeder Circuit With All Motor Loads.** Size the fuse at 150%♦ of the full load current of the largest motor plus the full load current of all other motors.

● **Feeder Circuit With Mixed Loads.** Size fuse at sum of
a. 150%♦ of the full load current of the largest motor.
b. 100% of the full load current of all other motors.
c. 125% of the continuous non-motor load†.
d. 100% of the non-continuous non-motor load.

● **Branch Circuit With No Motor Load.** The fuse size must be at least 125% of the continuous load† plus 100% of the non continuous load. Do not size the fuse larger than the ampacity of the conductor*.

● **Motor Branch Circuit With Overload Relays.** Where overload relays are sized for motor running overload protection, the following fuses provide back-up protection and short-circuit protection:
a. Motor 1.15 service factor or 40°C rise: size fuse at 125% of motor full load current or next higher standard size.
b. Motor less than 1.15 service factor or over 40°C rise: size the fuse at 115% of the motor full load current or the next higher standard fuse size.

● **Motor Branch Circuit With Fuse Protection Only.** Where the fuse is the only motor protection, the following fuses provide motor running overload protection and short-circuit protection:
a. Motor 1.15 service factor or 40°C rise: size the fuse at 110% to 125% of the motor full load current.
b. Motor less than 1.15 service factor or over 40°C rise: size fuse at 100% to 115% of motor full load current.

● **Large Motor Branch Circuit**—Fuse larger than 600 amps. For large motors, size KRP-C HI-CAP time-delay Fuse at 150% to 225% of the motor full load current, depending on the starting method; i.e. part-winding starting, reduced voltage starting, etc.

Non-Time-Delay Fuse

● **Main Service**—Size fuse according to method in ●.

● **Feeder Circuit With No Motor Loads.** The fuse size must be at least 125% of the continuous load† plus 100% of the non continuous load. Do not size the fuse larger than the ampacity of the wire*

● **Feeder Circuit With All Motor Loads.** Size the fuse at 300% of the full load current of the largest motor plus the full load current of all other motors.

● **Feeder Circuit With Mixed Loads.** Size fuse at sum of
a. 300% of the full load current of the largest motor.
b. 100% of the full load current of all other motors.
c. 125% of the continuous non-motor load†.
d. 100% of the non-continuous non-motor load.

● **Branch Circuit With No Motor Load.** The fuse size must be at least 125% of the continuous load† plus 100% of the non continuous load. Do not size the fuse larger than the ampacity of the conductor*.

● **Motor Branch Circuit With Overload Relays.** Size the fuse as close to but not exceeding 300% of the motor running full load current. This fuse size provides short-circuit protection only.

● **Motor Branch Circuit With Fuse Protection Only.** Non-time-delay fuses **cannot** be sized close enough to provide motor running overload protection. If sized for motor overload protection, non-time-delay fuses would open due to motor starting current. Use dual-element fuses.

Conductor Ampacity Selection

● **Feeder Circuit And Main Circuit With Mixed Loads.** Conductor ampacity at least sum of:
a. 125% of continuous non-motor load†.
b. 100% of non-continuous non-motor load.
c. 125% of the largest motor full load current.
d. 100% of all other motors' full load current.

● **Feeder Circuit With No Motor Load.** Conductor ampacity at least 125% of the continuous load† plus 100% of the non-continuous load.

● **Feeder Circuit With Motor Loads.** Conductor ampacity at least 125% of the largest motor full load amperes plus 100% of all other motors' full load amperes.

● **Feeder Circuit And Main Circuit With Mixed Loads.** Conductor ampacity at least sum of:
a. 125% of continuous non-motor load†.
b. 100% of non-continuous non-motor load.
c. 125% of the largest motor full load current.
d. 100% of all other motors' full load current.

● **Branch Circuit With No Motor Load.** Conductor ampacity at least 125% of the continuous load† plus 100% of the non-continuous load.

●, ●, & ● **Motor Branch Circuits.** Conductor ampacity at least 125% of the motor full load current.

†100% of the continuous load can be used rather than 125% when the switch and fuse are listed for continuous operation at 100% of rating. Most bolted pressure switches and high pressure contact switches 800A to 6000A with Class L fuses are listed for 100% continuous operation.
*Where conductor ampacity does not correspond to a standard fuse rating, next higher rating fuse is permitted when 800 amperes or less (240-3 Exc. 1)
♦In many motor feeder applications, dual-element fuses can be sized at ampacity of feeder conductors.

(Courtesy, Bussman Manufacturing, Division of McGraw-Edison Company.)

GUIDE FOR SIZING TRANSFORMERS

A transformer is used on all 24 V control systems. A general rule of thumb is to size the transformer to the largest total load occurring at one time.

On a heating-only system, the total heating load determines the transformer size. On a heating-cooling system, the total cooling load determines the transformer size, since it is almost always greater than the total heating load.

SIZING TO HEATING LOAD ONLY

1. For the total heating load, add the amperage draw of each parallel load in the system. FOR EXAMPLE:

Gas Valve	0.2 to 0.6 A
Heat Relay (if used)	0.4 A
Fan Timer (if used)	0.4 A
TOTAL	1.0 to 1.4 A

2. Now, multiply the total amperage draw by the transformer secondary voltage to equal the system VA rating.

IN OUR EXAMPLE: 1.0 A x 24 V = 24 VA

The tranformer must have a higher VA rating to allow for inrush VA. So, for our example, a tranformer with a minimum rating of 40 VA should be used.

SIZING HEATING-COOLING LOAD

To determine the total cooling load, add the sealed VA rating of each of the parallel loads. Typical loads are:

Blower Relay	10 VA
Cooling Contactor	15 VA
TOTAL	25 VA

Since the 25 VA cooling load is greater than the heating load in our example above, the transformer is sized for the cooling load. Allowing for inrush VA, we need a transformer with a VA of at least 40.

ADJUSTING THERMOSTAT HEAT ANTICIPATORS

Adjust the heat anticipator to match the current rating of the primary control; this rating is usually stamped on the control nameplate. Move the indicator on the scale to correspond with this rating and the anticipator will be properly adjusted for optimum comfort with most types of heating systems.

(Courtesy, Honeywell Inc.)

OHM'S LAW EQUATION WHEEL
Watts (*W*), amperes (*I*), volts (*E*), or ohms (*R*)

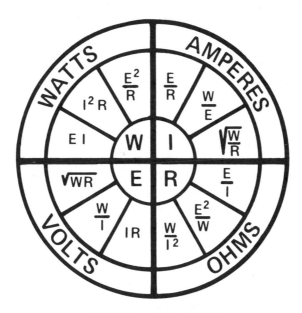

POWER AND HEAT

```
1 BTU . . . . . . . . . . . . . . . . 776 FT-LB, 0.293 WATT-HR, 252 CAL
1 CAL . . . . . . . . . . . . . . 0.003968 BTU, 0.0011619 WATT-HR
1 BTUH . . . . . . . . . . . . . . . . . . . . . 0.293 WATTS, 4.2 CAL/MIN
12,000 BTU . . . . . . . . . . . . . . . . . . . . 1 TON REFRIGERATION
1 WATT . . . . . . . . . . . . . . . . . . . . . . . . . . . . . . . 3.413 BTU
1 WATT-HR . . . . . . . . . . . . . . . . . . . . . . . . . . . . . 3.413 BTUH
1 KW (1000 WATTS) . . . . . . . . . . . . . . . . . . . . . . 3413 BTUH
1 KW-HR . . . . . . . . . . . . . . . . . . . . . . . . . . . . . . . 3413 BTU
1 HP . . . . . . . . . . . . . 0.746 KW, 2547 BTUH, 33,000 FT-LB/MIN
1 BOHP . . . . . . . . . . . . . . . . . . . . . . . . . . . . . . . 33,475 BTUH
```

BTU CONTENT OF FUELS

Grade or Type	Unit	Btu
No. 1 Oil	Gallon	137,400
No. 2 Oil	Gallon	139,600
No. 3 Oil	Gallon	141,800
No. 4 Oil	Gallon	145,100
No. 5 Oil	Gallon	148,800
No. 6 Oil	Gallon	152,400
Natural Gas	Cu. ft.	950 to 1,150
Propane	Cu. ft.	2,550
Butane	Cu. ft.	3,200

(Courtesy, Honeywell Inc.)

CONVERSION FACTORS

MULTIPLY	BY	TO OBTAIN
Atmospheres (Std.) 760 MM of Mercury at 32°F.	14.696	Lbs./sq. inch
Atmospheres	76.0	Cms. of mercury
Atmospheres	29.92	In. of mercury
Atmospheres	33.90	Feet of water
Atmospheres	1.0333	Kgs./sq.cm.
Atmospheres	14.70	Lbs./sq. inch
Atmospheres	1.058	Tons/sq. ft.
Brit. Therm. Units	0.2520	Kilogram-calories
Brit. Therm. Units	777.5	Foot-lbs.
Brit. Therm. Units	0.000393	Horse-power-hrs.
Brit. Therm. Units	0.293	Watt-hrs.
BTU/min.	12.96	Foot-lbs./sec.
BTU/min.	0.02356	Horse-power
BTU/min.	0.01757	Kilowatts
BTU/min.	17.57	Watts
Calorie	0.003968	BTU
Centimeters	0.3937	Inches
Centimeters	0.03280	Feet
Centimeters	0.01	Meters
Centimeters	10	Millimeters
Centmtrs. of Merc.	0.01316	Atmospheres
Centimtrs. of merc.	0.4461	Feet of water
Centimtrs. of merc.	136.0	Kgs./sq. meter
Centimtrs. of merc.	27.85	Lbs./sq. ft.
Centimtrs. of merc.	0.1934	Lbs./sq. inch
Cubic feet	2.832×10^4	Cubic cms.
Cubic feet	1728	Cubic inches
Cubic feet	0.02832	Cubic meters
Cubic feet	0.03704	Cubic yards
Cubic feet	7.48052	Gallons U.S.
Cubic feet/minute	472.0	Cubic cms./sec.
Cubic feet/minute	0.1247	Gallons/sec.
Cubic foot water	62.4	Pounds @ 60°F.
Feet	30.48	Centimeters
Feet	12	Inches
Feet	0.3048	Meters
Feet	1/3	Yards

MULTIPLY	BY	TO OBTAIN
Feet of water	0.02950	Atmospheres
Feet of water	0.8826	Inches of mercury
Feet of water	0.03048	Kgs./sq. cm.
Feet of water	62.43	Lbs./sq. ft.
Feet of water	0.4335	Lbs./sq. inch
Feet/min.	0.5080	Centimeters/sec.
Feet/min.	0.01667	Feet/sec.
Feet/min.	0.01829	Kilometers/hr.
Feet/min.	0.3048	Meters/min.
Feet/min.	0.01136	Miles/hr.
Foot-pounds	0.001286	BTU
Gallons	3785	Cu. centimeters
Gallons	0.1337	Cubic feet
Gallons	231	Cubic inches
Gallons	128	Fluid ounces
Gallons	3.785	Liters
Gallons water	8.35	Lbs. water @60°F.
Horse-power	42.44	BTU/min.
Horse-power	33,000	Foot-lbs./min.
Horse-power	550	Foot-lbs./sec.
Horse-power	0.7457	Kilowatts
Horse-power	745.7	Watts
Horse-power (boiler)	33,479	BTU/hr.
Horse-power (boiler)	9.803	Kilowatts
Horse-power-hours	2547	BTU
Horse-power-hours	0.7457	Kilowatt-hours
Inches	2,540	Centimeters
Inches	25.4	Millimeters
Inches	0.0254	Meters
Inches	0.0833	Foot
Inches of mercury	0.03342	Atmospheres
Inches of mercury	1.133	Feet of water
Inches of mercury	13.57	Inches of water
Inches of mercury	70.73	Lbs./sq. ft.
Inches of mercury	0.4912	Lbs./sq. inch
Inches of water	0.002458	Atmospheres
Inches of water	0.07355	In. of mercury
Inches of water	0.5781	Ounces/sq. inch
Inches of water	5.202	Lbs./sq. foot
Inches of water	0.03613	Lbs./sq. inch
Kilowatts	56.92	BTU/min.
Kilowatts	1.341	Horse-power
Kilowatts	1000	Watts
Kilowatt-hours	3415	BTU

MULTIPLY	BY	TO OBTAIN
Liters	0.2642	Gallons
Liters	2.113	Pints (liq.)
Liters	1.057	Quarts (liq.)
Meters	100	Centimeters
Meters	3.281	Feet
Meters	39.37	Inches
Meters	1000	Millimeters
Meters	1.094	Yards
Ounces (fluid)	1.805	Cubic inches
Ounces (fluid)	0.02957	Liters
Ounces/sq. inch	0.0625	Lbs./sq. inch
Ounces/sq. inch	1.73	Inches of water
Pints	0.4732	Liter
Pounds (avoir.)	16	Ounces
Pounds of water	0.01602	Cubic feet
Pounds of water	27.68	Cubic inches
Pounds of water	0.1198	Gallons
Pounds/sq. foot	0.01602	Feet of water
Pounds/sq. foot	0.006945	Pounds/sq. inch
Pounds/sq. inch	0.06804	Atmospheres
Pounds/sq. inch	2.307	Feet of water
Pounds/sq. inch	2.036	In. of mercury
Pounds/sq. inch	27.68	Inches of water
Temp.(°C.)+273	1	Abs. temp. (°C.)
Temp.(°C.)+17.78	1.8	Temp. (°F.)
Temp.(°F.)+460	1	Abs. temp. (°F.)
Temp.(°F.)−32	5/9	Temp. (°C.)
Therm	100,000	BTU
Tons(long)	2240	Pounds
Ton, Refrigeration	12,000	BTU/hr.
Tons (short)	2000	Pounds
Watts	3.415	BTU
Watts	0.05692	BTU/min.
Watts	44.26	Foot-pounds/min.
Watts	0.7376	Foot-pounds/sec.
Watts	0.001341	Horse-power
Watts	0.001	Kilowatts
Watt-hours	3.415	BTU/hr.
Watt-hours	2655	Foot-pounds
Watt-hours	0.001341	Horse-power hrs.
Watt-hours	0.001	Kilowatt-hours

PRESSURE CONVERSION TABLES

Equivalent Inches		Pressure Per Square Inch		Equivalent Inches		Pressure Per Square Inch	
Water	Mercury	Pounds	Ounces	Water	Mercury	Pounds	Ounces
0.10	0.007	0.0036	0.0577	8.0	0.588	0.289	4.62
0.20	0.015	0.0072	0.115	9.0	0.662	0.325	5.20
0.30	0.022	0.0108	4.173	10.0	0.74	0.361	5.77
0.40	0.029	0.0145	0.231	11.0	0.81	0.397	6.34
0.50	0.037	0.0181	0.289	12.0	0.88	0.433	6.92
0.60	0.044	0.0217	0.346	13.0	0.96	0.469	7.50
0.70	0.051	0.0253	0.404	13.6	1.00	0.491	7.86
0.80	0.059	0.0289	0.462	13.9	1.02	0.500	8.00
0.90	0.066	0.325	0.520	14.0	1.06	0.505	8.08
1.00	0.074	0.036	0.577	15.0	1.10	0.542	8.7
1.36	0.100	0.049	0.785	16.0	1.18	0.578	9.2
1.74	0.128	0.067	1.00	17.0	1.25	0.614	9.8
2.00	0.147	0.072	1.15	18.0	1.33	0.650	10.4
2.77	0.203	0.100	1.60	19.0	1.40	0.686	10.9
3.00	0.221	0.109	1.73	20.0	1.47	0.722	11.5
4.00	0.294	0.144	2.31	25.0	1.84	0.903	14.4
5.0	0.368	0.181	2.89	27.2	2.00	0.975	15.7
6.0	0.442	0.217	3.46	27.7	2.03	1.00	16.0
7.0	0.515	0.253	4.04				

(Courtesy, Robertshaw Controls Company.)

Abbreviations for Text and Drawings

A   Amperes

AC   Auxiliary contacts

ACCA   Air Conditioning Contractors of America

AFUE   Annual Fuel Utilization Efficiency

AGA   American Gas Association

AMP   Amperes

API   American Petroleum Institute

ARI   Air-Conditioning and Refrigeration Institute

ASHRAE   American Society of Heating, Refrigerating, and Air-Conditioning Engineers

AWG   American wire gauge

BK   Black-wire color

BL   Blue-wire color

Btu   British Thermal Unit

Btuh   British Thermal Units per Hour

C   24V Common connection

°C   Degrees Celsius

C.A.   California Seasonal Efficiency Percent

CAD   Cad cell

CAP   Capacitor

CB   Circuit breaker

CC   Compressor contractor

CCH   Compressor crankcase heater

cfh   Cubic feet per hour

cfm   Cubic feet per minute

CGV   Combination gas valve

CH   Crankcase heater

CO   Carbon monoxide

COMP   Compressor

COP   Coefficient of Performance

CO_2   Carbon dioxide

CPVC   Chlorinated polyvinyl chloride

CR   Control Relay

cu   Cubic

dB   Decibel

db   Dry bulb

DEG   Degree

DOE   Department of Energy

DPDT   Double-pole double-throw switch

DPST   Double-pole single-throw switch

DSI Direct spark ignition

E Electromotive force (volts)

EAC Electrostatic air cleaner

EMF Electromotive force

EP Electric pilot

EPS External Static Pressure

EWT Entering water temperature

F Farad

°F Degrees Fahrenheit

FC Fan control

FD Fuse disconnect

FL Fuse link

FLA Full-load amperes

FM Fan motor

FR Fan relay

ft Feet

ft^3 Cubic feet

ft^3/h Cubic feet per hour

ft^3/min Cubic feet per minute

FU Fuse

g Grams

G Green-wire color

G Neutral-ground

GFCI Ground fault circuit interrupter

gph Gallons per hour

gpm Gallons per minute

GV Gas valve

H Humidistat

HE High efficiency

HI: High speed

HP High pressure (control)

HR Heat relay

HS Humidification system

HSPF Heating Season Performance Factor

HTM Heat transfer multiplier

HTM™ Heat transfer module

H$_2$O Water

HU Humidifier

Hz Cycles/second

I Amperes

ID Inside diameter

IFR Inside fan relay

IPS International Pipe Standard

J Joule

kcal Kilocalorie

kg Kilogram

kW Kilowatt

kWh Kilowatt-hours

L Limit

LA Limit auxiliary

lb Pound

LO Low speed

L1 L2 Power supply

LP Liquid petroleum

LR Lockout relay

LRA Locked rotor amperes

M One thousand

mA Milliampere

MBh Thousands of BTU/hour

μF Microfarads

MFD Microfarads

mm Millimeter

m/s Meters per second

mV Millivolt

N Neutral

N Nitrogen

NC Normally closed

NO Normally open

O Oxygen

OBM Oil burner motor

OD Outside diameter

OL Overload

OT Outdoor thermostat

PC Printed circuit

Ph Phase

PPC Pilot power control

ppm Parts per million

PSC Permanent split phase capacitor

psi Pressure per square inch

psig Pounds per square inch gauge

PVC Polyvinyl chloride

R Red-wire color

R Resistance-Ohms

rev/min Revolutions per minute

rh Relative humidity

RH Resistance heater

RV Reversing valve

s Seconds

S Cad cell relay terminal

SAE Society of Automotive Engineers

SEER Seasonal Energy Efficient Ratio

SI International System

SOL Solenoid valve

SPDT Single-pole double-throw switch

SPST Single-pole single-throw switch

SQ Sequencer

SRN Sound Rating Number

T Thermostat terminal

T.C. Total capacity

TEL Total equivalent length

TEV Thermal expansion valve

TFS Time fan start

THR Thermocouple

TR Temperature rise

TR Transformer

U Overall heat transfer coefficient

UL Underwriters' Laboratories

V Volt (electromotive force)

VA Volt-amp

W Watt

W White-wire color

wb Wet bulb

wc water column in inches

w/lls (Units rated) with (accessory) liquid line solenoid

W1 First stage heat-thermostat

W2 Second stage heat-thermostat

Y Yellow-wire color

Y,R,G,W Thermostat terminals

Index

W